Remember This!

CONTEMPORARY INDIGENOUS ISSUES

Series Editor
Devon Abbott Mihesuah

Remember This!

Dakota Decolonization
and the Eli Taylor Narratives

Waziyatawin Angela Wilson

With translations from the Dakota text
by Wahpetunwin Carolynn Schommer

UNIVERSITY OF NEBRASKA PRESS · LINCOLN & LONDON

Acknowledgments
for the use
of previously published material
appear on page 269,
which constitutes
an extension
of the copyright page.

© 2005 by Waziyatawiŋ Angela Wilson
All rights reserved
Manufactured in the
United States of America

Library of Congress Cataloging-in-Publication Data
Wilson, Angela Cavender.
Remember this! : Dakota decolonization and the Eli Taylor narratives / Waziyatawiŋ
Angela Wilson ; with translations from the Dakota text by Wahpetunwin Carolynn Schommer.
p. cm. — (Contemporary indigenous issues)
English and Dakota.
Revision of the author's thesis (Ph. D.)—Cornell University, 2000.
Includes bibliographical references and index.
ISBN 0-8032-4814-8 (cloth : alk. paper) — ISBN 0-8032-9844-7 (pbk. : alk. paper)
1. Dakota Indians—Folklore.   2. Dakota Indians—History.   3. Dakota language—Texts.   4. Dakota
literature—History and criticism.   5. Tales—Great Plains.   6. Oral tradition—Great Plains.
I. Taylor, Eli, 1908–1999.   II. Title.   III. Series.
E99.D1W83 2005
398.2′089′975243—dc22   2004058826

The 1992 painting *The Crossing*, by Marian Anderson, was created
for the Treaty Site History Center in St. Peter, Minnesota,
to reflect the impact of the breaking of the Treaty of Traverse des Sioux,
negotiated between the Sisitunwan and Wahpetunwan bands
of Dakoṭa and the U.S. government at this site in 1851.
Uŋkaŋna Eli Taylor's image was used to embody the elder
in the painting whose "wisdom makes him aware of the future."
For further information contact Marian Anderson,
20101 Horseshoe Lane, Mankato MN 56001 / (507)388-1793,
www.mariananderson.com.

Set in Minion and MinDakota by G & S Typesetters, Inc.
Designed by R. W. Boeche.

Uŋḳaŋna,
Ohiŋni Dakoṭa wicoȟ'aŋ tewahiŋda kṭe.
Nitakoża, Waziyaṭawiŋ

Contents

List of Illustrations   viii

Acknowledgments   ix

Introduction: **Dauŋkoṭapi!** (We Are Dakoṭa!)   1

1. **Okiciyaḳa Uŋyaŋpi** (Oral Tradition)   23
2. **Owotaŋna Wohdaḳapo** (Tell It Straight)   37
3. **De Iapi Uŋk'upi** (We Were Given This Language)   51
4. **Dena Naḣ'uŋ Wauŋ** (These I Heard Growing Up)
   The First Historical Narrative   68
5. **Ṭaku Ociciyaḳe Waciŋ** (I Want to Tell You Something)   92
6. **Ṭoked Imacaġe** (How I Grew Up)
   The Second, Third, and Fourth Historical Narratives   102
7. **Dakoṭak Hena Wicawada** (I Believe in Those Dakoṭa Ways)   126
8. **Wahokuŋḳiyapi** (They Provide Guidance)
   The Fifth through the Tenth Historical Narratives   137
9. **Ṭaku Wakaŋ** (That Which Is Mysterious)   169
10. **Akicitapi** (They Are Warriors)
    The Eleventh Historical Narrative and the First War Story   184
11. **Wicoṭawaciŋ Yuwaṡṭe** (It Makes for Good Thoughts)   197
12. **Ṭoked Ḳapi Oyaḳapi** (Commentary)
    The First through the Fourth Commentaries   204
13. **Ṭaku Ṭoḳṭokca Iwohdaḳapi** (A Discussion of Different Things)   221

Conclusion: **Oyaṭe Nipi Ḳṭe** (The People Shall Live)   236

Appendix A: Explanation of Dakoṭa Orthography   243

Appendix B: Upper Sioux Resolution   246

Notes   249

Works Cited   263

Source Acknowledgments   271

Index   273

Illustrations

Following page 116

1. Uŋkaŋna Eli at Chris Mato Nuŋpa's adoption ceremony
2. Uŋkaŋna Eli during 1992 interviews
3. Uŋkaŋna Eli and Kuŋši Edna during 1992 visit
4. Kuŋši Waȟpetuŋwiŋ (Carolynn Schommer) during 1992 interviews
5. Uŋkaŋna Eli receiving honorary degree from Brandon University (1998)
6. Frances Maza Wasicuna, Uŋkaŋna Eli, and Kuŋši Edna
7. Uŋkaŋna Eli and Kuŋši Edna at birthday-anniversary celebration
8. Uŋkaŋna Eli speaking to children at the Mahkato Powwow

Acknowledgments

From the very beginning this project has been blessed with incredible support from those who believed in its significance. It has also been a lengthy project, years in the making, and I owe many for their kindness and support.

In 1991, when the planning for this oral-history work began, I had just started my senior year at the University of Minnesota. As an undergraduate trying to organize a major research trip for six people, I could have been discouraged by many. Instead, supporters rallied behind the project and helped get it off the ground. Financial contributions for the actual recording of Uŋkaŋna Eli's stories and some of the translations came from the University of Minnesota's Undergraduate Research Opportunities Program, an honors thesis grant, the Shakopee Mdewakanton Sioux community, the Prairie Island Tribal Council, the Minnesota Historical Society, and Ron Libertus. In addition I had the faculty mentorship and enthusiastic support of Jean O-Brien, Joel Samaha, and Carol Miller at the University of Minnesota. Tim Dunnigan, the linguist from the University of Minnesota assisting with the Dakota-English Dictionary project, has also shown tremendous interest in and support for this project. He was the person I called when I had questions about the written representations of the Dakota language or linguistic terminology.

I continued work on this project throughout my graduate career, and it formed the basis of my dissertation. Though many considered my historical research radical because it was based on oral rather than written history, I had several wonderful people comprising my graduate committee who were both challenging and encouraging: Dan Usner, Mary Roldan, Sherene Baugher, and Robert Venables. All of them recognized the importance of the inclusion of Indigenous voices in history and ardently explored with me the implications of my work. Dr. Bob, as he was affectionately called, was particularly influential during my years at Cornell, modeling a stance toward historical scholarship that began, first and foremost, with a commitment to Indigenous Peoples. Bob and Sherry offered their home and their classrooms as a safe haven to me, and they remain avid supporters and good friends. I am very pleased that Bob has also begun some treaty research for the Dakota Oyate since the formation of the Eastern Dakota Bands Treaty Council.

There are several other individuals I would like to recognize and thank for their special contributions. Alan Ominsky used his early days of retirement to help create a computer font for our written language, which many of us are now using. His efforts are obvious in the production of this book, and I hope there will be many more! Also, I would like to thank Bill Johnston, who first introduced me to Linda Tuhiwai Smith's work on one of his site visits to our Dakota language-immersion preschool. In doing so he started me on the important intellectual journey on which I am still traveling. In addition, Gary Dunham at the University of Nebraska Press has also been a supporter of my work. Because of the controversial nature of my research and writing, the publication of my work also requires a courageous editor. Gary is just such an editor, in addition to being wonderfully understanding and respectful of this project.

Since early versions of chapters 1 and 2 were published elsewhere, I would also like to thank the University of Nebraska Press and the University of New Mexico Press for permission to revise and reprint "American Indian History or Non-Indian Perceptions of American Indian History?" from *American Indian Quarterly* 20, no. 1 (Winter 1996), and "Power of the Spoken Word: Native Oral Traditions in American Indian History," from Donald L. Fixico, ed., *Rethinking American Indian History* (Albuquerque: University of New Mexico Press, 1997). In addition, chapter 5 and part of the conclusion are based on an essay that first appeared as "Walking into the Future: Dakota Oral Tradition and the Shaping of Historical Consciousness," in *The Forum*, Canadian Oral History Association, vol. 19–20 (1999–2000), which is used with permission here.

In addition to my undergraduate and graduate-school mentors, numerous individuals commented on various drafts of this project in sundry bits and pieces. I am extremely grateful for suggestions I received from Amy Lonetree, Myla Vicenti Carpio, Melissa Dyea, Anton Treuer, Peter Iverson, Michael Yellow Bird, Devon Mihesuah, Tony Clark, Tim Dunnigan, Susan Miller, Chris Mato Nunpa, Mary Beth Faimon, Winona Wheeler, and Neil McKay. I know this work benefited from their input. I would like to say a special thanks to Amy, Myla, and Lisa, who not only frequently commented on my writing but also burned up the phone lines in many long-distance conversations of support. These are the friends and colleagues who I knew were always standing beside me even when we were hundreds of miles apart. Not only did they offer a constant and limitless supply of strength, they always made me laugh in the process.

In the last several years two other important mentors have emerged in my life: Devon Mihesuah and Michael Yellow Bird. Early on, Devon showed tremendous support for my academic career by encouraging my honest (and radical) writing; she opened important doors. In working more closely with her in the last few years she has impressed me with her indefatigable work ethic and fervent commitment to the empowerment of Indigenous Peoples. Similarly, in the last several years as colleagues together at ASU, Michael Yellow Bird has turned into a most important mentor. Through our many and long conversations around our kitchen table or sitting outside Tibdo Michael has stimulated my intellectual growth and deeply affected the way I approach research and writing.

My love for the oral tradition was fostered by early exposure to engaging storytellers deeply committed to keeping our memories alive. I was privileged to hear stories from grandparents who enjoyed having a young audience and who were generous with their time. Kuŋśi Elsie Cavender, Kuŋśi Naomi Cavender, Kuŋśi Carolynn Schommer, and Uŋkaŋna Eli Taylor all took time with me and, in the process, ensured that our stories were well loved and never forgotten. By sharing with me, they inspired me. In listening to my Kuŋśi Elsie—who frequently said, "They never wrote that in a history book!"—I learned there were differences between how we presented our interpretation of our past and how we were (mis)represented by others. These elders taught me that taking back our history would be central to our survival.

I am extremely appreciative to all my family members who made this project possible. My father, Chris Mato Nunpa, helped make initial arrangements for our trip and has continued his support ever since. He helped with some of the initial translation work as did my grandmother, Naomi Cavender. My uncle, Caske Running Walker, patiently assisted with the transcription into Dakota, and the final translation work was completed with the help of my grandmother, Carolynn Schommer. All of them contributed to the interpretation with their valuable insights, though the contribution of Kuŋśi Carrie was especially great. I lost count of the number of hours I spent working with Kuŋśi Carrie on the translations over the years. She is unsurpassed in her dedication to our language. Her love for and commitment to it has now rubbed off—she has helped to produce a new generation of language warriors committed to reviving our language. Her dedication to this work is inspirational, and I am deeply grateful for the opportunity I have had to learn from her along the way.

I must also express thanks to the people who taught me I could achieve whatever I set my mind to, my mother and father, Edith Travers and Chris Mato Nunpa. As they are both well-educated, skilled writers in their own right, they were excellent models. Most important, they have maintained a firm belief in my skills and sense of purpose, which has helped me to succeed. I also extend a special thanks to my sister, Audrey Fuller, with whom I have shared many conversations about this project and who has always offered words of support, even when it seemed like I might never finish. In addition, my husband, Scott, has understood the immense importance of this undertaking from the first morning the interviews began in Sioux Valley; his support never once wavered. He saw me through every up and every down along the way, especially when the academic backlash came because of my defense of the oral tradition. Never once has he questioned the road I have chosen, and though he can't always walk beside me, he has been there to catch me every time I have fallen. My children have grown up with this project. Autumn was just a baby when we made the trip to Sioux Valley, and her baby chatter can be heard on the recordings with Uŋkaŋna's voice. Talon and Sage were born in the midst of my graduate school work and were well-familiar with Uŋkaŋna's voice and image because Ina (Mom) was always working with his stories. They have sacrificed a lot of time with their mother so this project could be completed, but I believe they, along with others from their generation, will be much enriched for its publication. To my entire family, nina wopida eciciyapi!

Finally, I would like to thank Uŋkaŋna Eli Taylor and the rest of our family in Sioux Valley. Bill Taylor was a tremendous help at the end of the project, compiling photos and tracking down information for me as well as supporting completion of this work for Uŋkaŋna. Uŋkaŋna generously left a tremendous gift to the Dakota of today and tomorrow. Hena kiksuya maunipi kte! (We will carry those memories!) He was extraordinarily patient in waiting for this work to be completed, and I am deeply sorry he is not alive to see the final results. He cherished and kept the stories well. I hope I have maintained their integrity.

Remember This!

Introduction
Dauŋkoṭapi! (We Are Dakoṭa!)

This work of Indigenous history is a profound departure from standard historical texts, and this departure is significant precisely because it marks a turning away from colonized interpretations of our past toward a decolonized tribal history. To the profession and field that has successfully colonized our past, maintaining hegemony over Indigenous historical discourse through the privileging of largely non-Indigenous written sources, this book is an unapologetic challenge. Rather than relying on and privileging Waṡicu written sources, this book relies on and privileges Indigenous oral tradition, specifically the stories of Dakoṭa elder Eli Taylor.[1] Ironically, this privileging of an Indigenous perspective in Indigenous history is cutting-edge work, a powerful testament to the colonial relationship Indigenous Peoples have to written history. Within this context, the stories of my grandfather, Eli Taylor, become a decolonizing agent, a means for Dakoṭa people to assert an identity and worldview that will carry us into the future while at the same time assisting us in resisting the colonizing forces.

This project also assumes value in an identity and worldview with relevance in the twenty-first century and beyond. It assumes that these have a potentially transformative power, not just for Dakoṭa people or Indigenous Peoples in general, but also for the world. Part of the challenge with this project has been how to articulate why such stories as this are so profoundly important. In a local or microcontext, the stories of Eli Taylor are positioned to contribute to the Dakoṭa recovery of our traditional knowledge, which we hope will spur new generations to carry on the struggle of resistance from a foundation of cultural strength. On a broader scale, decolonization concerns a simultaneous critical interrogation of the colonizing forces that have damaged our lives in profound ways, coupled with a return to those ways that nourished and sustained us as Indigenous Peoples for thousands of years. As we engage in this difficult process, we disrupt the world of the colonizer as well. From this angle, the recovery of Indigenous knowledge is a central component in the struggle for decolonization. This is precisely why the potential impact is so great and why the ripples will be felt far and wide.

Sioux Valley Uŋhipi (We Arrived at Sioux Valley)

In January 1992 a group of us traveled from Minnesota to the Sioux Valley Dakota Nation Reserve in Manitoba to begin a major oral-history project with my uŋkaŋna (grandfather), Eli Taylor. In the previous fall, as he did every year, Uŋkaŋna had come to Minnesota to attend the Mankato Powwow held at the Land of Memories Park in southern Minnesota.[2] While at the wacipi, he informed several people of his desire to have his stories recorded.[3] My dekśi (uncle), Gary Cavender, saw him at the powwow and heard this. He relayed this information to me and my kuŋśi (grandmother), Carrie Schommer, when the three of us were visiting in her office one day at the University of Minnesota. I was immediately interested as I knew the value of documenting stories in the oral tradition, which had been steadily declining for more than a century as a consequence of the military conquest of our people in 1862 and our subsequent diaspora and colonization. I had conducted a similar project with my kuŋśi, Elsie Cavender, in the previous few years in which I transcribed and edited the stories she shared. I understood the rewards associated with and the importance of such undertakings.

Uŋkaŋna Eli Taylor was not a blood relative of mine, but he became a part of our family, and we became a part of his, when my father, Dr. Chris (Cavender) Mato Nunpa, adopted him as a father in 1988.[4] My paternal grandfather had died about fifteen years previously, and Eli Taylor resembled him in so many ways (particularly with his singing and oratory skills) that my father wanted to cement the close bond he already felt with this man in a formal ceremony. So, in the Dakota way, Eli Taylor is my grandfather. Because of this family connection, I asked my father if he would contact Uŋkaŋna to determine if he would be interested in having me record his information. I was hesitant about doing this myself because I didn't know what type of information he had hoped to share, and we have some cultural norms about men relaying certain kinds of information only to other men, and women sharing only with other women. Apparently others had contacted Uŋkaŋna, but he had turned them down. When my father talked to him about the possibility of me doing the recording, he thought it was a good idea. Though I had reached a level of proficiency with the Dakota language, because I was not a fluent speaker, he also requested that my father be there to help provide translations from Dakota to English.

After the dates of January 11–19, 1992, were established for the trip, I spent time raising funds and organizing transportation, lodging, and equipment. My kuŋśi, Carolynn Schommer, came to assist with translations; my husband, Scott, was appointed the video and audio technician; and my stepmother, Laurie Cavender, came along to help keep us company and to assist in taking care of my daughter, Autumn (who was just sixteen months old at the time). Including my father and myself, there were six of us. All the plans fell into place fairly trouble free, and we were on our way to Sioux Valley.

While there, we were fortunate to be able to stay at my cousin Theresa's house, which allowed us to remain on the reserve instead of commuting daily to the city of Brandon where the nearest hotels were. It also enabled us to cook our own meals and do some of the recording there. Our entire family showed us incredible generosity and kindness throughout our stay in Sioux Valley.

We arrived late Saturday night, so our first meeting with Uŋkaŋna was Sunday morning over a wonderful breakfast prepared by Kuŋši Edna and my aunts, Tuŋwiŋ Marina and Tuŋwiŋ Margaret. In that first conversation over breakfast, Uŋkaŋna expressed many profound thoughts as he gave us an introduction to the project. He told us that he was going to be telling us things that would be hard, including some things about white people, and he apologized to Scott (who is non-Native) for this. He talked about people today living by "greed instead of need." He made sure to point out that this was going to be about Dakoṭa history and culture, not about any other groups. He said he wanted white people to remember that Indians are human. He discussed how he has had to live in two worlds, and that both of these worlds have helped him out at different times. He also said he was very glad we were there.

From my perspective, one of the most interesting comments made that morning dealt with the internal conflicts he had experienced over Indigenous and Wašicu knowledge and ways of knowing. While being raised by his elders who had never been to "school," he felt his teachers were as good as any we might have had with our formal, Western education. However, he talked about a period in his life in which he was "more into the white way of thinking" before he moved back to Sioux Valley. In describing that time in his life, he stated that he had been so afflicted by the white world that at one point he even thought the stories from the oral tradition might not be true.

He described feeling torn and in conflict with his first introduction to Christianity in the 1930s, and as a result began to question the Dakoṭa ways with which he was raised. He asked himself if the Christian Bible stories could "really be the way it happened." However, after hearing the story of Lazarus, which was quite similar to a Dakoṭa story, he said he realized that it did not matter who your people were: everyone prayed to the same God. This experience helped reaffirm his belief in the Dakoṭa ways and also solidified his belief in the Dakoṭa gift of memory. "He didn't give us pen and paper," he said, "we remember with our minds." These were important points, as all Dakoṭa are today trained to some degree in the thought of the colonizers and have to grapple with the anti-Indigenous sentiment we have begun to internalize.

Our week in Sioux Valley was filled with activities. We spent several exhausting hours a day recording information on audio- and videocassettes. We also were able to see a few hockey games, attend a couple of services where we enjoyed using the language in some good Dakota hymn singing, tour the beautiful sites around Griswold, Manitoba, and eat many wonderful meals! Another highlight was being able to observe a moccasin game, thanks to players from Pipestone (Lawrence Bell, Andrew Crow, and Mason Demas) and Sioux Valley (Gordon Bone, Carson Taylor, and John Hapa). It was an incredible week filled with many wonderful experiences that seemed to mark all of us in a profound way. I believe all of us who were there remember it very fondly.

Uŋkaŋna passed away on Sunday, January 10, 1999, at the age of ninety-one. He was a positive role model for the younger generations who knew him as he lived his life according to tribal teachings and his conception of what *being* Dakota meant. This including living with a tremendous sense of humanity and a desire to perpetuate goodness, but also a fierce adherence to Dakota teachings. Much of what Uŋkaŋna relayed I was not able to fully understand until we returned to Minnesota, as it was all told in Dakota. Even now, new realizations emerge and I understand things differently than I did when I first heard the stories. The things I have learned, and continue to learn, have had a deep impact on me and the direction of my life. As we struggle through translations and my own understanding is enhanced, I realize more and more the significance of his messages. I am continually impressed with his wisdom and knowledge, and I am not the only one. His cultural capital spread beyond the Dakota nation to non-Dakota institutions of higher learning. A year before he passed away, in the spring of 1998, Uŋkaŋna Eli Taylor was presented with an honorary doctorate from Brandon University. It was wonderful to have an academic institution recognize his breadth of knowledge and his gift as a teacher.

To understand the stories contained here, it is important to provide some information about our Oyaṭe and the context in which these stories were told.[5] *Dakota* is a term meaning *the friends* or *allies*.[6] This is the term we use to identify ourselves. Historians, as well as most Americans, have typically used the term *Sioux* to describe the Dakota as well as the Nakota and Lakota.[7] Our people, the Dakota, are composed of the Sisituŋwaŋ (Dwellers at the Fish Ground), Waȟpetuŋwaŋ (Dwellers among the Leaves), Bdewakaŋtuŋwaŋ (Dwellers by Mystic Lake), and the Waȟpekuṭe (Shooters among the Leaves). Further west are the Ihaŋktuŋwaŋ (Dwellers at the End) and Ihaŋktuŋwaŋna (Little Dwellers at the End), both considered to be Nakota, and the Tituŋwaŋ (Dwellers of the Plains) or Lakota. All of these groups are members of the original Oceti Šakowiŋ, or the Seven Council Fires of the Dakota Oyate (Dakota Nation). The Tituŋwaŋ (Lakota), who are the most populous group of the Oceti Šakowiŋ, are further divided into their own seven council fires. They speak a different dialect of our language (the primary difference being that they substitute an *l* where we would have a *d*), and, as their name implies, they are a people of the plains. The Dakota people—and, even more specifically, the Waḣpetuŋwaŋ people—are the primary focus of this work, as Uŋkaŋna Eli Taylor and I are both members of this council fire.

Hipi Itokab (After They Came)

Minisota Makoce (Land Where the Waters Reflect the Skies or Heavens), now known in English as Minnesota, is the ancient homeland of the Dakota people.[8] While at one time the Dakota would have lived and traveled through all portions of the state and well beyond, traversing freely across the now delineated state and national boundaries, by the mid-1800s our people were confined to reservations bordering the Minnesota River. The traditional way of life had been in a steady state of disruption from the time of first contact with Europeans in the 1600s until it climaxed with the U.S.-Dakota War of 1862.

The U.S.-Dakota War of 1862 remains the major point of demarcation in Dakota history. The loss associated with that seminal event has affected every Dakota alive since 1862, and it will continue to affect every Dakota person in the future. It was not just the fact that Dakota people were severed from the land that defined who we were, it was not just being confined to reservations in new lands, nor was it just the sense of disconnection suffered by the people. It was all these factors combining to change our relationship with the rest of the world, altering our existence with a seeming finality and irrevocability.

One of the most significant changes for the Eastern Dakota came in the summer of 1851, when under tremendous pressure we negotiated the Treaty of Traverse des Sioux and the Treaty of Mendota with the U.S. government. For the first time Dakota people were confined to reservations, which forever altered our seasonally based, hunting, planting, and gathering lifestyle. The 1850s were extremely difficult years for the Dakota people. In addition to facing reservation life, the Dakota confronted masses of white settlers who were flooding into areas ceded in the treaties (long before the treaties were ratified and the Dakota had received their compensation for the land cessions). Not only that, white settlers were also pushing the existing reservation boundaries, often illegally squatting on Indigenous lands. The invasion of the Dakota homeland was well under way, but the worst was yet to come.

In addition to provocation from the continual land invasions, the Dakota were also still angry and bitter about the involvement of Indian traders in swindling the bands out of thousands of dollars.⁹ To make matters worse, the Dakota people were subjected to major civilizing and Christianizing campaigns carried out by the missionaries. This perpetration of religious imperialism meant that all aspects of traditional Dakota life were under continual attack and disparagement. Missionaries worked hand-in-hand with government agents to liberally reward those Dakota who succumbed to their coercion.¹⁰ The federal government also played a major hand in the oppression of Dakota people in this era by violating the terms of the treaties. Throughout this period, the annuities due the Dakota according to the treaties were often late and incomplete, fueling the starvation that threatened the people. Little game was available on the reservations, and government provisions were inadequate to support the Dakota, making basic survival increasingly more challenging.

By the summer of 1862, even those Dakota who had taken up the full-time occupation of farming at the urging of the missionaries and agents were near starvation due to a crop failure the previous fall. In August 1862, when the gold coin had not arrived on schedule again, tensions were extremely high—there existed a climate of desperation, especially when food provisions sat undistributed in a warehouse. Our Dakota people had faced the invasion and theft of our homeland, loss of life due to disease, repeated incursions into what was left of the land-base, and daily assaults on our way of life.¹¹ Furthermore, a deliberate dependency on the Indian agency and other institutions of colonialism was created, crippling Dakota self-sufficiency and autonomy.

All these factors combined to compel the Dakota to strike out and attack those who were contributing to our impossible circumstances and threatening our survival in our own homeland. The war over Dakota land and resources had already begun, and the first strike did not come from the Dakota. However, the final event that would begin the Wasicus' war of extermination and elimination occurred on August 17, 1862, when four Dakota men from a Bdewakaŋtuŋwaŋ town killed five white settlers over an incident involving the taking of the settlers' eggs. Though the starting of the U.S.-Dakota War is often attributed to the actions of these men, when the war is examined from a critical perspective it becomes clear that these men and the others who participated in the war were only retaliating for assaults they had already endured. Brazilian educator Paulo Freire has characterized this phenomenon when, in reference to the relationship of violence to the oppressed, he stated, "With the establishment of a relationship of oppression, violence has already begun. Never in history has violence been initiated by the oppressed."¹²

The killing of the five Wasicu settlers was followed by an attack on the Indian agency at Lower Sioux the next day. Warfare continued, with many white casualties at first, until troops were brought in to put an end to the fighting. The final stage of the war was fought at the Battle of Wood Lake on September 23, 1862, at which time the Dakota were defeated and those who did not escape were imprisoned. Although many of the Dakota men were fighting in what they deemed a just war, they were not treated as prisoners of war. Instead, they were treated as war criminals. While women, children, and a small number of men were imprisoned in a concentration camp at Fort Snelling, most of the captured men were tried by a military tribunal set up by Gen. Henry Hastings Sibley.[13]

Three hundred and three of these men were sentenced to be hanged for their participation in the war. Sibley had the support of white settlers in the state of Minnesota, who clamored for Dakota blood and demanded the immediate extermination of over three hundred Dakota men, though many even thought him too lenient. Episcopal bishop Henry Whipple was one of only a few voices who actively spoke against the execution of the Dakota, citing it as a great injustice. It must be noted, nevertheless, that Whipple was convinced of Dakota savagery and only wanted the Dakota spared so that they could be converted to Christianity and "civilized." Ultimately, he believed the Dakota needed saving from their own cultural and spiritual traditions and thus was an advocate of what may be called ethnocide. At his urging, President Abraham Lincoln ordered a committee to review the trial records to determine if, indeed, these men should die. After reviewing the records, Lincoln ordered the execution of thirty-nine Dakota men and sentenced the remaining men to prison terms. At the last minute one additional man was pardoned. Then on December 26, 1862, the day after Christmas, thirty-eight Dakota men were killed in the largest mass execution in U.S. history.[14] Unfortunately, violence to those men did not end even then. Later that night Wašicu doctors dug up their bodies from the mass grave, and they were mutilated and desecrated in the name of science. Today the Dakota Oyate has only found and repatriated three of those original thirty-eight who were slain.

The remaining men were sent to Davenport, Iowa, where they were imprisoned for three years. Conditions were so horrendous there that one-third of those imprisoned died while in custody. After losing three hundred of their number in the concentration camp at Fort Snelling in the winter of 1862–63, the remaining group of primarily women and children was then shipped to a reservation at Crow Creek, South Dakota. They were later joined by the men who completed their prison sentences in Davenport. The total number of people who died as a result of this war is unknown, but the lives of Dakota people were changed forever.

As early as September 1862, when the war was still occurring, Gov. Alexander Ramsey stated unambiguously that "the Sioux Indians of Minnesota must be exterminated or driven forever beyond the borders of the State."¹⁵ This blatant call for the ethnic cleansing of Minnesota meant the impossibility of Dakota people remaining in our homeland. Of those who escaped, many fled to safety in Canada. Those who did return ran the risk of being killed for the bounty that was placed on Dakota scalps, a bounty that eventually reached the amount of two hundred dollars. This was the fate of Little Crow, the Bdewakaŋtuŋwaŋ chief who had led the fighting in 1862. He was murdered by white settlers in the summer of 1863 while out picking raspberries with his son. The Dakota could no longer return to our home in Minnesota.

Because living in our homeland meant the threat of extermination, Dakota people made their homes elsewhere. Those in Canada settled on various reserves, including Dakota Plains First Nation, Sioux Valley Dakota Nation, Dakota Tipi First Nation, Birdtail Dakota/Sioux First Nation, Oak Lake Dakota/Sioux First Nation, Standing Buffalo Dakota Nation, Whitecap Dakota/Sioux First Nation, and Wahpeton Dakota Nation. Eventually, many of those at Crow Creek were relocated to Santee, Nebraska, and others stayed at new reservations that had been established like Spirit Lake, Lake Traverse, and Flandreau. About twenty-five years after the 1862 war, Dakota people began returning in small numbers to Minnesota and began to reoccupy sites at Upper Sioux, Lower Sioux, Prior Lake, and Prairie Island. However, many chose to stay in the new homes and communities they had established.

I am still learning about the extent of loss and disconnection stemming from the 1862 war. In 1998 I learned for the first time that some of our Dakota people settled on the Wahpeton Reserve near Prince Albert, Saskatchewan, in Canada. We traveled there in the summers of 1998 and 1999 to attend a powwow the first year and the Dakota Summit the next.¹⁶ On our last trip I learned that some of the people living there are relatives with whom we had never had contact. Our ancestors fled a thousand miles to the northwest after the U.S.-Dakota War of 1862!

As a result of this turmoil, Dakota people and culture have gone through tremendous changes. Many of these changes in our lives are better characterized as loss, with much of our cultural identity sacrificed along the way. The values and traditions of mainstream contemporary society are often difficult to reconcile with those we consider to be Dakota values and traditions. However, the oral-history project with Uŋkaŋna Eli Taylor provides great hope in this area in that maintaining Dakota identity in the face of colonialism is a recurring theme throughout his testimony. Story after story shows not only how the Dakota once lived but also how this Dakota elder incorporated these values and ways of being into his everyday life.

I often ask myself whether our ancestors would recognize us as Dakota people today, and, if so, I think about what it is that makes us Dakota and separates us from other cultural groups. Uŋkaŋna had told us a story about a Native man he heard talk one time about the four things we would need for our ancestors to recognize us in the next world. He seemed to agree with this man's stated requirements of a Dakota name, a blanket, a pair of moccasins, and a song of our own. While those are requirements for the next life, in this life distinctions must also be made. In the context of the oral tradition, choices are made about what stories are passed on and about their relative importance. Those choices represent our sense of history because they are interpretations of the past that help to define our existence today.

Ṭoked Ecuŋuŋḳuŋpi (How We Did It)

Originally, when anticipating what stories would be included in this project, I expected a lot of information to be relayed about specific historical events. Certainly the stories conveyed here are historical in nature, but they also provide tremendous insight into the Dakota worldview. This set of stories is significant for all Dakota people because it represents a return to Dakota teachings, traversing the artificial boundaries that have been placed between us as members of the Dakota Oyate. As a collection, Uŋkaŋna's statement is a significant and valuable contribution to the understanding of the Dakota heart and mind. Much of the information has clearly been handed down orally for centuries.

When we arrived in Sioux Valley, Uŋkaŋna had a clear agenda for things he wanted to discuss. Therefore, he directed the recordings until he felt he had exhausted the topics about which he had prepared to talk. At that point, on the last day of recording, we were able to inquire about topics we were interested in and to some extent direct the conversation. In the entire recording process, he relayed some of his life experiences, a variety of stories, and in the end reflected on his hopes for the future of Dakota young people.

Initially, we had planned on providing just a free English translation of the Dakota stories, but as we encountered difficulties with accurately trying to convey the meaning of a word or phrase, and as we realized how much more valuable the record would be if the original Dakota were also preserved, we decided to offer both the Dakota transcription and an English translation. In so doing, students of the language can study the Dakota text and speakers of the language can provide their own translations. Furthermore, we decided to alternate between Dakota and English, sentence by sentence, while offering a more literal translation, which we hope will encourage even the non-Dakota–speaking reader to work at understanding Dakota meanings and translations. It must be noted that this more literal translation is not as smooth as a free translation would be, but we felt there were other benefits derived from a more literal translation, mainly the conveyance of differences in worldview. In addition, the selection of what we translate more literally is arbitrary; that is, there were certain words or phrases that were particularly striking to those of us involved in the transcription and translation process, and it is for those that we were more likely to provide a literal translation. In other instances we might have provided a freer translation in the text with further comment in the footnote.

We have privileged the Dakota text by positioning it first. The English text comes secondarily and is distinguished visually from the Dakota text. In addition, it is important to note that the Dakota language contained within these pages is conversational Dakota; that is, we have preserved the Dakota as it was spoken by Uŋkaŋna Eli Taylor. The contractions and informal speech are written as we heard them rather than edited into a formal style of Dakota. Examples of this are words such as *ociçiyakapi* written as *ociçiyakap*, with part of the ending dropped (this is often done when the plural *pi* appears at the end of a word), or *Dakota kiŋ* might be written as *Dakotak* with the *iŋ* dropped. We usually tried to indicate in a footnote the first time other contractions that might not be as clear were used.

The English-speaking reader will quickly become aware of the areas or topics in which cultural conceptions, categories, or ways of knowing do not convert easily from Dakota to English. In addition, the reader will become aware of familiar and conversational phrases, expressions, worldview, and values. In doing the translations, we struggled over how to translate certain words and phrases and recognized that they could always be improved upon and that other speakers would likely translate the text differently. In this process, Kuŋši Carrie Schommer explained to me that the language comes from within—it is part of us. Only a Dakota speaker who feels the language from within can understand and try to explain it to a nonspeaker. Therefore, this is not intended to be a definitive translation or text but rather is intended as a starting point for the reclamation of our own stories and our own language. We hope it will encourage increased examination of and interest in the teachings and language of our ancestors so that they will also be the teachings and language of our children. Of course, all the mistakes are mine, and I apologize to my Dakota elders for any that might be contained within these pages.

The more work I have completed on this project, the more I realize how small my part is in all of this. Uŋkaŋna had done more work than any of us, carrying this tremendous stock of information with him for so many years, and then being generous enough to share it with us. In 1992 I began the translation work with Kuŋši Naomi Cavender and miate, Chris Mato Nuŋpa.[17] This initial translation was done from videotape to ensure we could take into account gestures and body movements while completing the translations. After we decided to produce the stories in a bilingual format, Dekṡi Caskҽ (Harry) Running Walker helped me with the transcriptions of the Dakoṭa.[18] He would patiently repeat back to me very slowly what Uŋkaŋna had said on the tapes so that I could handwrite it in Dakoṭa. For the second set of translations, I worked with Kuŋṡi Carolynn Schommer directly from the Dakoṭa transcriptions. This was painstaking work, and we sometimes spent hours working on the translation of a single paragraph, either trying to decipher what was said or establishing a suitable translation. She has given diligently and generously to this project, and I learned a great deal during the many hours we spent together in extensive discussions about the meaning of the language or of specific words and phrases. The contribution of my elders to this project has been invaluable, and their insights have enhanced my understanding immeasurably.

We have encountered many difficulties while translating, such as finding appropriate words in English to convey the right meaning and, in some cases, being unfamiliar with the Dakoṭa words. Older words exist that are still used regularly by Sioux Valley elders but are rarely used in Minnesota Dakoṭa communities now because of language loss. My kuŋṡi, Carrie, pointed out that when the Dakoṭa is translated into English, some parts appear repetitious, although in Dakoṭa it does not appear that way. She has had over twenty years of experience teaching the Dakoṭa language at the University of Minnesota, translating words and phrases on a daily basis. As we were working on the translations she would agonize over how best to translate a word or phrase, not wanting to misrepresent the words of Uŋkaŋna and at the same time trying to create in English an imagery consistent with that gained when hearing the stories in Dakoṭa. This part of the work has been by far the most time-consuming.

Working within the Dakoṭa language presented its own unique problems to me as an Indigenous scholar. As historians in my field have ignored tribal languages and the writing of our history has been done in English, there were many issues to examine and overcome. Ngũgĩ wa Thiong'o has written extensively about the problems arising when colonized peoples have an established tradition in writing in the colonizer's language. As someone who has written in his native language as a means of reaching his own people as they continue their struggle of resistance, he has discussed what black Africans have faced as they reclaim their languages in literature: "[We have encountered] Problems of literacy. Problems of publishing. Problems of the lack of critical tradition. Problems of orthography. Problems of having very many languages in the same country. Problems of hostile governments with a colonised mentality. Abandonment by some of those who could have brought their genius—demonstrated by their excellent performance in foreign languages—to develop their own languages."[19] As Indigenous Peoples in North America we face these same issues, but we have the additional burden of the loss of our languages to take into consideration. We seek to develop a body of literature in those languages, but they must be recovered first. As our languages were devalued and disparaged for so long, it is a struggle in our era to reassert a commitment to them and overcome the above challenges.

For the Dakoṭa language we are fortunate to have a small body of written materials, primarily from the early work of missionaries (who believed developing our language in writing would facilitate the Christianizing process), especially the work of Stephen Riggs, John Williamson, and Samuel and Gideon Pond. In addition, there exists a small treasure of Lakoṭa language materials, in particular those collected, transcribed, and translated by Ella Deloria, made available to modern readers through the work of Julian Rice. Albert White Hat Sr. has also contributed greatly to the advancement of Lakoṭa language use and study in his recent work *Reading and Writing the Lakota Language*. However, little modern writing is done in the Dakoṭa language, outside of the important curricula developed for the purposes of language teaching. Thus this work will contribute to what I hope will be a developing body of Dakoṭa-language texts. I further hope that in the near future the analysis might also be presented in our language by fluent Dakoṭa-language speakers and writers, those with more skill than I. Perhaps one day we can begin to engage one another in a critical Dakoṭa-language discourse.

Initially, as these stories were relayed to us and as I began to imagine how to present them, it was my intent to publish Uŋkaŋna's narrative with as little comment as possible. I wanted the stories to stand on their own. However, I began to realize that with each telling of an account, Uŋkaŋna assumed a basic knowledge base among his listeners, something that, although I had taken it for granted as a Dakoṭa, became apparent as non-Dakoṭa people began to read his translated accounts and offered comments or questions. Clearly, what was needed was an analysis of what it is I take for granted or, more important, what a fluent speaker takes for granted when listening to Dakoṭa stories from a knowledgeable, fluent speaker. What became manifest was the notion that equally important to the understanding of the content of the accounts of the past was how the Dakoṭa conceptualize the past, and how that conceptualization is revealed in the use of language.

Ki Waṡicu Etaŋhaŋ Ihduḣdayapi (Decolonization)

In thinking about this project on a broader scale, I wrestled with how to articulate the importance of these stories within a broader theoretical framework.

Part of the colonization process for Indigenous Peoples has been the constant denigration of our intellectual, linguistic, and cultural contributions to the world. We have been trained by the dominant society to think of our stories and language as insignificant or even worthless. In our isolation from one another, especially in the United States, we have been taught that our small numbers make us inconsequential, and this has fueled a sense of powerlessness. However, in broadening our scope and linking with Indigenous movements on a global scale, a great sense of hope and empowerment arises. With 300 million Indigenous Peoples worldwide with common histories of struggle against colonialism and neocolonialism, we have tremendous potential to transform the world. Sharing our stories and linking our voices is one step in achieving a different vision of the world. We will help the world open its eyes and see the forest for the trees. Thus this project may be seen as one more link or one more step in that direction. It may be situated in the growing body of global literature on Indigenous decolonization.

In building a collective voice, as Indigenous Peoples we derive great strength from hearing words of truth spoken: truth is an ally of the oppressed. As Frantz Fanon has stated, "Truth is that which hurries on the break-up of the colonialist regime; it is that which promotes the emergence of the nation; it is all that protects the natives, and ruins the foreigners."[20] When other colonized peoples give voice to experiences we have struggled to articulate, we rejoice. When we see ourselves in words of their creation, we are affirmed. When we hear stories of resistance, we are inspired. Yet, as Indigenous Peoples, these experiences have been all too rare. As Maori scholar Linda Tuhiwai Smith points out about her experiences reading texts, "I frequently have to orientate myself to a text world in which the centre of academic knowledge is either Britain, the United States or Western Europe; in which words such as 'we,' 'us,' 'our,' and 'I' actually exclude me."[21] As Ngũgĩ wa Thiong'o would say, as Indigenous writers we are thus decentering the colonial language and recentering it for our purposes. In this work when the words such as *we* or *our* are used, it is inclusive of Dakota people specifically and, more broadly, of Indigenous Peoples or Indigenous scholars. This is part of the decolonization process.

As *decolonization* is a term I will use throughout this text, it is important to define it. As Cree scholar Winona Wheeler explains in this excellent passage, decolonization offers a strategy for empowerment:

> A large part of decolonization entails developing a critical consciousness about the cause(s) of our oppression, the distortion of history, our own collaboration, and the degrees to which we have internalized colonialist ideas and practices. Decolonization requires auto-criticism, self-reflection,

and a rejection of victimage. Decolonization is about empowerment—a belief that situations can be transformed, a belief and trust in our own peoples' values and abilities, and a willingness to make change. It is about transforming negative reactionary energy into the more positive rebuilding energy needed in our communities.[22]

Haunani-Kay Trask defines decolonization as "the collective resistance to colonialism, including cultural assertions, efforts toward self-determination, and armed struggle."[23] Decolonization is a most important undertaking for Indigenous Peoples. Without a critical understanding of the colonialist structure as well as a means to resist it, we are in danger of being incapacited in our dealings with the colonialist regimes and perpetuating a form of neocolonialism among ourselves in our own tribal structures. In many of our communities this is already occurring. If we desire freedom from oppression we must first release our own minds from the bonds that have held them.

Decolonization is a fancy term that would likely raise eyebrows and hackles in Indigenous communities where jargonistic language has been used by researchers to fuel colonial power. However, it is a term grasped easily by Indigenous people once it is explained, as we have lived the realities of a colonized existence and can recognize the need for a decolonizing agenda. For example, when attending an Eastern Dakota Bands Treaty Council meeting in 2002, both my father and I talked about decolonization and its applicability to Dakota treaty struggles of today. By the end of my father's presentation in which he broke down the terminology, one of the elderly women who sat in the audience stood up and said, "I hope you are going to bring these presentations around to the young people so they can learn about it and we can all decolonize ourselves!" It did not matter that she was newly exposed to a challenging term; she recognized its usefulness to our struggle and immediately appropriated it.

Therefore, as Indigenous scholars it is our responsibility to bring to our communities useful ways of talking about our experiences and co-creating a culture of resistance based both on the recovery of Indigenous knowledge and traditional means of resistance as well as the useful theoretical frameworks and language from outside of our cultures that can assist us in our struggle. My mentor, Hidatsa/Sahnish scholar Michael Yellow Bird, recently pointed out to me the importance of assisting our communities in developing mastery over this new language of decolonization. He stated that terms such as *critical consciousness* and *decolonization* should be in the vocabulary of all of our young people, as well as words from their traditional language. In this way we can raise a new generation of Indigenous Peoples deeply committed to their tribal traditions but also deeply critical of the institutions of colonialism. It is my hope that this text will serve both these purposes yet remain accessible and thought-provoking.

Dakota/Lakota scholars have recently recognized this need for critical language to define our contemporary circumstances as well as our vision for the future. We are working toward incorporating the conceptual framework of decolonization into our language. For example, in a conference of Dakota scholars in 2001, we discussed the need to devise Dakota-language terms that reflect the colonized status of our people and the need to work toward a precolonized state of mind. One of the fluent speaking elders present, Sioux Valley scholar Doris Pratt, provided a good basis to start addressing this need. In reference to the precolonized time, Tuŋwiŋ Doris suggested the phrase *hipi itokab*, which literally means *before they came*. In reference to the colonized time period she described it as *hipi ohakab*, which literally means *after they came*. The obvious "they" in these definitions are the Europeans, EuroAmericans, EuroCanadians, and the other invading colonizers. So in reference to seeking decolonization of our minds, we might seek *tawacin suta waŋ hipi itokab*, or *a strong mind before they came*.

More recently, the Dakota-language teacher at the University of Minnesota, Neil McKay, provided me with additional terms for decolonization and colonization. These were created by Charles White Elk from the Pine Ridge Reservation, who in a workshop discussed the phrase *ki wasicu etaŋhaŋ ihduhdayapi*, which might be translated as *tearing one's self away from that which is Wasicu*. *Ihduhdayapi* might also be translated as *peeling one's self* or *stripping one's self*, implying something that can be removed. This is an excellent term because of its descriptiveness. Furthermore, White Elk offered the term *ihdutakudasni*, or *making yourself into nothing* as a term for assimilation, but this might also be applied to colonization. I hope he develops this further, as he can help to provide the linguistic basis for a decolonization movement in our nation. Other Indigenous speakers have viewed the process of colonization similarly. In her work with Cree oral historians, Wheeler quotes the Cree elder she refers to as Uncle Smith, who says: "We start to believe we are not alive, what we believe is obliterated.... They will make us believe that black is white, that's how powerful it is.... A person will have to be very strong, like my môsom. He did turn into an animal, he did turn into a weasel, he did turn into a coyote, to get away from the people who were trying to kill him, to survive. I didn't get that stamina and thinking to make me into something. And so, really, I'm becoming nothing."[24] These Indigenous ways of viewing colonization are extremely powerful, not just because of their descriptiveness but also because of the critical consciousness they reflect.

The strength of this project is that it has remained an Indigenous project from beginning to end. It was initiated by my grandfather, and the subsequent work derived from that initial interview—such as transcribing, translating, interpreting, analyzing, and writing—was completed by Indigenous people. As choices of various kinds have been made by all of us involved in the project, we all have contributed to the interpretation of the stories. However, because of the circumstances surrounding the telling of these accounts, it has also been important to examine why Uŋkaŋna chose the stories he did. They certainly represent only a small number of the stories he held in his memory (both before and after the recording of these stories I heard a great many other stories from him), but he selected them to be documented for a purpose. In many of the stories this is indicated by the way he talks about them or for reasons suggested in the stories themselves, but as his audience, those of us working on the transcriptions and translations, we also have ideas about this. As Leslie Marmon Silko has written about the Laguna oral tradition:

> As with any generation
> the oral tradition depends upon each person
> listening and remembering a portion
> and it is together—
> all of us remembering what we have heard together—
> that creates the whole story
> the long story of the people.[25]

The stories contained here, then, do not represent the history of the Dakota nation. Rather, they represent a portion of one person's memory that helps to create the long story of our people. For all of us working on the project who have also been a part of the interpretive process, our voices are present in our translations, footnotes, and commentary.

Another decolonizing strategy employed in the publishing of this collection is the demonstration that stories from the oral tradition can stand on their own. While many prominent scholars in the field of American Indian history would argue that Indigenous oral tradition can only serve a supplementary role in written history, this work is a testament to the contrary. While it does not offer a complete history of the Dakota Oyate (an impossibility in both the written and oral tradition), the contribution it makes to understanding the past of Dakota people is no less significant, or valid, than any other work of history that relies on the written documentary record. The colonizers have worked very hard at trying to convince themselves and us that our history on its own is somehow inferior. As Albert Memmi states, "In order for the colonizer to be the complete master, it is not enough for him to be so in actual fact, he must also believe in its legitimacy. In order for that legitimacy to be complete, it is not enough for the colonized to be a slave, he must also accept his role."[26] Fortunately, the carriers of our oral traditions did not accept this role, rejecting the legitimacy of the colonizer's history and keeping our stories alive.

In addition, because these stories were told in our Native language, they also teach more about how we look into the past, how we make sense of that past, and how we remain affected today. A broader significance of these stories, then, also stems from our ability to define our history for ourselves, shaping our historical consciousness in a way that inextricably links it with our sense of identity. The stories themselves have a transformative effect in our contemptorary lives because they help determine our sense of who we are and where we are going. Through gifted storytellers the stories are interpreted through the generations, and we come to understand the meaning of being Dakota. This understanding and sense of identity is one that transcends time, the changing world, and modern technology. It is what will carry us into the future.

When I initially became involved with this oral-history project, I was unaware of how it would shape my life and become a driving force within it. While I knew it was my love of the oral tradition that fostered my interest in the professional discipline of history, I did not know quite how to bring the two together, or what would happen when I did. While other Dakota people such as Charles Alexander Eastman and Ella Cara Deloria brought the oral tradition to literature—and to anthropology, in Deloria's case—Dakota oral tradition has not been discussed in a historical context or from a historical perspective. Since 1992, when these accounts of my grandfather were first recorded, I've had an opportunity to explore the connection between the oral tradition and the academic discipline of history, and that exploration has given shape to the writings contained here. One of the major needs as I perceived it was for our oral tradition to break into the field of history, where it would have to be confronted as an alternative and radically different way of perceiving, ordering, and recording past experiences.

As an Indigenous scholar writing about my own culture, I came to realize that what we, as Dakota people, gained from our oral tradition differed from what my academic colleagues gained from their study of the past. I was writing and researching with a different purpose and, because of this, faced an isolation within the academic environment. The number of Indigenous academic historians is frighteningly low, and many of those who are established scholars have not felt compelled to write about their differing agendas. I have since grasped that my struggles are not unique to Dakota people but rather are part of a larger movement that is growing internationally among Indigenous scholars with a shared research agenda. Although Indigenous scholars are working in all areas of academics, history is one discipline in which Indigenous oral tradition and the academy collide. Linda Tuhiwai Smith, in her recent book *Decolonizing Methodologies: Research and Indigenous People*, discusses the relationship between history and our struggle for self-determination:

> A critical aspect of the struggle for self-determination has involved questions relating to our history as indigenous peoples and a critique of how we, as the Other, have been represented or excluded from various accounts. Every issue has been approached by indigenous peoples with a view to *rewriting* and *righting* our position in history. Indigenous peoples want to tell our own stories, write our own versions, in our own ways, for our own purposes.... [It is] a very powerful need to give testimony to and restore a spirit, to bring back into existence a world fragmented and dying.[27]

Dakota approaches to history are not easily aligned with the academic discipline's approach. Rather than dismissing them as incompatible, however, it is more sagacious for the academic discipline to expand itself to include approaches from non-Western peoples.

The first chapter in this book, "Okiciyaka Uŋyaŋpi (Oral Tradition)," may be more literally translated as "to tell as we go" and is a phrase used to signify the Dakota oral tradition. This section offers a critique of the area of "American Indian history" based upon the field's reliance on written documents. Historians of Indigenous history have paid little attention and given little credence to the oral traditions of Indigenous Peoples, thus excluding from their interpretations a vast number of authoritative Indigenous voices. This chapter further points out that scholars of Indigenous history have avoided learning and examining the Indigenous languages in which many of the oral traditions are transmitted. Scholars who have attempted to define oral tradition and oral history have fallen short in incorporating Indigenous worldviews into their definitions and have missed some crucial elements. This chapter offers a new way to view the oral tradition and oral history, highlighting the kind of training often received within Dakota culture as well as other Indigenous perspectives on the importance, power, and life of the stories.

The second chapter, entitled "Owotaŋna Wohdakapo (Tell It Straight)," addresses the accountability of scholars to the people about whom they are writing. It examines the benefits of studying Indigenous languages and developing respectful, collaborative relationships with Indigenous communities, as well as some of the problematic approaches scholars have taken in interviewing techniques and methodology. In addition, it provides commentary on the growing need for scholars to be attentive to the voices of Indigenous people as Indigenous people assert intellectual control over those things of value, including our history.

Bilingual formatting for Indigenous stories included in academic histories is unusual in the United States. Chapter 3, "De Iapi Uŋk'upi (We Were Given This Language)," is an exploration of the role and importance of Indigenous languages, both past and present, in the continuance of Indigenous identity. Central to this chapter is the idea that language is linked to cultural survival and is, therefore, part of a larger political and social struggle. Because the Dakota language is on the verge of extinction within Minnesota, the broader language preservation and revitalization efforts with which this bilingual project is linked will be highlighted. In consideration of the importance of language and its connection to historical conceptions, this chapter also analyzes categories of stories and their implications for inclusion in Dakota historical texts.

Chapter 4 begins the first section of Eli Taylor narratives. The term *ehaŋna woyakapi* used in this section may be literally translated as *the telling of long ago*, but it also serves as a categorical reference to a specific set of stories within the overarching oral tradition of the Dakota people. This chapter, "Dena Naḣ'uŋ Wauŋ (These I Heard Growing Up)," contains the first story relayed by Uŋkaŋna and is offered in a bilingual format. A brief introduction and summary preface each story. The main body of text is then offered in a sentence-by-sentence transcription and translation. Footnotes appear in places where clarification is needed, or in places where those of us working on the project felt it would be beneficial to add our insights or commentary. If any changes were made to the actual text, the additions are enclosed in brackets. The stories are divided in sections according to what seemed like natural breaks, either at the end of a taping session or when a clear change in subject matter occurred.

Next, chapter 5, "Ṭaku Ociciyake Waciŋ (I Want to Tell You Something)," relates the connection between the oral tradition, language, and contemporary Dakota identity. The formulation of historical consciousness within the oral tradition is in many ways the formulation of identity and sense of self. The language provides revealing insights into how this historical consciousness is shaped and notions about the past are constructed. This chapter extracts key passages from chapter 4 to illustrate these points, providing commentary on some of the important elements of the stories and revealing phrases, sentences, or thought patterns. The teachings from the oral tradition, relayed through the worldview inherent in the language, are key to maintaining the sense of identity that will carry Dakota people into the future.

Chapter 6, "Ṭoked Imacaġe (How I Grew Up)," presents Uŋkaŋna's stories on a variety of topics, most of which derive from his personal life, and is followed by chapter 7, "Dakotak Hena Wiçawada (I Believe in Those Dakota

Ways)," which provides a discussion of those accounts. Interestingly, we see in these chapters not only how personal experiences affect a person's life but also how missed experiences equally affect them. Thus he discusses in the earlier sections events or memories that shaped his thinking, but later points out that he missed out on participation in key ceremonial experiences such as the inipi (sweat lodge) and the wiwaŋyak wacipi (sundance). In this section we also see the role of Dakota women highlighted more prominently, beginning with a description of the care his mother took with him and continuing with discussions on a variety of issues more revealing about woman's position in Dakota society, such as menstruation and the buying of women for marriage.

Chapter 8, "Wahokuŋkiyapi (They Provide Guidance)," is divided into three sections, "Wapiya (Healing)," "Iŋyaŋ Śkaŋ Śkaŋ (Moving Stones)," and "Waehdepi (The Setting of Food)," but they are all united in the common theme of interaction with the spirit world. Although each of the stories conveyed here contains components that are mysterious in nature, they are nevertheless stories important to Dakota historical reality. The stories included within the first two sections occurred within Uŋkaŋna's lifetime, and they reflect the ability of an accomplished storyteller to interweave contemporary stories into the oral tradition. The last section of this chapter relates another meaningful account that reveals the important relationship Dakota people have with the spiritual world, but this story is older than the ones contained in the previous two sections. This story communicates the origin of a ceremonial offering to the spirit of a loved one after they have passed away, or the dedication of food.

Chapter 9, "Ṭaku Wakaŋ (That Which Is Mysterious)," then provides a commentary on the significance of these stories in conveying important aspects of tribally held values and belief systems. It illuminates the contrasting worldviews of the Dakota and the Wašicu by discussing more explicitly the themes and ideas contained in the stories from the previous chapter. It is important to point out here, however, that though these stories address things that are mysterious, or things that may have no scientific explanation, they are valued equally within the oral tradition as ehaŋna woyakapi or narratives of the past.

Chapter 10, "Akicitapi (They Are Warriors)," includes stories having to do with warriors or warfare, but only the last story might actually be considered an okicize story or more traditional war story. Uŋkaŋna begins with a discussion containing an important segment about the thirty-eight Dakota men who were hanged in Mankato, Minnesota, in 1862. Uŋkaŋna sends a powerful message by characterizing these men as heroes rather than as the killers and savages they are usually depicted as being. He uses this to lead into a story about four young men setting off on the warpath in search of honor. The second narrative is an okicize story about the Dakota code-talkers of World War I. In providing these stories, Uŋkaŋna is defining Dakota ideals about bravery, courage, and reasons for participation in war, all in stories completely unknown to mainstream Americans and Canadians. The commentary of these stories of warriors appears in chapter 11, "Wicotawaciŋ Yuwaṡte (It Makes for Good Thoughts)," which highlights these aspects and demonstrates the necessity of these stories to the building of a strong Dakota identity as well as a critical consciousness.

The last portion of the book is dedicated to Uŋkaŋna Eli Taylor's commentary and our discussions with him. While some of his commentary in between stories did not have a specific focus or a clear beginning and end, the content was valuable enough to warrant its own separate section. Chapter 12, "Ṯoked Ḳapi Oyaḳapi (Commentary)," is a collection of some of these narrations, with my commentary provided directly after his. Topics in this section of chapter 12 range from his thoughts on the possibility of future war, how the young people of today have been failed by their elders, how to take care of the iŋyaŋ ṡkaŋ ṡkaŋ, the story behind his Dakota name, to several amusing anecdotes.

Chapter 13, "Ṯaku Ṯoktokċa Iwohdaḳapi (A Discussion of Different Things)," provides a transcription of the discussion from our last day of recording. On that day we were able to ask several questions driven by our own curiosity, and his responses are recorded here. This, more than any other section of the text, is more characteristic of a conventional interviewing situation. This section is almost entirely in English, most likely because the questions were initially posed to Uŋkaŋna in English. Those of us in attendance made three queries to him: the first was on his thoughts about the wiŋkṭa (a third gender category within Dakota culture); the second was on the meaning of being Dakota; and the third on his wishes for Dakota young people today. In this chapter my commentary will, again, be presented directly after his interview responses.

Finally, the conclusion, "Oyaṭe Nipi Kṭe (The People Shall Live)," focuses on the contributions of this work, particularly to the Dakota Oyaṭe but also to the non-Indigenous world and the academic discipline of history. Much of the aim of the project has been to define Dakota identity, with linguistic analysis and stories of the past serving as the guide. But on a broader level, in training the next generations of Dakota young people in their own traditions and developing a culture of resistance to colonialism, this work also contributes to the growing global decolonization movement. Finally, this closing chapter offers some personal reflections about the importance of the Eli Taylor narratives for those of us who worked closely with the project. It reaffirms the powerful connection between identity, language, and history, all of which will ensure that the people will live.

As a historian, my challenge in bringing these ideas to the academic arena has been to articulate the need for Indigenous voices and perspectives, to push the boundaries of historical method and theory, and to call attention to the problematic way "Indian history" has been handled by many scholars. This is no easy task, since the academic discipline of history was not designed to accommodate non-Western conceptions of history (especially ones that challenge its colonialist rule) or to acknowledge other living sources of authority. Ultimately, as a Dakota historian, my task is to fashion a place for Indigenous historical scholarship that examines an Indigenous epistemology and utilizes Indigenous sources in an academic but Indigenous-centered framework.

As a Dakota, in these materials I am reminded of the beauty and richness of Dakota culture and the responsibility required to sustain its existence. Not only have I found a sense of purpose in recording this information so that others may share in the experience, but I have realized more of my responsibility in living up to the word *Dakota*. All of us have an obligation to remember our stories so that we may pass on the information to our children, not just in a written manuscript as presented here but in the way the information was originally given—through the oral tradition and language of our people.

A final comment must be made about Uŋkaŋna's intention in sharing these stories. Unlike many of the as-told-to stories or biographies of famous chiefs or medicine men, these are stories relayed by an ikće wićasta or common man, and they are not romantic in nature. He was an extremely humble man, often using self-deprecating humor to make others laugh. He would have resisted any attempt of mine to make him appear a hero or to glorify him in this book, preferring instead to be depicted as ordinary. However, many who knew him did consider him to be an exceptional human being precisely because of his selfless devotion to Dakota people, including those of us working on this project. The admiration for him contained in these pages is a reflection of that selflessness and belongs to us.

Because all the information presented here has been prompted by the teachings of Uŋkaŋna and the stories are written as he presented them to us, it is my hope that his voice and influence will come through above all else. If this is accomplished, it is certain his teachings will live on.

1. Okiciyaka Uŋyaŋpi (Oral Tradition)

Within Dakota culture, history is an interpretation of the past that becomes active only when a relationship has been developed between a storyteller and a listener. For thousands of years, stories deemed significant enough to perpetuate have been handed down orally through the generations, always reliant on the generosity and veracity of the storyteller and the eagerness and capacities of the listener. Most important, the continuation of these stories has been dependent on the meaning of the stories being conveyed and understood within the context of the worldview inherent in the Dakota language. This distinguishes it markedly from the Western academic historical interpretations of the Dakota past, which rely largely on documents written within the framework of the Western-European worldview.

One of my major goals is to promote the incorporation of Indigenous perspectives into the written historical record, with the hope and belief that this will lead to greater understanding and dialogue between the Indigenous and non-Indigenous peoples on the North American continent as well as a more comprehensive and broadly defined understanding of history. Since beginning my academic career, in discussions with colleagues about the importance of including Indigenous voices in history, I have been asked many times, "How might an Indigenous perspective on Indigenous history differ from those histories written by non-Indigenous historians?" Variations of this question have been asked in a number of other forums as well. There is no simple answer. Because there is no homogeneous Indigenous population, there is no homogeneous response, and there may be as many different responses as there are people asked. Based on my life experiences, my knowledge of Dakota history, culture, and language, and my work with the oral tradition, my answer to this may be markedly different from that of other scholars working in Indigenous history. This question, after all, is at the heart of what has fueled my ongoing examination of the role of the oral tradition.

To begin to address the question of how an Indigenous perspective of history might differ from a non-Indigenous one, we must first examine what constitutes an Indigenous perspective and how Indigenous voices are obtained. In an attempt to find Indigenous perspectives in Indigenous history, or to write a sound work in Indigenous history, it is absolutely essential to consult Indigenous sources. If there are written Indigenous sources available, those may be used cautiously, as many of the documents have been translated, written, and interpreted by non-Natives or others who might have altered dialogues to meet their own agendas.[1] However, the vast majority of authoritative Indigenous sources are oral. Our family and tribal historians, who belong to a long tradition in which information has been preserved and transmitted through the generations, possess the most thorough and vast accounts of our own perceptions of the historical past. Yet these spokespersons in our communities have been largely ignored by academic historians writing Indigenous history. An amazing number of Indigenous histories still are reviewed as being "balanced" and "thorough" by non-Indigenous scholars, when in many instances the histories contain an embarrassingly low number of Indigenous sources, if any.[2] This has somehow become acceptable historical scholarship when dealing with the history of Indigenous Peoples, and the ridiculous nature of this standard is revealed to non-Natives only when scholars are asked to apply the same standards to the writing of histories for other groups of people. For example, would it be acceptable to write a German history without consulting any German sources? Would it be acceptable to write a history of the French without using any French sources? Why, then, is it acceptable to write Indigenous history without consulting Indigenous sources? Is it because most of our sources are oral rather than written, or because actual people would have to be consulted instead of pieces of paper or microfiche? Clearly the latter approach is much easier, in which a historian would not have to deal with live people who might object to a study or who might have differing versions that could alter a thesis.

I would suggest that in addition to the above reasons for historians using double standards within the field, historians' views are also linked to their perceptions of Indigenous Peoples. For over thirty years Vine Deloria Jr. has articulated to the American public his concerns about various forms of racism, differences in Native and Western views, ways of life, and understandings of the world, as well as contemporary issues. In discussing racism in academia and scientific circles, he writes: "Some of the racism is doctrinaire and unforgiving—for instance, the belief that, for a person or community possessing any knowledge that is non-white/Western in origin, verification and articulation are unreliable. A corollary of this belief is that non-Western peoples tend to be excitable, are subjective and not objective, and consequently are unreliable observers."[3] While these views are certainly evident today in academia, both Indigenous and non-Indigenous historians must address these issues in open discussion.[4] Furthermore, this dismissal of Indigenous perspectives is symptomatic of the relationship of the colonizer to the colonized. Colonial dominance can be maintained only if the history of the subjugated is denied and that of the colonizer elevated and glorified.

Even for those desiring to break out of the academic historian's mold, they must address an accompanying problem with the collection of oral accounts among Indigenous groups, and that is the issue of language. Because many of our elders spoke their Indigenous languages first and are often more comfortable and eloquent speaking in their language, the linguistic element is one that historians working in Indigenous history need to consider. Would an English scholar doing German history be required to learn German? Would an English scholar of French history not bother to learn French? James Lockhart, in his work on the Nahua of Mexico, commented: "The gods of the disciplines seemed to have decreed that historians should study Indians indirectly, leaving it to others, mainly anthropologists, to approach them through their own language."[5]

Even scholars specializing in oral history, such as Jan Vansina, advocate long-term language study when examining traditions in an oral society.[6] While oral historians working with African groups have recognized the importance of linguistic studies, this seems to be an issue largely avoided by historians working in the United States and Canada. Prominent historians have developed rationales for not studying Indigenous languages, even while acknowledging the positive benefits to be gained from such study. Richard White, for example, recently wrote: "Historians have done very little with language because so few historians know any native languages. Our argument has been that there are no, or very few, documents in the language and very often no or very few speakers are left, so what is the point of learning it? To this we quite legitimately add a third objection: languages change like everything else. The language recorded at a given point is not necessarily the historical language."[7] Yes, Indigenous languages, like all living languages, change over time, but nowhere else would this type of argument be made as this would suggest that no languages should ever be learned because of their changing nature. And, yes, in many Indigenous cultures the languages are being lost at a rapid rate, but this does not decrease the value in learning them for academic purposes, especially since the only way to learn Indigenous languages with a degree of proficiency or fluency is through the help of a fluent speaker. If the language is still being passed on, it is still living! Few documents exist in which Indigenous voices are heard, and many of those are in Indigenous languages. White is asserting that for various reasons it is legitimate to ignore the voices of Indigenous people if those voices are in Indigenous languages, either oral or written, as well as arguing the acceptability of only utilizing sources that speak to him in the English language. Furthermore, his comments suggest that contemporary speakers wouldn't have the skills to understand the cultural change necessary to contribute insight into historical texts and/or interpretations of current analyses.

Some others might claim that the diversity of Indigenous populations precludes the study of specific languages, but again, the question must be raised, does a scholar specializing in comparative European history not bother to study or develop a working knowledge of any of the languages of the European groups? I think not. In fact, the tendency would be to become at least familiar, if not fluent, in several languages. Knowledge of Indigenous languages will only deepen understanding and enhance interpretations of Indigenous history, but the learning of Indigenous languages requires a lengthy, if not a lifetime, commitment. This certainly cannot be accomplished on six months of funding from a research grant, and it may mean that publications on various Indigenous groups will only be produced after many years of research.

The acquisition and understanding of Indigenous oral accounts, including language, is of vital importance in understanding Indigenous perspectives and is, I believe, the greatest resource with which the discipline of Indigenous history will proceed. However, it is also the area that is the most difficult to engage in, to interpret, and to incorporate into standard texts, because for non-Natives it means attempting to understand a completely foreign worldview that often does not conform to Western standards of historical analysis and writing. Because of this, many established scholars in the field of Indigenous history will meet these ideas with resistance. However, as more Indigenous people are trained as historians and begin to examine their own histories with all the analytical, research, and writing skills that graduate training provides, it is inevitable that ideas, theories, and interpretations held by non-Natives who have dominated the field will be challenged. In addition, new ideas will emerge, these new worldviews will be incorporated, and Native history will be forever altered.

I have briefly discussed why Indigenous perspectives must be included in histories related to their group or nation, and I have also suggested that the most valuable resources for gaining this perspective are contained within the oral tradition. In his book *Oral Historiography*, David Henige differentiates between oral history and oral tradition when he writes: "As normally used nowadays, 'oral history' refers to the study of the recent past by means of life histories or personal recollections, where informants speak about their own experiences. . . . Oral tradition should by widely practised or understood in a society and it must be handed down for at least a few generations."[8]

Vansina has a similar definition for oral history but further divides the area into categories, and he differs from Henige in the definition of oral tradition only by excluding the need for a collective memory: "The sources of oral historians are reminiscences, hearsay, or eyewitness accounts about events and situations which are contemporary, that is, which occurred during the lifetime of the informants. This differs from oral traditions in that oral traditions are no longer contemporary. They have passed from mouth to mouth, for a period beyond the lifetime of the informants."[9]

Aside from being derogatory in nature, these definitions may be applicable to Indigenous oral history and oral tradition only in a limited way.[10] Indigenous people's life histories, for example, often incorporate the experiences of both human and nonhuman beings as well as the experiences of their ancestors. In addition, by suggesting that people living today are outside an oral tradition, these definitions assume that the contemporary person is not part of a living tradition that can incorporate new information.

For my purposes here, from a Dakota perspective, I would suggest that the definition of oral history is contained within that of the oral tradition. For the Dakota and, I suspect, for many other Indigenous nations, "oral tradition" refers to the way in which information has been passed on rather than to the length of time something has been told. Hence, personal experiences, pieces of information, events, incidents, and so forth can become a part of the oral tradition at the moment they happen, or the moment they are spoken of, as long as the person adopting the memory is part of an oral tradition. Oral history can also exist outside the oral tradition since many individuals may provide authoritative oral-historical accounts based on their own experiences without necessarily belonging to an oral tradition themselves. These definitions imply that even though this may be the case, those belonging to an oral tradition would also be able to relate oral-historical accounts.

Charles Eastman, a Waȟpetuŋwaŋ Dakota, reveals in his autobiography, *Indian Boyhood*, the distinct way in which oral skills were developed in our culture:

> Very early, the Indian boy assumed the task of preserving and transmitting the legends of his ancestors and his race. Almost every evening a myth, or a true story of some deed done in the past was narrated by one of the parents or grandparents, while the boy listened with parted lips and glistening eyes. On the following evening, he was usually required to repeat it. If he was not an apt scholar, he struggled long with his task; but as a rule, the Indian boy is a good listener and has a good memory, so that his stories were tolerably well mastered. The household became his audience by which he was alternately criticized and applauded.[11]

This excerpt highlights the rigorous and extensive training required of young boys, as Eastman is speaking of his own upbringing, but it would certainly be applicable to the training of girls also. In my own family, my father's older siblings (who were fortunate enough to receive extensive training from their great-grandparents) would spend hours listening to the stories of their elders. Upon leaving their grandparents, they would be instructed to return home and relate to their mother the stories they had just learned. Since she had also received her training from them, it was clear that they could test their storytelling skills on her and that she would be able to verify their accuracy.

In the present, this training may take a different form. For example, although growing up I was not required to recite back to my grandmother accounts I had heard, I find myself in that position more frequently today. I have given numerous presentations among Dakota people, including some of the elders who have trained me. As a junior scholar and storyteller, I often begin my presentation by asking them to correct me if I make any errors. They usually very kindly make suggestions when they need to or reaffirm the information as I have presented it. In public presentations to Dakota people who are unfamiliar with me or my work, I have also been quizzed on both my knowledge of and perspective on Dakota topics, both in English and Dakota. These interactions serve the same fundamental purpose: they help preserve the integrity of the collective historical memory of the Oyate.

Consequently, the Dakota definition of oral tradition is at least partially based on the assumption that the ability to remember is an acquired skill—one that is acutely developed or neglected. In addition, in his first story Uŋkaŋna Eli Taylor tells about a spiritual figure who came among the Dakota many centuries ago. As he passed on information to our people, he said, "What I am going to tell you now, I want you to pass on every year, from one generation to the next, from your grandchild to your great-grandchild, and your great-great-grandchild on down. Ḳiksuyapo (Remember this)!" "I will help you remember these things that I have told you," he said. In another instance, the Dakota were told, "I will give you a strong mind to remember." This story suggests that not only are our stories meant to be told orally because our tradition is of divine origin, but also that we have divine help in remembering them!

However, today not all Indigenous people have been trained in an oral tradition. While all accounts collected from Indigenous people may be valuable if those people are speaking from a position of authority about their own life experiences, here I am addressing oral history as it applies specifically to those belonging to an oral tradition. In many cases, this means working with the elders of our communities. These same people are often the carriers of such other traditions as language, ceremonies, and customs, which all help to better understand differing worldviews.

Eastman also describes the differentiation between myth and true stories, which would necessarily mean that both these types of stories would be part of the oral tradition, and all would require this intensive training. The distinction highlighted by Eastman might also signify his understanding of Western categories and his desire to give credence to Dakota historical accounts within their conceptual framework. As academic historians begin to consider what aspects of stories may be of historical value, or what constitutes a "true" story, they are treading on culturally sensitive turf. As we delve into these topics, we begin to consider how the Indigenous perspective may differ from the academic historian's. Over thirty years ago archeologist Bernard Fontana perceptively offered his views on this subject in his essay "American Indian Oral History: An Anthropologist's Note," stating: "What is relevant is that someone else defines truth differently and sees history in a different way. If in collecting oral histories one aims to get the Indians' point of view, the question of veracity in our terms has little to do with it. It is veracity in their terms which counts."[12] For a research commitment made three decades ago by an anthropologist, it is disheartening to note that little progress has been made in this area in the discipline of history. A few scholars, however, are making headway in this area.

Joanne Rappaport, for example, has intentionally and quite persuasively worked to break down the history/myth dichotomy in her work on the Nasa of Colombia, instead framing the focus of the discussion much more productively on Native interpretations of historical evidence.[13] In her work *Indeh*, Eve Ball also provides readers important access to the historical knowledge conveyed by Asa Daklugie and other Apaches, fortunately with very little interpretation from Ball. While not always agreeing with or understanding the worldview from which Daklugie and other Apaches were speaking, she does acknowledge their memory skills and ability to relay knowledge competently.[14] Moreover, the results of her years of work provide a valuable Indigenous perspective that would be unobtainable from the written documents found in archives.

Another scholar, David William Cohen, has argued that rigidity in thinking about oral history is highly problematic. He instead argues that scholars are presented with a unique opportunity when examining the history of people from oral cultures. "They invite us to see individuals," he remarks, "making and holding historical knowledge in all their complexity and individuality—considerably concerned with interests, objectives, recreation, and esteem, and rather less concerned with performing history according to some given cultural design.... They call us to strengthen our approach to the reconstruction of the past through the reworking of our logic of the production of historical knowledge."[15] This is the crux of the challenge to academics writing history about those from oral cultures. This is an issue that will become increasingly more pressing, and the drive for understanding more compelling, as more Indigenous scholars articulate their own tribal perspectives in the production of historical knowledge. However, because the oral traditions from which Indigenous people come are linked to cultural survival (not to mention land and treaty claims), the invitations to "see" will likely be framed as demands.

After growing up in a family with a rich oral tradition and deciding to spend my life working with that tradition, I have come to the realization that our oral tradition is a kind of web in which each strand is part of a whole. The individual strands, which may be compared to a single story, are most powerful when connected to make an entire web—that is, when as many stories as possible are examined in their entirety. Each of our stories possess meaning and power, but they are most significant when understood in relation to other stories in the same oral tradition.

For example, while stories of "shape-shifting" are part of the Dakota reality and would belong to our categories of "true" stories, they make much more sense when understood in combination with some of the stories outside of what academics might call the "historical" realm—such as some of our Uŋktomi stories. Uŋktomi is a sort of trickster figure, as well as a spiritual entity, who has the capacity to change form. While Uŋktomi stories are often told to teach and entertain, he is very much a part of our reality, and our very being would be in question if he had never existed. In addition, Uŋktomi stories contain meaningful elements that are important in understanding our worldview as relayed in many of our historical accounts. Furthermore, they solidly contain what we perceive as truth, especially about human nature. Uŋktomi is a notorious shape-shifter, and understanding this helps provide a context for understanding shape-shifting stories in the historical context. An example of such an account is one Uŋkaŋna Eli Taylor relayed to us. Shortly after the U.S.-Dakota War of 1862, two Dakota men turned themselves into snakes to flee to Canada, thereby escaping extermination or imprisonment. Ironically, and somewhat humorously, one of them wasn't a good swimmer as a snake and drowned. The other one, a man by the name of Oyate Yaŋke, made it to Canada and resided there for years.[16] Without an understanding of our worldview, such a story as this might be dismissed as fiction. However, in accordance with Dakota worldview, we would consider this particular story to be historical. Common threads run through many of the stories and are a reflection of our reality, unexplainable perhaps, but reality nevertheless. To reach through the depths of the layers of meaning then, it is valuable and necessary for historians to acquaint themselves with accounts outside the traditional historical domain.

The differentiation between myth and true stories has been a source of contention between Natives and non-Natives for centuries. As Deloria points out, "Regardless of what Indians have said concerning their origins, their migrations, their experiences with birds, animals, lands, waters, mountains, and other peoples, the scientists have maintained a stranglehold on the definitions of what respectable and reliable human experiences are. The Indian explanation is always cast aside as a superstition, precluding Indians from having an acceptable status as human beings, and reducing them in the eyes of educated people to a pre-human level of ignorance."[17] In addition to what many non-Natives dismiss as "impossible," they have also dismissed the possibility of a distinction between myth and history, not understanding how those from within a culture make those distinctions. Much of the conflict and misunderstanding in this area arises because within Indigenous culture the spiritual and material worlds are intimately interconnected and mutually constitutive of Indigenous "reality." This is certainly reflected in the Dakota conception of history. For most Indigenous people, these things are perfectly "natural," "real," and "factual." Therefore, those from outside the culture would be hard-pressed to prove what is truth from the perspective of someone else's worldview.[18]

Moreover, in notions of truth and myth, an Indigenous perspective may differ from a Western historian's in the emphasis each places on time and place and its role in history. While many historical stories from Indigenous oral traditions do not contain information on when a particular event occurred (especially according to a Julian or Gregorian calendar), the stories often contain detailed information about where specific events took place. In the Dakota language, my kuŋśi, Elsie Cavender, began dozens of stories with *ehaŋna*, meaning *long ago*, to indicate that the story took place long before the lifetimes of those present but that the exact length of time was unknown. In this way I learned about many events and important places in my family's and nation's history. Another phrase used to indicate the antiquity of a story is *otokahe hekta*, which would literally translate as *in the beginning*. This invokes the origins of the people or the origins of the topic of the story.

A reference to "long ago" is common among Indigenous Peoples. For example, the Anishinaabe use the word *mewinzha*,[19] and as Luci Tapahonso points out, "Many Diné stories begin with the expression, 'alk' idaa' jini' (a long time they said) if the event requires it; otherwise, they start with 'Jini' or 'they said,' and who 'they' are is not questioned, because inherent in Diné storytelling is the belief that, indeed, the events or the story did occur at some time in the past."[20] Similarly, Wheeler explains, "The idea of time and its referents are expressed in specific contexts: *Long ago*, kayas, or, *a long long long time ago*, mitone kayas, or kayas kayas mitone kayas, so far back it doesn't matter how long ago."[21] As Indigenous people we have different values underpinning our examination of time.

In the Minnesota and Mississippi River valleys (where my people have lived for thousands of years) there are numerous places described in the stories that I have personally visited, which have solidified the concept of Dakota history within my own mind. For example, I learned about Bdoṭe (now called *Mendota* in English), where the Dakota were first created according to the Bdewakaŋtuŋwaŋ creation story. According to that same story in the first attempts at our creation, two bluffs were formed from the earth, one called Caskẹ Taŋka (large, first-born, and male child) and the other Caskẹ Cisṭinna (small, first-born, and male child). These bluffs are still important today.

I also knew early the sight at Wood Lake where my great-great-great-grandfather Mazomani (Chief Walking Iron) was shot by white soldiers while carrying a white flag of truce during the final battle of the U.S.-Dakota War of 1862. In addition, the location of the homes and missions of early missionaries Williamson and Riggs near Upper Sioux was part of my early education, although I never learned exactly when these missions were established until I read some of the non-Native texts on the subject. Visiting these sites reinforces the connection to place taught in the oral tradition, and many times I have walked with elders in search of a "place" attached to a story from the oral tradition. The sheer magnitude of sites is a reflection of the special relationship those who are indigenous to an area develop after thousands of years of interaction with it. As Wheeler points out, places also help to recover historical memory: "The land is mnemonic, it has its own set of memories, and when the old people go out on the land it nudges or reminds them, and their memories are rekindled."[22]

Keith Basso has done important research on place, and particularly its significance to the Western Apache. As an anthropologist and someone who has worked closely with tribal historians, Basso is fully aware of the discrepancy between how the Apache interpret their history and how academics approach the past.[23] He also is aware of how place is of fundamental importance in the Apache reconstruction of the past, saying, "For what matters most to Apaches is where events occurred, not when, and what they serve to reveal about the development and character of Apache social life. In light of these priorities, temporal considerations, though certainly not irrelevant, are accorded secondary importance."[24]

Though many Indigenous Peoples, including the Dakota, do not possess a concept of "time," it is not that the Dakota or other Indigenous groups had no sense of the passing of time or that they did not record any events chronologically. Some of the different means used to record events include winter counts, notched and bundled sticks, song boards, and other mnemonic devices that varied among Indigenous groups. Often things were placed in relation to one another. They might be placed in the context of lineage and who was alive when a specific event took place, or when natural or man-made events or disasters occurred. However, for many of the stories reaching into the distant past, exact dates remain unknown. Many of the origin stories of creation, ceremonies, and traditions, do not have specific dates associated with them.

For many Indigenous people, this does not pose any particular problem. While working on the life story of Mabel McKay, a Pomo woman, Greg Sarris had the following discussion with her:

> "How you going to do my book?" she asked.
>
> "That's what I always ask you," I shot back. She gave me an admonishing look. Not the answer she was looking for, I thought to myself.
>
> "I'm going to come back in the spring, like I said," I told her. "I'll finish getting the exact dates and figures that go with the stories."
>
> She looked perplexed.
>
> "You know," I said, "so I can get things right. I mean your life, the story."
>
> She focused. "It has nothing to do with dates and that. I don't know about dates. It's everlasting what I'm talking about."[25]

To give another example, Oren Lyons, in his interview with Bill Moyers, said: "The great Peacemaker came amongst us, brought peace amongst the Mohawk, the Oneida, the Onondaga, the Cayuga, and the Seneca. He laid down the rules at that time. We don't know how long ago, maybe a thousand years ago, maybe two, maybe more. It doesn't matter."[26] So, while those raised in a Western tradition are preoccupied with knowing exact dates, for many Indigenous people time is of peripheral importance to the experiential lessons and understandings. From this perspective, a lack of exact dates does not represent a shortcoming of the oral tradition; rather, it simply demonstrates differences in emphasis regarding important matters. Any scholar persisting in the need for dates has essentially "missed the boat."

Deloria describes the difficulties those from a Western European tradition have had in understanding the Indigenous connection to land, and he highlights these ideological differences between Indigenes and Europeans in *God Is Red*:

> Western European peoples have never learned to consider the nature of the world discerned from a spatial point of view. And a singular difficulty faces people of Western European heritage in making a transition from thinking in terms of space. The very essence of Western European identity involves the assumption that time proceeds in a linear fashion; further it assumes that at a particular point in the unraveling of this sequence, the peoples of Western Europe became the guardians of mankind. The same ideology that sparked the Crusades, the Age of Exploration, the Age of Imperialism, and the [more] recent crusade against Communism all involve the affir-

mation that time is peculiarly related to the destiny of the people of Western Europe. And later, of course, the United States.[27]

While linear time has certainly dominated the way history has thus far been written, we may be in an age where divisions of time become less useful than dimensions of space. In this same work, Deloria points out that "in a world in which communications are nearly instantaneous and simultaneous experiences are possible, it must be space that in a fundamental way distinguishes us from one another, not time."[28] It may, after all, be in the historian's best interest to begin to examine spatial relationships more thoroughly, not only to consider other peoples' perceptions of time but also because our current age may demand it.

Where I disagree with Deloria in *God Is Red* is in his characterization of Indigenous conceptions of history. "The scholars have had a difficult time piecing together the maps of pre-Discovery America because of the vague nature of tribal remembrances," he states. "The result of this casual attitude toward history was, of course, that history had virtually no place in the religious life of the tribe."[29] Although he has since revised his opinion, in this text Deloria is clearly using a definition of history that is largely employed today, but one that is overwhelmingly biased toward Western thought. If scholars have had a difficult time piecing together the maps of "pre-Discovery America," perhaps it is because they have been trying to use the wrong puzzle pieces. If, for example, historians used puzzle pieces of place, rather than time, a comprehensive and detailed map would emerge. If the standards of evaluation would shift, and place were emphasized over time, then history and spiritual beliefs would also be closely intertwined.

When this issue is examined more closely, it becomes apparent that a fundamental difference in the perception of history exists, and that it is connected to its basic definition. According to the *New Standard Encyclopedia*, history is "a record of past events, usually a written account of the development of human civilization and an explanation of how and why events occurred."[30] This definition highlights the emphasis on written versus oral, a chronological order and thus emphasis on time, and the human element being of utmost importance. In fact, many historians utilizing a similar definition may even suggest that events not placed within a chronological time frame are, indeed, ahistorical or antihistorical. In addition, this definition suggests a connection between "civilization" and history, a mark of classification for which most Indigenous groups have not qualified—that is, according to many academicians, specifically anthropologists. If this were true, according to this definition and the one that Deloria used, Indigenous people's lack of a sense of history would be a shortcoming.

Deloria, however, has recently produced a strong defense of Indigenous oral traditions in his book *Red Earth White Lies*.[31] In this work his views on oral history are more closely aligned with my own understandings according to the oral tradition with which I grew up. Within Indigenous cultures I have seen great concern over and investment in history, and it was my experience in the oral tradition that fueled my love for history, not the written texts that I grew to regard with mistrust and dislike from an early age. It is not Indigenous people's perspective of history, then, that presents a "problem," but rather the limited definition of history employed by historians today.

To elaborate this concept, it is necessary to address the function of the oral tradition within Indigenous societies. Our stories have served and continue to serve very important functions: both the historical and mythical stories provide moral guidelines by which one should live; they teach the young and remind the old what appropriate and inappropriate behavior consists of in our cultures; they provide a sense of identity and belonging, situating community members within their lineage and establishing their relationship to the natural world; and they always serve as a source of entertainment as well as a source of bonding and intimacy between the storyteller and the audience. Perhaps, most important, our oral tradition helps us to reclaim our past for ourselves and stands as a body of knowledge to be differentiated from that body of knowledge written and understood by the dominant society.

James W. Loewen, in his national best-seller *Lies My Teacher Told Me*, describes how history is the least favorite and is considered the "most irrelevant" of subjects by American high-school students.[32] I believe students are unable to relate in a meaningful way to their past, largely because of the content of the material and the way it is presented. In addition, Loewen points out:

> African American, Native American, and Latino students view history with a special dislike. They also learn history especially poorly. Students of color do only slightly worse than white students in mathematics. If you'll pardon my grammar, non-white students do more worse in English and most worse in history. Something intriguing is going on here: surely history is not more difficult for minorities than trigonometry or Faulkner. Students don't even know they are alienated, only that they "don't like social studies" or "aren't any good at history." In college, most students of color give history departments a wide berth.[33]

For Indigenous students who have been exposed to an oral tradition growing up, there is a conscious sense of alienation and a realization that discrepancies occur between the way Indigenous people are depicted in written texts, or absent from texts, in contrast to how we are depicted in the oral stories about our own people. It was while in high school that I first went to my father and asked why the "Sioux" I was reading about in high school were so different from the people my grandmother talked about.

In another discussion on the oral tradition with my father during my sophomore year of college in 1989, he described the reverse verification process he uses in attempting to determine if a history of our people is accurate. After that discussion, I realized I had unconsciously been doing the same thing. While most academic historians examine oral tradition and look for written evidence to validate it, for us, we knew a written story actually had merit if we had heard the same stories from our elders.

In addition, our stories, much more so than the written documents written by non-Natives, give detailed descriptions about our historical players. They provide information such as our motivations and our decision-making processes and how nonmaterial, nonphysical circumstances (or those belonging to the unseen or spirit world) have shaped our past and our understanding of the present. They also answer many other "why" and "how" questions typically asked by the academic community. Moreover, stories are considered by many Indigenous people to be living entities, with a power and spirit of their own. Greg Sarris, in one of his essays on his work with Mabel McKay, relates her perspective on this subject and the non-Native's inability to appreciate the stories as Indigenous people do. She tells him, "Our stories, like our lives, are living. Might as well give white man your leg or arm. No matter what he gets, he just does with it how he likes. Like our land."[34]

Consequently, ours are not merely interesting stories or simple dissemination of historical facts. They are, more important, transmissions of culture upon which our survival as a people depends. In addition, as the stories are heard repeatedly through time, they cease to be just the stories of the elders and ancestors—the elders' and ancestors' memories become our own. Often the messages contained within the stories are not easily decipherable, even for those from within a culture. Often it takes years, or even a lifetime, to understand the full meaning and implications of a story heard as a child. These stories are reflected upon throughout our lifetimes, first as we hear our elders tell the stories and then as we retell them as the elders. Thus, our historical consciousness is well developed and our connection to the past is intimate. That a people's history is only properly called history if it meets the criteria set by the culture of the colonizer is a form of intellectual racism and a testament to the ongoing process of colonization.

2. Owotaŋna Wohdakapo (Tell It Straight)

Imagine a scholar sitting before a room full of elders from the culture he has been studying after his first book on them has just been published. Imagine him having to be accountable for his methodology, his translations, his editing, his terminology, his analysis, his interpretation, and his use of their stories. While a discussion like this between a scholar and his subjects of study may never occur in this formal forum, the dialogue will occur somewhere. The time for accountability of the work of historians and anthropologists has definitely come.

Prior to engaging in the collection of oral data from an Indigenous community, a scholar should consider the following:

> What are the motivations behind this interest?
> How will the information be used, and in what kind of context?
> Is enough known about the culture from which the information will be extracted?
> Who initiated the topic to be studied, Indigenous people or a scholar interested in a particular aspect of Indigenous history?
> And, perhaps most important, who will benefit from its documentation?[1]

Establishing answers to these questions will be the first step in engaging in a process loaded with moral considerations and acknowledging the ethics involved when working with live subjects who are quite capable of speaking for themselves.

In addition, concerns important to Indigenous people should also be taken into consideration. Within Dakota culture, we are taught that we must also learn to think with our hearts, and that those people who can only think with their minds are not only seriously lacking important understandings but whatever they produce will also be lacking important understandings and will ultimately create an undesirable outome. I've heard elders speak very openly about good minds being meaningless without good hearts. *Caŋte* is the word for *heart* in our language, and many words are derived from that root word (nearly fifty listings exist with the base word *caŋte* in Riggs's *Dakota-English Dictionary*). One such word is *caŋteyuza*, which means *to think, form an opinion*.[2] From a Dakota perspective, *thinking with our heart* encompasses the ethical considerations that must be at the forefront of any endeavor. Even academic endeavors would not be deemed worthwhile if heart did not have equal weight.

For those interested in pursuing a collection of stories from the oral tradition, additional issues of language and interpretation can be huge stumbling blocks for those outside the Indigenous culture and can be problems even for those from within a culture. There is no quick-fix solution for this. Learning the language requires a lengthy commitment. A number of universities currently have Indigenous language programs, which can be a starting point for some.[3] In most instances, however, and always eventually, becoming involved with Indigenous people, befriending them, and placing oneself in a position of vulnerability (not interacting with Indigenous people as an authority or expert on their history and culture but as a student of theirs) will reap positive benefits. Taking this route will also allow the scholar the opportunity to build relationships with those who are often the most knowledgeable about the culture—the fluent speakers of the language.

Ideally, sustained interaction with a culture different from one's own should also produce a sense in the scholar of some of the basic concepts that seem common to many Indigenous groups, such as the importance of community and the notion of reciprocity. As close relationships are developed with Indigenous people, even "outsiders" are often made a part of the community. This "making of relatives" is not unusual and may mean a formalized adoption into a specific family or community. Privileges come from such a relationship, but an equal number of responsibilities are attached. One has only to glance through many of the "as-told-to autobiographies" of Indigenous people written through this century, primarily by anthropologists, to get a glimpse of the trust Indigenous people have placed in these newly made relatives. It is unfortunate that not all scholars have understood their responsibilities.[4]

Furthermore, familiarity with the concept of reciprocity brings a realization of the need to give something back to the individual and the culture from which one has taken knowledge. This goes far beyond the economic compensation that many scholars have used in exchange for their "informant's" time and information. The scholar has a commitment to return the gift of stories and education by giving in a more difficult and profound way; that is, to use the information in a good way and to make research materials and skills available to the community.

Maori researchers in New Zealand have articulated an ethical framework for researchers to follow in regard to Maori research. This is now identified among Maori scholars as Kaupapa Maori research and crosses a broad range of both scholarly and community-initiated research projects. In discussing this framework, Linda Tuhiwai Smith points out that "Kaupapa Maori approaches to research are based on the assumption that research that involves Maori people, as individuals or as communities, should set out to make a positive difference for the researched."[5] Indigenous people may not have control over those who choose not to follow ethical principles of research and to work collaboratively with those about whom they are writing, but Indigenous people worldwide are beginning to codify research principles, with one of the fundamental claims being that in some way, Indigenous people should benefit from being researched. In the past Indigenous people have seen little positive outcomes from those who have conducted research about us and, in fact, have suffered greater oppression and other negative repercussions because of governmental policies informed by researchers, particularly anthropologists, and through misinformation reaching the general public. Because of this, the push for useful research is tied to self-preservation and self-determination.

One of the most beneficial and powerful ways a scholar can give back to a community is through the language. Because many Indigenous communities are grappling with the issue of language retention, bilingual texts that may be used for language study are extremely valuable. An excellent example of work of this nature is that of John Nichols, who has dedicated a lifetime to work among the Anishinaabe of Minnesota, specifically with elders Maude Kegg and Earl Nyhom. Together Nichols and Kegg produced a number of source materials based on the oral accounts narrated by Kegg to Nichols. Their works represent truly collaborative projects in which the Indigenous voice is not overpowered by that of the scholar, and which will contribute a great deal to the furtherance of Ojibwe language. In addition to these bilingual texts, Nichols and Nyhom have together produced the second edition of *A Concise Dictionary of Minnesota Ojibwe*, which demonstrates a great deal of tenacity and commitment.[6] Because processes like this are painfully slow and tedious, particularly for those learning about a culture foreign to them, it means spending an unusually long time in the research process and becoming comfortable with the idea that publications may only result after years of work.

Once mutually satisfactory arrangements about the subject are agreed upon, culturally appropriate protocols should be observed. In some Indigenous communities this may mean offering tobacco to an elder, providing gifts of food or money, or asking for help in some other specific way. Until the appropriate process for the collection of data is determined, no attempt should be made to collect oral accounts. Understanding and respecting this protocol will ensure that the relationship between the scholar and tribal historian gets off to a good start.

Because Indigenous people have varying concerns about how stories should be written down, or whether they should be written at all, whether their Indigenous language should be used, what time of day or season of year the stories should be told, and in what setting the stories will most comfortably be told, these should be considered early on in the process. All involved parties should discuss these issues, and decisions about them should be made in advance of any recording. The wishes of the narrator should be honored in all instances. Videotaping, with backup audio recordings, is ideal in my opinion, because the gestures and facial expressions are captured and preserved and may greatly enhance interpretations in the translation process. In addition, as mentioned earlier, it is important to record Indigenous people in the language in which they are the most comfortable and eloquent. While this may put the recorder or scholar at a disadvantage, I would rather see the scholar struggling with lack of eloquence and discomfort than see our elders placed in such a position.

The process of recording stories may then commence. But how does one begin the transference of a culturally specific oral tradition to a written academic tradition? This methodological question has often been discussed in the context of technique, but rarely within a moral framework. In an essay from *The Past Meets the Present*, William Moss, who defines oral history and oral tradition similarly to Henige and Vansina, offers this version of an ideal interviewing process for working with oral history: "The role of the interviewer in oral history is never entirely passive. It is always active, a dynamic interaction with the person being interviewed. The interviewer searches out memories and provokes reflections and evaluations of significance, even hypotheses that may be tested against an individual's personal experience, and challenges the respondent into further examination and reflection on assumptions and assertions made in the first instance."[7]

Moss and other scholars may believe this is an appropriate interviewing technique for members of the communities with whom they work, but I would not recommend it for working with Indigenous elders, as this type of behavior would be construed as disrespectful and aggressive. Eastman comments on the proper etiquette of an audience in Dakota society when they are privileged enough to hear a story, saying: "I sat facing him, wholly wrapped in the words of the story-teller, and now I took a deep breath and settled myself so that I might not disturb him by the slightest movement while he was reciting his tale. We were taught this courtesy to our elders, but I was impulsive and sometimes forgot."[8] While children might be excused for improper etiquette, adults would be expected to have mastered the subtleties of appropriate interaction. In addition, I was taught not to ask questions until after the story had ended, and even at that time it would be entirely inappropriate to "provoke," "test," or "challenge" the elder's assertions. Indeed, as an interviewer, it is important that the expert's flow of thought be interfered with as little as possible. This is a concrete example of how the usual scholarly methods of inquiry may be inappropriate to cross-cultural work.

James LaGrand points out differences between methods of inquiry based on his definitions of oral history and oral tradition. About the oral tradition he says, "Often the message passes through a formal, structured, and even ritualized process of transmission. Through the process, narrators of oral traditions try to stay as close as possible to the original message.... In the recounting of an oral tradition, the listener or person who asked the question which elicited the telling of the oral tradition plays little role as the message is repeated."[9] He contrasts that with the "collaborative relationship between narrator and interviewer" in the transmission of oral history, which he describes as a "type of oral source in which an individual addresses experiences and feelings experienced first-hand in narrative form."[10] In many instances this may be an accurate description of the process. However, skilled and trained tribal historians are also very apt at interpreting contemporary events and incorporating them into their oral tradition and can often convey seamless accounts that blend old and new with little or no prompting or provocation from an interviewer. Oral traditions, then, are not simply accounts handed down from another generation but are continual and always expanding. This becomes apparent in the presence of a gifted observer and storyteller.

Another obstacle to introducing Indigenous stories into an academic arena exists in the lack of communication between disciplines. The information contained within Indigenous oral tradition necessitates an interdisciplinary approach, which sometimes encroaches upon the intellectual territory of various departments in institutions where biologists rarely communicate with historians or anthropologists with geographers. This is further impaired by the technical jargon each academic discipline employs, which, by nature, tends to exclude those from outside their field. Indigenous understandings of history tend to be more holistic and all-encompassing; therefore, they articulate a deeper understanding of how we and our cultures came to be. Again, broadening the definition of history as it applies to Indigenous understandings of the past will allow varying understandings of history to enter into academe.

Mention must also be made of the differing goals of academic and tribal historians. Typically graduate programs strive to produce a population of historians who are thorough and meticulous in their gathering of written sources, who weigh and test each hypothesis to generate a single account of the piece of the past they are studying, and who finally create a history that provides some revealing perspective, slant, or model that has not been articulated the same way previously and which allows the intended audience to view that topic in a new way. Admirable as these goals are, they are not necessarily compatible with the responsibilities of tribal historians in many Indigenous cultures, and they present a special dilemma for those academic historians who are attempting to contribute Indigenous perceptions of the past to the written collections of Indigenous history.

In order to expand the field to accommodate the historical traditions of non-English-speaking peoples, it would be helpful to understand the goals and responsibilities of other nonacademic historians. The first and primary responsibility of a Dakota historian has always been to "tell it straight." A new interpretation is not necessary and in many instances is entirely inappropriate. Moreover, at present our elders, who have been charged with the intense responsibility of passing on history through the oral tradition, are very much consumed with the industry required in remembering the stories and finding an audience when the loss of the oral tradition is occurring at an alarming rate. In this way they differ from the academic historians who are playing with historical theories, reconstructing, revising, deconstructing, and examining history as an intellectual exercise, albeit one about which they may be passionate.

In addition, the goal of Dakota historians is not to collect data from every available source on a given topic or event but to make sure that the Dakota perspectives entrusted to them are preserved and transmitted. Rather than trying to disprove other theories about history, Dakota historians often begin with the basic supposition that every perspective will be different. Rather than that being proof of an error in an account, it is accepted as a reality. It is quite easy, for example, for the Dakota to accept that the Anishinaabe might have a different perspective on a specific Anishinaabe-Dakota battle, just as it is perfectly acceptable that perspectives of the maple tree or robin witnessing the same event might also be radically different. All these Dakota concepts of history are based on its orality and the worldview inherent in the language. These ideas, however, are often alien to the academic perspective, which usually discounts unverifiable information, attempts to keep biases in check, and ultimately attempts to draw a conclusion about what "actually" happened in the historical past based upon a thorough examination of the available written documents.

Once written accounts are made from oral-historical stories, differing views or interpretations of history held by Natives and non-Natives continue to influence decisions about how the material should be handled. Scholars may, and have, attempted to treat oral-historical material as they would other written source materials. Many scholars working with oral history today recognize that oral accounts do not represent "raw data," but they nevertheless recommend using the same process of analysis as one would use for written sources. Vansina suggests that oral traditions should be treated as hypotheses, similar to a historian's hypothesis about the past, and should thus be tested as such before a scholar considers other hypotheses. "To consider them first means not to accept them literally, uncritically," he writes. "It means give them the attention they deserve, to take pains to prove or disprove them systematically for each case on its own merits. . . . [The historian] must continue the historiological process that has been underway. This by no means is to say that the historian's interpretations should be literal. Only at the least should they be more believable than the already existing oral hypothesis."[11]

How one from outside the culture would be able to "continue the historiological process that has been underway" or how the historian decides what a "more believable" hypothesis might be is beyond my comprehension. Rather, what I see happening with those specializing in the field of oral history is an attempt to make oral accounts from oppressed cultures conform to the colonizers' notions of respectability, truth, narrative format, categories, significance, terminology, and sensibility as a means to discredit and eliminate them. While I would argue that oral accounts certainly are interpretations of the past and should not be treated as raw data, I don't believe they should be tested and evaluated by the colonizer's standards or by standards from other cultures, for that matter. The purpose of the written sources should not be to validate, verify, or negate the Indigenous perspective. Rather, they should be used for what is significant about them according to the culture from which they were created. Indigenous stories must be respected in their own right, and historians must be willing to let them stand on their own. The only standards that matter are those set from within the culture, and if stories are being told within that oral tradition by respected carriers of that tradition, then they have passed the necessary internal standards. Once historians have obtained stories that have passed the internal verifiability mechanisms within the culture and reflect that Indigenous worldview, they can begin to be placed within a larger historical context and presented alongside other non-Native interpretations.

Many from the academic community might be concerned that without historians policing the integrity of sources through their own analysis, the result will be the publication of stories that ultimately have no authority because they have not passed an acceptable validation process. If scholars can agree that there are other legitimate sources of authority, there is little need for concern. As has been pointed out, the training process for those belonging to an oral tradition is extensive. In addition, if stories are still being relayed (sometimes for thousands of years), that is testimony in itself to the tenacity and commitment Indigenous people have in regard to their own history. Also, communities have their own stringent requirements for determining who has authority to speak about what topic, whose stories are reliable, what kind of upbringing and training of individuals is necessary, and who is the most knowledgeable about a specific topic. These tight regulations are not easily recognizable to those outside the community, but they do exist. With these ideas taken into consideration, the expertise of tribal historians may find a valued place among academic historians willing to place tribal interpretations on equal par with their own.

Nez Perce ethnographer Josiah Pinkham offers us a contemporary example of this internal mechanism for validating tribal authorities in an Indigenous community. He is working among his own people to perpetuate and revitalize Nez Perce traditions. As one article points out, "Tribal members observed Pinkham's ability to sit, listen and absorb the stories and truths he heard. Thus, he was set apart and entrusted with carrying on the Tribe's cultural heritage." Now engaged in transmitting teachings to the next generation, Pinkham also "watches for those who internalize and understand the stories and who, with the same upbringing, could take his place in the future."[12] In Indigenous societies, community members are ever vigilant in their quest for gifted and committed purveyors of knowledge and stories, and these individuals are apprenticed with a tremendous sense of responsibility to their own people.

Some historians have recognized the distinctions about who has authority to speak in a given community, but issues of credibility and accuracy still dominate discussions, while issues of respect for the culture are seldom discussed.[13] Tribal people and scholars need to work together at developing and understanding the rigorous evaluation mechanisms existing in Indigenous communities and at developing a mutually agreeable code of ethics and methodological processes. This may vary between nations and even communities within the same nation.

The notion of objectivity is another topic that needs to be addressed. As Peter Novick points out on the first page of his book *That Noble Dream*:

> At the very center of the professional historical venture is the idea and ideal of "objectivity." It was the rock on which the venture was constituted, its continuing raison d'être. It has been the quality which the profession has prized and praised above all others—whether in historians or in their works. It has been the key term in defining progress in historical scholarship: moving ever closer to the objective truth about the past. Anyone interested in what professional historians are up to—what they think they are doing, or ought to be doing, when they write history—might well begin by considering the "objectivity question."[14]

Because of the pervasiveness of this thought about the need for objectivity within the field of American history, some historians might argue that Indigenous scholars in America are not the most appropriate people to research and write Indigenous history because of their emotional involvement.[15] Many Indigenous intellectuals see this issue in a different light. Fanon states that "for the native, objectivity is always directed against him."[16] As an institution of colonialism, the academy has used the veil of objectivity to normalize and codify their own vision of the world, so that other visions may be characterized as subjective. Furthermore, I would argue that it is precisely our deep commitment to and concern for our nations that makes us the best interpreters of our history to the academic world, particularly because, in addition to the training we have received from our tribal backgrounds, we have also learned much about the dominant society. Those of us who have received academic training in institutions of the United States and Canada are also well versed in Western traditions. Perhaps most of all, many Indigenous scholars have become especially astute at recognizing methods of oppression and the colonialist tactics employed by non-Native scholars who have used us as their objects of study. We are thus in the unique position of being well trained in the culture of the colonizers, with valuable insights because of our knowledge in two modes of thought, two worlds. As Paulo Freire states, "Who are better prepared than the oppressed to understand the terrible significance of an oppressive society? Who suffer the effects of oppression more than the oppressed? Who can better understand the necessity of liberation?"[17] Since much of our history in the last several centuries is about our resistance to oppression, are we not in a privileged position to engage in the writing about this history?

The idea, then, of someone outside of the culture, or of the colonizer's culture, studying our stories word by word and line by line, categorizing them, scrutinizing the narrative format, dissecting their structure, analyzing their changes, and testing their credibility by the colonizer's standards is downright offensive to many Indigenous people and indicative of their power and privilege. In addition, the idea that historians can extract the information they want and discard the rest is presumptuous. As I discussed these issues with other Indigenous scholars using oral history in their own work, they used such phrases to describe this analysis as "robbing the stories of their context" and "sucking the life out of the stories." Certainly this is not what our elders intend to have happen when they share the stories.

Some Indigenous scholars, however, are attempting to reconcile their oral stories with archaeological, geological, and historical evidence. For example, Roger Echo-Hawk (Pawnee) is linking his nation's origin/migration story to the Bering Strait Theory and is thus creating a history in which both are mutually validated in the process.[18] While this type of mediation work may be an interesting exercise when academic and tribal theories conveniently overlap, I believe this is an ultimately dangerous approach for Indigenous people to promote. On this topic, for example, what about the hundreds of other Indigenous groups who have stories about their creation/transformation occurring in North America and absolutely do not subscribe to the Bering Strait Theory because it is in conflict with their own cultural understanding of the past? This is not to suggest that the Pawnee never came across the Bering Strait; that is not at issue. What is at issue is that the Bering Strait Theory explicitly states that *all* American Indians came across from Asia, and those who subscribe to this theory will cling vigorously to the Pawnee experience articulated by Echo-Hawk as evidence of the immigration of the rest of the Indigenous Peoples into the Americas.

So much of what is contained within the oral tradition, on a variety of subjects, may never be corroborated by any written evidence, and every inch of the the continent could be excavated by archaeologists and still there may be nothing that could prove or disprove many of the stories. Because of this, it is important to note that scholars of any discipline trying to verify every story with additional evidence will quite often engage in an exercise in futility. If we as Indigenous people are willing to put our stories forward with faith in our culture and elders, no further evidence is necessary—that is, if one's aim is to truly understand Indigenous perspectives on Indigenous history.

One might ask, But how do Indigenous people reconcile differing accounts, or what happens if oral sources are in direct contradiction to written sources? To respond to this, I would like to use a concept from my own culture to explain my perspective. One of the ceremonies still practiced among my people is called in our language haŋbdeceya or, literally, crying for a vision. While this term usually makes reference to the formal ceremony in which men would go off by themselves, usually for a four-day period, fasting, praying, and singing until they received a vision, visions were given to both men and women in a number of other ways as well. An important aspect of this concept is that when one receives a vision, it is not for others to question. Thus, I grew up with a belief that you "respect another person's vision." This concept naturally extends to communities and cultures and seems particularly relevant to the question of what should be done with various "visions" of history.

This is a fundamentally different approach from the one embraced by a Western/European scholarly tradition that is largely based on Christian values and promotes a belief in only one truth, one way, one right.[19] Michael Dorris commented on this phenomenon when he stated, "To admit that other, culturally divergent viewpoints are equally plausible is to cast doubt on the monolithic center of Judeo-Christian belief: that there is but one of everything—God, right way, truth—and Europeans alone knew what that was."[20] Most indigenous people would never presume to define these for the rest of the world or even for other Indigenous nations.

Consequently, while there might be differing stories on the same topic within any given Indigenous community, and families and individuals may differ in opinion about these stories, there is acknowledgment that there may be more than one "right" version, that stories differ according to perspective, and some individuals may be more adept than others at relaying specific stories. This does not lessen the importance of the stories, however. In her book *Ghost Singer*, Anna Lee Walters impressively explores the conflict between tribal and academic perspectives through fictionalized characters. In this exchange, the Diné character Jimmy Tom says to his grandfather, "'Grandfather, there is something I have been confused about. Who were the four original clans? There is some disagreement, I have heard.' 'There is no disagreement,' the old man answered. 'All the stories are right, no matter who the four clans were.'"[21]

My impressions are that most Indigenous Peoples would not expect people from other cultural traditions to discard their belief systems, culture, and stories and subscribe instead to Indigenous beliefs, cultures, and stories. Instead, there is a respect among Indigenous people, especially concerning the stories, in which we can appreciate the wonderful nature of another group's stories, believe those stories, and then share ours with them, knowing we will receive the same courtesy. As a Dakota, I do not expect all non-Dakota to subscribe to our notions of truth, reality, or history. However, it is only this simple if we are sharing with others in an atmosphere of equality as we might with Indigenous Peoples worldwide, and this is generally not the context in which the validity of our stories is discussed. Our written history has not been dominated by those who viewed us as equals. Our written history has been dominated by our colonizers, our cultural perspective systematically suppressed, and our stories subjugated in favor of those of the colonizers. Therefore, when we challenge those who have disregarded our cultural perspective and attempted to make what is Dakota conform to the colonizer's standards as a means to deny its validity, we are resisting.

This hands-off approach I am recommending to the analysis of Indigenous oral historical accounts will be, understandably, very disturbing to academic historians. After all, what I am suggesting is that the vast majority of what has passed thus far in the field as Indigenous history has not had the one component that legitimizes that label, the perspective of Indigenous people; and also, that what is truly Indigenous history, that is, our history as we perceive it, should not be subject to the usual rules of historical analysis. Rather, Native histories should be examined according to cultural and historical standards from which they derive.

I do not mean to suggest that histories based solely on non-Indigenous–produced written documents are of no value. The contributions they make to the understanding of the written word is significant, but their limitations must also be acknowledged.[22] The idea that scholars can "sift through" the biases of non-Native written sources enough to get at the Native perspective is both naïve and erroneous. While vast oral accounts go unrecognized, very few scholars have attempted to ascertain how Indigenous people would interpret, analyze, and question the written documents they confront, nor have they asked if the Indigenous people they are studying have their own versions or stories of their past that might be pertinent to their analysis. If the majority of our sources were written and not oral, and scholars continued to neglect this valuable information, accusations of sloppy scholarship would be hurled from all directions. Because of this double standard, what I am suggesting is that those writing history in this manner should abandon the pretension that they are truly understanding Indigenous history or that they speak for an Indigenous society and perspective.

Increasingly today, Indigenous nations are attempting to gain a sense of intellectual control over information dispersed to people outside their culture. The Cattaraugus Seneca Nation in 1994 required a fellow graduate student at Cornell to make a formal presentation on her research intentions to the tribal council because she was interested in interviewing an elder from their community. Theodore S. Jojola, in his essay "On Revision and Revisionism: American Indian Representations in New Mexico," describes how the Zuni have actively taken charge through the Zuni History Project, which was "initiated to bring back non-Native academics who had used Zuni knowledge in their scholarship. The invitation was laced with a warning that individuals who did not cooperate would be banished from conducting any future research. Their reports to the community were retained by the tribe and became the basis for expert testimony concerning Zuni land claims."[23] It is necessary for Indigenous Peoples to articulate their traditional positions on these topics and to codify a set of precedures for addressing them. Among the Cree, Wheeler describes what elder Harold Cardinal and others refer to as "traditional copyright," saying: "In the Cree world all knowledge is not knowable. Some knowledge is kept in family lines, other kinds of knowledge have to be earned. While all knowledge is intended for community well-being and welfare, to acquire certain specific kinds of knowledge one is obligated to adhere to its rules of acquisition."[24] Along these same lines, Linda Smith argues that "communities and indigenous activists have openly challenged the research community about such things as racist practices and attitudes, ethnocentric assumptions and exploitative research, sounding warning bells that research can no longer be conducted with indigenous communities as if their views did not count or their lives did not matter."[25]

As we continue to promote this new agenda in the researching and writing of Indigenous history, we will likely face severe backlash in the academy. For example, after some heated debates in the academy with gatekeeping scholars desiring to maintain the status quo, opportunities available to me have been lost precisely because I have held to these views about the oral tradition. In fact, after one particularly painful experience in 1997 in which I had put many of these ideas forward and was subsequently attacked, I sought support from my tribal community. Believing that I was advocating an approach that would be beneficial to my nation, I asked my tribal council if they would be willing to read some of my writings and pass a resolution in support of my key arguments (see appendix B). It was important for me to know that my community supported in principle what I was trying to do, and by doing so they provided me considerable strength, strength I would clearly need as I continued to challenge the academy. It was also important because I wanted to ensure that Uŋkaŋna's stories were published with support—that is, a fierce defense of their importance and validity.

Other nations are deciding that they do not wish to have non-Natives studying their language.[26] This is something scholars should investigate before deciding to focus their investigative study on a specific Indigenous group. In the next few decades issues of cultural and intellectual property rights will be coming to the forefront, and more and more bodies of tribal leadership may codify procedures for others to either access or be denied access to tribally valued information. Despite what some scholars may believe, a Ph.D. does not give automatic entrance into all source material archives, whether oral or written, especially when dealing with live people and cultures.[27] Furthermore, in the academy there exists an accompanying belief that once stories are documented, scholars have a right to do with them whatever they wish.[28] Many scholars may be indignant about Natives exerting aggressive control over their tribal resources and knowledge, but the trend in this direction will ultimately make non-Native scholars more aware of their ethical responsibilities and will serve to protect Indigenous communities.

Ramón Gutiérrez's work on the Pueblo peoples, *When Jesus Came, the Corn Mothers Went Away*, is testimony to this.[29] His work has been highly acclaimed by other non-Native scholars and has won numerous book awards, in spite of the many Pueblo leaders and scholars who have come forward to discredit his work. Jojola captured many Indigenous sentiments when he described it as "the most recent mythologizing about the Pueblo Indians by outsiders seeking to fulfill their own career agendas."[30] Deloria also sheds light on this topic by offering a general explanation of where the obligations for academics truly lie: "But who is the responsible scholar responsible to? Not to the public, not to science, or history, or anthropology, but to the small group of similarly situated people who will make recommendations on behalf of his or her scholarship, award the prizes which each discipline holds dear, and write letters advocating his or her advancement."[31] As Indigenous scholars become more numerous and find their places in institutions throughout the country, this will be increasingly more difficult for non-Native scholars to do. Furthermore, as the nonwhite population becomes the majority in the United States, the demand will become even greater in this country for histories to include accurate depictions of the populations they represent, with each group's own cultures and experiences as part of the written text. I challenge academic historians to embrace this change and work with nonwhite populations, including Indigenous Peoples.

As Indigenous Peoples, we have our own theories about history, as well as our own interpretations and sense of history, in which our stories play a central role. It is time for a major change in the field of history, for a movement away from colonialist versions of our past. It is time the field acknowledges, values, and accepts as valid Indigenous conceptions of our past. Only then will there be an understanding of Indigenous history. This is not to suggest there is no place for non-Native scholars in the writing of Indigenous history. On the contrary, we need non-Indigenous allies who will assist us in challenging colonialist representations of our past and will contribute to collaborative projects in which there is mutual respect for the authority and skills everyone might bring to those projects. We will all be richly rewarded when scholars contribute research and writing beneficial to Indigenous Peoples and when those scholars, in turn, have the endorsement of Indigenous Peoples.

3. De Iapi Uŋk'upi (We Were Given This Language)

Dakoṭa wohdakapi ṭakomni niuŋkiyapi kṭe. He uŋkiyepi. Uŋciŋcapi hena teuŋhiŋdapi heuŋ tokaṭakiya yapi he Dakoṭa wohdakapi kṭe. Peżihuṭazizi Wahoḣpi Wohdakapi Uŋspe ed śiceca ķiŋ hena awaŋuŋhdakapi kṭe. Ṭohan Dakoṭa wohdakapi hena uŋspepi ķiŋhaŋ iyokpiya uŋpṭe, naġi he yuwaśṭepi kṭe, Dakoṭa iapi he teḣiŋdapi kṭe, hehan naķuŋ Dakoṭa Oyaṭe teḣiŋdapi kṭe, hehan naķuŋ makoce he teḣiŋdapi kṭe, hehan naķuŋ Dakoṭa wicoḣaŋ hena teḣiŋdapi kṭe.

> We must bring to life the Dakoṭa language. It is who we are. We treasure our children, and so they will carry the Dakoṭa language into the future. At the Peżihuṭazizi Wahoḣpi Wohdakapi Uŋspe, the children will be watched over. When they learn the Dakoṭa language they will feel a sense of fulfillment, their spirit will be enriched, and they will cherish the Dakoṭa language, they will cherish the Dakoṭa nation, they will cherish the land, and also they will cherish the Dakoṭa way of life.

This mission statement of the Peżihuṭazizi Wahoḣpi Wohdakapi Uŋspe, the Dakoṭa-language immersion preschool of the Upper Sioux Community, was written in September 1999, one month before the school opened its doors.[1] Recognizing the crisis in language existing among the Dakoṭa, the establishment of the school was viewed as a means of revitalizing the Dakoṭa langauge, culture, and worldview by attempting to produce a new generation of fluent speakers.

The history of an Indigenous people cannot be cut from its roots. The Indigenous perspective is holistic and inescapably linked to language. Language is linked to systems of thought, which are linked to history and to identity. Every description of the world depends on language, every ceremony conducted depends on language, every teaching about the past depends on language; language conveys the meaning of life. Because of this connection, history cannot be discussed without consideration of the state of Dakoṭa language and where they intersect and apply to one another. Furthermore, language preservation and the struggle to exert Indigenous voices must be seen within the larger framework of the struggle for self-determination.

In light of this, it is important to ask difficult questions about the meaning behind using the colonizer's language or our own. Kenyan intellectual Ngũgĩ wa Thiong'o has posed such a challenging question about his own people's use of language in a straightforward manner: "What is the difference between a politician who says Africa cannot do without imperialism and the writer who says Africa cannot do without European languages?"[2] As Indigenous Peoples we must ask this question of ourselves. We have brilliant minds among our people, but why do we not have a wealth of literature in our Indigenous languages? How can we resist colonialism if we have abandoned the languages that will allow us to resist in one of the most meaningful ways? Granted, our circumstances differ from those of the millions of Africans who are struggling against neocolonialism. Within the United States, we are in an ongoing state of colonization since our colonizers never left, forcefully and unmercifully destroying our most sacred tribal treasures, including our languages. This chapter will explore the reasons why we have adopted the colonizer's language as our primary language of resistance, but it will also explore why it is essential that we develop further resistance through the taking back of our languages.

To further this aim, this chapter will discuss the importance of Uŋkaŋna's stories in this language project in the context of the broader Indigenous struggle for language preservation and renewal, as most of our languages face an imminent threat of extinction. Language loss has become the most pressing cultural issue facing Indigenous Peoples in the twenty-first century, but this has implications far beyond the realm of culture. To illustrate the worldview in jeopardy, if Dakoṭa were to be spoken no longer, examples will be provided of key words and phrases formative in the development of Dakoṭa consciousness that convey important cultural meanings. Without an internalization of these concepts, what has existed for thousands of years as Dakoṭa identity and worldview would be severely undermined. Because language also affects how the Dakoṭa conceptualize the past, a discussion is also provided of the various categories encompassing stories within the Dakoṭa oral tradition.

Since languages are linked to worldview, loss of language in essence means loss of worldview. Many Indigenous communities are in imminent danger of losing their languages and all that this implies. Prior to European contact, anywhere from about 300 to 600 Indigenous languages were spoken in North America. In the United States and Canada, it is estimated that 210 Indigenous languages now remain, with the vast majority of those threatened with extinction.[3] Unless drastic efforts are made to rescue Indigenous languages, the future looks terribly bleak. Dr. Stephen Greymorning, an Arapaho scholar and language specialist, has stated that "if we are not able to effectively pass our languages on to our youth, within the next 15 years we could witness the loss of as much as 85 percent of the Indian languages that are still presently spoken."[4] The situation has reached crisis proportions for much of Native America.

Attacks on Indigenous languages began with missionary efforts in which Indigenous languages were utilized to speed the conversion of Native people to Christianity, with the teaching of English or Spanish closely following as a means of eradicating Indigenous cultures, values, and spirituality. Among the Dakota, the work missionaries invested in the Dakota language was closely aligned with the attempt to destroy Dakota lifeways. The first book translated into Dakota was the New Testament of the Bible, and missionaries preached their sermons in Dakota to reach more potential converts.

By assuming control over the written language, missionaries were able to appropriate Dakota words and assign new meanings, which served to linguistically internalize for Dakota people the missionaries' racist and ethnocentric attitudes. Examples of these may be found in Stephen Riggs's *Dakota-English Dictionary*, first published in 1890. In defining Dakota spirituality and ceremonies, for example, Riggs would use such explanations as "to conjure the sick, to powwow in the Indian way" for our word *wapiya*, which we would translate as *to heal the sick*.[5] In the case of *waziya* (who we would define as a spiritual entity from the North responsible for bringing the cold weather), Riggs defines it as "the northern god or god of the north; a fabled giant who lives at the north and blows cold out of his mouth."[6] The derogatory usage of words employed by Riggs (such as *conjure, powwow*, and *fabled*) was an attempt to diminish the importance of traditional Dakota healing practices and spirituality. They were so successful in their work, and Christian influences were so great, even some contemporary Dakota people refer to these words in the same derogatory vein. In addition they helped to create new words such as *wakaŋśica* (meaning something mysterious and bad) for the devil and *maȟpiya* (meaning clouds) for heaven, thus giving old words new meanings.

More severe blows to the language were dealt in mandated federal boarding schools, where Indigenous children were punished, often severely, for speaking their Indigenous languages. In her book *Boarding School Seasons*, Brenda Child writes: "Beatings, swats with rulers, having one's mouth washed with soap or lye, or being locked in the school jail were not uncommon punishments. . . . Government school education, both on-and-off-reservation, bears a large responsibility for the decline of Ojibwe and other tribal languages."[7] This is a major understatement.

The suppression of Indigenous languages is part of a colonial enterprise designed to completely subjugate everything Indigenous while establishing the dominance of the colonizing class. As bell hooks points out, "When I realize how long it has taken for white Americans to acknowledge diverse languages of Native Americans, to accept that the speech their ancestral colonizers declared was merely grunts or gibberish was indeed *language*, it is difficult not to hear in standard English always the sound of slaughter and conquest."[8] It was with extreme violence that our languages were silenced. The brutality of the federal government and church-run boarding schools is still being realized as Indigenous Peoples continue to suffer the long-term consequences of those experiences and begin to place them in their proper context. The boarding schools themselves meet the criteria of the *United Nations Convention on the Prevention and Punishment of the Crime of Genocide*, which states that "forcibly transferring children of the group to another group" constitutes a form of genocide. The United States leadership has yet to take ownership of and responsibility for this government-mandated genocidal policy, and thus part of the colonization process has been to minimize the severity of boarding-school violence on the most vulnerable and impressionable segments of Indigenous populations—the children. These assaults perpetrated against the children were profoundly damaging to whole generations of Indigenous Peoples and threatened the very foundations of our cultural and spiritual life. The forbidding of speaking Indigenous languages in itself constitutes ethnocide, yet these issues remain swept under the vast rug of American history. Our stories of pain surrounding this issue have been silenced in American society, just as our children's voices speaking our beautiful languages were silenced in schools across North America.

Because of these genocidal efforts, a legacy of cultural shame has become intertwined with the speaking of Indigenous languages, and this is apparent in many Indigenous communties where even fluent speakers correlate the language with "savagery."[9] The problem has been compounded among many populations because the boarding-school experience was intergenerational, making the transmission and maintenance of language nearly impossible and the assault on our cultures that much more thorough. This association with shame and savagery has occurred precisely because suppression of the language was not the only goal. Indigenous children were indoctrinated with harmful beliefs about the inferiority of Indigenous languages, beliefs still prevalent today among both Indigenous and non-Indigenous people. However, as Ngũgĩ wa Thiong'o articulates, one language is not inherently more progressive or backward than any another, but this did not stop the colonizers from asserting this myth.[10] In reference to the repression of African languages, he states: "Our languages were suppressed so that we, the captives, would not have our own mirrors in which to observe ourselves and our enemies." Along with elevating the language of the conquerer, he goes on to say that "humiliation in relation to our languages was the key."[11] Certainly this is also applicable to the boarding-school experiences of Indigenous children in North America.

Thus, even today, the teaching of an Indigenous language as a first language to children is a concept laden with extreme emotion. Those who attended the boarding schools and faced severe punishment for speaking their languages, or who saw the difficulty first-language speakers had when they needed to maneuver in an English-speaking environment, had to make a choice when it came to rearing their own children about which language would be the primary language taught in the home. As Darrell Kipp, a language activist and cofounder of the Piegan Institute in Browning, Montana, has stated, ultimately many parents chose not to teach their children the Indigenous language because they loved them and did not want to see them suffer the negative repercussions experienced by those who were first taught in their Indigenous language.[12] Adults who have little or no knowledge of their Indigenous language have often felt betrayed by those elders around them who possessed language skills but did not teach them the language while growing up. Many have difficulty working through these feelings of hurt and anger, and efforts to learn the language later in life can be hampered by the shame they feel for not speaking their language. Unfortunately, the long-term consequence of this is that Indigenous people now are struggling fiercely with issues of identity and are losing ground in terms of an essential component that makes Indigenous people unique. Cultural survival is deeply threatened.

In a 1998 article entitled "Indians Striving to Preserve Their Languages," James Brooke wrote: "Despite five centuries of population decline, assimilation and linguistic oppression, most of North America's Indian languages have survived to the end of the twentieth century. Of the approximately 300 Indian languages that existed when Europeans first arrived in what is now the United States and Canada, 211 are still spoken today. But with the impact of television and radio and increased mobility among Indians, North America's Indigenous languages are suffering their sharpest free fall in recorded history." He goes on to say that "about half of the world's 6,000 languages are expected to disappear over the next century."[13]

The Dakota language is one of those languages in danger. In 1997 in Sioux Valley, Manitoba, at the Dakota Summit, an annual gathering of representatives from Dakota, Lakota, and Nakota communities in both the United States and Canada, the issue of language loss was foremost on the agenda. Two of the tribal council members from Upper Sioux who attended reported back that in the ensuing discussions in Sioux Valley, what became apparent was that language loss was a problem with all three dialects of the language. The Lakota, who far outnumber the Dakota, had more fluent speakers, but proportionately they were losing the language at about the same rate as the Dakota. All the communities were reporting that the young people were not able to speak the language and that the fluent speakers were of the older generations.

After returning from the summit, tribal leaders from the Upper Sioux Community were determined to promote efforts to revitalize the Dakota language.

They requested that I write a comprehensive language revitalization plan that could begin to be implemented at Upper Sioux by the following winter. At that time we still were unaware of the extent of language loss, even within our own small community. We visited two other Indigenous language programs in the Midwest to see what the possibilities were and to gain ideas for our approach.

The Hocak Wazija Haci Language & Culture Program in Mauston, Wisconsin, was an impressive facility housing such language components as CD-ROM development, video creation, an archive for Hocuŋk videos, photographs, and manuscripts, Hocuŋk language Headstart programming, and curriculum development. Then–cultural director Kenneth Funmaker Sr. shared with us their long-term vision for the Hocak language: that within the next twenty years they hoped to have produced a new generation of fluent speakers. The revolutionary nature of his comment and its effect upon me cannot be overstated. After years of watching a steady decline in the use and knowledge of the Dakota language, and even teaching the language to encourage its conversational usage, it had never occurred to me that the production of a new generation of fluent speakers might be an achievable goal. So thorough had the inevitibility of language decline been ingrained in my conscious mind, even in my imagination I did not dare to dream this dream. Colonization had dictated the parameters of my vision. For the first time I knew this had to be the long-term objective that would save our language. I knew as Dakota people we had the economic means to conceivably design and implement programs to achieve that end if steps were immediately taken. This was the awakening.

We then visited Shelly Ceglar, an Ojibwe language instructor at the College of St. Scholastica in Duluth, Minnesota, to learn more about the Ojibwe Language CD-ROM she created with the help of Tom Gibbons, an assistant professor of computer information science. There, we received a step-by-step demonstration on how they created the CD-ROM with information about their software programs and the required equipment. The realization that other Indigenous people were successfully creating exciting language materials left us with a sense that, indeed, it could be a reality for the Dakota Oyate.

To explain the language crisis and the need for immediate language efforts, the experience at Upper Sioux can offer some insight. Our language plan was conceived as a three-pronged approach to preservation and revitalization. The first component was to facilitate support for the already existing Dakota-English Dictionary Project (DEDP), coordinated by Chris Mato Nuŋpa and based on the Upper Sioux Reservation. In creating a Dakota-authored dictionary, we are reclaiming control over defining ourselves and our culture. The second component consisted of the development of a Dakota-language CD-ROM tutorial, based on the dialect spoken at Upper Sioux and targeted toward the youth. The third component was the creation of a Dakota-language immersion preschool, which would target children between the ages of one year and five years.[14] However, a necessary additional element was a community survey which needed to be conducted in order to assess the status of language knowledge, usage, and interest within the Upper Sioux Community.

The results were shocking. When the survey was completed in October 1998, only twenty fluent speakers of Dakota remained at Upper Sioux, all of whom were over the age of sixty. Between 1998 and 2003 three more fluent speakers have been lost, reducing the total number to seventeen. In addition, according to the survey even the fluent speakers were not using the Dakota language on a daily basis, as many of the elders did not have daily contact with other fluent speakers. They commented that even when they were gathered together socially as a group, English was still the primary language used to communicate. One positive aspect of the survey, however, was the overwhelming interest (95 percent) in language learning stated by the respondents and their belief in the importance of teaching the language to the children.

All aspects of the language-preservation and renewal plan were being implemented by late 1999. The preschool immersion program opened in October of that year, and within three months the children were producing sentences and were beginning to communicate with one another using the language. This language program was viewed as an exciting chance to reverse the trend in language loss and to begin producing fluent language speakers within the Upper Sioux community. The Peżihutazizi Wahohpi Wohdakapi Uŋspe preschool was the first language immersion program among the Dakota, although it is hoped many more will follow.

Upper Sioux's immersion program was based on the examples set by other Indigenous communities. In the last twenty years a language revolution has occurred in New Zealand for the Maori people, which has had positive effects on other aspects of their lives, including research. For example, Linda Tuhiwai Smith attributes the shift in approach to Maori research to "(1) the establishment of the Waitangi Tribunal; (2) the development of a language revitalization movement known as the Te Kohanga Reo; and (3) the spaces opened up in social sciences by more critical and reflexive approaches to research."[15] They opened their first Te Kohanga Reo (Language Nest) in 1982. By 1994 they had eight hundred preschools serving fourteen thousand children and as a consequence have completely reversed the trend in language loss and are ensuring their cultural survival.[16] At a recent conference on Native language curriculum development, we were shown videotape from a Maori program in which fluent high-school students were translating their treaties and other legal documents into Maori.[17] Their youth are being trained to enter all phases of the struggle against colonial oppression while maintaining their cultural practices.

Native Hawaiians have embarked on similar language-rescue efforts. At the time their language revolution began, the Hawaiian language was on the verge of extinction, and it was close to fulfilling a 1965 prediction by Bruce Briggs (a scholar of oceanic linguistics from the University of Auckland in New Zealand), that Hawaiian would be the first Polynesian language to die.[18] Instead, following the example set by the Maori, they took active steps to revitalize and stabilize their indigenous language. They also have become knowledgeable about the political process in their language revitalization efforts. When I attended the "Sixth Stabilizing Indigenous Languages Conference" in June 1999 in Tucson, Native Hawaiian language activists, though happy to be at our conference, lamented the fact that they were missing the graduation of the first class of students from twelfth grade who had received an entire immersion education in Hawaiian. This is a dream held by many of us.

Many other Indigenous Peoples in the United States and Canada are using immersion as a means of revitalizing and stabilizing their indigenous languages. Strong programs exist among the Mohawk, the Blackfeet, the Arapaho, the Inuit, and the Navajo. Many language programs are geared toward the very young because of the proven ability of small children to learn languages. Because language ability diminishes with age, it makes sense to reach children as early as possible.

Unfortunately, the language program at Upper Sioux did not last, and six months after opening its doors the immersion preschool closed. While this program cannot be considered a failure, the closure of the school and the ending for the CD-ROM work were terribly disheartening. While operational, great strides were made in promoting language interest and language learning, and the children in the preschool program had begun to speak in complete Dakota sentences. However, within weeks of opening, it was evident that there was not enough support for the language at that time and place to warrant the sustained financial expense and political turmoil caused by the issues that emerged around the language school. Upon further reflection, it appears that a sustained effort at language recovery would have to be combined with a community decolonization agenda, first to confront the damage wrought by previous assaults on our language and then to attempt to heal that damage. Once a critical mass of support is attained by which community members can fuel one another in their language efforts, the chances of further success will increase exponentially.

In the meantime, Dakota-language efforts are taking on heightened visibility and growing importance as both Indigenous and non-Indigenous Peoples become increasingly aware of the language crisis. For example, the Shakopee

Mdewakanton Dakota community, located just outside of Minneapolis, began an innovative and comprehensive language-renewal effort in the summer of 2001 when they hired five trainees to work under the guidance of Dakota speakers Carrie Schommer and Glen Wasicuna. Their two-year goal was to produce fluent Dakota-language speakers and writers who had also amassed a wealth of teaching skills. Upon completion of the program, these trainees will then be able to offer their skills where they are needed, as the pool of qualified Dakota language teachers is exceedingly small. The fruits of these intensive efforts should be observable within the next decade.

The Grotto Foundation has also emerged as not only an important contributor to Indigenous language-renewal efforts in the Minnesota region but also an advocate of endangered-language awareness and support within the world of foundations. After completing extensive research into Native language revitalization (largely through the work of Richard LaFortune and the commitment of Peg Thomas), the foundation dedicated $5.6 million in 2001 toward these efforts over the next fifteen years. They are now supporting a variety of Anishinaabe and Dakota language projects, including the Dakota Preschool Immersion Program at Lake Andes and the Master/Apprentice Program at Mendota and Upper Sioux. It is hoped that their lead in supporting important language projects through a substantial monetary commitment will be followed by other foundations around the country. Their geographic location in our Dakota homeland as well as their commitment to the local Indigenous populations fortunately offer us a source of support independent of tribal councils and the accompanying political turbulence.

Within Dakota culture, Dakota is the language in which our stories are told, our ceremonies conducted, our prayers said, and our songs sung. Without the language, much of the meaning is lost. Those who are fluent speakers of the language and who participate in Dakota ceremonial life recognize this and fear what the future will bring if the language is no longer spoken. Those nonspeakers who participate in ceremonial life also have an understanding of the importance of language, which becomes obvious to them when they cannot understand the prayers or follow the directions being given to them. In some ceremonial circumstances today English is used at times to accommodate the non-Dakota speakers, but prayers and songs still require knowledge and understanding of the Dakota language. In fact, in a statement made in 2003 by Chief Arvol Looking Horse, the Nineteenth-Generation Keeper of the Sacred White Buffalo Calf Pipe, after the Protection of Ceremonies Ominiciyapi, the importance of the language in ceremony was confirmed. In reference to the Inipi, or purification ceremony, he stated that "those that run this sacred rite should be able to communicate with Tun-ca-si-la (our Sacred Grandfather) in their Native Plains tongue."[19] Language is profoundly important for maintaining our relationships and conceptions of the world.

A fundamental element when examining Dakota conceptions of history, then, must be language. Thousands of cultures around the world speak languages other than English. If one assumes that language is linked to worldview, then it makes sense that there are thousands of cultures in the world that do not share the same worldview as the English-speaking population. If this is the case, it also makes sense that those who look at their past within a different cultural framework might also have different theories of history. Or, more basically, it makes sense that different peoples conceptualize, interpret, relate, and understand history differently.

If we can agree that other cultures might have different theories of history, then we have to ask ourselves the following questions: Do we compare one with the other to determine which one has more "truth" value? Do we dismiss one in favor of another? Is one inherently more "right" than another? Does one approach/transcend all cultural boundaries in a way that makes universal sense? If every culture has its own way of interpreting and recording history, relaying historical knowledge, and contextualizing the past, an examination of the language will provide some powerful insights into this. Specialized uses of language, conceptual categories, and frequency of usage of specific words or word groupings are all revealing about worldview and ways of thinking. Anna Wierzbicka, in her 1997 book *Understanding Cultures Through Their Key Words*, defines key words as "words which are particularly important and revealing in a given culture.... There is no finite set of such words in a language and there is no 'objective discovery procedure' for identifying them. To show that a particular word is of special importance in a given culture, one has to make a case for it."[20] In describing the connection between language and culture, Wierzbicka points out: "It is often debated whether words encapsulating culture-specific conceptual categories... 'reflect' or 'shape' ways of thinking, but the debate seems misconceived: clearly they do both.... Culture-specific words are conceptual tools that reflect a society's past experience of doing and thinking about things in certain ways; and they help to perpetuate these ways."[21] It is essential then, to understand how languages have shaped and reflected the Indigenous cultures from which they come and the serious danger of language loss in Indigenous communities. It means the conceptual tools are no longer at work in the same powerful way, and if we are not careful, Indigenous people will begin to assume the same conceptual tools and ways of thinking as the dominant society—doing so, however, from the margins.

Daniel Rodgers, a historian who has examined uses of language and meaning, based his book *Contested Truths: Keywords in American Politics Since Inde-*

pendence on the exploration of the notion of seven keywords from American history. According to Rodgers, keywords are "words which matter enough for persons to fight over them. Not to fight for them, though that may happen, but to fight for control over them—for the power to redefine, redeploy, and gain possession of them."[22] This contestation becomes much more profound and one-sided in the context of imperialism. The language of imperialism was forced upon Indigenous Peoples, not to gain possession over the Indigenous languages, at least not for the long term, but to wipe them out of existence. Control over language in this context is part of the colonial enterprise in which the entire way of life, language, and land was redefined in the colonizer's language. The fact that we have any language speakers left at all is a testament to the fierce resistance offered by our ancestors to maintain our languages even under seemingly impossible conditions. However, because Indigenous languages have been recipients of treatment running the spectrum from appropriation to obliteration, two levels of contestation over words still exist: one level is the internal contestation among Dakota people who speak the language, and the other is the Native-white contestation.

This latter conflict over keywords existed primarily in missionary times, and generally most fervently with religious terms, as missionaries labored to immediately appropriate Dakota-language vocabulary to serve their own imperialist aims. This kind of contestation was relatively short-lived, especially as Dakota converts to Christianity began assuming the role of the colonizing missionary. We are just now reasserting control over the religious terminology in the written form, although orally this battle has been waged continually by those practitioners of our traditional ceremonies and customs. Internally, Dakota people debate, vehemently at times, the meanings of words. This happens regularly in such contexts as the Dakota-English Dictionary Project meetings designated for discussion of translation. As contemporary Dakota people struggle with issues of identity and leadership, individuals and groups use keywords to argue political positions.[23] In light of the threatened extinction of tribal languages and the extensive measures taken by the United States government to extirpate them, today the contest is not just a battle over keywords; rather, the battle is waged over language survival.

When talking to various elders and asking them what it is that makes us distinct as Dakota people, language is always one of several things mentioned. The term *wakaŋ* is used in reference to the language, meaning *mysterious, sacred,* or *holy*. It is viewed this way because according to our teachings, our language was given to us by Wakaŋtaŋka, "The Great Mystery." Thus, it is a sacred language. In line with the comments from Looking Horse cited earlier, as a young girl I repeatedly heard elders state that if we are unable to pray in Dakota, we must first apologize to Wakaŋtaŋka for not speaking in the language that was given to us. Loss of language then, from this perspective, calls into question our relationship with our Creator.

Furthermore, loss of language calls into question our relationship to the rest of the world. For example, concepts of kinship are fundamental to the Dakota worldview, and yet they would be hard to reproduce in English without loss of meaning. The many kinship terms within the Dakota language reflect an important Dakota value about the relatedness of all beings. We have a comprehensive list of kinship terms, quite extensive relative to that existing in the English language. Many of our single-word terms require a three or more word English translation because English equivalents simply do not exist. For example, if the word *tibdo* is used among siblings, it is understood that this is a reference to a brother, but because this term is only used by a woman to address her older brother, it also relays information about gender and age relationship. If the situation were reversed and a younger male was referring to his older sister, the single Dakota term *taŋke* is used. After observing a family a short time, an outsider would quickly understand the birth order of all the children in a family, just by observing these kinship references. However, these kinship terms would be difficult to employ in the English language. I have heard my uncle, Harry Running Walker, frequently refer to my father as "younger brother" when talking to an English speaker, but because this English translation doesn't account for the gender of the speaker—since "younger brother" could also be spoken by an older sister—the extensiveness of Dakota relatedness is lost. Because these kinship references become cumbersome in English, few young families on our reservation retain any of these kinship references among siblings.

Along these same lines, the term *Mitakuyapi Owas'iŋ* is a phrase central to Dakota culture and even those with limited language knowledge are familiar with its usage and the weightiness of its meaning. Literally, this would translate as *All My Relations*, and while it translates easily enough, the worldview associated with this phrase becomes apparent only when used in the context of the extensive network of other kinship terms. This is language that reflects the sacredness and interconnectedness of all creation and is used to encompass all living beings, in essence, all the natural world. It is used in greetings, in prayers, in ceremonies, in speeches, and any other time one wants to call upon all or part of creation. Thus, uttering the phrase in English does not have the same depth of meaning, because in English, other spiritual beings are not referred to with a kinship term in everyday speech, even siblings.

Furthermore, the designation of a spiritual being among the Dakota differs from the designation often used by English speakers. For example, *tuŋkaŋśida*, *grandfather*, may apply to a human being or a number of human beings as a kinship term, but it also is applied to other spiritual beings. The term may refer to Wakaŋtaŋka (The Great Mystery), the rocks used in the sweat lodge, or the gigantic granite boulders that appear in our area of the country and whom the Dakota recognize as the oldest, most ancient beings. Interestingly, scientists have now dated those rocks from 3.6 to 3.8 billion years old, identifying them as some of the oldest exposed rocks in the world.[24] Kinship terms are used to discuss all of creation—terms of elder brother or elder sister may be used to describe the animals, the sun may be talked about as grandfather and the moon as grandmother. For those who grow up in a Dakota-speaking household, from the time of birth a different relationship with the universe and all of its beings is developed and then nurtured throughout a lifetime. For a student of the Dakota language, these references and understandings open doors to an entirely new set of values and move stated ideals about kinship from mere rhetoric in an intellectual argument to one based solidly in language and worldview.

In what manner do the Dakota conceptualize our historical past? Language terminology used to describe the stories reveals that they are divided into categories quite different from those in the Western academic tradition. This makes distinguishing these categories difficult, as they do not easily translate into English, and the English terms are inadequate as they are heavily laden with meanings that diminish the authenticity or truth within the stories themselves. Terms such as *myth*, *legend*, or even *stories* all carry connotations that are typically associated with mere entertainment, fiction, tall tales, or untruth. Even finding a single Dakota word that directly translates to *history* is difficult. The closest appropriate word, *ehaŋna*, refers to *long ago*, but to signify the telling of long ago, *ehaŋna* must be accompanied with a term like *woyakapi*, which may be translated as a *narration*. Together, *ehaŋna woyakapi* may be translated as a *narration or telling of the past*, which has an implicit oral meaning. While this category or phrase that the Dakota use to identify a type of stories may be the one most easily grasped by and recognizable to academic historians, stories of this type are not the only ones of historical significance.

Another category, which we call *hituŋkaŋkaŋpi*, refers in general to stories from the elders that teach about the past and often involve things of a mysterious nature, not easily explainable. In reference to these, Dale Childs (one of our gifted storytellers from the Prairie Island Reservation who passed away in 2001) said, "These stories were given to the people for their survival so they could learn from these stories."[25] Because many of these narratives contain elements that may be viewed by the non-Native world as "impossible," with the frequent occurrence of miracles, they have been dismissed as fiction or myth. They are, instead, part of our reality. Some of the kinds of stories included in this category are the Uŋktomi stories, those of the Oceti Śakowiŋ, or the Seven Council Fires, stories about animals (whether the rabbit, wolf, bear, eagle, or others), caŋ otida (little dwellers among the trees), ciżanna (the grandson character of a former storyteller), wicapapṡuŋpśuŋna (the head-menace character), and other "how they came to be stories." These are stories that have been passed down through the generations and should only be told in the winter when snow is on the ground.

Another interesting feature of these stories is that they *mark* the listener; they leave an imprint on the listener. The Dakota term *owaŋke* is used to identify this act. When discussing this concept, my grandmother, Naomi Cavender, described how a child is influenced by someone with whom they spend time. A man, for instance, may have certain habits, and if a child sees this he may also develop these habits because he has been marked by his relationship to the man. These stories may have this same kind of influence in that they become imprinted on you and become a part of your thoughts. In essence, they become a part of you. Songs, dances, and gestures are central components of many of these stories. They undoubtedly contribute greatly to the impression they leave on the audience, and one cannot help but marvel at the accompanying sounds of an ancient song or the expressiveness of ancient movements.

A third major category of stories is that of the *okicize*, or *the stories of war*. Being Dakota, war was a central component of our lives. About this important tradition, Charles Eastman remarks: "Warfare we regarded as an institution of the 'Great Mystery'—an organized tournament or trial of courage and skill, with elaborate rules and 'counts' for the coveted honor of the eagle feather. It was held to develop the quality of manliness, and its motive was chivalric or patriotic, but never the aggrandizement or the overthrow of a brother nation. It was common, in early times, for a battle or skirmish to last all day, with great display of daring and horsemanship, but with scarcely more killed and wounded than may be carried from the field during a university game of football."[26] Because of this central theme in the lives of Dakota people, both men and women enjoyed hearing about the feats of their ancestors and notable acts of bravery, or hilarity, as the case may be. Having an entire genre of stories to accommodate the value placed on war, then, becomes noteworthy. Several of the stories contained here might be categorized as okicize stories, and all of them may be categorized as ehaŋna woyakapi.

The okicize stories are primarily told by men, as it was primarily the men who were the warriors. As in many instances in Dakota culture, it is usually those who have firsthand knowledge of a given experience who are the best qualified to relate those experiences to others; empirical knowledge is highly valued. However, in the absence of qualified men, or if they have participated in war themselves, women also tell oḳicize stories. Women have often been tellers of the hituŋkaŋkaŋpi stories, although men may also tell these. Stories falling within the category of ehaŋna woyaḳapi may be relayed by either gender. In my own family, my kuŋśi, Elsie Cavender, grew up hearing many ehaŋna woyaḳapi stories from her grandmother, who carried detailed memories of the traumatic and rapidly changing times she had survived. She also described her grandfather as a great storyteller, and his repertoire would have included stories in all three of these categories. In my lifetime, with the male relatives in my direct ancestral line deceased, it is through my grandmother that I heard the oḳicize stories of my ancestors, as well as the stories in the hituŋkaŋkaŋ and ehaŋna woyaḳapi categories, as she felt all of these were important to my education.

In a recent conversation with Kuŋśi Carrie Schommer, she was relaying a discussion she had with another Dakoṭa elder and reminded me of another important lesson. The Dakoṭa language does not have an equivalent to the English word *sorry*. There is no way to apologize for bad deeds or words. It is understood that as a Dakoṭa, it is important to think carefully before acting or speaking so that there is no need for an apology. She pointed out that once something is spoken, it cannot be taken back. When discussing this she referenced Uŋkaŋna, who once told us this was like ringing a bell—once it is rung, it cannot be taken back. Certainly this notion is relevant to a discussion on the oral tradition, as it sheds additional light on the need for veracity to maintain cultural and societal standards.

Uŋkaŋna Eli understood well the importance of our language. Believing in the necessity of reading and writing in our language, Uŋkaŋna was involved in a variety of language projects over the years. For example, he and Doris Pratt served as translators for a very colorful 1987 children's book.[27] This particular book, rather than focusing on "traditional" Dakoṭa life, focused on the modern world, attempting to show the young reader that our language has relevance for and a way to discuss all the things in the world today. As there weren't words in common usage for many of the modern items contained in the book, Uŋkaŋna and Tuŋwiŋ Doris created many new words, understanding fully the necessity of change and development in a living language. The two of them also collaborated on a *Dakota Word Dictionary* published in 1986. The foreword to that project states: "The aim of the Dakota Language Retention Program is to develop and utilize as much material in the Dakota Language as possible. We have reached a crucial point in time as our language is in danger of dying out."[28] They both understood deeply the significance of language retention and worked hard at trying to reverse the trend in language loss. Tuŋwiŋ Doris is still working daily with our language and remains a leader in our language recovery efforts. They also could articulate much better than I what is at stake.

Our language and the stories perpetuated within that language are not only about telling stories that have some historical data, they are about the perpetuation of a worldview that has its own distinct theories about the past and its significance to the Dakota of today and tomorrow. The language of our people has always been the foundation of this worldview. For those who want to learn about the history of the Dakota from us, not from what the written sources might reveal about our people, an understanding of our language, and thus worldview, is key. As Kuŋśi Naomi Cavender says, "We are caretakers of a great heritage, a tradition which is a valuable inheritance." The Dakota have a rich and complex past that far exceeds what can be found in an archive.

When we use our Indigenous languages in writing, unlike colonized peoples in other parts of the world, we are not doing so to make them accessible to the masses of our people, as today the masses of our people, especially the younger generations, do not yet understand them. Rather, we are using the recovery of our languages as part of a larger decolonization project and as a means of conscious resistance. When discussing the attempts of Indigenous people to transform our lives and the world of the powerful, Linda Tuhiwai Smith states: "Part of the exercise is about recovering our own stories of the past. This is inextricably bound to a recovery of our language and epistemological foundations."[29] Language, stories, and epistemology are connected to who we are and where we will go in the future. In recognizing the significance of Indigenous languages and the history of their loss, revitalization and preservation become not just struggles for cultural survival but struggles for justice and equality. In fighting for the legitimacy and value of our languages and worldview, we are saying that they matter, they are important, and they have something to contribute to the world, and that somehow the contributions we make in these areas will assist us in our fight for self-determination. Ngũgĩ wa Thiong'o eloquently describes this struggle in more poetic terms:

> A world of many languages should be like a field of flowers of different colours. There is no flower which becomes more of a flower on account of its colour or its shape. All such flowers express their common "floralness" in their diverse colours and shapes. In the same way our different languages can, should, and must express our common being. So we should let our languages sing of the unity of the people of the earth, of our common

humanity, and above all of the people's love for peace, equality, independence, and social justice.³⁰

While we struggle to achieve recognition of our language as a flower, as Dakota people we are also grappling with how to maintain our Dakota worldview in contemporary times. Uŋkaŋna's stories help to guide our way.

4. Dena Naȟ'uŋ Wauŋ (These I Heard Growing Up)

Of all the stories Uŋkaŋna relayed during this 1992 visit, this first narrative is perhaps the most significant because it lays the groundwork for many of the other stories and reveals much about our oral tradition and how we, as Dakoṭa people, were instructed to conduct ourselves. Uŋkaŋna begins by describing his childhood and from whom he received his teachings, essentially laying out his credentials. This serves as an introduction to the first account he relayed to us. On a hunting and trapping trip with his uncle, he hears an ancient story about a very different man encountered by a group of Dakoṭa warriors on their journey to find the end of the land. Throughout the story the audience is reminded that this is not his personal story but rather one that has been passed on through many generations and which belongs to all Dakoṭa people. He follows this with a discussion of what happened after contact with Europeans and how we as Dakoṭa need to proceed into the future.

Ehaŋna Woyaḳapi Ṭokaheya (The First Historical Narrative)

Uŋkaŋ,[1] he ṭaku haȟ'aŋna de ṭokaheya ociciyaḳap waciŋ dena nakap dena.
   And so, first of all this morning, I want to tell something to all of you sitting here.

Uŋkaŋ, ṭaku ociciyaḳapṭe kuŋ he waciŋ.
   And so, I want to tell you something.

Ehaŋna hekṭa, ṭokaheya homakśida he ehaŋ iapi ṭaku hena naȟ'uŋ wauŋ.
   Way back a long time ago, I heard those things that were said when I was growing up.

Wabdawa śni uŋ eṭaŋhaŋś wicaȟcada wakaŋkada hena wicopeya imacaġe ka ṭaku ṭoked aŋpeṭu wakan yamni imacaġe iyohakap aŋpeṭu wakan iyamni uŋkaŋ Aṭe t'e.
   It didn't make any difference that I didn't go to school, I grew up amongst the old men and the old women and what happened was that three Sundays after I was born, the third Sunday, father died.

---

1. *Uŋkaŋ* is a word that may be translated as *and so*, but often within the text it doesn't get translated as it may not make sense in the English translation. This should not be confused with the Dakoṭa word for *grandfather*, *uŋkaŋ* or *uŋkaŋna*.

Ina išnana icaḣmaye.

Mother raised me by herself.[2]

Uŋkaŋ heye he "Wiuŋcoṭapi uŋkaŋ, nitaŋke ka niciŋye hena, boarding school Brandon hed wayawapi uŋ hece nawaḣ'uŋ ka hdip ehan ekṭa ṭaku uŋspep hena uŋġe iyeceṭu śni, wadake ce eya.

And so, she said that "We are many, and so, your older sister and your older brothers, they went to Brandon Boarding School I heard,[3] and when they returned, what they learned over there, I didn't agree with.

"He uŋ etaŋhaŋ wadawa kṭe śni, mihakap yauŋ ka icaḣciye, ka waecanuŋ kṭa ce, nibdiheca ka haḣ'aŋna ecada yekṭap.

"For that reason, you are not going to school, you will follow me and I will raise you and you will do things, you will be industrious and you will wake up early.

"Hehaŋ nakuŋ, ṭaku wicoḣan hena ecanuŋ kinhaŋ heced inicaġe kṭa ce.

"Then, also, if you do those tasks, that is the way you will develop.

"Waciŋic'iye inicaġe ka nakuŋ waciŋciye kṭa dena ekeś tohni waŋna waciŋwicawaye kṭa śni naceca ce ka iyayap okaŋ iyayap ce."

"You will grow up to depend only on yourself and I will depend on you also—these here ones, I will probably never depend on them, and they are gone from there now."

Eye waŋna de wabdawa kṭa keyapi iyehaŋtu kaŋhaŋ ho hece kaś wabdawa śni.

It was time for me to start school they said, but even so, I didn't go.

You know, ihnuḣ nine years henamakca caŋku ohna waśkaṭa, Aṭeyapi[4] Model T ohna inaźiŋ.

You know, suddenly, when I was nine years old I was playing in the road, the Indian agent came in a Model T and stopped.

"De niṭuwe he?"

"Who are you?"

---

2. Because his father died when he was so young, Uŋkaŋna knew very little about him, not even his Dakoṭa name, though he suspected it might have been Taŋkaya Omani, or "Travels Far." His mother's Dakoṭa name was Wayak Hiyaye Wiŋ, which might be translated as "Woman Who Watches as She Goes" or, more simply, "Watchful Woman" or "Alert Woman."

3. The term *nawaḣ'uŋ* here, meaning *I heard*, may have been used here instead of something more authoritative, indicating that perhaps his mother never actually saw them at the boarding school but was told that's where her children were.

4. *Aṭeyapi* refers here to the *Indian agent*, but it may be used to describe any *fatherlike figure*, or *authority figure*.

"Ho,[5] de de Eli Taylor he miye do."

"Well now, Eli Taylor, that is who I am."

"Wadawa he?

"Do you go to school?

"De ṭoḳed uŋ naḣmayahdiyaḳu?" he deye.

"Did you sneak away?" he said that.

"Hiya, de wabdawa śni do.

"No, I don't go to school.

"Mom wabdawa kṭe ciŋ śni do."

"Mom doesn't want me to go to school."

"Ho, ded opa wo!

"Well, get in here!

"Wadawa de kṭe do!"

"You will go to school!"

Ho eceś[6] de taŋḳad waśḳaṭamaka, uŋkaŋ heṭaŋhaŋ owape wayawa wai, day school heced ded Reserve ded akan.

I was playing outside and from there got in, and I went to school, day school, on this Reserve here.

Hokśipida heciya owas yupiyaked opiya ob waśḳaṭapi, hena heciya śḳaṭapi.

The boys I usually played with nicely, they were playing over there.

Nina iyokpiya wauŋ.

I was very happy.

Naḳuŋ uŋġe kośkap taŋḳiŋḳiŋyaŋpi.

Some of the boys had gotten bigger.

Ho uŋkaŋ hehan waniyeṭuwaŋ waŋżi hed wabdawa.

And so, I went to school there a year, one year.

Hehan ake inuŋpa he bde hehan haŋḳeya.

In the second [year], I went half.

Ina heciya hihnatuŋ.

Mother got married over there.

Ho hece heṭaŋhaŋ wayawatip eṭaŋhaŋ imacu hehaŋ amakip hece heciya wauŋ.

She took me from the school, they took me back over there, so there I stayed.

---

5. *Ho* is usually a male term of greeting or assent, but in this case we thought it would be better translated as *Well, now*.

6. *Eceś* is an interjection indicating an unwillingness but was difficult to translate into English here.

Hece ḳaṡ waŋna ḳa nine years hehaŋya imacub ḳa ten years heca ḳa eleven, twelve etḳiya bde heci, heciya wauŋ.

> Now it has been nine years since they got me, then it was ten years and eleven, when I was going on twelve over there.

Twelve years hena makca hehan okitaŋna kape ibdabde hehan waŋna waṡicuŋṭa wicoȟan iyewaya.

> When I went a little bit past twelve years, now I found a job with a Waṡicu.

Heciya wauŋ tiyaṭa wauŋ ṡni.

> I stayed over there, I didn't live at home.

Waṡicu ṭaḳu eyap hena naȟ'uŋ wauŋ.[7]

> I heard what the Waṡicu said.

Taḳ ecuŋ ṭoḳed uŋpi ḳa ṭaḳu yutapi, ṭoḳed waŋḳapi heca hena iyeced imacaġe.

> What they do, how they are, what they eat, how they live, I learned to live in that way, too.

Ḳaṡ hehan hed waŋna itokab ten years hehanya Dakoṭa dena ṭaḳu eyap naȟ'uŋ wauŋ.

> Now ten years before this, I always heard what these Dakoṭa said.

Hehan waniyeṭu ṭop heciya Bde Wataŋḳada, *Lake Manitoba*, eyapi heci ḳahdaya heciya wauŋ.

> For four years I was over there, Bde Wataŋḳada, Lake Manitoba, they call it, I was over there by it.

Heciya wauŋ ye wouŋspe makiya ḳa Aṭe waye iyeced Waṡicu uŋṡimadaḳe ḳa omakiye ṭaḳu heyake opemicituŋ micażażużu hehan kaṡpapida mak'u.

> I stayed over there and the Waṡicu taught me and cared about me like a father, he helped me, bought me clothes, paid me, and gave me coins [money].

Ho hehan waŋna komaṡkaga hehan waŋna he Dakoṭaḳ he deci ṭuwe nineteen, eighteen iṡ nineteen, heca kiŋhaŋ kounṡkapi.

> And so, now, when I became a young man, now over here, when a Dakoṭa becomes nineteen, eighteen or nineteen, we become young men.

Ho hehan hinaȟ hehaŋyaŋ tawaciŋ uŋsuṭap ṡni, ḳaeṡ, hehan waŋna he ho hece deciya wahdi ḳa ake deci waṡuŋṭa waecamuŋ.

> But still, we are not strong-willed in our thinking, but still I returned over here and again I worked for the Waṡicu.

---

7. *Naȟ'uŋ wauŋ* is a phrase that may be translated as *I heard growing up*, but also implies *that what was heard became a part of the state of being*, *wauŋ* also meaning *I am*.

Weṭu hehan wahmuŋkapi iyap bde.
   When it was spring, I went along with them in their trapping.
Ṭokiya sinkpe ohmuŋkapi capa uŋkuwapi, iś ṭaḳu bdoḳeṭu kiŋhan ihnuḣ nakuŋ suŋktokca hena nakpaḳ de yuksap ḳa wiyopeyapi.
   Where they trapped muskrats, we hunted after beaver, when it was summer sometimes they cut wolves' ears and sold them.
Hena waciŋyapi bounty hena eyapi Waśicu he heca unḳicuŋpi
   They depended on the bounty, the Waśicu call it that, that is what we got.
Ho hena heced uŋyaŋkuŋpi.
   That is the way we lived.
Uŋkaŋ he de Saskatchewan heciya Dekśi waya waŋ heciya ihdaḳe.
   And an uncle of mine moved over there to Saskatchewan.
He ecan waŋna Ina ṭoḳ ye śni, owaŋżida tiyata yaŋke.
   At this time, mom didn't go anywhere, she sat at home.[8]
Deci wakpada, Oak River, akasaŋpaṭaŋhaŋ heciya uŋtipi hed yaŋke.
   Over here, the river, Oak River, across from over there we lived, that's where she stayed.
Iża ake he wicaḣcada he kci hdi ḳa hed yaŋkapi.
   The old man, he too again came back with her and they stayed there.
Cinye wihni he kci wihni wahdi maġaksica unkuṭepi ḳa taḣca uŋkuṭepi ṭaku.
   I came back from hunting with older brother, we shot ducks and we shot deer and others.
Uŋkaŋ, tawicukciça ḳa hehan Dekśi iś tawicukciça hena wakeya num, ti num, Saskatchewan heciya wauŋ.
   And then, I was over there in Saskatchewan with his wife, and uncle with his wife, two tents, two dwellings.
Uŋ he, he ecuŋhaŋ waŋna Dekśi waye (miś, nakaeś eighteen, nineteen hed wauŋ) ḳaeś iyekśe waŋna he seventy-five or eighty years heciya henakca heced waŋna oḣ'aŋ iyehaŋṭu śni.
   And so, in the meantime, my uncle (as for me I was just eighteen, nineteen) as for him, he was now right about seventy-five or eighty years old so he was not up to doing much.
Wakpada de opta copa ibdabde aḳasaŋpaṭan ḳa aṭanuka kci maza ewauŋpe.
   I waded across the river to the other side and on both sides we laid traps.
Ihanke heci uŋkipi ḳa hehan hed opta icipaś wahdiyaḳu hehan ṭaku uŋkṭep hena uŋḳiŋp uŋḳupi çee.

---

8. Phrased in this way the implication is that because of her age his mother didn't go many places any more.

When we got over to the end and then there I came back across, we came with our kill packed on our backs.

Hah'aŋna waśtedahcaka hah'aŋna he.
That morning was a particularly beautiful morning.

Uŋkaŋ heya, "Haw Tośka, ito kaeś ded ded oziuŋkiye kte do."
And so he said, "Okay nephew, here we will rest for a little while here."

"Ded," eya ka iyotaŋke hece miża isakib ibdotke.
"Here," he said and he sat down and so I too sat down beside him.

"Ṭaku ociciyake kta ce.
"I will tell you something.

"Ito wowahdake kte, anahoptaŋ wo!"
"Ito,[9] I'm going to talk, you listen!"

"Haw," epe, ecin ṭohaŋtaŋnaśṭa wicahcada hena anawicawahoptaŋ, macistiŋna hetaŋhaŋ, wauŋ naka.
"Yes," I said, because for so long, from the time I was little I have listened to the old men.

"Ṭaku ociciyake kte.
"I'm going to tell you something.

"He tokata kiksuya uŋ wo!
"Remember that in the future!

"Tokatakiya okiciciyapta, keyapi.
"Share with one another in the future, they say.

"He niciŋca ka niṭakoża hena owicakiyaka wo!
"Those who are your children and your grandchildren, tell them!

"Hekta deciya uŋyaŋkuŋpi tka do.
"Back then, we were living over here.

"Makato Icu, Caŋśayapi ṭaku hena makoçe heciya.
"Where They Get Blue Earth,[10] Painting the Trees Red,[11] those were that kind of land.

"Ded uŋyaŋkuŋpi tka uŋġe deci uŋkub uŋġe deciya Mnidiheye heciya he ehaŋ owicaġe wanice do, heciya uŋyaŋkuŋpi do.
"We are here, but some of us that came over here, from over there at

---

9. *Ito* is an expression that can mean *well* or even *perhaps*.
10. This refers to the Mankato area of Minnesota. The city of Mankato has retained the ancient Dakota word for the land there.
11. This refers to the Lower Sioux Community today but is a reference to the area's large number of redwoods. Redwood Falls is the name of a nearby town, again, retaining the Dakota place-name.

Mnidiheye,[12] at that time there were no boundaries, we were over there.

"Uŋkaŋ homakśida macistiŋna he ehaŋ wohdakapi.

"And so, when I was a little boy, at that time they spoke.

"Uŋkaŋ taku oyakapi he ehaŋ okiciyakap uŋyaŋpta keyapi, wicowicaheg iyohi tka heced Taŋkśida k'a Haŋkaśida niyuhe ka taŋhaŋ ed uŋ śni.

"What they told at that time through oral tradition, they said to carry on every generation, but then younger sister and little female cousin, they raised you and they passed on.

"Tuweda taku oniciyake śni ce.

"No one has told you anything.

"Heuŋ etaŋhaŋ ociciyake."

"For that reason, I'm telling you."

"Ho," epe.

"Yes," I said.

"Haw heced anahoptaŋ.

"Yes, so then listen.

"Ehaŋna nakab, haw ded kaki uŋyaŋkab heciya hed Pežihutazizi Ode heciya hena Caŋśayapi he heciya hehaŋya makoce hena oyate hena uŋkitawapi do.

"Long ago, yes here now, we were way over there at Looking for Yellow Medicine,[13] over there where They Painted the Trees Red, those people on that land over there are ours.

"Haw hena wicahca wohdakapi, uŋkaŋ heyapi do," eye.

"Yes, those old men spoke, and this is what they said," he said.

"Poh'osaŋ waŋ yuhap keyapi do.

"They said they had a leader.

"Uŋkaŋ, Poh'osaŋ he Eyapaha yuhap okiyake, 'Ka ya wo, ito hah'aŋna kaŋhaŋ kośka uŋǧe upte do.'

"And so, the Poh'osaŋ[14] told the Eyapaha[15] they had, 'Go and in the morning some young men should come.'

---

12. Mnidiheye refers to Niagara Falls, which indicates the great distance Dakota people traveled at various times.

13. Pezihutazizi today refers to the Upper Sioux Community outside of Granite Falls, Minnesota. Historically, the yellow medicine grew in abundance in this area, and Dakota people would gather it to use for healing purposes. It has been identified as moonseed or *Menispermum canadense* in Alma R. Hutchens, *Handbook of Native American Herbs* (Boston: Shambhala, 1992), 236, and is documented as a Native medicinal plant in Virgil J. Vogel, *American Indian Medicine* (Norman: University of Oklahoma Press, 1970), 289.

14. *Poh'osaŋ* is an older Dakota word referring to a *leader or chief*. It is rarely used in this way today.

"Uŋkaŋ, wicakco, keyapi do.

"And so, he invited them, they say.

"Ṭuweda tawicutuŋp śni, cinca wanicapṭe do.

"No one who is married [should come], they should be without children.

"Hehan wipe yuhapṭe do ka wihnipi woṭe henipi taŋyaŋ uŋspepṭe do ka haŋpa uŋġe akab yuhapṭe do.

"They must have a weapon and they must be an expert hunter and a hunter of game and have some extra pairs of moccasins.

"Ḳiŋhaŋ hena wawicabdaka waciŋ ce.

"If so, I want to see them [the men].

"Ded upṭa ce.

"They will come here.

"Tiyopa tipi ded upṭa do.

"They will come into my home.

"Ob wowahdaḳe kṭe do.

"I will speak with them.

"Hah'aŋna he wicaśta he eyapaha aye, 'Ṭona tawicu yatuŋp śni ka nicinca wanicapi hecihaŋ P'oh'osaŋ ti heciya dapṭa he eciŋ ṭaku iwaciŋniyaŋpṭa ḳeye oniciyaḳapṭa.'

"That morning, that man, he went calling out, 'Those who are not married and who are without children, you go where Poh'osaŋ lives over there because he will depend on you for something, he said he will tell you.'

"Ho hehan hah'aŋna ḳaeś waŋna wiŋyaŋ waŋśpayaŋpi taŋkad he ecan, he ecan hena waŋna kośkag ahi.

"So then it was morning, and already now the women were cooking outside and already now those young men had arrived.

"Ṭonakcaŋ ḳeye śni tḳa wicotapi nacece nakaha ahibayakaŋpi.

"He didn't say how many there were, but there must have been many of them because they came and sat.

"Uŋkaŋ heya ḳeyapi, 'Haw wotap canuŋpa po canuŋpa opuġi.

"And so, they say he said, 'Yes eat, smoke your pipe, fill your pipe.

"'Ṭaku waŋżi dena waciŋciyapi de kośka dena,' eya ḳeyapi.

"'I'm depending on you young men for one thing,' they say he said.

"'Waŋna awanihdakapi oyaḳihipi do.

"'You are able to take care of yourselves now.

---

15. The *Eyapaha* is the *town crier*. He would go from dwelling to dwelling announcing important messages to keep the village abreast of the latest news.

"'Hehan nakuŋ tokatakiya ninic'iyapta wokahniġe hena duhapte.
  "'Then also, you will have the understanding of survival in the future.
"'Ho de poh'osaŋ maya duhapi.
  "'You have me as your leader.
"'Ṭaku waŋżi sdodwaye śni do.
  "'There is one thing I don't know.
"'Ṭaku ota sdodwaye ka nawah'uŋ ka wauŋ, tka ṭaku waŋżi sdodwaye śni do.
  "'Many things I know and have heard, but there is one thing I don't know.
"'Makoce de he ṭokeca he sdodwaye śni do.
  "'I don't know what this land is like.
"'Taŋkaya omani wauŋ kaeś ṭukte ed ihaŋke ṭohni wabdake śni do.
  "'I have traveled all over but I've never seen where it ends.
"'Heced iṭo ṭonakca tawat'ed ya kaŋhaŋ omakiya po!
  "'And so, for as many of you who are up to it, help me.
"'Wi de kaki iyaye heciya taŋhaŋ yapo.
  "'Beyond where the sun sets, go over there.
"'Ake yabadaba ṭukṭed he makoce ihaŋke hecihaŋ ṭokiya iś mayasaŋ k'aiś ṭokeca hecihan he.
  "'Again, you go to exactly where the end of the land is, whether where the gray cliff bank is or whatever it might be like.
"'He wowayake mayakahdib kaŋhaŋ ka sdodwaye kte.
  "'Bring me back the account and I will know.
"'He iyokpiya wauŋ kte do,' eya keyapi.
  "'I will be happy,' they say he said.
"'Ho,' eyap keyapi.
  "'Yes,' they say, they said.
"Heced uŋġe ṭonakca hetaŋhaŋ waŋeya ic'icaġap haŋpa ic'icaġap wicahcakap.
  "So therefore, so many of them from there made food to carry, made shoes for themselves, [shoes] were made for them.
"Wik he iyayek hehaŋya okope oyaṭe ṭoktokca yuke.
  "From where the sun sets, it's frightening that far, there are different tribes of people.
"Ic'i ktep çe ihnunah.
  "They sometimes kill one another.
"Hena okiciçakahniġap śni.
  "They don't understand each other.
"Oyate obe ota Dakoṭa kaeś hena owas'ina ṭokaŋ uŋ etaŋhaŋ nakaha iap tokca.

"There are many different nations, even all of the Dakoṭa, the language they speak is different now.

"Okiciçakaȟniġap śni uŋkaġap.
"We were made so we don't understand each other.

"Haw itokab hihaŋna ṭaku hena nakuŋ nawahuŋ.
"Yes, I also heard those things a long time before.

"Haw he ṭoked uŋ hena hecuŋ he?
"Yes, why did he do those things?

"Oṭoiyohi ikce wicaṡṭa hena owas ouŋtokca ḳa iapi tokca uŋk'upi.
"All of them, each and every common man, we were given a way of life and different language.

"He iap heuŋ wahoḳuŋciciyapi wouŋkciyap ḳa wowaecuŋ ṭak uŋkekciyapi ḳaŋhaŋ tamahed, tawaciŋ, mahed heci iyouŋḣpayap caŋte ekṭa iyoḣpaye ṭaŋyaŋ oḳaḣniġ wicauŋdapi.
"Using that language to give direction to help each other and to do for each other, if we say these things to one another, inside, in our minds, taking something within ourselves, reaching our heart, with a good understanding we believe.

"Heca uŋ he iapi tokca oyaṭe iyohi uŋk'upi.
"Therefore, every nation, we were given a different language.

"Ḳa iża heced wicak'up ḳa nakuŋ uŋḳiża hena heced uŋk'upi.
"And so they were also given that and we were also given those.

"Yaba ake wi iyaye ca ake, ṭukṭe ed can k'aiṡ makośiceke ḳa kiŋhaŋ ṭuŋwewaŋ iyaye, çe ḳeyapi, he ṭuŋwewan iyayeyap çe ḳeyapi ekṭa eṭuŋwaŋ yaŋkapi.
"If they go till the sun sets again, again where there were trees, where the land is bad, and a scout would go out they said, the scout that went out they said they would watch the direction he went.

"Pahaḳ, iṡ isiŋyaŋked iyaye ekṭa, itokab wayaḳ yaŋkapi.
"Before, they sat looking that direction where he disappeared into the hill.

"Ho, heciya ṭaŋhaŋ ṭana waŋna ḳu ḳiŋhaŋ, aokas'iŋ ḳu yukśaŋkśaŋkiya deced, kutkiya iyaŋka ḳu.
"And when he was returning from over there, looking here and there, zigzagging, he came running down.

"Haw hed he ṭaku owas ṭaŋyaŋ yaŋke ṭaku oḳokipe hena wanica hena.
"Everything is fine there, there are none of those things to fear.

"Ca hece dena aye ḳa ake waŋna tehan yap keyapi waŋna he wetu kṭe iyayap hed wi iyaya eṭopṭaya iyaye.
"So therefore they went again, and now they have been going a long time, they say, it was going to be spring now, the sun set in the direction that they went.

"Iȟnunaȟ ȟeśica waŋ ed ipi ḳeyapi do.

"Sometimes they arrived at ȟeśica.[16]

"Pahaha ḳa ȟeśica ḳa iŋyaŋ ȟe ḳa hehan maḳaṭa hehan ṭaḳu heca ed obeya, eyap ḳeyapi.

"It is hilly and ȟeśica and rocky hills and the ground was all of those things, they say they said.

"Iyus'eya yapi ṭukṭed iyaḳapṭe ake heṭaŋhaŋya heced yapi.

"They were barely making it to where they made it over, from there again, that is the way they went.

"'Haw hed naḳuŋ pahawaŋ nina wakaŋṭuya yaŋḳ,' ḳeyap ce.

"'Yes, and also a very high hill was there,' they said.

"'Waŋ, niśṭo ye ḳa nu ito ṭuŋweya wo ito ded uŋyaŋḳapṭe do.'

"'Waŋ,[17] you go this time, nu,[18] to scout and we will sit here.'

"'Haw,' eye, he eciŋ ekṭa eṭuŋwaŋ yaŋḳapi do.

"'Yes,' he said, because they were sitting there looking in that direction.

"Ekṭa eṭuŋwaŋ yaŋḳapṭe uŋkaŋ, ye ḳa pahaḳ heciya aoḳas'iŋ ḳa nusḳe ekṭa eṭuŋwaŋ yaŋḳapi.

"They were sitting looking in the direction and he started over to the hill and looked into the hills at something, they were sitting looking in the direction.

"Iȟnunaȟ ȟeyaṭa ḳiya ṭohanyaŋked sdohaŋ ḳu naḳuŋ ḳa hehan nažiŋ owoṭaŋna kud itoheya. 'Waŋ, ṭaḳu, ṭaḳu[19] waŋ wokokipe waŋżi wayake do.'

"Suddenly he came crawling back for a distance and he stood up and came straight down. 'Waŋ, he saw something that was frightening!'

"Wakṭayaŋḳapi. 'Waŋca itḳouŋkipapi kṭe.'

"They were waiting expectantly. 'We had better meet him at once.'

"Ed hdi ḳa 'Ṭaḳu ṭokeṭu he?' eyap.

"He returned there and they said, 'What happened?'

"'Huŋhe, waŋ he ṭaḳu waŋ wabdake tḳa, haw he owakaȟniġe śni do,' eya ḳeyapi.

"'Huŋhe, I saw something but I don't understand it,' they say he said.

---

16. *Ȟeśica* may refer to *hills, buttes, mountains,* or *badlands*. In this case it is not clear which of these is described.

17. *Waŋ* is a Dakoṭa exclamation similar to the English *oh* and is used by male speakers.

18. *Nu,* or *nusḳe,* is a Dakoṭa term used when the speaker cannot recall information immediately, similar to the English *ah* or *um.*

19. Often in Dakoṭa words are repeated for emphasis, or in this case to convey the excitement of the situation. It doesn't make sense when translated into English and so has been left out.

"'Haw ekta uŋyaŋpa wauŋyakapte do,' eyapi.
  "'Yes, we'll go there and we will see it,' they said.
"Heced takci śni śkaŋ do, haw heced, iś he makowaśteĥce do.
  "He is focusing on what he is doing, yes, as for that place it's really beautiful.
"Wato ḳa otaŋkaye owaśtecake do, eyap ḳeyapi.
  "It was a beautiful open space with green grass, they say they said.
"He cokaheya hed śkaŋyaŋḳe do.
  "He was right in the middle of that.
"Tka hece ṭaḳuḳ owakaĥinige śni do, eyap ḳeyap.
  "But I didn't understand what it was, they say they said.
"Yaba, owas abeya ḳaked hoiyohikciyapṭa heced aya.
  "They went and spread out within hearing distance of each other.
"Haw aoḳas'in owas wayaḳapi ḳaeś hece iźa ṭaḳu he sdodyap śni.
  "They all looked on and saw, but they did not understand what it was, either.
"He ecaŋ ḳakiya hukuya ṭuwe śkaŋ uŋġe he wicaśta ekśe śkaŋ.
  "Meanwhile, over down there, whoever was there, it was a human who was there.
"Hukuya iyeic'iye ḳa makaḳ de uŋġe içu.
  "He stooped down and took some of this earth.
"Napopopaġe ake kaĥoiyeye eṭaŋhaŋ śota heceĥ p'o heceĥ ye ḳa ṭohan p'oḳ he ḳaska ca ṭaḳuwaŋ huha ṭopa he mani iyaye çe.
  "He rubbed it in his hands and threw it, from it went something smokelike, foglike and when the foglike cleared, something four-legged went walking away.
"Ye ḳa ḳaki waŋna uŋġe śkaŋpi uŋ heciya ope iyaye.
  "It would go and over there now it would go and join some that were over there.
"Haw heced, ṭokedked de ṭuwe ṭaḳṭoḳuŋ he?"
  "Yes, and so just how is this person doing this?"
Hed de dekśi oyakeca, "'De kiksuya wo,' eya ca."
  When uncle told this he said, "'Remember this,' they said."
"Ihnunaĥ ḳa ayuśtaŋ ahituŋwaŋ.
  Suddenly he stopped and looked this way.
"'Ḳuya upo deciya,' eya ḳeyap çe.
  "'All of you come down here,' they say he said.
"'Waŋ, Dakoṭ ie do.'"
  "'Hey, he speaks Dakota!'"
"Ḳuya u wicaśi. 'Ḳuya uŋyaŋpta?' he eyap.

"He told them to come down. 'Shall we go down?' they said.

"'Haw, upo!' eya keyapi.

"'Yes, you all come!' they say he said.

"Haw heced ekta uŋyaŋp kiŋhaŋ waśte do.

"Yes, it would be good if we all go there.

"Haw uŋġe eya kokipap ka kaeś wadidake ic'iyapi uŋġe ihakab uŋġe kokipapi.

"Yes, some were fearful but they strengthened themselves, some of them following, some of them fearful.

"'Komakipapśnipo, upo,' eya keyapi.

"'Don't be afraid of me, all of you come,' they say he said.

"'Dena he wociciyakapte do,' eya keyapi.

"'I am to tell you all these,' they say he said.

"Haw heced yaba ikiyadeyapi, ikiyadeyapi kaeś taku he?

"Yes, so they went and closer, closer they went, but what was it?

"Ekśe he wicaśta tka hehan haŋpo kiŋhaŋ cehnakituŋpi śina taku taha śina iaŋ uŋpi, heced tak uŋ śni.

"He was a human, but the footwear . . . if they [the Dakota] wore the breechcloth robe, some leather robe they wore, he didn't wear any of this.

"Kaeś itek de ataya hituŋ, itek ataya hituŋ hehan takuwaŋ ohdiheya uŋ he akantu uŋ.

"The face was all bearded, it was hairy all over, then he wore something draped over.

"Hehan nakuŋ, haŋpa uŋktaya abdezap sicuda kaeś decekced optaptayeya tak iyutaŋ.

"Then also, they observed the footwear he wore was the sole only with straps strung over and across.

"Haw, heced wayakapi heced.

Yes, that is what they saw, that was.

"Uŋkaŋ heya keyapi, 'Haw, hed he iyotaŋkapo, ociciyakapte do.'

And here, they say he said, 'Yes, sit down there, I will tell you something.'

"'Poh'osaŋ nitawap he de maka tukted ihaŋke he wayak niśipi do," eya, "tka de he ituya iyotaŋ iyekiya mayanipi do.

"'Your leader told you to see where the land ends," he said, "but you have suffered with a lot of walking for nothing.

"'Toked taku wooyake ayakipta cin heciŋhaŋ deda ociciyakapta detaŋhaŋ hena yuha yahdapta do."

"'How you will take back the story he wants, I will tell you here and now, you will take those back with you from here."

"'Haw,' eya keyapi.

"'Yes,' they say he said.

"Ṭokedked he dena he ṭuwe sdodye kṭa?"
"How is anyone going to know these?"
"Waŋna iża sdodyap śni awiyukçaŋpi.
They didn't know, now they were thinking.
"'Haw de de de he de wociciyakapṭa ka de wau do,' eyap.
"'I am here to tell you something, and that is why I come,' they said.
"'Haw dena Danikoṭapi heced wociciyakapṭe do.
"'Yes, you are all Dakota and so I will tell you.
"'Uŋkaŋ, ṭaku ociciyakapṭa he ka ked maka ded akan niya uŋpṭa do.'
"'And so what I am to tell you is the manner in which you are to live on this earth.'
"Eya ka ṭak ṭoked ṭukṭe ohna opiic'iyapṭe ka ṭukṭe ohnaya icaġapṭa wicotapṭa hena hena owas ṭaŋyaŋ owicakiyake.
"However, in what way they will do for themselves and in what way they will grow, how they will multiply, all of these he will tell in the right way.
"Unkaŋ, uŋśikcidakap kiciniya he wowahicuŋ hena sdodkiya wowahicuŋ hehan ohokcidapa ho he wowahicuŋ eya opiic'iyapṭe.
"And so, have compassion for one another, know your relatives, honor your relatives, respect them, and treat each other as relatives.
"Hena ṭaŋyaŋ owas awicakiyake.
"He explained these clearly.
Haw, hena, hena he de ṭakuda uŋġe add iyewaye kṭe śni, ṭoked dekśi oyakek hecihan nawah'uŋ, haw hena de iyeced obdake kṭe.
Yes, those, I will not add something to those things, how uncle told I heard, that is the way I tell it here.
"Hena owicakiyaka hehan heya keyapi, 'Haw hopo inażiŋ po decitkiya uŋ-yapṭe do.'
"And so, he told them so, and then they say he said, 'Yes now, stand up and we will go in this direction.'
"Ho, hetkiya ob ye ka he yapṭa unkaŋ peżi, keya, peżi hutkaŋ.
Yes, that way he went with them, and as they were going there were some grass and grass roots.
"'Wayakapo de wadakapi he?'
"Look, do you see this?
"'Haw, dena peżihuṭa he ṭukṭed panihuŋ kaiś niyazaŋp kaiś ṭoketu kiŋhaŋ pa de niyazaŋp kaŋhaŋ de iś ee do de.'
"'Yes, these medicines, if you get a cut or have pain or something, if you have a headache, this is it for that.'
"'Iśta niyazaŋp kaŋhaŋ iś de ihnunah ṭukṭed ṭaku uŋ huhu waŋżi napaksapi de huhu peżihuṭa dena ee.'

"'If your eyes are sore this is it and if suddenly you break a bone, these are the bone medicines.'

"'Haw, ṭukṭed ihnunah, haw dodyaciŋp śni kaŋhaŋ de peżihuṭa uŋ woyuṭe yapṭe [20] yaciŋp kaŋhaŋ.'

"'Yes, if you should suddenly lose your appetite, you will use this medicine as food if you want.'

"Hena owas ṭaŋyaŋ owicakiyake.

He explained all those clearly.

"Ho woyazan obek oṭa, tka hena iṭoiyohi he ehaŋ hena iś woyazan heca.

"Yes, there are different kinds of illnesses, but each and every one of those were common.[21]

"Dehan he de woyazank obe oṭa.

"There are many kinds of illnesses now.

"Heced hena peżihuṭa hena owicakiyake.

"Thus he explained all the medicines to them.

"Hehan can kiŋ heciya awicayak.

"Then he took them toward the woods.

"'Haw caŋk dena he waciŋyeyapṭa[22] do.'

"'You will depend on these woods.'

"'Hena uŋ ceyatipṭe hena ṭaŋyaŋ, haw he.'

"'With those you will build your fires, those are good, that's that.'

"Uŋkaŋ eya keyapi, 'Dena ṭaku ociciyakap dena ṭohaŋya śṭa tokaṭakiya kiksuya uŋpo ka okiciyak yeya po omaka iyohi ka wowicaġe iyohi, ka saŋpa nitakożap ka nakuŋ saŋpa nitakożap hena okiciyak yeya po,' eya keyapi.

"And so, they say he said, 'These things that I am telling you, always remember these as long as you can in the future, tell each other every year and every generation, and your grandchildren and your great-grandchildren, continue telling each other,' they say he said.

"'Tokśta tawacin he suṭa cicaġapi, hena kiksuya mayanipṭe do.

"'For certain, I made your minds strong, you will carry those memories.

"'Tuwe wiċakeya ohna manipṭa, hena kiksuyap, ohna manipṭe,' eya keyapi.

"'Those who walk with commitment, they will walk in that path of what they remember,' they say he said.

"Haw hdaba ake, ṭaku eya kahabiyewicaye yaŋkek hed yakuŋpi.

---

20. This is a contraction of the phrase *peżihuṭa uŋ woyuṭe yayapṭe*, which means to *eat the medicine for food*.

21. The implication here is that there weren't so many illnesses then.

22. Contraction of *waciŋ yeyapi kṭe*.

"They were going back again, they were there where he was shooing those things out of the way.

"'Haw dena awicayadapte do,' eya keyapi.

"'Yes, you are going to take these back with you,' they say he said.

"'De mani yauŋpi ka iyotaŋ iyekiyap yauŋpi do.

"'You are on foot and you are suffering hardship.

"'Tokiya dapi kiŋhaŋ kaŋ hena wicayak'iŋp ka nakuŋ taku woyute ka taku hena, hena nakuŋ, iyotaŋ iyekiya k'iŋ mayanipte do.

"'Whenever you go you carry the old and also different foods, other things, and those also, you suffer carrying them.

"'Dena, dena śuŋka wakaŋ ewicakiyapte do.

"'These, these will be called horses.[23]

"'Kiŋhaŋ hena waĥbapida ka haw dena okiŋ waśtepi heced tukte ohnaya, tukte ohnaya yaciŋp kaŋhaŋ waĥbada wicayakauŋspepta, hena.

"'They are gentle and they are easy to handle and so whatever way, which way you want, you can train them to be gentle, those.

"'De uman bdoka ka wiyeda de ka iża wicota ayapi kte do.

"'This other is a male and this a female and they will multiply.

"'Dena wicaduhapta do.

"'You will have these.

"'Yuha iyahdakapta ka yakip kaŋhaŋ owotaŋna wohdakapo,' eya keyapi.

"'You will have them in your moving and when you return, tell it straight!' they say he said.

"'De de wociciyakap de taŋhaŋ haw de dap heciya mniwaŋ hed kokab waŋke, he tuweda tohnina opta mani ka ohomni kte okihi śni do.

"'What I've told you from here, yes, over where you are going a body of water lies in front of you, no one could ever walk across and could not go around it.

"'Haw de wihinapek heciya iża he nakuŋ ka hececa waŋ waŋke.

"'Yes, where the sun rises, over there also lies another one like it.

"'Haw, heciya akasam bde kte do.

"'Yes, I will go over there on the other side.

"'He de inaĥni ya de wociciyakapta[24] wahi do.

"'I'm just here briefly, I came here to tell you something.

---

23. Śuŋka wakaŋ is literally translated as *mysterious dog*.
24. This word is used in instances when something is told about what's going to happen, perhaps as in a prophecy.

"'Heciya bde ka ekta maktep śni kiŋhaŋ ake wau ka ake wociciyakapta do,' eya keyapi.

"'I will go over there and if they don't kill me there, I will come again and talk to you,' they say he said.

"'Ka maktep kiŋhaŋ ho toksta tuwek eya iyohakab wonociyakapte keyap upta do,' eya keyapi.

"'And if they should kill me, some others will come after, the ones they say will come, they will come,' they say he said.

"Haw heced de de tiyata kupa ded omani tokitkiya eyayek he wicoti awicakitapi dena ciŋca takożakpaku eya.

"And so they came home, here from where they left someplace walking, the ones who lived there were watching out for these, their children, grandchildren that went for that reason.

"Haw ihnunah watohaŋya śuŋ akaŋtuŋpa²⁵ śuŋokpe hena ihakab aupi.

"Yes, suddenly, about then, the ones on horseback brought these other horses following them.

"Hena wikaŋ peżi yuśda ka wikaŋ uŋ wicakcage.

"Those ropes, he pulled grass and made rope for them with it.

"Haw hena, tak wicaya ka taŋiŋ śni.

"Yes, it was hard to understand what they were saying.

"Oyate dena de tokiya taŋhaŋ taku kiŋ eya aup çe ake timahed aki yahde wakeyadak woinape śni kaiś eyokas'iŋ yaŋkap kiŋ he hena eyayek hena de śuŋ wakaŋ eya awicahdipi.

"These people are bringing something from somewhere, they went back in the tent, even though it was not a place to seek refuge in, but they sat peeking out [at] the ones who were bringing home those horses.

"'Haw,' eyapaha okiyaka.

"'Yes,' he told the crier.

"Hahaŋna kaeś kośkak hena wicakço ka oyate eya wok'u owote wicakiya.

"In the morning they summoned the young men, and the people gave them food and feasted them.

"Wicakçoba de oyakap keyapi.

"They summoned them, this is what they told, they say.

"Uŋkaŋ, heciya hehaŋyeda, heciya taŋhaŋna hena wahokuŋkiyab hehan iyaye iyecetu.

"And so, even back then, from back then, those predictions were confirmed.

---

25. Contraction of *śuŋ akaŋtuŋpi ka uŋpa*.

Aškatuya detaŋhaŋ, waŋna waniyetu tonakca, waniyetu kektopa wiŋġe, waŋžida saŋpa iyaye okiciyaka uŋkuba ihnunah oyate tokca ahihunu ka walibayada caṇte wašteya uŋpi ciŋpa²⁶ ahiuŋ.

> Recently, from here, how many years now, one thousand and one years have passed with the oral tradition, and then different nations arrived here and because they wanted to be content and serene, they came and stayed.

Haw, de he ded wata ohna bdiwaŋca de ahihuni.

> Yes, they arrived here in this place in a ship through the ocean.

Uŋkaŋ Dakotak heya, "Waŋ, hena skaskapi do he haskap lica ke do!"

> And so, the Dakota said, "Wow, they are white, their skin is very white!"

Hena Dakotap šni do kaeš hece tawaciŋ mahed okciyapi wicakcidapo eya wowicakiyaka.

> In saying this he shared with them, they are not Dakota, but even so in your minds have faith in one another, help each other.

Haw heced de wica, wicada wica heuŋ etaŋhaŋ.

> For that reason, he told them to believe in this way.

Uŋġe ptaŋyetu waŋna ošni ke kte hehan ahi ka ptewaniyaŋpi ka šuŋkawakaŋ ka hehan nakuŋ aŋpahotuŋna uŋġe kukuše nakuŋ awicahipi.

> Now that it was getting cold in fall, some arrived then and there were cattle and horses and then also chickens, some also brought pigs.

Haw hena wiwicakihnipi hena tipi hena, caŋ hena heced ehnakapi wicakcaġapi.

> Yes, they helped them establish the dwellings they made for them by putting the wood in place.

Watak²⁷ taŋka nakaha uŋspe ka caŋibakse, takuku hena yuha ahik hena taku uŋ²⁸ kte hena.

> Because the ship was large, they brought those other things that they will make use of, axes and saws.

Owicakiyapa hena awaŋwicayakap awetu awicayapa.

> They helped them and took care of them, they saw them through spring.

Hehan nakuŋ yuoowatan makoce hena de Dakotak sdodyapi naka.

> They cleared the land for them, these things the Dakota understood.

West hetkiya uŋġe aupa²⁹ heced ahitipi.

> Some came westward and made their homes.

---

26. Contraction of *ciŋpi ka*.
27. Contraction of *wata kiŋ*.
28. *Uŋ* in this instance referring to them, instead of an individual.
29. Contraction of *aupi ka*.

Hena owicaḳiyapi hena wiwicaḳihnipi.

They helped them get established.

Wica wicauŋdapa[30] **wiçakeya owicauŋḳiyapi.**

We earnestly believed in them and we helped them.

Uŋkaŋ miś dehan maḳek de wicakeyahaŋ iciṗaś he iye ouŋḳiyap śni eś ecan ṭaḳuwaŋ amanuŋ uŋkipi.[31]

As for me, now as I sit here, they did not help us in return, instead they took something away from us by stealing.[32]

Cistiyeda waniye iyeced de makoce ṭaḳ aḳan naḳuŋ euhnaḳap hena naḳuŋ hinah ciŋpi hena . . . hed opeya iyauŋyaŋpte.

Like the little while that I've lived, what we put on this land, those also they still want, they will put us amongst them there.[33]

Uŋkiye ṭokaheya ded uŋyaŋkuŋpa[34] **he de uŋkiye hed ded Columbus de iyeyega he de de. "He uŋkitawapi do," eyapi.**

We were here first, we were here and what Columbus found was us, here. "That is ours," they said.

Dakoṭap hena Ṭaḳu Wakaŋ wicakaġe hed aḳan wicakaġe ḳakiya hiṗ śni he ehaŋna wahokuŋwicaḳiyaḳe wowicakiye ḳa ṭok ye ḳta ḳeye.

What is Wakaŋ created the Dakoṭa, he put them there long before they came, he shared those predictions, and then he told them he was going somewhere.

Ho he hecuŋś wiçakeyehan hetaŋhaŋ waŋna miś tawaciŋ we c'uŋ.

As for me now, from that time on, I use my own mind with a strong will.

Waśicuḳ[35] **de ṭaku wahokuŋḳiya ahib wouŋkiyaḳap ḳa ṭukṭe ohnaya wouŋkiyaḳap ohna uŋyaḳuŋpta opiuŋkiciyapta ḳeyap uŋ he waśṭeḳ henana uŋkicupi śica hena anauŋpta.**

The Waśicu, what teachings they brought here (what they told us and in

---

30. Contraction of *wicauŋdapi ḳa*.
31. At this point Uŋkaŋna shifts from relaying his uncle's story and teachings to relaying his own personal thoughts.
32. In this case, *ṭaḳuwaŋ* refers to something more than land or material things. The implication is that something from our very being was taken, something was stolen from our existence as a people.
33. The deeper meaning of this is that by being put out there amongst them, we are not allowed to maintain our cultural identity, we are not allowed to be separate.
34. Contraction of *uŋyaŋkuŋpi ḳa*.
35. Contraction of *waśicu ḳiŋ*.

what way), they told us how to be, how to conduct ourselves, because of what they say we take only what is good and we stop what is bad.

Maunipta.

We will walk in that way.

He okihiuŋciŋpta ca Dakoṭak wicotawaciŋ he hduha, he hduha maunipta.

If we are going to try to do that, then we will keep our very own Dakota thoughts, we will carry them as we journey through life.

Dakoṭa he hekta ṭaku šica iyecetu šni cokada.

Way back, the Dakota were without things that were bad and not right.

Wicoicaġe ṭaku dehan ṭaku ekta, mni wakaŋ eyaba haw ṭaku iyecetu šni.

The younger generation, now what they call alcohol takes them to something that is not right.

Nakuŋ hena uŋġe candi šni ḳaeš uŋpapa uŋtawaciŋ wicotawaciŋ iyuṭokca.

Also, some of them smoke what is not tobacco, it makes their mind different.[36]

Uŋġe iš nakuŋ hena wizica Dakoṭa wacaŋġa ka haŋte ṭaku hena obe oṭa hena wizica ka ḳaŋhaŋ oziṭe hena wakaŋtkiya ayapṭe, he uŋk'up.

As for some, they gave to us the Dakota sweetgrass and cedar and many different kinds for smudging which sends the smoke from them upward.

Hena heca šni ḳaeš ṭaku tokca izidyap hena omnapa nakuŋ ṭak tokca oṭa omnapa hena.

That is not what they are, but something different they use to smudge, and they also inhale many different things.

Mni wakan he iš nakuŋ yatkaŋpta kaġapi šni tka hena ko yatkaŋp he wicataᴄaŋ iyušica, tawacin he iyušiçe uŋ etaŋ uŋšika ṭuwe taŋyaŋ awaciŋp ḳiŋhaŋ hena owas iyoyakapi.

There is alcohol that is not made for drinking, but they also drink that, it ruins their body, it makes their mind bad, poor thing, when someone really thinks about them they all feel the pain.

Wakiwoakipe tehihika uŋkakipap wocaŋte šica tona uŋkakipapi hecihan, haw hena, hena he hena ṭaku etaŋhaŋna u he.

If some of us have come up against some heartbreaking happenings, those things are coming from that.

Tka Dakoṭa wicotawaciŋ de suṭaya uŋ hduhapi ḳiŋhaŋ ṭaku wašṭek dena henanakeda uŋkidakapa[37] ka ṭaku wašṭe šni hena....

---

36. Uŋkaŋna is referring to different drugs used by Dakota people today that can be smoked. Drug use remains a major problem in all Dakota communities in both the United States and Canada.

37. Contraction of *uŋkidakapi ka*.

But if we keep a strong Dakota mind, we will have control over only those things that are good and those things that are not good. . . .

Haw, Wakaŋtaŋka tawacin uŋk'upi he, he hdus uŋyakuŋpa[38] **he ohnaya śice ka waśte ka**[39] **wauŋyakapṭe taŋka ka cistiŋna ka wauŋyakaŋpte.**

Yes, if we hold on to the mind that Wakaŋtaŋka gave us, through that we will see the good and the bad, the great and the small, and we will see.

Wiśica waciŋ śni ṭaku ṭonakca Ṭak Wakaŋ[40] **uŋiyokpiya caŋte waśteya mauŋipṭa, he uŋk'upi hecihan.**

If it is so that What Is Sacred gave to us many things to walk with a good heart, I don't want to have ill feelings.

Henana awacin iyokpiya mauniṗ kaŋhaŋ ṭukṭe ohnaya mauniṗ kaśṭa hena oyaṭe iṭoiyohi ṭukṭe ohna oyeg wicaśṭa wicak'up hena ṭaŋyaŋ owotaŋna hduha śkaŋpa[41] **uŋkiża de Dakoṭak hena heced uŋśkaŋṗ kiŋhaŋ ṭaku he amaunipi hecihan uŋkokihipte.**

If we walk with only [the good] in our thoughts, we will walk happily and no matter where or how we walk—because each and every nation was given a direction—if they live in a good way and if we as Dakota do the same, we will accomplish what we have been journeying toward.

Woiwahoye uŋkaŋ wicanaġi ikoyake uŋk'upi Ṭak Wakaŋ he tokaṭa aŋpeṭu ed hdi kṭek he, hena amaunipṭa.

And so, Ṭak Wakaŋ gave us the spirit that ties in with that promise that he will one day in the future return, we will journey on that [promise].

He makak hena uŋyaŋkuŋṗ he ecan ṭuwek owasina waŋżi iyeced wakiciyak okciyapi iciyokpiya wicakeyahaŋ wiċakcidapi he mauniṗ kiŋhaŋ he ṭaku uŋkihdeġapṭe.

While we are here on earth, each and everyone as one, if we walk seeing one another, helping each other in a happy way, believing in each other in earnest, we will overcome.

Ṭokiya uŋkiṭakuyapi uŋpi hecihan ka wicanaġi omnaya heciya uŋkiṭakuyapi eyayega yakuŋṗ de maka ded maka uŋyakuŋṗ he ecan kihdeġ waciŋ ṭaŋyaŋ awaŋic'ihdakaṗ uŋśikśida ohokcida okiciya mauniṗṭa.

Wherever our relatives are with the gathering of the spirits over there, where our relatives went and are at while we are here on this earth, we

---

38. Contraction of *uŋyakuŋpi ka*.
39. In this case *ka* is a contraction of *kaŋhaŋ*.
40. While *ṭak wakaŋ* translates as *something mysterious, something sacred, what is mysterious,* or *what is sacred* and could refer to any number of things, in instances where it is capitalized it is a specific reference to Wakaŋtaŋka, "The Great Mystery."
41. Contraction of *śkaŋpi ka*.

should try to overcome by taking care of each other with compassion, respect, helping one another as we walk.

Kiŋhaŋ he woie aŋpetu waŋ maka akaŋ wiconi de ihaŋke ka hehan tuweda sdoduŋkiyap śni.

No one will know of the word if and when one day life on this earth ends.

Tka, ihankek he itkuŋza hehaŋyaŋ akokitkiya he ded maka akan uŋyaŋkuŋp hecan awohouŋkic'iyapte he uŋśkaŋpte caŋku cistiŋna tuwe toked uŋspe.

While we are here on this earth, we will promise ourselves we will do in a small way, however one knows.[42]

Uŋkiye kaŋk[43] dena śicece ka dena wouŋcikiyakapte hee tkah[44] okpaniya uŋśika śicecek hena kuya iyayewicuŋyaŋpi.

Us, these elders, what we should have shared with the children was lacking, those poor children, we let them down.

Uŋġe hena huŋkakek hena tokiya akab iwicacupi wayawa awicakiyap wauŋspe wicakiyap huŋkakek hena ciŋca wauŋspe wicakiyap takożakpaku wauŋspe wicakiyap hena uŋkipa[45] iyeśkaŋpa[46] nuniyaŋpi.

Some of those parents, they took them somewhere [outside their home], they sent them to school, they took the education of our children and grandchildren away from us, they did this, causing us to lose our way.

Onunipi tka sdoduŋkiyap śni.

We were lost but we didn't realize it.

Tka etaŋhaś iyeiyataya itoiyohi woicada uŋyuhap kiŋhaŋ, tukted ohna uŋkuŋspep śta.

But even so, if we have our own belief, in each and everyone's own way, it doesn't matter what way we learn.

He ohna hoyeuŋyaŋpa taku owotaŋna uŋkihduhap kaŋhaŋ he aŋpetuwaŋ uŋkitakuyapi uŋp heciya wicoopeya aŋpetu ihaŋke kaki nauŋżiŋpte.

We will send forth our voice if we keep ourselves honest one day the day it ends, we will stand over there amongst them, where our relatives are gathered over there.

He wicadawo heced maunipta hecihan Dakotak de woope hena uŋkiksuyapta ka Waśicu ahi ka wowapi taku wowaśte uŋġe taku iyecetu śni ahipi hecihan hena iwaŋyaŋkap.

---

42. A freer translation might be, "While we are here on this earth we should all do whatever we are capable of—even in a small way."
43. Contraction of *kaŋ kiŋ*.
44. Contraction of *tka hce*.
45. Contraction of *uŋkipi ka*.
46. Contraction of *iyeśkaŋpi ka*.

If we are to walk in that way, the Dakota, we will remember those traditions and what the Wašicu brought here, and the book of goodness,[47] those things they brought that were not right we will examine.

Iapi nuŋpak̇ de waŋna maunip k̇iŋhaŋ uŋkihdeġap nacece wakiye, he ohnaya miš opimic'iye.

If we are going in the path of the second language [English], I believe we have an understanding of the language.

Haw, ṭak̇u ota obdake kṭe.

Yes, I have a lot to share.

He bduhe tk̇a hehan miš miye ṭoked opimic'iye hecihan hena nak̇uŋ ṭak̇u awacami hecihan hena obdake kṭa nak̇uŋ bduhe.

I have that, but as for myself, if that is so, I also have to share the way I live and those things that I also think about.

Ṭk̇a he de Dekši womakiyake de he de k̇iksuya nak̇ap k̇iŋhaŋ eciŋ wowahdak̇e k̇iŋhaŋ ṭohan heciya eṭaŋhaŋ ṭak̇u iyowak̇ahniġa heca uŋġe heciya iwowahdak̇e kṭa.

But this here is what Uncle told me, if you sit here and remember, because when I speak I will talk about some of what I understand from what he told from over there.

Haw he uŋ de Cinš dena ociciyakek̇ Mitakoża dena ṭaŋyaŋ de owotaŋna iwoyahdak̇e kṭe okiŋni ṭak̇u iwowahdak̇e dena uŋġe ok̇ahniġe šni nacece, uŋġe ok̇ahniġe.

Yes, for that reason, Son, these things I have told you, my grandchild, you can talk about these well and straight, some of the things I talk about, some of these she probably doesn't understand, some she understands.[48]

Haw, niża kiṭaŋna oṭa niye oyak̇ahniġa tk̇a uŋġe okinni niża ṭak̇ wakek̇[49] uŋġe oyak̇ahniġe šni.

Yes, you too understand a little more, but maybe you also don't understand some of what I'm saying.

Ṭk̇a tożaŋ iye he tehan waniyeṭu hekṭa opa hece hena ṭoked wakek̇ hena ok̇ahniġe kṭa, haw heced wiċawada.

But niece, she's been with us many winters, I believe that she understands what I'm saying, yes, that's what I believe.

---

47. The Bible.
48. Uŋkaŋna is directing his words at his son, Chris Mato Nuŋpa, about me, his granddaughter.
49. Contraction for *wake k̇iŋ*.

Haw heuŋ etaŋhaŋ he ihnuḣ ded makoce ded uŋyaŋkuŋpi, he iś he waŋna, so much for that story.

Yes, for that reason we came to be here on this land, so much for that now, so much for that story.

5. Ṭaku Ociciyake Waciŋ
(I Want to Tell You Something)

While initially these stories were collected to provide a Waḣpetuŋwaŋ Dakoṭa historical perspective on specific events transmitted within the oral tradition, what became apparent within the first few stories recited was that the history presented from this perspective was also tremendously important for the information it provided about the meaning of being Dakoṭa. During his lifetime Unḳaŋna Eli Taylor was respected by many Dakoṭa people for the language he spoke, the stories he told, the songs he sang, the beliefs he held, and the values he lived by, precisely because he lived as a Dakoṭa; "Dakoṭa" itself implying a certain code of behavior. Because he was viewed this way by Dakoṭa people, and because we as Dakoṭa wanted to see ourselves in him, his stories represent more than a personal account. They divulge much about Dakoṭa consciousness, historical and contemporary, because of what can be inferred from the language, the narrative strategy, and the content of the stories themselves. The stories are interwoven with the creation of Dakoṭa identity and the sense of belonging stemming from an understanding of the shared Dakoṭa past and present.

In an examination of identity, language is of vital importance because in a larger contextual framework it is the key to patterns of thought. This may be exemplified by examining a saying that is often repeated in Dakoṭa culture when an elder is about to offer an educational lesson. They might begin with the simple phrase, *Ṭaku ociciyake waciŋ* or *I want to tell you something*. While this translates into English easily enough, the patterns of thought that occur in the Dakoṭa mind go beyond what one might experience in English. When this phrase is uttered, unlike in English where this might be a joke, an afterthought, a bit of gossip, or some other trivial bit of information, in Dakoṭa the implicit meaning is that some important information is about to be bestowed upon the listener and that it is something that needs to be remembered. In addition, since this would almost always be spoken by an elder to a younger person within the culture and family, there would be an unspoken understanding that the listener has a kinship responsibility to listen, learn, and remember.

This kinship responsibility is of great significance because of the role kinship plays within Dakoṭa culture. While Ella Deloria's comment on Dakoṭa kinship is often quoted, its eloquence bears repeating:

> The ultimate aim of Dakota life, stripped of accessories, was quite simple: One must obey kinship rules; one must be a good relative. No Dakota who has participated in that life will dispute that. In the last analysis every other consideration was secondary—property, personal ambition, glory, good times, life itself. Without that aim and the constant struggle to attain it, the people would no longer be Dakotas in truth. They would no longer even be human.[1]

These kinship responsibilities are enormously influential, and I find they pervade all aspects of life, even academic life. For example, while some scholars might scoff at the subjective use of kinship terms in academic writing, because I was taught that it is disrespectful not to use kinship terms, especially with elders, I am unable to write without them. This is due to the sense of respect and obligation I feel toward respected elders at all times and in all settings. Within Dakota culture, violating the trust an elder places in you is tantamount to losing one's identity as a Dakota, even as a human. This is one of the most powerful incentives to fulfill your kinship responsibilities and to listen, learn, and remember your teachings, not just for yourself but for your elders, your ancestors, your descendants, and, indeed, for your nation.

In this first story conveyed by Uŋkaŋna, he provides insight into some of the devices in place for establishing and understanding that important historical knowledge is about to be conveyed. At the age of nineteen on an outing with his uncle, his uncle said to him:

> **Uŋkaŋ hehaŋ, "Haw Tuŋṡka, ito kaeṡ ded ded oziuŋkiye kte do.... Ṭaku ociciyake kta çe. Ito, wowahdake kte, anahoptaŋ wo!" "Haw," epe, ecin ṭohaŋtaŋnaṡta wicahcada hena anawicawahoptaŋ, macistiŋna hetaŋhaŋ waun naka. "Ṭaku ociciyake kte. He ṭokata kiksuya uŋ wo!... He niciŋca k'a nitakoża hena owicakiyaka wo!"**
>
> And so he said, "Okay nephew, for a little while here we will rest here.... I will tell you something. Now I'm going to talk, you listen!" "Yes," I said, because for so long from the time I was little, I have listened to the old men. "I'm going to tell you something. Remember that in the future!... Those who are your children and your grandchildren, tell them!"

This excerpt from the main body of text illustrates a number of points. The first is my grandfather's uncle's invoking of kinship obligation. This kinship obligation not only includes the nephew's obligation to listen, learn, remember, and retell the stories but also the obligation of an uncle to his nephew. The mother's brothers play a key role in the life of a male child. This would be especially true if that child had no other male relatives to assist him in his maturation into manhood. Also, by telling him, "I'm going to tell you something," he captures his nephew's attention. In this situation, there would have been no question as to the graveness of this exchange. Uŋkaŋna Eli Taylor knew his understanding of what his uncle told him was intended to stay with him throughout his lifetime.

Sixty-six years after participating in this exchange, Uŋkaŋna was continuing to fulfill his obligation by repeating the story to those of us present, his niece, son, and granddaughter, the younger generations. Revealing the success of his teaching, the first words he spoke to us when he realized the recorders were on were these:

> Uŋkaŋ, he ṭaku haĥ'aŋna de ṭokaheya ociçiyakap waciŋ dena nakap dena.
>
> And so, first of all this morning, I want to tell something to all of you sitting here.

We had been called upon to assist in the documentation of a life's worth of stories, a serious task, and my grandfather had begun his instruction.

In the first story he relates, a group of men on a long journey encounter a mysterious and divine being. As he begins to offer them instruction, he tells them in Dakoṭa, "Haw, hed he iyoṭaŋkapo wociciyakapṭe do" (Yes, sit down there, I will tell you something). The Dakoṭa men understand immediately that they are to be instructed in a matter of importance.

Another phrase Dakoṭa people use in reference to teachings they have received is *naĥ'uŋ wauŋ*. *Naĥ'uŋ* is a verb meaning *to hear*, and *wauŋ* may be translated as *I am*, as in a *state of being*. Although *nawaĥ'uŋ*, meaning *I hear or I heard*, is the first person form of the verb *naĥ'uŋ*, the two have very different meanings. *Naĥ'uŋ wauŋ* suggests more than *I hear or I heard* and implies something much greater, perhaps *what I heard has become a part of my state of being*. In essence, it refers to teachings that have become internalized and comprise an aspect of one's identity. In everyday conversation with a Dakoṭa speaker, it would be a reference to what one heard growing up, how one was taught, or how someone was raised and linked closely with the individual's sense of identity.

Along these same lines, the verb *içu*, meaning *to take, accept or receive*, is used in reference to *teachings being taken* as in the following sentence:

> Ḣṭanihaŋ uŋġe wociciyakap hena nakuŋ uŋġe iyaçupi nacece.
>
> You all probably took in some of the things I told you yesterday.

The implicit understanding is that when a Dakoṭa person is told something, the message or teaching is internalized. Knowledge or wisdom, then, comes not simply from hearing but from receiving new information at a deeper level.

Regardless of the type of story told, it is imperative that all of them be told correctly. This concept is relayed linguistically in a number of ways. For example, phrases my grandmother, Elsie Cavender, used frequently were *eceḣ eya*, or *say it right*, and *yat'iŋt'is eya*, or *you tell the truth*. She would give reminders such as "Ṭohnina iṭu śni wahdaḳe śni. Ekṭa opa ḳaŋhaŋ iyaṭuŋ śni he ed nihi kṭe" (Do not tell an untruth. That lie you told will come back to you). In one of my grandfather's accounts, another common phrase was used: "Ḳa yakip ḳaŋhaŋ owotaŋna wohdaḳapo" (When you get back home over there, tell it straight).² To verify a story, the phrase *He wicaḳapi* would be used, translated as *That is true*. Another phrase with the same meaning is *Ṭaŋyaŋ wohdaḳapo!* (Tell it well!). In a culture based on orality, the significance of these types of phrases cannot be overestimated. They all make reference to the notion of telling it the same way it was heard, with no fictitious additions or deletions of unfavorable parts. The implication here is that the original story was our concept of truth, and by straying from the original story, one is not a reliable teller of tales. Recognizing this, midway through the first story, Uŋḳaŋna tells us:

> **Haw, hena, hena he de ṭakuda uŋġe add iyewaye kṭe śni, ṭoḳed dekśi oyakeḳ hecihan nawaḣ'uŋ, haw hena de iyeced obdaḳe kṭe.**
>
> Yes, I will not add something to those things, how uncle told I heard, that is the way I tell it here.

Uŋḳaŋna knew he was obligated to tell it to us straight and, more important, wanted us to understand his sense of responsibility toward an accurate transmission.

Because these stories are centered in the personal, by the very telling of the story the listener is drawn inclusively in and a sense of personal connection with the storyteller or narrator is created. Uŋḳaŋna Eli Taylor bound the telling and the living together in this excerpt from the first story:

> **Haw, ṭaku oṭa obdaḳe kṭe. He bduhe tḳa hehan miś miye ṭoḳed opimic'iye hecihaŋ hena naḳuŋ ṭaku awacami hecihaŋ hena obdaḳe kṭe naḳuŋ bduhe.**
>
> Yes, I have a lot to share. I have that but then, as for myself, if that is so, I also have to share the way I live and also those things that I think about.

In a sense, knowledge becomes responsibility. For Uŋḳaŋna Eli Taylor, when the knowledge was gained, a certain way of living was required, and that way of life, in the telling, became an important aspect of what was shared. The power of these stories stems from the connection created between the shaped historical understanding and living within the present. The oral tradition, in all its forms, has the potential to cultivate thoughts, worldview, and to dictate a pattern for living.

Within the Dakoṭa process of narration, when the storyteller is about to begin with an account of some kind, the first information to be transmitted often centers around the training and background of the storyteller. The listener immediately comes to understand by whom the narrator was trained and what kind of Dakoṭa education they received. By evoking previous authorities and demonstrating their right to relate specific information, the credibility of the storyteller is established. This is usually followed by a brief description of when and where the story was originally heard, thus establishing continuity between past and present tellings.

By the time Uŋkaŋna had begun his first story, we knew that he had been kept home from school by his mother so that he could receive a Dakoṭa education rather than the boarding-school education that was producing results in his older siblings his mother didn't like. We understood that the elders in his life were entrusting him with their valuable knowledge and that he spent much time in the company of those elders listening to them speak. In sharing this kind of information he was letting his audience know that he had received proper training, that his elders had faith in him, and he was being entrusted with the responsibility of transmitting information, according to custom within the oral tradition.

In the preservation and transmission of the stories, a common technique used to remind the listener about the Dakoṭa Oyaṭe, or Dakoṭa Nation, is to relate our connections with one another across geopolitical boundaries imposed by the United States and Canada. This has become particularly important today because of the vast distances that separate our nation. Minisoṭa Makoce, or present-day Minnesota, is considered the ancient homeland of the Dakoṭa Oyaṭe. While the various bands of Dakoṭa historically occupied a larger territory, Minnesota is believed to be the place where Dakoṭa people originated. The Bdewakaŋtuŋwaŋ Dakoṭa creation story places the exact point of origin at the site referred to by the Dakoṭa as Bdote,[3] literally meaning "the joining or juncture of two bodies of water." In this case it refers to the place where the Minnesota River joins the Mississippi River, an area that lies between the Twin Cities of Minneapolis and St. Paul. A suburb there carries the name Mendota, from the ancient Dakoṭa name for this sacred spot.

For Dakoṭa people, the connection to homeland was broken after the U.S.-Dakoṭa War of 1862 when the Dakoṭa were either imprisoned in the concentration camps established in Minnesota during the winter of 1862–63 and then forcibly removed, or when they chose flight to Canada to avoid that horrific treatment.[4] In June 1863 bounties were placed on the scalps of "Sioux" people, beginning at twenty-five dollars and eventually increasing to two hundred dollar.[5] Although bounties on human scalps were illegal at the time, knowing they were still enforced made it virtually impossible for the Dakota to consider returning to Minnesota. For some of those who fled to Canada, a return to Dakota ancestral lands did not begin until the late 1880s, and then only by small groups of people.[6] Most of those who fled chose to remain in places they had come to call home. Today, Dakota populations are scattered in smaller groups in Manitoba and Saskatchewan in Canada and in Minnesota, South and North Dakota, Nebraska, and Montana in the United States. Perhaps because of this diaspora, there is a greater need to remind one another of our connection and bond, which transcends distance and state and national boundaries.

The U.S.-Dakota War of 1862 is a pivotal point around which many stories within the oral tradition are referenced—not just because this was a traumatic period in Dakota history but because this is the event that marks the separation from homeland. Minnesota is the place that unites us as a people, and it is often referred to in the oral tradition. This fundamental connection to place and homeland is apparent and becomes more meaningful when examined in context, with an understanding of the historical circumstances it recalls.

Uŋkaŋna Eli Taylor, throughout his stories, consistently referenced the connection between the Dakota in Canada and the Dakota in the United States, in this way affirming our connection to one another as relatives and members of a broader cultural group, the Dakota Oyate. The first story he chose to relate is one told to him by his uncle, when he was a young man of eighteen or nineteen years of age. His uncle told him a story of Dakota warriors who, many centuries earlier, had been sent out by their leader to find where the land ended. While on their search they encountered a strange man who provided the Dakota with many gifts and words of advice about how the Dakota were to live and treat one another. Uŋkaŋna relayed to us what had been passed down to him regarding the connection to the Dakota of Minnesota:

> **Makato Içu, Caŋśayapi ṭaku hena makoce heciya.... Ehaŋna nakab, haw ded ḳaki uŋyaŋḳap heciya hed Peżihuṭazizi Ode heciya hena Caŋśayapi he heciya hehaŋyaŋ makoce hena oyate hena unkitawapi do.**
>
> Where They Get Blue Earth,[7] Painting the Trees Red,[8] those were that kind of land.... Long ago, yes here now, we were way over there at Looking for Yellow Medicine,[9] over there where They Painted the Trees Red, those people on that land over there are ours.

Shared and familiar places served to unite the storyteller and the audience, bridging the distance of the present and returning us to the connections of the past.

Out of all the stories Uŋkaŋna Eli Taylor could have relayed to us first as we began the taping, he chose this particular story, which very powerfully validates the significance of the oral tradition and empowers the carriers of the tradition. The wakan[10] man the Dakoṭa men encountered instructed them in this way:

> Uŋkaŋ eya ḳeyapi, "Dena ṭaḳu ociciyaḳap dena ṭohaŋya śta toḳaṭakiya ḳiksuya uŋpo ḳa okiciyaḳ yeya po omaka iyohi ḳa wowicaġe iyohi, ḳa saŋpa nitakożap ḳa naḳuŋ saŋpa nitakożap hena okiciyaḳ yeya po," eya ḳeyapi. "Ṭokśta tawaciŋ he suṭa cicaġapi, hena ḳiksuya mayanipṭe do. Ṭuwe wicakeya ohna manipṭa, hena ḳiksuyap, ohna manipṭe," eya ḳeyapi.

> And so, they say he said, "These things that I am telling you, always remember these as long as you can in the future, tell each other every year and every generation, and your grandchildren and your great-grandchildren, continue telling each other," they say he said. "For certain, I made your minds strong, you will carry those memories. Those who walk with commitment, they will walk in that path of what they remember," they say he said.

It is not surprising that the taping of Uŋkaŋna's stories for an oral-history project would begin with a story that emphasizes not only the importance of the transmission of the oral tradition but also that Dakoṭa minds were made strong by a wakan source so that we would have divine help in remembering. Also, the memories shared with us with each telling become more a part of who we are, influencing how we carry ourselves in our lives and thus connecting our past, present, and future. Because many of the stories of the past embody values fundamental to being Dakoṭa, with each telling the listener is reminded how to walk in the future.

Within this story, the wakan man encountered by the Dakoṭa taught the people how to relate to one another and how to live as Dakoṭa. Here Uŋkaŋna Taylor's uncle relates the message given to the Dakoṭa by this man:

> He makaḳ hena uŋyaŋkuŋp he ecan ṭuwek owas'ina waŋżi iyeced wakiciyaḳ okiciyapi iciyokpiya wicakeyahaŋ wicakcidapi he mauniṇ ḳiŋhaŋ he ṭaḳu uŋkihdeġapṭe. Ṭoḳiya uŋkiṭaḳuyapi uŋpi hecihaŋ ḳa wicanaġi omnaya heciya uŋkiṭaḳuyapi eyaye ḳa yakuŋp de maka ded maka uŋyaŋkuŋp he ecan kihdeḳ waciŋ ṭaŋyaŋ awanic'ihdaḳap uŋśikśida ohokcida okiciya maunipṭa.... Tḳa, ihaŋkeḳ he itkuŋza hehaŋyaŋ akokitḳiya he ded maka akan uŋyaŋkuŋp hecan awohouŋkic'iyapṭe he uŋśkaŋpṭe caŋku cistiŋna ṭuwe ṭoked uŋspe.

> While we are here on this earth, each and everyone as one, if we walk seeing one another, helping each other in a happy way, believing in each other

in earnest, we will overcome. Wherever our relatives are with the gathering of the spirits over there, where our relatives went and are at, while we are here on this earth, we should try to overcome by taking care of each other with compassion, respect, helping one another as we walk. . . . While we are here on this earth, we will promise ourselves we will do in a small way, however one knows.

The encounter with this wakan being influences the world of the Dakota, and his teachings are incorporated into Dakota tribal ideals. What had started as a historical account about an event in the Dakota past evolved into a larger story about how the Dakota were to live with one another, shaping and reaffirming the Dakota sense of self.

Also contained within the story is a validation of cultural identity; as Dakota people we are taught we are unique and our culture is of divine origin, a sentiment characteristic to many Indigenous Peoples. As the Dakota are traveling in search of the end of the land, they encounter many different tribes of people. Although a lack of understanding might exist between the various groups, there is also a recognition that each group was created as they were for a reason. Uŋkaŋna Eli Taylor was told by his uncle:

> Okicicakahiniġap śni uŋkaġap. Haw, itokab hihanna ṭaku hena nakuŋ nawahuŋ. Haw he toḳed uŋ hena hecun he? Otoiyohi ikçe wicaśta hena owas ouŋtokça ḳa iapi tokça uŋk'upi.

> We were made so we don't understand each other. Yes, I also heard those things a long time before. Yes, why did he do those things? All of them, each and every common man, we were given a way of life and different language.

These comments about the differences among different nations necessitates a belief in the equality of people and their divine creation. Central to this is an understanding that every living being was created with a purpose and with a divine right to exist.[11] In times of turmoil when questions arise over the tenacity and resiliency of Indigenous cultures, this particular cultural value and belief offers hope and a reminder that the Dakota language and way of life is also of divine origin and that it was given expressly to us.[12] For that reason alone it must live, and we must ensure its continuity.

In another excerpt relaying what he learned from this story told by his uncle, Uŋkaŋna Eli Taylor explained to us:

> Wiśica waciŋ śni ṭaku tonakça Ṭak Wakaŋ uŋiyokpiya caŋte waśteya maunipta, he uŋk'upi hecihaŋ. Henana awaciŋ iyokpiya maunip ḳaŋhaŋ ṭukṭe ohnaya maunip ḳaśṭa hena oyaṭe otiyohi ṭukṭe ohna oyeḳ

> wicaśta wicak'up hena ṭaŋyaŋ owotaŋna hduha śkaŋpa uŋkiża de Dakoṭak hena heced uŋśkaŋp kiŋhaŋ ṭaku he amaunipi hecihaŋ uŋkokihipṭe.

> If it is so that Tak Wakan[13] gave to us many things to walk with a good heart, I don't want to have ill feelings. If we walk with only those [the good] in our thoughts, we will walk happily and no matter where or how we walk—because each and every nation was given a direction—if they live in a good way and if we as Dakoṭa do the same, we will accomplish what we have been journeying toward.

This interpretation of the significance of the wakan being's message is an empowering one in that it places the responsibility for the success of the nation upon the individual. If we as individuals all do this, our nation will flourish and we will accomplish our dreams. This provides a rationale for living, an ideal code of ethics Dakoṭa people were expected to try to live by.

Many of the messages implanted in a young mind may take years to reach fruition, however. Within the oral tradition there is also an understanding that comprehension of this historical interpretation, as with many things in life, develops with age and maturity. There is not always immediate understanding or instant gratification for the listener. After relaying his first account and as we were preparing for a break in the taping, Uŋkaŋna Eli Taylor addressed the different generations present (me as his grandchild, my father, Chris Mato Nunpa, as his son, and my grandmother, Carrie Schommer, as his niece) at this particular telling:

> **Haw heuŋ de, Cinś, dena ociciyakek mitakoża dena ṭaŋyaŋ de owotaŋna iwoyahdake kṭe okiŋni ṭaku iwowahdake dena uŋġe okahiniġe śni nacece, uŋġe okahiniġe. Haw, niża kiṭaŋna oṭa niye oyakahiniġe tka uŋġe okiŋni niża ṭak wakek uŋġe oyakahiniġe śni. Tka, tożaŋ iye he tehan waniyeṭu hekṭa opa hece hena ṭoked wakek hena okahiniġe kṭa, haw heced wiçawada.**

> Yes, for that reason, Son, these things I have told you, my grandchild, you can talk about these well and straight, some of these things I talk about, some of these she probably doesn't understand, some she understands. Yes, you too understand a little more, but maybe you don't understand some of what I'm saying. But niece, she's been with us many winters, I believe that she understands what I'm saying, yes, that's what I believe.

Thus the stories may be related to an audience, but the meaning and implications of a story may not be revealed for many years into the future, or they may be understood to varying degrees by the listeners.

Stories within the oral tradition are not easily categorized in academic terms of "history" and "myth," and as historical accounts are examined within the tradition, it is apparent that what occurs is not just a promulgation of a set of historical facts. Instead, the stories themselves, while presenting historical information, also serve as a teaching ground for the perpetuation of concepts firmly embedded in Dakota identity. They provide a code of ethics for carrying oneself as a Dakota in contemporary times and furnish the tools with which to walk into the future.

Historical consciousness is shaped in myriad ways within various cultures, but within Dakota culture the oral tradition has been the primary means through which our historical consciousness has been constructed and by which a deeply rooted investment in the past is created. As is the case in other societies, the understanding of the Dakota past is closely linked with notions of identity and self, which serve both to affect the present and to shape the future. Oral tradition, then, and the language used to convey it, along with identity, are all inextricably linked within Dakota culture and central to our sense of historical consciousness. What eventually evolves into historical consciousness is a simultaneous evolution into Dakota self-identity, the oral tradition weaving one into the other.

6. Ṭoked Imacaġe (How I Grew Up)

The following narratives are more personal in nature, relaying information about a variety of topics but all told in the broader context of Uŋḳaŋna Eli Taylor's life. Thus, as with the last account, he begins with a discussion of his own childhood, though this time providing new details. He discusses the importance of song in his life, offering a couple examples of childhood songs that stayed in his memory. In the following accounts we also hear about his early adult life, including his marriages and participation in the Omaha Society. The last section is devoted to a discussion about the experiences Uŋḳaŋna was unable to participate in either because of his age or because of cultural loss as a consequence of colonialism.

Ehaŋna Woyaḳapi Inuŋpa (The Second Historical Narrative)

Uŋkaŋ, iṡṭo ake hehan takoża nu ṭaḳu ociciyaḳe kṭa heciŋhaŋ.

And then again, next, grandchild, nu, I am going to tell you something if it is so.

Toḳaheya ekṭa imacaġe aŋpeṭu wakaŋ yamni he ehan aṭe wayeḳ wanice, keyapi.

In the beginning, three holy days[1] after I was born, I did not have a father at that time, they say.

Uŋkaŋ he, miye ṭoked imacaġe heciŋhaŋ he ociciyaḳe kṭe.

And so, I will tell you myself how it was that I was born.

Uŋkaŋ Ina heye waŋna mataŋka ḳa waŋna owaḳahniġe kṭe.

And so my mother said I was big enough now and I would understand now.

Hehan wayawa bde kṭe, ḳeyapi.

Then I will go to school, they said.

Uŋkaŋ, wicada ṡni, "Hiya, de kṭe ṡni ye.

And so, she did not agree, "No, you will not go.

"Niciŋye ḳa nitaŋka, hena owas niye nihaḳa kṭa ye, niye nihaḳa kṭa ye, heuŋ eṭaŋhaŋ wayawa ṡni tiyaṭa yauŋ kṭe.

---

1. *Aŋpeṭu Wakaŋ* (Holy Day) is the phrase for Sunday, so three Holy Days would refer to three weeks in English.

"Your older brother and your older sister, you are younger than all of them, you are the youngest, for that reason you will stay at home with no schooling.

"Niciŋye ka nitaŋka wayawapa wouŋspepa hena ṭaku waśtewadake śni ye.

"Your older brother and your older sister, they are studying and those things that they have learned I do not like.

"Ṭakuku iyecetu śni.

"Some things are not correct.

"Dakoṭa wihduwi etaŋhaŋ iyanuŋ uŋspeic'ic'iyapi.

"From the Dakoṭa way of life, they are learning another on top of that.

"Hena tokaṭakiya waciŋuŋyaŋpṭa śni nacece," eye.

"In the future we will probably not be depending on those," she said.

"Iyehaŋyaŋ wouŋspe hena iyehaŋyaŋ yuhap śni ce.

"They do not have the knowledge for that level of understanding.

"Inicaġe kte tkak tokye inicaġe ye.

"You grew up differently from the way you were supposed to grow up.

"Miye dehan he, icaḣciye ka haḣ'aŋna kaŋhaŋ ciyuḣice ka idotaŋke ka mni hwe de ka caŋ ayaku waecanuŋ ka ṭaku dena omayakiye kṭe.

"Me, at this time I will raise you, and when it is morning I will wake you and you will get up and go after water and bring wood, other tasks, and with these things you will help me.

"Ḳiŋhaŋ miniheca inicaġe kṭe.

"Then you will grow up to be industrious.

"Heced dehan icaġap śni, dehan wouŋspepa waśtewadake śni ye, de kṭe śni ye."

"At this time they are not growing up that way, what they have learned now I do not like, you will not go."

"Ṭaku he de ke, ṭaku?"

"What is she saying, what?"[2]

Hehan nakuŋ macistiŋna naka he sdodwaye śni.

Then I was still little and so I did not understand that.

Whatever she says, she's my mother, well then, that's the way it has to go, kecanmi, that's all there is to it.

Whatever she says, she's my mother, well then, that's the way it has to go, I think, that's all there is to it.

Haw heced he, wayawa bde śni wauŋ ka waŋna, oh I must be about nine, nine years old, hehan ṭukṭed ihnuhanaḣ Aṭeyapi uŋ hi.

---

2. Uŋkaŋna Eli was asking this of himself, trying to understand what his mother meant.

And so I was not going to school, I was around, and now, oh I must have been about nine, nine years old, then came a time when suddenly the Ateyapi[3] came.

"Wadawa kte."

"You are going to school."

Caŋku ohna wamayake.

He saw me on the road.

"Wadawa de heciya taŋhaŋ yaku?"

"Are you coming from school?"

"Hiya, wabdawa śni do."

"No, I don't go to school."

"Tokeca he?"

"Why?"

"Mom wicada śni do."

"Mom does not believe [in school]."

"Haw, ed opa wo wayawa de kte do."

"Yes, get in, you are going to school."

He wowaś'ake yuha hiyeye naka waŋca ake owape.

He carried that authority with him so I just got in.

Haw hece wai ka ḣtayetu hehan waku, "Ṭoki yaun ka yaku śni he?"

And so I went and when it was evening I came back, "Where were you that you did not come home for this long?"

Wakik hece henana, "Ded wayawa wai do."

Just as soon as I got home, "I went to school."

"Waciŋyaŋtaŋka hece wayawa yai he?" he śida.

"Did you go strong-minded?" she was saddened.[4]

Ateyap he hdoki nicap kaeś he Wicaśtayatapi heya heca wabdawa kta keya heced day school ed wabdawa waniyetu waŋżi hehaŋyaŋ wabdawa.

She kind of argued with Ateyapi but Wicaśtayatapi[5] says it, and so he said I had to go to school, and so I went to school at the day school, I studied one year, for that long.

Ṭaku ota ibototo ked wauŋ.

I bumped into a whole lot of things.[6]

Haw kaeś hece (cinye, taŋke) hena wayawa iap ca iwohdakapi hena naḣ'uŋ imacaġe.

---

3. *Ateyapi* might be translated as *Father Figure*, but in this case it refers to the *Indian Agent*.
4. In asking this his mother likely meant, "Did you feel like you could handle it?"
5. Most likely referring to the superintendent or higher government official.
6. Free translation: "I ran into so many obstacles."

Yes and so I grew up hearing them (older brother, older sister) talk school, and talk about it.

Haw heced ṭaku ṭukṭed waciŋ śni ca, waciŋ śni ca, "No," haw hekśe waŋna omaspe."

And so, when I do not want something, when I do not want [it], "No," I had already learned that."

Ṭaku waŋżi waciŋ ḳiŋhaŋ hecetu ḳiŋhaŋ, "yes, yes."

When I want something, if that is right, then "yes, yes."

Hena uŋmaspeḳ hehan different things, you know, hena uŋmaspe he.

Then I learned those different things, you know, those I learned.

Ḳaiś ṭokiya yapṭe ca, bda waciŋ śni ḳiŋhaŋ (hena naḳuŋ he heya uŋpi) heced naḳuŋ uŋmaspe, "No, I don't want to go."

Or if they were going somewhere and if I did not want to go (they also go around saying those) I also learned in that way and "No, I don't want to go," [I would say].

Hecekced hena uŋmaspe ṭaku, haw heced Waśicu iyae ked wauŋ naka when I went to that school, I got along pretty good with the teacher, ṭaŋyaŋ kci wohdaḳ wauŋ.

I learned those in that way, yes, because I went around kind of speaking Waśicu, when I went to that school, I got along pretty good with the teacher, I spoke well with her.

Haw heced naḳuŋ he, odowaŋ ṭaku iś odowaŋ uŋspe uŋkiyapi naḳuŋ hehan.

Yes, and so also songs, they taught us some songs then also.

Haw he ehan wowahdaḳe ḳa naḳuŋ ṭuwe śicecaḳ hena uŋġe ṭaku eyapi oḳihip śni ḳaŋhaŋ naḳuŋ uŋġe iyewicawaḳiske ce, heced wauŋ.

Yes, at that time I spoke and also I translated for some of those who were unable to speak some things, that's the way I was.

Iyokpiya wauŋ.

I was happy.

Waśṭewadake wayawa waiḳ he.

I liked that I went to school.

Ṭka he ṭaku waŋżi śica ecamuŋ ceḳ he ihnunaḣ haḣ'aŋna ḳaŋhaŋ bde ḳa ḳa uŋ ṭip akotaŋhaŋ wakpada waŋ ḳa dusya oḣidate iyaye pahaḳ aḳan wayawa ṭipidaḳ he he bde wakpada he oḣidateya ibdabde, wakonaḳ he ibdabde heṭaŋhaŋ.

But, there was one thing bad that I would do, sometimes when I was going in the morning, on the other side of where we lived there was a flowing creek that ran below the schoolhouse on top of the hill, I went below the creek-pool, I went through the mist from there.

I disappeared, caŋ mahed ibdabde ḳa I stayed in the bush all day.

I disappeared, I went into the forest and I stayed in the bush all day.

Ekṭa awaŋyakwicawakuwa waŋna śicecek haḣ'aŋna kupi ca ake he ed owape ake.

I was on the lookout for them, now the children, when the children came back in the morning, I joined them again.

Uŋ heced taŋke wicawayek he de waŋżi wayawa.

The older sisters that I had, one of them was in school.

He sdodyek he hed ikiyeda ti do.

The one that knew, she lived close by.

Taŋhaŋ wayek de Indian Agency hed ieska uŋ he.

My brother-in-law here at the Indian Agency was the interpreter.

Hehan śicece wayawaṗ hena wiyotaŋhaŋ ca we get a bowl of soup hehan hardtack eyapi ṭaku or biscuit heca waŋ ee dececa heuŋ uŋṭaṗ ce, haw hehan cokaheya kakse ka uŋk'up ce.

At that time, the children who were in school got a bowl of soup when it was noon, then what they called hardtack, or biscuit like this [as he knocked on the table], we ate with that, he broke it in the middle and gave it to us.

Uŋkaŋ, they come up with an idea that I missed some different days.

And so, they come up with an idea that I missed some different days.

Waki kaŋhaŋ hena Ina owakiyake, "De aŋpeṭu ṭokeṭu wadake he waśṭe do," iyokpiya wauŋ.

When I got home I told my mother about those, "I liked how my day was," and I was happy.

Hena iwatuŋśni.

I didn't tell the truth about those.

Kaeś heced taŋke de ṭakuda waŋ syrup pail heca waŋ ahi ka śicecek soup oyaptapi.

But even so, my older sister, she brought something, a syrup pail, that is what it was, and the children's leftover soup.

Haw, "De ecin dena uŋġe mama yakahde kṭe.

Yes, "Later you will take some of this home to mama."

Haw he half of when I'm in school he awaki, he mama wak'u, "Haŋ waśṭe ye."

Yes, half of [what I got] when I'm in school I took home, I gave it to mama, "Yes, that is good."

Ṭaŋyaŋ yużaża ka haḣ'aŋna saŋpa, "De wicakcaya" eya ca ake bde ka ake awai, that kept me going to school for a while, steady.

She washes it well and the day after tomorrow, when she says, "Take it back for them," again I go and again I take it there, that kept me going to school for a while, steady.

Ihnunaḣ ceġadak̇ he kci inawaḣbe do.
> Unexpectedly, I hid with the pail.

Up the side of the hill, I hid, I hid in the bush there, pail and all.

I left that pail there and waki k̇a "Wahaŋpi ayahdi śni he?"
> I left that pail there and I arrived home and, "Didn't you bring soup home?"

"Waŋ, de aŋpetu de śiceca hena wotehdapa owas wahaŋpi yahepapi do."
> "Today the children were hungry, and they drank all of the soup up."

So they got suspicious I guess, heced.
> So therefore they got suspicious, I guess.

Ihaŋḣ'aŋna k̇aeś ekta ake wai pail heced hek̇ ohna wahaŋpi awaki.
> The next morning I went over there again to get the pail, to pick it up where it was sitting.

They got me to go pick it up wherever I left it.

So heced yak̇ed waśkaŋ k̇a eced term iwahuni.
> So, I did things in that way, and then finally I finished the term.

Uŋkaŋ taku waŋżi ecamuŋ s'a hehan taku waŋżi waśtewadaka he eciŋ dowaŋp de waśtewadake.
> And so, one thing I like doing a lot of is that I like singing.

Dowaŋp de waśtewadake k̇a teacher uŋk̇itap[7] he dowaŋ he waśtedake.
> I liked to sing and our teacher liked singing.

Heca uŋ etaŋhaŋ, Indian Day School Oak River ehapi it wasn't Sioux Valley then, Oak River Indian Day School etaŋhaŋ, concerts hena Virden, Hamiota, Brandon, Seward, heciya hena concerts hece k̇aŋhaŋ ekta uŋkiza uŋyaŋpi.
> For that reason, from that time they called it Indian Day School Oak River, it wasn't Sioux Valley then, if those concerts are over there at Virden, Hamiota, Brandon, Seward, we also all go from Oak River Day School.

Hed wadowaŋ ce, odowaŋpi owahiya k̇a haw tak̇uk̇u waśteśte k̇a after we finished k̇a wowapi uŋk'upa wayawatiŋ ed otk̇eyapi owas otk̇eya he.
> I would always sing there, I sang songs, they gave us nice things after we finished and certificates, they would hang them up at the school and they all hang there.

Haw he, he waśtewadake.
> Yes, that, that I liked.

Uŋkaŋ he, heced wauŋ k̇a ake next year he ake waniyetu opta bde k̇a ake bdoketu k̇a next term ake, half, half of the term, hehan ihnuḣ Ina, ake hihnatuŋ Portage heciya, wicaḣcada waŋ heci hihnaye.

---

7. This is a contraction of uŋkitawapi.

> And so, I went around like that and again next year and again through the winter and again in the summer and next term again, half, half of the term and then here mother married again, she married an old man over there in Portage.

I had to graduate then, after a year and a half. Nobody told me what grade I was in.

Haw heci heciya wai, we stayed over there for about two years.

> Yes, over, over [where] I had gone, we stayed over there for about two years.

Hehan, when I got twelve, wahecedya hehan, I went out on a farm, haw hena heced wauŋ.

> Then when I got twelve, right around then, I went out on a farm, yes, that's the way I lived.

Haw hehan, hehan he he Ina tokek he ehan, toke ecaḣmayek he ehan he macistiŋna he ehan taŋyaŋ awamayake.

> Yes, then, in the beginning, at the time my mother first raised me, at that time I was small, at that time she took care of me well.

Ate waye ka nakuŋ Ina wayak naka taŋyaŋ awamayake wimakihni takuku mak'u.

> She was my father and also my mother and so she took care of me well, she looked out for me, different things she shared with me.[8]

Hehan hokṡiyopa mayuhe, miye hakakta mayuhe.

> Then she had me as her last one.

Haw heced he mihakab wanice.

> Yes, and so there was not another one after me.

Haw heuŋ taŋyaŋ mayuhe.

> Yes, for that reason she took good care of me.

Uŋkaŋ he ḣtayetu waŋżi ihnunaḣ imuŋke kiŋhaŋ waŋna uŋkiwakapa de misakib de isakib miża muŋke.

> And so one evening I suddenly lay down, when we all had laid down, she lay beside me and I lay beside her.

"Waŋna iṡtiŋma," de eyakeṡ heced.

> "Sleep now," she said this.

Heced maḣiba ṡni ca heced he Dakota ia mihna ce.

> But I was not sleepy, so then she comforts me in Dakota.

Hekta ehaŋna he ehan when my mother's age, he ehan he heced wiŋyaŋ hena ṡicecak wicakihnap he ohna mihma cee.

---

8. *Wimakihni* can mean *she looked out for me*, as in a protective way, or that *she sought out things for me*.

At that time way back then, when my mother's age, at that time that was the way the women comforted the children,⁹ she comforted me in that way.

Iaŋ hena Dakoṭa iapi yuke do tḵa hehan owas tokca ḵa ṭokiḵiya tokca.

There are those words found in the Dakota language, but then they are all different and in different places it is different.

They don't rhyme hece he muŋḵe ḵa anaġopṭaŋ muŋḵa çe, that word does not go with this word, trying to put the two and two together, pretty soon I'd get sleepy heced misṭiŋma.

They don't rhyme and so I lay and lay listening, that word does not go with this word, trying to put the two and two together, pretty soon I'd get sleepy and so I slept.

Haw hehan he anaġopṭaŋ muŋḵe ḵa odowaŋna he ahiyaye çe.

Yes, then I lay listening and she carries a little song.¹⁰

Hehan naḵuŋ tawaciŋ deci mahed ṭaḵu tehan Ṭaḵ Wakaŋ ḵiksuye uŋ-yaŋk'uŋpta uŋk'upi.

Then also, here inside the mind, Ṭaḵ Wakaŋ gives us a place where we put things to remember for a long time.

Haw deci paḵ ekṭa mauŋ naka ḵiksuya wauŋ.

Yes, it is here in my head, that is why I am remembering.

Haw heced ded isakib muŋḵe ḵiŋhaŋ Ina maki dowaŋ:

And so, when I lay here beside her, my mother sings for me:

Wica tataŋkada	Little big men
Deciya deciya	Over here, over here
Eḵṭahiya kud waŋḵe	Over there laying down
Ninaha Nihaha	You are unsteady, you are unsteady
Ti taŋka oho	Big house
Çeġ'osṭaŋ, ho ho	Kettle with a cover
Śuŋka niyapopo, śuŋka niyapopo	Dog gnaws on you
Winuhca nuŋpap ḵa sḵuyaya, sḵuyaya	Two sweet, sweet women
Wicanaġi, Wicanaġi	Human spirit, human spirit
Ni ya we, ni ya we	[vocables?]
Ġood day, ġood day, çaŋsicahpu	Good day, good day, little bird
Wicaṡta waŋ peżiteṡdaḵa	A man wearing a crown of grass
He yuhpeya, he yuhpeya	He buys her, he buys her

---

9. *Wicaḵihnapi* implies that they follow the ancestor's ways, traditions.
10. *Ahiyaye* means *to carry [a tune]*, or *to sing*.

Wi san, wi san	When the sun is bright, sunrise
Tawicu, tawicu	Wife, wife
Ticanice, taŋka waŋna se	Just like the big snipe, now
Wašuŋ snake waŋna se	Just like the den now
Śiyo wani u śiyo wani u	My life is bad, my life is bad
Wiŋyaŋ ob wakaŋheża dehaŋhaŋ żożo	Women with children now whistle
De nape, tibdo totoya, tibdo totoya	This hand my older brother makes blue
Eça niçiiçepaŋśi okiciyaka okiciya	Your cousin, tell it to her, help her
Hehaka tośkiśke tośkiśke	The elk, his life is rough
Mani mani	Walking, walking
Śiyo śiyo	Prairie chicken, prairie chicken
Abdo huŋhuŋ titaŋkapo heya ośtaŋpo	Shoulder blade [exp.] big house [voc.]
A, a, a, epa ça witohan wahdi ca	When I say, "A, a, a," the month when I return home
Hokśid ob napciŋwaŋk	With nine boys
Wiciŋciŋye ciŋ	I want a girl
Waśtewadake, waśtewadake	I like it, I like it
A, A, A, eya keyapi ye	"A, a, a," they say he said

"Waŋna niśtiŋma he?"
    "Are you sleeping now?"
"Hiya nihaŋh," ho umaŋk he iśto ake ahiyaye.
    "No not yet," the other one she sang again.

Wicataŋtaŋkada	The older ones
Deciya deciya	Over here, over here
Ekta hiya kud waki	Over that way I returned below
Nihaha nihaha	You are unsteady, you are unsteady
Titaŋka po po	Old unsteady big house
Çeġ hośtaŋ po po	Loose kettle cover
Šuŋka niyapo po	Dog is chewing you ragged
Šuŋka niyapo po	Dog is chewing you ragged

Heptecedak ahiyaye, "Waŋna niśtiŋma he?"
    A short one she sang, "Are you sleeping now?"
By that time I was long gone.
Haw heced, he he de tohan he de hena onispe kta, ospenic'iciya kta tohan niśtiŋma kte.

Yes, and so this one, when this one, as you go you will learn those, teach yourself when you are going to sleep.

De wicohaŋ waśte duhe do.

You have a good task.

Śiceca yuha woyak'up he.

The children you have, you feed them.[11]

CMN [to Angela]: Maybe you can learn that song.[12]

WAW: Yes, I'll try it.

Haw hena he waśte do.

Those are good things.

Heced imacaġe.

I was raised in that way.

Haw ehan de ḳakiya waŋna wai ḳa twelve years henamakca hehan waśicuŋṭa waecamuŋ.

Yes, then over there I went now, twelve years, I was that many, then I worked for the Waśicu.

He wahdi, wahdi ḳa hehan deci waŋna hehan sixteen or seventeen hed wauŋ.

I came home then over here, now then I was sixteen or seventeen and stayed around here.

Ḳaeś ed Portage heciya ḳa fifteen and sixteen henamakceḳ hehan waŋna Dakoṭa okodakiciye wacipi ed ciŋye wicawayeḳ ed dowaŋp çe, opap çe.

And so over there at Portage, fifteen and sixteen, I was that many by that time now, at the Dakoṭa dance group older brothers of mine would sing and I would join them.

Hena ciŋye wicawayeḳ hena wicaśta Halls yamnipi, waŋżi John Hall eciyapi, Tom Hall ee ḳa Reuben Hall, Alex Hall he iś opṭa hena ob wadowaŋ çe.

Those older brothers of mine, those three Halls men, one they called John Hall, there was Tom Hall and Reuben Hall, as for Alex Hall he was in the group, I sang with them all.

Homakśida ḳaeś ob wadowaŋ çe.

Even though I was just a boy I would sing with them.

Haw he de wahdiḳ hehan wadowaŋ de dowaŋp ca owicawakiya çe.

Yes, when I returned then I sang, when they sang here I would help them.

---

11. In saying "you feed them," Uŋḳaŋna is referring to breastfeeding them rather than bottle-feeding them. I was still nursing Autumn on this visit.

12. "CMN" is used to indicate the speech of Chris Mato Nunpa, "CCS" for Carrie Cavender Schommer, and "WAW" for Waziyatawiŋ Angela Wilson.

Heced wau ḳa haw eced ihnunaḣ 1923 he ecan Omaha tokaḣ oḳaḣ'u hed owicawakiya hed owape.

That is the way I came and, yes, then finally when it was 1923 when the first Omaha came to be, I helped them and joined them there.

He dowaŋ top dowaŋp çe he waŋżi miye odowaŋ ḳa Omaha wacipa ceġtaŋḳa piyapa ṭoked wicaṡkaŋ hena owas aŋpeṭu de dehan decedya yuha wauŋ.

There are four who sing and I was one of them, song and Omaha dance, they prepare the big kettle, how they did all those things, today at this time I carry these things in this way.

Odowaŋ hena owaciŋhaŋ ahiyapi wamihnake yuheḳ hena naḳuŋ odowaŋ ahiyapi.

They sing those songs in order, those that have wamihnake[13] those also sing a song.

"Caŋwiyus'ayaya" eyapi naḳuŋ hehan waŋżi "Wiyohnaŋkwicakiyapi" eyapi, "Tukiha Ceġa Ehde."

"Caŋwiyus'ayaya,"[14] they say, also then one called "Wiyohnaŋkwicakiyapi,"[15] "Tukiha Ceġa Ehde."[16]

Hena owas odowaŋ, hena ḳiksuya wauŋ.

All of those songs, those I remember.

Hena ekṡe tape iyewaye tiyaṭa wahnake.

All of those I did tape, I keep them at home.

Haw he icabu he ehan mak'upa he aŋpeṭu dehaŋyaŋ hinaḣ he tiyaṭa wahnaka tḳa de miciŋkṡi umaŋ naḳakṭa, "De waŋna eṭaŋhaṡ he de Omaha hena owas nit'api do, ṭakuda duhap ṡni do, Okodakiciyeḳ.

Yes, that drumstick they gave me at that time and up to this day I still keep it at home, but this my son, the other young one, "This now anyway, those Omaha, all of them, you are all dead, you don't have anything, the Society."

Hekṭa wiŋyaŋ hena iża okodakiciya yuhapi, Iwakci[17] Okodakiciye yuhapi.

But then the women, they also had a society, they had the Scalp-Dance Society.

Haw heced okodakiciye num ded Sioux Valley ded uŋhapi naka he wiŋyaŋḳ iṡ iṡnana wacipa wicaḳ iṡnana wacip.

---

13. *Wamihnake* means *something I put away for myself* and seems to refer to a separate group that sings a different song.
14. This means "taking the staff in hand while singing."
15. "They put food in their mouth."
16. "Set the kettle and spoon."
17. *Iwakci* is a contraction of *iwakicipi*.

So then we had here these two societies here in Sioux Valley and so the women, they danced alone, and the men danced alone.

Ihnuȟ Iwakci dowaŋp hena ito (Omahaȟ) uŋkaŋ Iwakci wicakidowaŋpi kte do itoptayap kaŋhaŋ ka odowaŋpi itopta wiŋyaŋ iża ake we call on them too.

Sometimes those scalp dance singers, they (Omaha) will sing for the Iwakci and then they in turn sing back to them, then again the women also, we call on them too.

Heced okciya wauŋ cip.

We helped each other dance.

Hehaŋyaŋ uŋkupa.

That far we have come.

Hehan de aṡkatuyeda about ten years ago, kaiṡ eight years ago, hehan de miciŋkṡi hakakta Gordon, you saw him yesterday, didn't you?

Then recently, about ten years ago, or eight years ago, then this my youngest son, Gordon, you saw him yesterday, didn't you?

Haw he he traditional dancer hecek hehan he nuske, haw heced hed otaheda abduṡtaŋ.

Yes, he was a traditional dancer and so there, in between there, I quit.

Our first boy he, we lost him.

Haw hehan he wacipa icabu de ewahnake wicawacu.

Yes, so then this dancing and drumstick I put away, I gave it back to them.

Uŋkaŋ about a year after ake hokṡida waŋ, Hepaŋ Marshall he ake eṡ uŋhapi.

And so, about a year after again, a boy, Hepaŋ Marshall, we had then again.

Uŋkaŋ he aŋpetu ed ihnunaȟ haw he ehnakapa Omaha pikiyapi.

And here one day, suddenly they put him in as one of the singers, and the Omaha were making preparations.

Uŋkaŋ he Omaha itaŋcaŋ he inażiŋ ka haw he icabu he hokṡida mitawak he he k'up kak[18] uŋ he.

And so the Omaha leader stood up and that drumstick, the one, my boy, that is the one thing that they had given him.

He ake bduhe haw heced hehan, he hece hena weciyuhe . . . haw he wanice kaeṡ icabu tawa he aŋpetu dehaŋya yuha wauŋ.

I have it again and then I still carry that for him . . . it is no longer [the Omaha Society], but I still carry his drumstick to this day.[19]

De recently Gordon he waci ciŋ hinaȟ yuha waci, it's all beaded.

---

18. *K'up kak* is used here as a contraction for *k'up tka kiŋ he*.
19. The ellipses indicate a deleted phrase that was indecipherable.

Recently, sometimes when Gordon wants to dance, he dances with it, it's all beaded.

Yuha waci çe.
He dances with it.

Hehaŋyaŋ waŋna waniyetu ota okodakciye[20] ed dowaŋ hed ope imacaġe.
It has been many winters now, that long [since] I was raised to be a part of the brotherhood's way of singing.

Ehaŋna Woyakapi Iyamni (The Third Historical Narrative)

Uŋkaŋ tokek ekta ehaŋna Dakotak oihduha ekta he wiŋyaŋ wicak'upa he wiŋyaŋ opetuŋpi taku hecetu.
And so in the beginning, way back then in the Dakota tradition, they gave women and they bought women, those things happened.

Uŋkaŋ ciŋye, ciŋye omakiyake ka dekśi wayawaŋ haw he wabdenica icaḣwicaye wiŋyaŋ nuŋpapi hehan dekśi tawicu he haw he takożakpaku hena.
And so older brother, older brother told me and the one who was my uncle, he raised two women orphans, then uncle's wife, those were her grandchildren.

Umaŋ wayawa umaŋ iś tiyata uŋ wayawa śni ye.
The one went to school and the other one stayed at home and did not go to school.

Waŋna eighteen hece ka nineteeen hece ka ku kte kaeś tukteda ku kte yuhe śni.
Now she was eighteen and she was nineteen, she could come home, but she did not have any place to come back to.

Haw hece haw he kci uŋ maśi.
He told me to be with her.

"Taŋyaŋ kci yauŋ kta do, atkuku ka huŋku wanice do.
"You will get along well with her, she doesn't have a father and mother.

"Haw hece he taŋyaŋ kci yauŋ kte do," eye.
"And so, you will be fine with her," he said.

"Aho," epe, haw heced kci wauŋ.
"Yes," I said, so I was with her.

---

20. In reference to the Omaha Society, up to this point Uŋkaŋna used the word *okodakiciye*, which can be translated as *society* or *organization*. Here he uses the word *okodakciye*, which is better translated as a *brotherhood*, implying that the people within this group are very close and together.

Waniyetu num taŋyaŋ kci wauŋ.
> Two years I was fine with her.

Uŋkaŋ ihnunaḣ wasicu wakaŋk kiŋ ekta ipa woope kuwapi keyapa wakaŋyuzapta çe eyapa dena woopek dena Dakota hena takuda śni çe.
> And here the missionaries went there and they said they were studying law and they will be in holy matrimony, they said the Dakota do not have these laws.

Ho ekśe wakaŋciyuzapi ecuŋk'uŋpi Ladsworth ed he ehnaked tak owas toked iyaye.
> After we did the marriage ceremony in Ladsworth, just like that everything went wrong.[21]

Heced two years okciŋwaste uŋyak'uŋp he iyeced uŋyak'uŋpi śni.
> So two years we were getting along well together, we were no longer that way.

Eced eś Dakota wicotawaciŋ heciya taŋhaŋ wakiyahde ka takuda iyomakpi śni kaŋhaŋ etaŋhaŋ tokan iyaye maśi.
> Finally I went back over there to the side of Dakota thought and, when nothing would make me happy, then she told me to go away from there.

Haw hena he ecamuŋ tokaŋ ibdabde ka iźa tokaŋya.
> I did those, I left and went away and she too went away.

Hehan iyohakab hehan he de waŋźi de dehan kçi wauŋ dehan waŋna waniyetu wikçemna . . . ake waŋźi itaŋcaŋ he he waŋna hehaŋyaŋ sixty-two years etkiya kçi wauŋ.
> After that time, then this one I am with at this time, now at this time tens of winter . . . and one, for that long, going on sixty-two years I have been with the one who is the boss.

Haw hena he heced imacaġe ka wau.
> Yes, that's the way I have been raised and I have come.

Hehan nakuŋ, nonsupport uŋ mayuzapi, otokak ekta nakuŋ makaskapi.
> Then also, they arrested me for nonsupport, in the beginning they also put me in jail.

Hde maśipi ciŋpi.
> They wanted to send me home.

"Hiya, he de etaŋhaś he taku omaśicaya kaŋhaŋ inuŋpa ed amayawaciŋpi śni po."
> "No, it does not make any difference whatever happens to me, if I have a bad happening again, do not try to take me again."

---

21. Literally this would be "everything went every which way."

Haw he ecan iś de de de kci wauŋ ecan he iś tibdo ḳuŋwaŋ he iś ake ḳa wiŋyaŋ waŋ he iś kçi uŋ.

> Yes, then this one, the one that I am with, then her older brother, that one in the meantime again, he was with that woman there.[22]

She raised a very good family over there, they can get along, uŋḳiźa deciya ded śiceca icaġapi.

> She raised a very good family over there, they can get along, as for us also, the children were being raised over here.

He ehan Dakoṭa uŋyak'uŋpi.

> At that time we were all living as Dakoṭa.[23]

Haw heced uŋkicaġapi, heuŋ eṭaŋhaŋ dehanṭu ekṭa ouŋ num ikoyaḳ wauŋ.

> Yes, that is how we were raised, for that reason at this time I live in two worlds.[24]

Dakoṭaḳ hena wicawiçada hehan naḳuŋ Waśicu hena wicawicada tka hehan tawaciŋ mitawaḳ de uŋ ṭaḳu wiçawada ḳa wiçawada śni ḳaŋhaŋ hena ohnaya mitawaciŋ wec'uŋ.

> She believes in those Dakoṭa [ways], then also, she believes in those Waśicu [ways], but then with my mind, I use my mind in that direction for what I believe and do not believe.

Oḳaḣniġaya ṭukṭe waśṭe kecanmi ḳaŋhaŋ he ohna oḳiic'iya wauŋ.

> In understanding what I think is good, I help myself in that way.

Hena iyeced niźa hena tawaciŋ yahduhapi heced ṭukṭe ohna ded yaupi uŋkaŋ deced waśṭe ḳa yaupa hece henana wiçakeya yaup ḳiŋhaŋ tokaṭakiya waniyeṭu ota wakiciyaḳ, ṭohanya wani ḳiŋhaŋ waciyaḳapi wauŋ kṭe.

> In that same way you also have those, a mind that is yours and so the way in which you came here is good and if you continue to come in a truthful and strong way in the future, for many winters we will be seeing each other, for however long I live I will be seeing you.

Haw heced wiçawada wauŋ ṭohaŋya owic'iye wauŋ iyeced wauŋ opimic'iye, kṭa ibduṭe.

> I believe in that way and so for as long as I help others in that way, I am trying to live that way.

Haw he he iś wiconi he mitawaḳ he heced opimic'iye he haw heced ociciyaḳap.

> Yes, as for that, for the life that is mine I live in that way, that is why I am telling you this.

---

22. Kuŋśi Edna's older brother married Uŋḳaŋna's first wife.
23. "Living as Dakoṭa" here refers to living with Dakoṭa traditions.
24. The literal translation here refers to being tied to two states of being.

1. In 1988 Chris Mato Nuŋpa adopted Eli Taylor (shown here) as his father in a formal ceremony in Granite Falls, Minnesota, just outside the Upper Sioux Reservation. (Author's collection)

2. Uŋkaŋna Eli during the 1992 interviews, Sioux Valley, Manitoba. (Author's collection)

3. Uŋkaŋna Eli and Kuŋśi Edna during the 1992 interview in Sioux Valley, Manitoba. (Author's collection)

4. Kuŋśi Waḣpetuŋwiŋ (Carolynn Schommer) during the 1992 interviews in Sioux Valley, Manitoba. She served as the primary translator for the project. (Author's collection)

5. Uŋkaŋna Eli in 1998, when Brandon University of Brandon, Manitoba, bestowed on him an honorary doctoral degree. (Author's collection)

6. Uŋkaŋna Eli, Kuŋśi Edna (*right*), and Eli's niece, Frances Maza Wasicuna, in the late 1990s. (Photo courtesy of Bill Taylor)

7. Uŋkaŋna Eli and Kuŋši Edna at a birthday-anniversary celebration in the 1980s, Sioux Valley, Manitoba. (Photo courtesy of Bill Taylor)

8. Uŋkaŋna Eli speaking to children during Education Day at one of the Mahkato Powwows in Mankato, Minnesota, late 1990s. (Photo courtesy of Bruce Dowlin and Sheryl Dowlin, Ph.D.)

Kiŋhaŋ he hena he eś he.
>That is the way that those are.

He naka wadowaŋ makek he nakuŋ odowaŋ waŋ ed ikowayek kte do.
>I will also put another verse on what I was singing a while ago.

He nakuŋ when I was , when I was a young kid going to that day school, that was during the war, First World War, in 1914 I was about eight, nine years old.
>Then also, when I was, when I was a young kid going to that day school, that was during the war, First World War, in 1914 I was about eight, nine years old.

Uŋkaŋ he wauŋyawapi uŋ he, the teacher liked my singing so she takes me around to, to picnics and taku heced iyaza, parties.
>And here when we were at school, the teacher likes my singing, so she takes me around to picnics and things like that here and there, parties.

Uŋkaŋ he, some songs that they call the patriotic songs that she had taught me to sing about the war and the boys are over there and allies, and all these are over there.
>And so, some songs that they call the patriotic songs that she had taught me to sing about the war and the boys are over there and allies, and all these are over there.

So she taught me this song to sing at one of those parties.

Aŋpetu dehaŋyaŋ, like I told you this morning, our Creator says whatever you like and what you want in your body, it's going to stick in your head.
>To this day, like I told you this morning, our Creator says whatever you like and what you want in your body, it's going to stick in your head.

Wowapi uŋk'uŋ śni tka hena heciya hena taku computer ka iyeced kagapi do, epe.
>They did not give us any books but over there they made those, something like a computer, I said.

"Uŋkaŋ, he uŋspeuŋkiyap kiŋhaŋ tukted uŋkahiyapte çe."
>"Grandfather, if you teach it to us we'll sing it somewhere."

You're going to have to teach us that song, we'll sing it somewhere, those three girls that were singing last night.[25]

Uŋkaŋ odowaŋnak he this is the way it goes:
>And so that little song, this is the way it goes:
>>We are the men of the very far north, the land of the maple spread around us.

---

25. This refers to the three daughters of Donald Pratt whom we had heard singing the night before.

> Here shall we live, not an inch we'll give, men shall confound us.
> For we have the brains and the brawn and the blood of the Saxon
>   and the Celts and the Gauls.
> Any fight that we can fight when we know we are in the right, then
>   we'll march at the country call.
> Canada, dear Canada, men of the North are we.
> For thee we'll live and for thee we'll die, but forever more thou
>   shall be free.

I've never heard that song in writing, or nobody's ever sung it, you don't hear it over the TVs or anything now, yet that's stuck in my mind. That's the kind of mind that the Indian people are meant to have. That's a long time ago, that's a long ways back that I can remember. Today I forgot what day yesterday was, my memory is getting that short.

Ehaŋna Woyakapi Itopa (The Fourth Historical Narrative)

Haw he, he heuŋ etaŋhaŋ, he waŋżi waŋna woyuśtaŋ de haħ'aŋnaŋk de ṭaku iwouŋhdakap kṭe do.

> Yes, for that reason that one is finished this morning, we will talk about something.

Uŋkaŋ inip de inim he de okiŋni wayakap okiŋni mitakoża he de hena kci aki ka dena itoyap ko ayaki ka iyawaya dena nuske kiŋhaŋ nakuŋ eś ṭukṭed ihnunah wicaśta taŋka ka wiŋyaŋ taŋkana nah'uŋpṭe.

> And so, the life, they will look at the life that was, maybe when my grandchild takes these home with her, these videos and these writings, also just maybe somewhere the male elders and female elders will listen.

Inip de, inip de de wicaśta peżihuta yuhap he ka inipa wiŋyaŋ taŋkad yakap he he ka hehan, hehan nakuŋ he wicaśta he naġiyewicayapi kaŋhaŋ hena he wo wo ṭaku wośape ikoyakapi hena hena inip de uŋ ihduskapi.

> This inipi, this inipi, the men that carry the medicine and the women sit on the outside of the inipi, if the men are bothered by them they go in the inipi and cleanse themselves from the wośape[26] they [the women] have within themselves.

Wica ka hehan wiŋyaŋ ekśe inip, inip śni ṭohnina.

---

26. *Wośape* is one of those words that is difficult to translate accurately. Riggs describes it as *anything that blackens or defiles*, but this is usually used in reference to women's condition during menstruation. In Dakoṭa there is not a bad or evil connotation associated with this, but it is a time when women shouldn't be around others because of the power deriving from this natural occurrence.

Men and then women sweat but they [women] never sweat.[27]

Sdodwaye śni, aśkaṭuyada de wiŋyaŋ dena inip̣ çe ḳeyapi naḳuŋ ḳa hekṭa imaçaġe he ehan hena wiŋyaŋ ṭohnina inip̣ śni.

I don't know, lately they say these women also sweat, [but] back then when I was growing up, the women never did sweat.

Iyekśe hena wiŋyaŋ ihuŋniya sḳaya yaḳuŋpi.

They themselves, the women, always walked in cleanliness.

Wi waŋżi ca ake ṭaḳu we iyeceṭu śni uŋ taŋcaŋ ekṭa ikoyaḳ uŋpi hecihaŋ hena wiŋyaŋ wakaŋyaŋ wicaḳaġapi ḳa hena weḳ hena hiyu ḳa ake eṭaŋhaŋ tecaniyaŋ ake manipi.

In a month when they bleed they are not well, whatever is not right hangs in their body, those women were created in a sacred way and the blood comes out and after that happens, from then on they walk again with new life.

Ṭona ca taŋḳad yakaŋpi ḳaŋhaŋ he ecan peżihuṭa hena ṭuweda ikiyeda up śni, ṭaḳu wakaŋ uŋpa ṭaḳu ot'iŋsya hena ed ayap śni.

The many times that they sit on the outside, during that time no one brought any of the medicine near them, whatever was sacred that they used, they did not take those there.

He aŋpeṭu tonakça taŋḳad yakaŋpi hecihan asnip ḳaŋhaŋ ṭokiya mni waŋżi ekṭa ipa ṭaŋyaŋ ihdużażapi hehaŋyaŋ waŋna ihduskapi he.

So many days that they sit there, they go to where there is water and wash themselves really well, but by that time they have cleansed themselves.

Uŋḳiye hena wicaḳ hena hed isam iyaye naḳuŋ ṭaḳu wowahṭani ikoyaḳ uŋḳic'iyapi hena.

As for us, the hardships we have brought on ourselves as men are worse than that.

Ṭukṭe kted ṭaḳu śica ikoyaḳ uŋkic'iyapi ḳiŋhaŋ hed inip he uŋyaŋpa teuŋmni yap iŋyaŋ hena ḳad yapa.

Sometimes when we bring the bad things on ourselves, we go into the inip̣i, they heat the stones and we sweat.

Haw hena iŋyaŋ hena dena ṭuweda wicaśta kaġe śni hena iŋyaŋ Ṭaḳ Wakaŋ kaġe ḳa hehan he iŋyaŋ he ṭukṭe obe waŋ he he he uŋ kadyapi.

---

27. "Sweat" here is used to indicate participation in an inip̣i ceremony, though it should be noted that the purpose of the ceremony is not "to sweat." As George Sword pointed out, "When a Lakota says ni, or ini, or inipi, or initi, he does not think about sweat. He thinks about making his ni [life-force] strong so that it will purify him." See James R. Walker (with Raymond J. DeMallie and Elaine A. Jahner, eds.), *Lakota Belief and Ritual* (Lincoln: University of Nebraska Press, 1991), 100.

Yes, those stones, no man made those stones, Ṭaḵ Wakaŋ made those stones and then, one certain stone, that is the one they use to heat up.

Heca śni śta kadyapi ḵaŋhaŋ nabdebde çe kṭe.

If that is not the right kind [that they heat], it cracks up.

Mini sni akaśṭaŋp ḵaŋ nabdece.

If they pour cold water on it, it will crack up.

Haw hena sdodye wicakiya hena owicakiyake ḵa woiśṭiŋpa ecan wowahoḵuŋḵiya wicakipazo wawayaḵ wicakiye.

He lets them know, he tells them and during their sleep, he advises them, shows them, he causes them to see.

Haw hena hena uŋ de inip çeeḵ he he uŋkaŋ Waśicu mawaśṭeḵa ṭohiŋni inip he waŋżi timahed bde śni.

Yes, those [reasons] are why they do the inipi, as if I was such a good Waśicu, I never went into a sweat.[28]

Ṭohniŋna waŋżida bde śni.

Never did I go to one.

He he inim de imacaġe ḵa waŋna inim timahed bde kṭe, iyemahaŋṭu waniyeṭu iyenamakca he ecan waŋna wicaḣica inip ceḵ hena owas wanicap.

The inipi, when I was growing up and I was going to go into the inipi, I was old enough and ready, there were no more old men who had the inipi.

Iża okicize inuŋpa uŋkaŋ ehaeś homakśida umaŋḵ de owakihi śni, and twenty years later no okicize uŋkaŋ waŋna ehaeś wimacaḣica owakihi śni.

Also, I was just a boy during the second war,[29] I couldn't do one or the other and twenty years later, now I was too old, I couldn't do it.

Nakaeś notice mak'upi he ecan inażiŋ okicize.

They gave me a notice, but the war had already ended.

Hed otaheda iża inip he iyeced umaŋna iyemahaŋṭu śni iyaye hena.

In between there, just like the inipi, those went by because I wasn't ready for either one.

Haw heced tka iwohdakapi naḣ'uŋ wauŋ.

But, by being around I heard them talking about it.

Uŋkaŋ hena heca inip hena heca uŋ ihduśḵapi wicaḵ he ḵa wiŋyaŋ iś hena, haw weḵ hena śicaḵ hena hiyu ḵa hena wowaḣṭani yuhapi ecehna ikoyaḵ

---

28. This is an interesting reference to the Waśicu by Uŋḵaŋna, likely used here as a way of saying he was speaking with authority about something he had not experienced, as white people have been known to do, especially academics.

29. We think he intended to say "first war" here, a reference to World War I.

hena hiyu, hiyu ka hehan etaŋhaŋ ake tecahani ihduźaźapa ake hetaŋhaŋ skaya manipi, wakaŋya manipi.

And so, the men, they cleanse themselves in the inipi, and as for the women, when they pass the bad blood, the hardships they have and everything that clings to them all those come [out], and then at that time they wash themselves, and then again from there they walk clean in a sacred way with a new beginning.

Dakotak de he i etaŋhaŋ taku enape ka uŋkeyap kaŋhaŋ he wakaŋ he i wakaŋ uŋkaǵapa heuŋ etaŋhaŋ taku, taku śica uŋkeyapta kaŋhaŋ nape uŋyaŋpta śni.

We say what appears from the mouth is sacred because they made whatever we say to be sacred for that reason, the bad things that we say will not cause us to flee [be afraid].

Taku waśte kiŋhaŋ he napeya maunipte tuka dehaŋtu ekta hena waŋna tokca owahaŋ ihat'a hekta yakuŋp hena iś tokca dehaŋtuk ekta akicibdezapa akiciiapi kiciyaśica ihdawaśtepa etaŋhaŋś.

We will walk with the good that was put forth but at this time those are different now, back then when they were having fun and laughing, those were different, now they are watching each other and making themselves look good.[30]

Hena dehaŋtuk ekta wuŋke hena hena tokiya taŋhaŋ uŋkuspepi hecihaŋ?

That's the way things are at this time, from where did we learn those?

Oyate tokca ahi heciya taŋhaŋ uŋkuŋspepi.

We learned those from the different nations that have arrived here.

He Dakota iapi uŋkitawap de aŋpetu waŋźi ka num, yamni tohaŋyaŋ tuweda ia Dakota iap de wohdake yaŋke kaśta tukteda icaptapa iapi śica Tak Wakaŋ icaźeya icaptaia wanice takuda śni.

In our Dakota language, someone who speaks one day, two, three, that long, no one is speaking the Lord's name[31] in the Dakota language, no matter how long they sit and speak, no place, there is no bad swearing language, there is no using Tak Wakaŋ's name in swearing, nothing.

Iye he uŋkeyapi uŋkaŋ de eś de tahaŋśi, Jim Blacksmith, owa ewahnake he he de oie obdake.

We said this and here I wrote this and told my cousin Jim Blacksmith what he said.

---

30. This is a reference to bragging.
31. In saying this Uŋkaŋna does not mean we have no word for the Lord, but rather in Dakota there is no way to use the Lord's name in vain, as there is in English.

Dakotak de ṭaku śice icapṭapi ṭaku hena uŋḳuŋspepi śni.

The bad swearing, the Dakota never learned those things.

Haw heced, eca ṭaku śica eyap he he ekśe ṭaku śica he kapi, he sdoduŋyaŋpi do.

[When] they say something bad, we know that it means something bad for sure, we know that.

Uŋkaŋ "śica" eyap de yamni akihde uŋkeyap ḳaŋhaŋ he ehaŋkeyap ṭak śica uŋḳeyapi he haŋhaŋyeda uŋḳuŋspepi do.

And so, when they say "bad," if we were to say it three times we are saying something really bad, that is what we have learned.

"Heced ṭoḳed ehe kṭa he?" eyapi, uŋkaŋ ṭuwe caŋze maye ḳiŋhaŋ, "Śiceḣca, niśice do, śica!"

"So how would you say that then?" they said, and so if someone were to make me mad, "Really bad, you are bad, bad!"

Haw he ihaŋḳe śidya ṭak epe kṭe he miciyaŋḳe.

For my place, that was the worst that I could ever say.

De Dakoṭa ekṭa iyanum ṭaḳuda ṭokca eye do.

The second time he did not say anything different.

Haw hena uŋ he hena uŋ he de inipi de iś hena deced u.

For those reasons, for those, that is how the inipi came to be.

Dekśi wicawaḳ hena ehaŋna inip s'a do.

The ones who were my uncles long ago, they always had sweat ceremonies.

Ṭukṭekṭed wacekiyapa inipa timahed ḣmu se dowaŋpi.

Sometimes they prayed inside the inipi and they sang with a loud humming-like sound.

Haw he, that's the purpose for that inip he.

Yes, that's the purpose for that inipi.

CMN: Do you know a song, do you know any of the songs?

Hiya he ekśe he ṭohiŋni heced ed bde śni epe tḳa dehaŋṭuk ekṭa dena mitakożak uŋspepi uŋkaŋ uŋ wiwaŋyaḳ wacipi heca uŋp ḳeyapi hena.

I said that I never went to one but at this time my grandchildren they know, and they say that they use the ones for the sundance.

But before that he wiwanyaḳ wacipi de nakuŋ ṭaku inażiŋ hehan imacaġe.

But before that, the sundance, that also stopped when I was growing up.

Heced iyohakab ded aśḳaṭuyeda eṭaŋhaŋ wiwaŋyaḳ wacipi wabdaḳe tḳa hece ḳakiya ṭokik ekṭa Dakoṭa uŋyaŋḳap heciya he ehan teḣika ṭaku dehan he de wacip ḳaŋhaŋ waśakayeda ḳeyapi hehan.

Then after that, just recently I saw a sundance here, but then over there where we were as Dakota, they said it was difficult over there back then, now when they dance they say it is easy.

Ozikiyaṗ ca ake ozikiyaṗ çee hekṭa ehaŋna heca waciṗ he iyamni ca waciṗ ḳaŋhaŋ iṭopaḳ hehaŋyaŋ waŋna woṭe hdapa ipuza çe ḳeyapi hena hehaŋyaŋ ṭuweda ihuŋniya mini yatḳe śni ḳa waciṗ ḳeyapi.

They rest and again they rest usually, but long ago when they did that dance, the third dance[32] and then when they got to the fourth, by then they were hungry, they thirsted they say, no one drank water during that length of time and they danced, they say.

Naka he otawat'e teḣike he.

And so it was a tremendous hardship.

Wakaŋ kidapa teḣiŋdapi ḳeyaṗ tḳa dehaŋtuḳ toḳye, toḳye waciṗ.

They hold that sacred they say, but at this time it is different, they dance differently.

Haw he deciya ded sundance iyeyaṗ he de waŋna he hena he he waceḳiyapi ṭukṭed ṭuwe ṭuwe woyazaŋ waŋżi ḳicicuwapṭa wicaśṭa wapiya hena wasdodyaṗ hena he dena wiwaŋyaḳ wacipi he de iyopṭayapi hena ḳaġapi heced nawaḣ'uŋ.

Over here they do the sundance now, they are praying for someone someplace, someone with a sickness the medicine men have the knowledge to treat, these are the ones who conduct the sundance and they make those, that is what I hear.

Uŋkaŋ he ṭuweḳ wapiyaḳ he ye ḳa ṭuwe wacipi hena omaka opṭa ṭukṭed ṭuwe wayazaŋḳe ḳa ho śicayaḳ ḳaeś pikiyapa Ṭaḳ Wakaŋ hoyekiyapa woyasni kicidapi okihi wicaya ḳa asniṗ ḳaŋhaŋ.

And so, the one who heals goes and the ones who danced over the year wherever one was sick and in a bad way, they would treat them and they would send forth their cries to Ṭaḳ Wakaŋ and they would ask for healing and with their help, they are healed.

Haw he wopida eṭaŋhaŋ de wicaśṭa waŋ asniyeḳ de wiwaŋyaḳ waci ḳaŋhaŋ de ṭuwe asniyaṗ heciḣaŋ he wopida uŋ.

Yes, through his gratefulness the man who was cured, when he dances looking at the sun, this person who was healed, if that is so, that is for what he was grateful.

Ekṭa i ḳa okiye ḳiciwaci hecetu ḳeyapi he.

He would go there and help and dance for him, that is the way it was they say.

---

32. He likely means the third day of the sundance.

Heuŋ wicokcoṭa wacipi śni do ded nuske ḳiŋhaŋ bdokeṭu ca June ed heca wacipi ḳaŋhaŋṭuk de nakaha nuŋpakiya de heca wacipi.

> Therefore, a lot of people who do not dance in the summertime, in June when they have that dance—recently they have two places they have this dance.

Uŋkaŋ umaŋ wikçemna yamni saŋpa wacipa he wicota wacip hena.

> And so the other thirty-plus they danced, those were a lot of dancers.

Wiwaŋyak uŋkipi ekṭa uŋkipa hed uŋyaŋkaŋpi.

> We went to observe at the place we went and we were there.

Waŋna imahed uŋyapṭe uŋkokip śni hena caŋpaḣpipa canuŋpak hena ekihnakapi.

> Now we could not go inside the wooden enclosure because they had placed their pipes there.

Haw canuŋpek hena hdutecapa ake waŋna wacipi ḳiŋhaŋ ed yuha hoyeya manipṭa eṭaŋhaŋ uŋ wiwaŋyak wacipi hena ṭuwehehe yuhaśkaŋ hecihaŋ.

> They renew their pipes so that when they dance again they send forth their voice and they walk carrying that, the one who takes care of things for those who sundance.

Haw he ṭaŋyaŋ ṭak wakaŋ wauŋyakapṭaŋ.

> Yes, Ṭak Wakaŋ will look upon us clearly.

He iża nakuŋ heced wicaśkaŋ waŋbdi hena hi çee waŋbdi hena ahi ka iś he hoic'iyakap do owas waŋkan.

> Also, while this is going on, even the eagles also come, the eagles come and all of them from up above make their voice heard.

It got so nu awiçakiṭapi çee do.[33]

> It got so they search for them.[33]

Hena ṭukṭeda waŋżi de deciya uŋkaŋ ṭop ipi.

> Not just one, but over here there were four who came.

Ṭukṭed Dakoṭa aye ḳaŋhaŋ waŋbdik he awaŋwicayakap.

> Wherever the Dakoṭa go, the eagle watches over them.

He dowaŋ waŋbdi wocekiya he he he Dakoṭa awaŋwicayakapi.

> The song is the eagle's prayer, that is how they watch over them.

He he he de bdokehaŋ Mankato heci uŋkipi uŋkaŋ ake num hed ḳiŋyaŋ yakuŋpi waŋkan.

> Last summer we went to Mankato, and here there were twelve flying around above.

---

33. In using the word *awiçakiṭapi*, there is an implication of anticipation. The people know the eagles come so they look for them.

Uŋkaŋ, fourteen ṭuwe yawa ḳeyapi miś num wicabdu śna nacece.
And here someone counted fourteen, they said, as for me I missed two of them.³⁴

Iyohaḳab nakuŋ ake every day hed wakaŋ ḳiŋyaŋ yaḳuŋpi.
After that, also every day they were flying around above again.

---

34. This comment shows a generosity of spirit. Rather than accusing someone of miscounting, Uŋkaŋna states that he missed two, taking responsibility for a discrepancy that may or may not be his.

7. Dakoṭaḵ Hena Wiçawada
(I Believe in Those Dakoṭa Ways)

In the last chapter, Uŋḵaŋna Eli Taylor covers a variety of topics that offer additional insight into the Dakoṭa mind and worldview. While they differ greatly in form and content, they are presented in their original order[1] and demonstrate a conversational flow. This section offers a brief glimpse into Uŋḵaŋna's personal past and allows us to understand more clearly how his experiences shaped his sense of identity and belief systems.

Uŋḵaŋna first restates the conditions surrounding his birth and upbringing. This is a narrative strategy used frequently within the oral tradition in which the storyteller is not only providing a reaffirmation of the position and teachings from which he speaks but also using repetition as an instrument for teaching. It is precisely this kind of repetition that facilitates the learning and remembering of stories within the oral tradition. However, it also demonstrates the fluidity of the oral tradition. In this case, for example, he is not citing the same information verbatim, but much of the same information is relayed using slightly different phrasing, though we learn new details as well. While some oral traditions are remembered verbatim, among the Dakoṭa this is not usually the case, as every storyteller has his or her own distinctive way of presenting information and may place stories within the context of their own upbringing and understandings. Furthermore, once a storyteller has mastered the knowledge or the content, he or she has the ability and the freedom to describe events in his or her own terms.

In this instance, the content is Uŋḵaŋna's own life. Here we learn in further detail why his mother does not want him to attend school, and we see a fascinating challenge to the ideology of the dominant society. Europeans, and later Euro-Americans and Euro-Canadians, firmly believed they were bringing "civilization" to Indigenous Peoples, just as Christian missionaries believed they were bringing "lightness" to the dark. Beliefs such as these can only be maintained through a firmly entrenched sense of superiority over others. Rather than eroding through time, this sense of superiority, which is part and parcel of the colonial mind-set, is still prevalent today. Missionary efforts of many faiths (which are by their nature enterprises of religious imperialism) are still going strong in all corners of the globe. We still frequently hear the term "uncivilized" applied to whomever is the current enemy of today's world powers, and when this term is invoked, it usually precedes a new "civilizing" campaign, often with the use of military force. Thus, in terms of Indigenous populations, the educational agenda was implemented with the youngest generation and accompanied a larger colonial civilization project, not necessarily unique to North America. However, not all Indigenous Peoples succumbed to an ideology of inferiority, maintaining instead their traditional beliefs about the importance of Indigenous forms of education.

In this section we are offered a glimpse into this culture of resistance maintained through an era of intensive policies of colonization in the early twentieth century. Uŋkaŋna's mother, Wayak Hiyaye Wiŋ, was one of those who recognized the importance of resisting agents of colonialism and in this case was acting in response to the changes she had already observed in her other children. Maintaining a belief in the importance of Dakota traditions and a suspicion of the education of the Wasicu, she tells him:

"Hena tokatakiya waciŋuŋyaŋpta śni nacece," eye.

"In the future we will probably not be depending on those," she said.

It is clear from this statement that her faith for the future still rests with those ways of life that had sustained the Dakota for thousands of years. It is this way of life she wants to perpetuate and which she believes will be of help to the Dakota of the future. These pockets of resistance, both then and now, offer great hope and inspiration to the current decolonization movement, as they remind us of the confidence born from traditions of strength and beauty.

When Uŋkaŋna Eli was picked up by the agent and brought to school against his will, his mother's concern is evident from her comment:

"Waciŋyaŋtaŋka hece wayawa yai he?" he śida.

"Did you go strong-minded?" she was saddened.

As a mother she understood the educational transformation that was likely to occur with her youngest son, as it had with her older children, but she was also concerned with how difficult it might be for him.

From his accounts it appears that Uŋkaŋna made the transition quite well, despite the obstacles he faced and his days of playing hooky. He attributes some of his adaptability to his previous exposure to older siblings and the bits of English language he had learned from them. As a consequence of the language skills he had acquired, he got along well with the teacher and was able to serve as translator for some of the students who had greater difficulty learning English. However, it is also at school that his talent for singing was recognized and put to use to serve the institution's colonialist agenda.

Uŋkaŋna attended school for a brief period during World War I. As a favored student of the teachers with a gift for singing, Uŋkaŋna comments that he was taken around to perform for different audiences at picnics and parties. However, rather than being encouraged to sing Dakota songs, which would not facilitate the colonizing process, he was taught and asked to sing what he called the "patriotic songs," which were of special importance during wartime with Canadian troops overseas. However, this support of the troops would have been particularly important to Uŋkaŋna, not only because of the participation of Dakota men in the war but also because he had an older brother who was lost in World War I. As he explains later in another section in an upcoming chapter:

> Haw, he he hena wocaŋte śice hena etaŋś tokeḋ dehaŋ ekta tokeḋ uŋ hena heced waŋkap̄ maka tehiŋda.
>
> Yes, those are heartaches, but in these times the reason why they are lying there is because of the love of their land.

Thus, in their participation in the wars of the world, Dakota men did so believing they were helping to defend their homeland. This thinking would have been encouraged by military recruiters, no doubt, as they attempted to solicit support among Indigenous populations for the war efforts. However, it must be pointed out that the sense of "patriotism" instilled by the dominant society was not patriotism toward the Dakota Oyate but rather patriotism toward the colonizer's society. For Uŋkaŋna Eli this patriotic influence was conveyed through song and must have made a powerful impression, since he was able to recall it flawlessly after almost eighty years.

The other example of song relayed in this section also draws on childhood remembrances of his mother and the sweetness of his bedtime ritual. As it was time for him to go to sleep, his mother would speak gently to him in Dakota, comforting him, as was the Dakota tradition. If this did not put him to sleep, she would sing a "nonsense" lullaby, one with no rhyme or reason for the words strung together, but with a beautiful melody. At one time this song must have been widely known as I have heard two versions from Dakota communities widely separated geographically. When I played the tape of Uŋkaŋna singing this song for my Kuŋśi Naomi Cavender, she recalled a slightly different version of the song that she learned growing up on the Santee Reservation in Nebraska. The song and its description here invoke all the feelings of warmth and comfort that Dakota mothers extended to their young. Uŋkaŋna reminds us: "Haw hena he waśte do" or "Those are good things."

In this section Uŋkaŋna also makes mention of the Omaha Okodakiciye and the Iwakci Okodakiciye, two societies previously important among the Dakota, though, to my knowledge, no longer in existence. He briefly describes aspects of the men's Omaha Society here, which started in Sioux Valley in 1923, but he does not go into much detail. Based on later discussions with him about the Omaha Society, it was clear this was not a religious organization but a social organization. He described it as a society in which men could come together in brotherhood and support one another in living up to the ideals of Dakota manhood. They would encourage positive codes of behavior and ethics, and punishment would be inflicted if they were violated. For example, if a man from the society was found to have beaten his wife, all the men in the society would be subject to a group punishment. Thus they each had a vested interest in supporting one another to live life according to the highest Dakota morals. This also meant that it was not a brotherhood in which one could loosely participate. It required a serious commitment on behalf of each of its members, as that was the only way the ideals of the society could be sustained. As Thomas Tyon stated about the Omaha Society in the early 1900s: "Whoever is an Omaha member is commanded to think nothing bad. And when they hear anything bad about people, they pay no attention to it. They are commanded not to fight with anyone. They are commanded not to lie. And whatever they give, they are commanded not to take back. Each day they are commanded to think good thoughts."[2] Many who knew Uŋkaŋna Eli Taylor would say that even after he left the Omaha Society he continued to live by these difficult standards. Although the society is no longer in existence in Sioux Valley, former members retain knowledge of the society.

In 1996, with growing problems in my own community of Upper Sioux, particularly among the population of young men, we discussed the possibility of resurrecting the Omaha Okodakiciye. Our belief was that a society like this was desperately needed to provide guidance and teachings to the young men according to our own traditions and values. With many of the spiritual teachings lacking on our reservation, opportunities for this kind of learning were scarce. We also hoped that with such an organization, the men of all ages would be able to develop trust in and support for one another, especially in maintaining chemical-free lives and positive family relationships. With the support and participation of the tribal council, about a dozen of us traveled to Sioux Valley in the summer of 1996 to record Uŋkaŋna's stories about the Omaha and to receive guidance from him about how we might revitalize this important men's society. However, it was clear midway through the process that establishing a serious commitment to the creation of the society in our community was going to be extremely difficult at that point in time. Several of the key men left early, before the first phase of teachings had been completed, to attend to a developing political situation in our community. That, at least temporarily, ended further discussion.

However, the recovery of this traditional knowledge and its implementation in our communities is crucial to the decolonization process, and it is my hope that it will eventually be restored. When we examine the current men's issues in our communities, many of which involve alcohol and drug abuse and/or forms of violence against women and children, we see that these are responses to colonization. These abuses are not characteristic of Dakota values; indeed, these types of problems were virtually nonexistent in our society prior to invasion and conquest, as they would have been among most Indigenous societies. However, Indigenous Peoples around the world have responded similarly to the forces of colonialism, and, in that regard, our responses are utterly predictable and normal. Now, if we are to meaningfully resist the oppressive forces to which we are subjected, it is necessary to understand and rechannel the colonized responses into something positive for our nations. In his "Model of the Effects of Colonialism," Sahnish/Hidatsa scholar Michael Yellow Bird describes the colonized adaptation to which many Indigenous Peoples have succumbed. In the "Social" area, he points out that one aspect of this is "Low or no cultural gender role training or rites of passage." The antidote then, as he points out, is to "implement community-driven gender rites of passage."[3] This would obviously also be applicable for the gender-role training that a society like the Omaha could provide.

The other society made mention of in this section is the Iwakci Okodakiciye, or the "Scalp-Dance Society" as Riggs would define it. Uŋkaŋna discussed this society as predominantly a women's organization, with some male involvement, especially with male singers and drummers. Written sources on the topic also describe both male and female participation, with women playing the prominent role in the actual dancing. Wilson Wallis provides a more detailed description of the society based on accounts he collected and his own observations. In an account received from a man who was at least a hundred years old, Wallis told of the origin of the society as such: "A medicineman dreamed that they would kill many Chippewa and that afterwards they would hold a dance. They went to fight, all returned the following morning, and brought scalps. In the afternoon, they began the dance. They secured a long oak pole, painted it red, and tied scalps to its top. This pole is called *tca wakan*. The dance was held out in the open."[4] He also comments that in the era when he observed the dance, the male members were not the men who had obtained the scalps but rather their sons and grandsons. This helps to explain the decline of the Iwakci

Okodakiciye. If scalps are no longer collected, it is hard to maintain a social organization grounded in the celebration of taking enemy scalps. However, in light of Eastman's comments cited earlier on warfare among the Dakota, it seems that prior to invasion the taking of scalps would have been unheard of, and even killing in warfare would have been extremely rare. Either this was a society created within a limited historical context, or when the taking of scalps became more common, a society was adapted to accommodate this new practice.

Riggs also highlights the scalps as a central component of the iwakicipi. He describes the dance as one which "follows the bringing home of the scalps of their enemies. A circle is formed, on one side of which stand the young men, with their bodies painted, with their feathers in their heads, and their drums, rattles, and other instruments of music in their hands; while on the other side stand the young women in their best attire, carrying the scalp or scalps stretched on a hoop."[5] However, as Riggs also points out, the term *Iwakici* may more broadly mean *to dance for one, as in praise of one*.[6]

Perhaps this broader definition would allow for the eventual revitalization of the society. Recovery of this knowledge will be an important task for Dakota women in future years, but equally important might be a consciously critical assessment of what aspects of the former society are of value and how it might be adapted for beneficial purposes today. It might be decided, for example, that the usual context for enemy scalp-taking no longer exists but that dancing in praise of one's male relatives is worth resuscitating. While our male relatives today participate in military combat, it is usually in the context of fighting for the U.S. or Canadian governments rather than in defense of the Dakota Oyate. Thus, as a nation of people we may need to reexamine what kind of warrior actions are worthy of celebration and praise by the women of an Iwakci Okodakiciye.

The Scalp Dance Society is not the only tradition in need of examination and recovery. For example, there is a current movement among the Dakota to revitalize the traditional rites of passage into womanhood. In recent years women from the Pine Ridge reservation have been teaching women from the Upper Sioux community about these practices, helping them to rejuvenate traditions lost to the Eastern Dakota after the 1862 war. This indicates a growing understanding of the importance of Dakota traditions and also offers a vital and viable means of engaging in decolonization practices.

In another discussion of Dakota practices, the subject of women in the society was approached when Uŋkaŋna discussed his first wife and the Dakota tradition of the giving and buying of women, or the trading of women. He mentions this in his account, suggesting that this is how he came to be married the first time, though not providing any specific details. A comment on this must be made, as many non-Dakota might interpret this as evidence of the inferiority of women in Dakota society. While there was a clearly defined sexual division of labor in our traditional culture, all people within the society were valued for their contributions, though those contributions differed according to gender.

Nonnative observers of Dakota culture sometimes mischaracterized the relationship between genders, stating that women "lead worse than a dog's life" or that a Dakota wife "is subject to all the whims of her husband."[7] One Waśicu observer claimed that Dakota women were nothing more than men's property with no power whatsoever. He even goes so far as to suggest that the men could kill their wives at their discretion, without fear of public protest. And, if he killed another man's wife, he was usually required only to compensate the husband in some manner.[8] To anyone familiar with Dakota culture, this seems a ridiculous assertion. As Dakota men are responsible for the protection of their female relatives, mistreatment of a Dakota woman would be impossible without severe backlash from her male relatives. Furthermore, the killing of another Dakota, by Dakota accounts, has always been a crime of the most serious offense. Deloria comments that "the murder of a fellow Dakota was a crime punishable either through immediate reprisal by the kinsmen of the slain or a resort to the ancient ordeals, supervised by the council" (the "ancient ordeals" being nearly impossible to survive).[9]

Indeed, Dakota sources reveal a different perspective regarding the status of women in Dakota society. For example, concerning the privileges held by Dakota women, Eastman states: "The wife did not take the name of her husband nor enter his clan, and the children belonged to the clan of the mother. All of the family property was held by her, descent was traced in the maternal line, and the honor of the house was in her hands."[10] Thus women maintained a secure status within society, regardless of their relationship to men. Even if men from their immediate household were no longer available to provide food for them, societal structure allowed for other men from the village to help them. Unlike in Western society, where homes have typically been the property of the men, in Dakota society women maintained considerable influence over everything that happened in the home. Because all the household possessions belonged to the woman, she never had to worry economically about losing her basic material goods with the loss or death of a husband. Furthermore, because children belonged to the lineage of their mother, women were not dependent on men for children to be recognized as lineage members. There was never a fear that if a woman left her husband that her children could not be claimed.

Perhaps the most important defense of the status of Dakota women in our society is the reverence shown to the White Buffalo Calf Woman, a major spiritual figure for the entire Oyaṯe. She is a wakaŋ being, regarded with tremendous veneration as bringer of the sacred pipe and the seven ceremonies of the Oyaṯe. William Powers points out from an anthropological perspective that the White Buffalo Calf Woman brought the sacred rites so that the people could live, changing into a buffalo as she departed the camp circle and "enunciating that the source of life and the source of food are inseparably one." Furthermore, in reference to several of the traditional narratives, he states: "The myths and metaphors in everyday usage underscore the fact that woman generates food, as she generates mankind."[11] Although we would not characterize the story of the White Buffalo Calf Woman as "myth," he is correct in asserting the connection between life itself and the powers of women, which ultimately creates a cultural consciousness that necessitates a profound respect for women.

The particular marriage custom mentioned by Uŋkaŋna Eli seems to be one of the most misunderstood institutions of the Dakoṯa. Reactions from the dominant society in regard to the practice of trading or buying women are usually quite negative, as if it were a degrading practice. For example, a former professor of mine in graduate school, a Waṡicu, female, feminist anthropologist, actually suggested to me that in instances when women do not object to practices such as this it is because they are so oppressed they cannot even recognize it. She felt as if it was her prerogative, indeed obligation, to free Third World women from their sexist societies and, of course, to impart to them the feminist ideals of gender equality from the Western world. She completely misinterpreted the status of women in Dakoṯa society and instead projected the inferior status of Euro-American women onto our Indigenous society. She could not conceive of a society in which women were highly regarded while gendered divisions remained, and therefore, in her eyes, that was an impossibility. Always serving as the backdrop of this colonialist mind-set is the assumption that Indigenous societies could not have developed a gender equality yet to be attained in the Western world.

For Dakoṯa women, the practice of buying women in marriage is far from degrading and is instead considered a high honor. One of the missionaries among the Dakoṯa, Samuel Pond, commented that "it was as disreputable for a young woman to become the wife of one who had not purchased her, as it is with us for a woman to cohabit with a man without the ceremony of marriage."[12] While Pond was attempting to understand the significance of this practice for the Dakoṯa, he also missed the mark. Deloria and Eastman paint a different picture of this practice. About the second marriage of Waterlily in her book by the same title, Deloria writes: "This time she married in the other sanctioned way, the way most women married who had good sense not to elope—

the way of mutual agreement openly declared."[13] Thus while being bought for marriage gave prestige to the bride, it was not the only way to acceptably enter a marriage. Eastman reinforces this perspective in his comment on marriage:

> We believed that two who love should be united in secret, before the public acknowledgement of their union, and should taste their apotheosis alone with nature. The betrothal might or might not be discussed and approved by the parents, but in either case it was customary for the young pair to disappear into the wilderness, there to pass some days or weeks in perfect seclusion and dual solitude, afterward returning to the village as man and wife. An exchange of presents and entertainments between two families usually followed, but the nuptial blessing was given by the High Priest of God, the most reverend and holy Nature.[14]

It is clear from the quotes of Deloria and Eastman that the buying of women was not as widespread or necessary to a woman's reputation as Pond suggests, but it certainly did occur and was considered an honor. In a culture where women are revered and celebrated for their contributions to society, this particular tradition of buying women for marriage represents nothing shameful or objectifying. Indeed, the man who risked public humiliation by so forthrightly declaring his interest in a woman might face more disgrace in this process. On the other hand, a woman might be very much relieved to be asked for her hand in marriage by someone who had demonstrated himself as a successful hunter and provider and/or with the family support to pay a handsome amount.

In this instance, Uŋkaŋna does not discuss what he paid or even if he paid for his first wife, but this might be inferred from his mentioning of it as the lead-in to a discussion of his marriage to her and then his discussion of their breakup. Ironically, after they legalized their marriage in the Waṡicu way, their marriage began to fall apart. As he then returned to a Dakota way of thinking, it sounds as if he went through a period of depression, even spending a period of time in jail for nonsupport. However, his family situation improved when he married Kuŋṡi Edna, and they remained together until he passed away.

After discussing his marriage to Kuŋṡi Edna, he makes an important comment about the conflicting worlds of which he was a part:

> **Haw heced uŋkicaġapi, heuŋ etaŋhaŋ dehantu ekta ouŋ num ikoyak wauŋ.**
>
> Yes, that is how we were raised, for that reason at this time I live in two worlds.

The literal translation of the last portion is "I am tied to two ways of living," or "I am tied to two ways of knowing." Since one does not usually tie oneself, the implication is that the external forces help to bind an individual to ways of being or ways of living. Because of Uŋkaŋna's Dakota upbringing, the teachings so deeply ingrained in him would remain a driving force in how he would live his own life. But implicit in this statement is also the recognition that there was no escaping the other world, constructed from the teachings and values of the Wašicu. However, rather than becoming dismissive of Dakota teachings after being exposed more thoroughly to the non-Indigenous world, his convictions about the importance of Dakota traditions seemed to deepen. An important point here is that he did not reject all the Wašicu teachings; rather, he selectively chose those that seemed of most value to him while maintaining Dakota traditions as well.

In the last commentary in this section, rather than focusing on the teachings he did receive, Uŋkaŋna wistfully focuses on those experiences he was denied because of age and circumstance, both in the Wašicu world and in the Dakota world. In the Wašicu world he missed out on participating in both World War I and World War II. In the Dakota world he missed what he felt was his window of opportunity to participate in important ceremonial traditions including the inipi and the wiwaŋyak wacipi.

He begins by relaying information about women's connection to the inipi, or purification ceremony, often referred to in English as the sweat lodge ceremony. While he never participated in an inipi because of the loss of the ceremonial leaders by the time he came of age, clearly he received teachings about it and felt there were some important messages that needed to be transmitted. His comment that "wiŋyaŋ inip šni" ("women do not sweat" or, more appropriately, "women do not participate in the sweat lodge ceremony") is an important, if controversial, teaching. Uŋkaŋna did not say this for the purpose of casting judgment on women who might participate in sweat lodge ceremonies today or, for that matter, on spiritual leaders who conduct sweat lodge ceremonies for women. This was clarified in a later conversation with him in which he stated that he had heard some spiritual leaders have even received visions about opening up the sweat lodge ceremonies to women and non-Dakota people. At that time he expressed the attitude that it is important to respect another person's vision and that he has no right to question what others do. However, in broaching this subject, his intent was to transmit the teachings he received as a means for us to educate ourselves and others about the place of this ceremony in traditional life.

Prior to colonization—when the entire Dakota cultural system was intact—women did not need to participate in what might be called a consciously constructed (even if divinely given) purification ceremony. After menstruation, women were naturally cleansed of any impurities with each cycle of the moon and essentially made pure again. During menstruation, women were relieved of daily household responsibilities so that they could spend time alone and isolated from the rest of the community. The terms *išnati* (*she lives alone*) or *iš-natipi* (*they live alone* to refer to the lodge where menstruating women would stay) are used in reference to this period of isolation. This solitude would allow the menstruating woman time for prayer and meditation. Women are deemed too powerful during this time to be around men, especially their ceremonial, hunting, and war accoutrements, which might be rendered impotent or even harmful upon exposure. However, as men have no natural bodily mechanism for achieving this purity through a natural cycle, the inipi takes on particular significance. While in contemporary times women obviously still maintain this natural cleansing process, rarely do they have the familial and societal support to seek solitude and meditation during menstruation. Thus the inipi in recent years has become a means for women to purify themselves with prayer and ceremony. Ideally, as Dakota people engage in the decolonization process and restore the communal structures that once supported the entire village, these practices can also be restored.

Similar to his experience with the inipi, the timing for participation in the wiwaŋyak wacipi (sundance) also passed him by. The ceremony ceased at Sioux Valley during his childhood, as it had decades before in Minnesota. By the time it was revitalized, he felt himself too old to participate, but he did have the fortune of seeing his grandchildren sundancing. Though he noticed some changes in the way the ceremony was performed, based on teachings he had received previously versus what he observed in later life, Uŋkaŋna felt the purpose of the dance had remained consistent as well as important.

These personal narratives provide more insight into Uŋkaŋna's worldview and provide a strong basis for developing decolonizing strategies. His own mother's opposition to his participation in the colonizer's education system provides an example of a culture of resistance existent among the Dakota. While still participating briefly in the Wašicu educational institutions and being exposed to the patriotic influences of that education, clearly the foundation his mother built with him helped to shape his own choices in adulthood. Deeply committed to Dakota traditions, Uŋkaŋna also did not deny the reality of living in two worlds. Ultimately, however, the stories he wanted transmitted are those that illuminate the importance of Dakota traditions, not just as remnants of a lost past but as bits of information that will help future Dakota survive and flourish.

8. Wahokuŋkiyapi (They Provide Guidance)

Among Dakota people it is common knowledge that scientifically unexplainable events occur frequently and that some individuals are gifted in their abilities to facilitate these occurrences themselves or to interact with spiritual entities who participate in them. No attempt is made to explain them in scientific terms or to verify their occurrence, rather they are accepted as mysterious and left to the realm of those things never completely understood. *Ṭaku wakaŋ*, or *things that are mysterious*, are elements of the next set of stories. This first set of stories is revealing of Dakota healing practices, including the role that the *iŋyaŋ škaŋ škaŋ* can play and the faith Uŋkaŋna had in them.

While the *ṭak škaŋ škaŋ*, or *traveling stones*, can play a significant role for those medicine people engaging in healing practices, they may also be called on to help protect loved ones. They are spiritual beings embodied in physical matter who maintain their own distinct personalities and agendas. These stories provide valuable insight into the Dakota relationship to the past and how a sense of Dakota identity is created. The next section in this chapter includes two accounts about the *iŋyaŋ škaŋ škaŋ*[1] when they helped in the protection of and communication with men who had gone off to war. The first narrative describes the experiences of John Duta, who was accompanied by a stone in World War I, and the second narrative similarly relays Peter White Cloud's experience in World War II.

The final story in this chapter relates the origin of the *waehdepi*, the ceremonial setting or dedication of food. This story begins with the description of two men with a very close bond between them. After years of sharing meals together in friendship, even after one of the men died there was the desire by the other to maintain this sharing of food. The spirit of his friend arrived to partake of his offering, and a tradition of the setting out of food had begun. This story offers another example of the importance of spiritual messengers to the Dakota as well as the importance of nurturing and feeding the spiritual beings around us.

---

1. The terms *iŋyaŋ škaŋ škaŋ* and *ṭaku škaŋ škaŋ* are used interchangeably here to describe the *moving stones or traveling stones*. *Ṭaku škaŋ škaŋ* may more literally be translated as *that which moves*, but is clearly a reference in these stories to the stones. *Iŋyaŋ* is the Dakota term for *stone* or *rock*, so accompanied with the *škaŋ škaŋ*, which translates as *to stir, move about, or change place*, it literally means *moving stone*.

Ehaŋna Woyakapi Izaptaŋ (The Fifth Historical Narrative)
WAPIYA (HEALING)

Uŋkaŋ taŋhaŋ waya waŋ ye he hi k̇a ṭokiya ṭaŋhaŋ.
Here the one I have as a brother-in-law, he came from somewhere.

Winyaŋ mitawa ded napek̇ de ṭokeca aġuyap k̇aġa okihi śni.
There was something wrong with my wife's hand and she couldn't make bread.

Tiyopak̇ yuġaŋk̇[2] napek̇ hena owas deced iyeġa, ṭak̇uda ecuŋ okihi śni.
She couldn't open the door with her hand, the hand was all gnarled and she couldn't do anything.

Uŋkaŋ he wicaśta wapiye do he Little Crow, Willie Little Crow, eciyapi.
And so a man called Little Crow, Willie Little Crow, was a medicine man.

Uŋkaŋ he wicaśtak̇ Prince Isle, no Sasketoon heciya uŋ.
And so that man was over at Prince Isle, no, Sasketoon.

Waśicu winuḣca waŋ kci uŋ.
He was with a Waśicu woman.

K̇aŋyehaŋ iś wapiya he, hehan tawicu iś wayawa wicakiye.
As for him, he lives as a medicine man and then, as for his wife, she is a teacher.

Uŋkaŋ okpaza iwaŋka uŋkaŋ he ṭak̇u messengers wicayuhek̇ he, ṭak̇ śk̇aŋ śk̇aŋ eyap çe ...
And when it got dark he laid down and here what messengers he had "that which moves" they say ...

He ek̇śe he niye ṭożaŋ sdodyaye, de miciŋk̇si sdodye śni, k'a nak̇uŋ iś sdodye śni nacece tka ṭak̇ śk̇aŋ śk̇aŋ—those are little spirits—hena wahokuŋ-wicakiyapi wowicakiyak̇api k̇a awaŋwicayak̇api.
As for you, my niece, you know this, my son doesn't know and also, as for her, she probably doesn't know, but ṭak̇ śk̇aŋ śk̇aŋ—those are little spirits—those provide guidance and counseling and they take care of them.

Waŋżi iśṭimmak̇ ecan i k'a heya k̇eyapi, "Waŋ, de niṭankci de ṭok̇iya iyoṭaŋhaŋ iyekiya do," eya k̇eyapi.
While he slept one went and said, they said, "Oh, your younger sister is suffering somewhere," he said they said.

"Wayazaŋk̇e teḣiya iyoṭaŋ iyekiya ecan de ṭak̇ce śni ded nakanak̇ahe de.
"She's sick and really suffering while here you sit without a care.

---

2. *Yuġaŋk̇* is a contraction of *yuġaŋ okihi śni* in this instance, but only the *k̇* from *okihi* was audible.

"Waŋ, ekta ye ka ed etuŋwaŋ wo.
    "Go there and look after her.
"Eya iyopemaye do," eye.
    "Saying that, he got after me," he said.
He, atkuku hena takukciyapi heciya taŋhaŋ taŋkśi yek hehan on top of that, he, he was a twin, he had a twin sister.
    They were related to one another from his father's side, she was his younger sister, and then on top of that, he was a twin, he had a twin sister.
Uŋkaŋ heced, he lost his sister.
    And so he lost his sister.
Uŋkaŋ deciya hi uŋkaŋ de wiŋyaŋ mitawa taŋkśi hed uŋkaŋ he heceh wayake heced nuŋpa owicaŋ he, taŋkśi ye he.
    And when he came over here he saw my wife as a younger sister twice, one right after the other, he took her as a younger sister.[3]
Ekśa he napek sani ekśe he wahpe kadye iś taku ecuŋ dehan iśto ake deciya taŋhaŋ yazaŋ hena iś nuŋske hena de uŋ aġuyapi kaġe taku hena.
    And so she can heat the tea with the other hand, she can do things, so now again this one on this side hurts, she makes bread and other things.
Hed ehan Carlisle ded taŋhaŋ Little Crow tawicu he wayawicakiyaka hed tipi do, Hohe tipi hed.
    At that time at Carlisle here my brother-in-law, Little Crow, his wife, she taught and lived there among the Assiniboine.
Saskatchewan ipa, Hohe taŋhaŋ hi.
    They went to Saskatchewan and from the Assiniboine he came here.
Hi ka he de wahpe owicawakaśtaŋ de tak śpaŋyeda kik hena nuŋske owahnake wowicawak'u.

---

3. The "one right after the other" refers to him taking Uŋkaŋna's wife as a sister, in a second way, right after Little Crow's twin sister passed away, thus seeing her as a younger sister twice. This is an example of the meaning being clear when spoken in Dakota, but as it is translated into English the meaning becomes blurred. Uŋkaŋna is referring to the Dakota kinship ties that include a closer relationship with those considered in English to be "extended family." For example, a Dakota sees each of his/her father's brothers as a father and his/her father's sisters as aunts. Her children would be his/her cousins, but their father's brother's children would be his/her siblings. So in the Dakota way, Edna, Uŋkaŋna's wife, would be the sister of this medicine man, Willie Little Crow, because their fathers were related. Also, in Dakota families, if someone loses a close relative, a form of adoption may take place so that another person can step in and fulfill that role (for example, my father, Chris Mato Nunpa, adopted Uŋkaŋna as a father in 1988, to fill that important role in his life). In this case because Willie Little Crow had lost his twin sister, Edna was replacing that position in the family for him. Thus, they were related twice.

He came and I poured them tea and what she had cooked up, this I put in something and fed them.

Uŋkaŋ waŋna ayaśtaŋp hehan, "Ḣeyaṭa uŋkiyataŋḳapte."

And so when they finished now, then "We'll go sit back."

Hehan eye, "Haw Taŋkśi, ṭaku waŋżi uŋ dewahi do, ociciyaḳe kṭe do."

Then he said, "Hello, Taŋkśi, I came here for one thing, I will tell you."

"Haŋ," eye.

"Yes," she said.

"Hiŋhaŋ de wahmuŋḳa uŋkaŋ he ṭaḳ śḳaŋ śḳaŋ he wicabdu he waŋżi iyopemaye koyaŋna uŋmaśi do," eya.

"Last night I was trapping and ṭaḳ śḳaŋ śḳaŋ that I have, one got after me and told me to come right away," he said.

"Hehan waniyazaŋḳa ḳeye ḳa omakiyake do.

"Then, it told me that you were sick.

"Uŋkaŋ woyazaŋ nitawa de, de uŋ ṭaḳu uŋ oniciya kṭa he au maśi hece he de awahi do.

"And so, he told me to bring something to help you for this sickness, and so for that I brought it.

"Hecic'u kṭe do."

"I will give that to you."

"Haŋ," eye.

"Yes," she said.

Haw he de kokadaḳ de de Dakoṭa peżihuṭa de wicak'upi ḳin de ḳa de heca de eṭaŋhaŋ icahi de Waśicu eçupa uŋḳaġapi do.

This little box, they gave this medicine to the Dakoṭa and from that the Waśicu took and mixed it and made it.

Hena alfalfa tablets heca.

Those are alfalfa tablets.

Uŋkaŋ he he deced cicahi do, de two hundred uŋ do.

And so, this is what I brought you, there are two hundred here.

De waŋżi do, de koka dusota ḳaŋhaŋ waŋna ṭokeca, nuŋpa iyamni se dusota ḳaŋhaŋ iyeced iniyaye kṭe do.

This is one, when you use up the box it will be different now, like about the second and maybe the third [box], when you use those up you'll be back to the way you were.

De cic'uceḣ kiksuya wo.

Remember I gave this to you.

Heṭaŋhaŋ uŋ waśtenic'iye kṭe do, eye ḳa hehan wamayaḳe ḳa "taŋhaŋ, ṭaku ociciyaḳe kṭe do," eye.

From that you will get well he said, and then he looked at me and he said, "brother-in-law, I want to tell you something."

Saskatchewan ed Moseman hed eceeda de ṭaku ḳiŋ yuke do.

There at Moseman, Saskatchewan, is the only place they have that.

He hehan deciya north ekṭa Dauphin, eyapi do, heciya naḳuŋ he ṭaku yuke do.

They have them north of there in Dauphin, they said, they also have it over there.

Ṭohiŋni Dauphin hena ekṭa ye śni nacece ḳaiś heya omakiyaḳe.

He probably never goes to Dauphin, yet that was the way he told me.

Eya heced ye ḳa waŋna de yusoteḳ kṭe hehan heceŋna I was driving a school bus that Saturday.

That was what he said and so she was already close to using them up, and I was driving a school bus that Saturday.

He ecan waŋna tiyopa hena iyehdugaŋ okihi naḳuŋ.

But now she was also able to open her own doors.

Waŋca ake num awahdi heciya ṭaŋhaŋ.

And so I brought back two at once from over there.

It's a long trip, you go over the mountains and it's on the other side.

Haw awahdi ḳa uŋkaŋ nuŋske uŋ hehan, pretty soon, owas asni aye ḳa waŋna eye i naḳuŋ tiyopak iyeyugaŋ taŋkad iyaye ḳa ihnunah tiyopak ed wokipaye ibdabde kṭe uŋkaŋ naḳuŋ ważuyaŋke, she was doing beadwork.

Yes, I brought it and then she used it, pretty soon all of her aches and pains were healing, now she could even open the door and go outside and I just happened to go through the door and here she was doing beadwork.

Aġuyapi kaġe eced ye ḳa nu waśṭe.

She went with her bread-making and then it was good.

Haw heceŋna ehaŋna witaŋtaŋka waŋ Uŋkṭomi[4] eyap çe he ḳaŋpceḳ hehan he nayahuŋpi çe nacece.

You probably have heard the elders talk about a proud one called Uŋkṭomi.

Ee se waŋna he de miciŋkśi he waŋżi arthritis ecece ośice uŋ decaeś, hecak eya taŋhaŋ ahi uŋkaŋ de wiŋyaŋ mitawa asni do, epe.

Just like that one of my sons was bad with arthritis, "Some of that my brother-in-law brought here and my wife was healed," I said.

Haw he uŋkaŋ he haw waśṭeye do he ṭukṭed etu owakiyaḳa, alfalfa tablets, eyapi do.

---

4. Uŋkṭomi, as a reminder, is a spiritual being as well as a trickster figure within Dakota culture. Uŋkṭomi is always getting into trouble in the many Dakota stories about him, sometimes from imitating or impersonating others.

Yes, and so that is good, I told him where it was at, they call it alfalfa tablets.

Waŋżi opetuŋ iyuṭe ḳaeś owa icu śni.

He bought one to try, but he didn't take it all.

Haw heced hehan he he ecan de miciŋkśi de tawicu (wiwawaġa) he nakuŋ iża arthritis ecece do.

And so then in the meantime, my son, his wife (the daughter-in-law) she also got arthritis.

He iś de, my wife, Waŋbdi Sḳa etaŋhaŋ he he iś he he tużaŋ ku he.

The one here that is my wife, she is from White Eagle, and that one there is her niece.

Haw he de waŋżi opetuŋ ahdi ḳa haw de tużaŋ de uŋ asnimayaŋpi ye heced de heced iyuṭa niża.

He bought and brought one home and, this niece, they healed me with this and so you try this also.

Haw heced iye, iyee k'u hee uŋ.

And so, the one that she gave her was the one that she used.

Takoś he asni ḳa de Uŋkṭomi iye ded ṭaḳu wicak'u iyeced waecuŋ śni.

Daughter-in-law was healed and with Uŋkṭomi here, what he gave them didn't work the way he thought.[5]

Hece medicine man he ṭuwe de peżihuṭa waŋżi k'upi ḳiŋhaŋ he he he k'upi he he iyeceṭu kṭe.

And so when the medicine man gives medicine to someone, that which was given him would be right.

Ehaŋna Woyaḳapi Iśakpe (The Sixth Historical Narrative)

Back when I was going to the school there, one-year school, the second term bdek'u he, a bigger boy kicked me on the shins and broke my leg.

Back when I was going to the school there, one-year school, the second term that I was going, a bigger boy kicked me on the shins and broke my leg.

Haw heced he ehan taŋhaŋ waya waŋ hed, he was an interpreter there and was working for the Indian agent.

And so at that time a brother-in-law of mine there, he was an interpreter there and was working for the Indian agent.

He picked me up and the Indian agent brought me down to dekśi waya waŋ, Waŋ Duṭa eciyapi, he wapiya ed uŋḳayapi.

---

5. A reference to the medicine Little Crow gave them.

He picked me up and the Indian agent brought me down over here to an uncle of mine named Waŋ Duṭa, a medicine man, they brought us to him.
Haw de wicaoȟa ded uŋ kṭa nacece tḳa, tḳa heced nu, ṭaŋyaŋ naȟ'uŋ kṭe śni ḳa ihuŋniyaŋ.
This son-in-law will probably be here but he would not hear it well all the way through.[6]
Haw he waśiçuŋ ia wahociciyakapṭe do, iyute ibdute kṭe do.
I will send it to you in Waśicu, I am going to try to do that.
I'm going to try to translate.[7]
I'm going to try to tell my stories in a language that we can all understand, heṭaŋhaŋś ded de u śni.
I'm going to try to tell my stories in a language that we can all understand, he doesn't come here.[8]
When I broke my leg my brother-in-law brought me down to my uncle. He felt around my legs. He is a medicine man and he told my brother-in-law to bring in a piece of stick, a flat stick, and he got him to pull my leg and set it back in place and put some poultice, or some medicine, on it and wrapped rags around it. In about a week or so he was looking after it, he says, "You're okay now." I got up and walked and I played a lot of soccer and hockey and baseball since.

CMN: In one week?

In one week, yeah. I didn't start to play and run around with it because I was limping yet.

Ehaŋna Woyaḳapi Iśakowiŋ (The Seventh Historical Narrative)

Another story that I want you to take with you—you're taping, eh?
Ṭaḳu waŋżi nakuŋ ociciyaḳapṭe do.
Also, I'm going to tell you one thing.
I'm going to do that in English too, as well, so we can all at the same time hear what I am talking about. I guess you can understand me. My translation may not be that accurate, but I'll do the best I can. We had an Indian agent come out from Ottawa to do fieldwork, and he came to our reserve, and his wife took sick.

---

6. This is a reference to Scott, *wicaoȟa* being a term used to address a son-in-law, or in this case a grandson-in-law. He means that Scott might not understand the Dakoṭa even though he was present.
7. Uŋḳaŋna shifts to English here, providing his own translation.
8. "He" may refer to his uncle or brother-in-law here.

Before that he lost a girl and the girl was buried here. He had two girls. And, of course, somebody as usual, they told him from Ottawa that I was the chief here, that I was very sports-minded, and he was also sports-minded, so the Ottawa figured that I could get along with him. Well, so they sent him down here and his wife took sick. We had about seven or eight medicine people here, like my uncle, but they had all died and there was only one old woman left at that time, that she could still doctor. And he took her to the doctor—he took her to two or three different doctors, but she was slowly going down. So, by that time they moved out from this agency and moved into Virden, which is more central to Pipestone and Virden, so they moved right plumb in the middle of town there. They got an office in there. They came up to my place one day and they said, "Eli," he says, "I'm going to ask you something." He said, "Some of the people here had told me that you have a medicine woman here that might be able to help." This was in the fall. "That might be able to help my wife, that she might be able to help."

"Yeah, we have one, but I don't know whether she's going to be able to help. She's not here right now—she's over in Elkhorn," I said.

"Oh well, they told me you'd know how to go about it and we are desperate for some help because she's going down."

"Okay, I'll take you to Oak Lake, or to Elkhorn." On the way I says, "You buy some tobacco." So I went down there, took that tobacco down. I get out of that pickup—he had a pickup—"Get out and come with me."

"Well you know what I want."

"Come on with me, it's your wife that is sick, it is not my wife."

So he came out and he says, "Here is the tobacco."

I says, "I'm not the medicine man, you give it to her and I'll interpret. She doesn't know a word of English and she never went to school."

She was fairly old then. That's back in the sixties when he came along. They were sitting out there at the tent, you know they were out doing fall work, seasonal work, putting up stalks so they can thrash them then. There were not too many combines in them days. That's the way they make their money.

"Haŋ śic'e ṭak uŋ yahi he?"

"Hello brother-in-law, why did you come here?"

"Haw de he de wicaṡta de Waśicu ķiŋ de tawicu he wayazaŋķe do.

"Hello, the wife of this Waśicu man is sick.

"His wife is sick heced haw de opaġi nicahi caŋdi de he."

"His wife is sick and so he brought you tobacco for pipe-filling."

"Haŋ," eye.

"Yes," she said.

"**Haw heced iyotaŋke ka haw caŋdi he k'u wo.**"
   "And so, sit down and give her the tobacco."
"Give her that tobacco, give her tobacco."
She took out her pipe and opened up the tobacco. She smoked.
"**Haŋ, tuktetu he de?**"
   "So, where is this at?"
"**Haw de de, Virden ed otuŋwe hed tiwatayapi ded ti he, hecetu.**"
   "In the town of Virden there they make their home."
"**Tośta ake uŋkaŋ nihdapa ake uŋkaŋ niyupta do.**"
   "Presently we will take you back with us, we will bring you again."
"**Haŋ,**" eye.
   "Yes," she said.
So she got in the pickup there between the two of us. And I was sitting there and we were talking on the way home. He dropped us off where they lived from the middle of town.

He says, "I'm going to the office, somebody might want something and they are going to come there and I won't be there, so, ah, how long is it going to take?" One thing he keeps trying to ask me is, "How much is she going to charge?"

"She's not going to charge you nothing. You have already given her tobacco and that's why the Creator give her that gift, to be able to look after the sick people. You think, give what you think it's worth. It's up to you. If you want to give to her that's fine and dandy, she'll accept it. But, she's not going to charge you for it."

"How long is it going to take, about two hours?"

"No," I said, "it might take about half an hour or so."

"Well then, I'll be back in about an hour and I'll take her back. I've got to go to the bank, if you tell me how much this is going to . . ."

"Man, you're worrying about the money, worry about your wife for a change, hope that and pray that she gets better."

So she set up her altar in front of, on the sofa like that, where the sick woman was laying down, eh? She says she gets up and around but this time she was laying down. So in front of her she set up her altar—sweetgrass, and her little, what do you call that thing, gourd.

Hena kihnake ka hece canuŋpa, caŋdi okpaġi ehnake etuŋwaŋ, ed etuŋwaŋ waŋka waŋke.

   She set something for herself, she filled the pipe with tobacco, set it down and sat and gazed at it.

She was looking and watching and she closed her eyes. She started praying to our Creator. I can understand what she is saying.

Before she started she said, "We as Indian people don't go by names. We commute to one another through our relations. So now, sic'e, this wašicu winuȟca de icepaŋši owaye kte."

So now, brother-in-law, I will take this Wašicu woman as a cousin.

"Haw," epe.

"Yes," I said.

"Haw heced he wacekiya Ṭak Wakaŋ icepaŋši taŋcaŋ uŋšpa iyehaŋtu šni ye," wacekiya.

"Ṭak Wakaŋ, part of my cousin's body is not functioning like it should," she prayed.

Wacekiya ka haw yuštaŋ, hduštaŋ ka dowaŋ ka hehaŋ ŋakuŋ wacekiya.

She prayed and she finished, she finished and sang and then she prayed again.

Haw ayaštaŋ ka hehaŋ de hehaŋ miye omakiyake he eciŋ etaŋhaŋš he okiyake kaeš, she can't speak.

She stopped and then, then she told me later, because even if she were to tell her, she can't speak [English].

She can't understand, so I had to act as an interpreter.

"Icepaŋši haw ṭaku ṭoked ocicyaka hecihan, . . ." eye.

"Cousin, if whatever I told you, . . ." she said.

Anaȟoptaŋ make ake.

I sat listening again.

"Caŋtek de kaŋ obe owi ṭonakca iyanihdi niye.

"The heart has many different veins that are connected to you.

"Uŋkaŋ he waŋżi, waŋżi na obdute ka taŋyaŋ waecuŋ šni heuŋ etaŋhaŋ waš'ak ye ṭaku waecanuŋ yaškaŋ kiŋ hena ocib kutkiya ye."

And here one, one is plugged and isn't working well, for that reason, more and more you are getting weaker when you do things that are difficult."

Haw heced wabdaka he ociciyake ye.

Yes, I tell you, that is what I saw.

Haw heced ayaštaŋ ka canuŋpa hehaŋ Mrs. Ballington he owakiyake.

She was quiet and smoked, then I told Mrs. Ballington that.

What she said was that she was telling you that of course you don't understand but she was telling you that, well, your problem was that there's a lot of veins, at least to your heart, which feeds your heart, to function all parts of your body. One of those veins is getting plugged and it's not working right, it's why you're not strong enough to get going and vacuum and do different things, you're coming down all the time.

Her face lit up and she said, "Yes," she says, "I was in Brandon yesterday and I went to the doctor and they took x-rays of me." She said, "Look up there on the cupboard, you see that pill box? They gave me that box of pills. They told me the same thing and I was to take one of those to thin out my blood so it would circulate. I was quite sure that the old lady didn't phone that doctor and had no communication between them, but the x-ray showed the same thing that she said over here."

So that's who I thought ihakab ṭuwe uŋ wahokuŋ uŋkiyapṭa hena, that's who I thought they were then.

>So that's who I thought, those who came behind us direct us, that's who I thought they were then.

And then we were going back. On the way back he was driving and she was sitting in between and "Haw de haŋka de nu peźihuṭa heca duha hecihan?" hepe.

>On the way back he was driving and she was sitting in between and I said, "Is it so that you have this kind of medicine?"

He kci ṭohaŋyaŋ wohdake ka hehan etaŋhaŋś he when we speak English she doesn't understand so, "I'm quite sure she has some medicine that might help her but it's up to you to ask her for it."

>I talked with her for a while and then, it didn't matter, when we speak English she doesn't understand so, "I'm quite sure she has some medicine that might help her but it's up to you to ask her for it."

"Ask her for it and, how much is she going to charge?"

I says, "You give her what you think it's worth." Haw heced, "Haw hececa heca bduhe ye hena ake, haŋ de ṭokśṭa de uŋkip kiŋhaŋ ecin kadwakiye kṭe."

>And so, "Yes, I do have those kind, later when we get back I'll warm it up for her."

Heced, but I had to say a lie there.

>So, but I had to say a lie there.

I'm not a Catholic, but I'm confessing now. I turned around and asked, I told the old lady that, that Indian agent wants you to make some medicine for his wife which I put him wise to it, and then I got to reverse it around. Yeah, I said, she's got medicine I think, to give it to you. Okay, she's going to make some medicine for her when we get there.

So when we got there we stopped. To her daughter, who's still around, says, "You go back there, up in that tree is my medicine bag," she said.

Wiŋyaŋ taŋkad yaŋkapi timahed ded uṗ.

>The women who were sitting outside came into the house.

Hena peźihuṭa hee kiŋ he yuhe, yuhuŋke śni waś'ake śni, that's why they have to have that medicine feast now and again.

>That medicine that she had was weak, it wasn't strong, that's why they have that medicine feast now and again.

Heced taŋkad otkekiye aku ka heced ahdi, she opened it up.

And so, she hung it outside, she brought it, brought it back home and she opened it up.

Etaŋhaŋ taku icu ka, "Mni uŋge huwe iyayap," cuŋwiŋtku iyaye ka she got some water in a pan and put it on the stove, water, and put something in it.

From it she took something and then, "Go fetch some water," her daughter went and she got some water in a pan and put it on the stove, water, and put something in it.

He said, "How long is this going to take?"

"Well, I don't know, it will take about ten, fifteen, twenty minutes."

"Well let's go to town and have some coffee."

So even while doctoring his wife he got to have that coffee too. So we went and had coffee, came back, she had a quart sealer, oh just about to the top. She had this all strained and just the pure liquid in there. She says, she has to drink a little bit of that, but she's going to have to take four of those.

"When she finishes you can come back and I'll make you some more again. I can't make the four at once."

But, she says, she is to finish four of them. So I brought it, she brought it over and then gave it to him so he puts it in the center and took off for Virden.

"Oh, I forgot to ask her how much she wanted for it." That's before we left.

I said, "You give her what you think."

So he got out of the car and went over to the old lady and pulled out his billfold. I know he gave her some bills but I don't know whether it's a dollar, or ten dollars, or five dollars, or what it is, but he gave her some money anyway. I guess he gave her what he thought his wife was worth so then we got home. And this lady, the Indian agent's wife, in about four days she was supposed to finish that in four days, when she finished that she was doing her own vacuuming. And he came back, and he didn't come back no more.

And I said, "Did you get the other three that you're supposed to get?"

"No," he says, "I didn't go back because of the fact that she had some of her grandchildren down here. Doug was supposed to go to school, but she's keeping him over here and Indian Affairs, got after me, and wanted me to come down and get them kids into school. And I had an argument with her. She was working to get some decent clothes for those kids to go back to school in. So if I get mad, she got mad at me and so I don't want to go back there and talk to her again, get some more medicine."

Haw hena he nina iyomakpi šni, haw heced.

And so, I wasn't very happy.

"It does not matter, it's a gift that she's got from up above. And you didn't finish what she'd asked you and told you that you had to do, violated some of the rights that she's supposed to have. Maybe you think it will cost too much. I don't know, but you should come. They don't charge, she's going to give you those other three to complete, complete what she's working for is to cure that lady."

Anyway, they left the Indian nation, his wife left and went back to Ottawa. Three or four years later he sent me a note his wife passed away, four years. I often wonder, and I'm still wondering about whether if he did come back and got those three, other three, it might cure her, even more better.

CMN: She would have lived longer. Little Crow, what was he to Little Crow in Minnesota?

Yeah, there are two or three different Little Crows over there. One was a war leader and the others weren't. So this group had, they belonged to the other group. They are not the agitators. But there was one Little Crow who was related to that leader that we read about. I think his great-grandson, he's still in Fort Qu'Appelle.

CMN: There's about four of them, I think, down there in Minnesota that were called Little Crow.

Yeah, oh there's all kinds of stories.

CMN: Well, how are you feeling now?

Oh, I'm feeling all right. I'm just enjoying it and that's all there is to it.

Ehaŋna Woyaḳapi Iśahdoġaŋ (The Eighth Historical Narrative)
IŊYAŊ ŚḲAŊ ŚḲAŊ (MOVING STONES, TRAVELING STONES)

He Dakoṭak kci iciṭokċa iŋyaŋḳ de heceeda waawayaŋḳa heca.
There is a difference with the Dakota, the rock alone is the only caretaker.
Uŋkaŋ dekśi waya waŋ ḣtayed oiye obdaḳe.
Last evening I told about something an uncle of mine said.
"Uŋkaŋ he tawicuḳ waniceḳ hehan ake wiŋyaŋ waŋ ṭokċa kci uŋ uŋkaŋ wiŋyaŋ he wapiya.
"When I was without a wife, I took another woman to be with, and here that woman was a healer.
"Haw wapiya he waŋżi he he ṭaḳu wakicuŋza wowaciŋyaŋ ṭaḳ ḳ'upi hena heced eṭaŋhaŋ icaġa ka he yuhe."
"As a healer her purpose was to be depended on, what she was given came from being born into that, and she carried that."

He kci uŋ uŋkaŋ tokaheya okicizek de, tokahaŋ okicize uŋ ded.
He was with her the first war, the beginning of the war he was here.

Haw Dekśi wayek he ciŋca kośka waŋ, John Duta, ded ninety, ninety-two, ninety-eight etu kepçe hehan ed uŋ śni, about four years ago.
My uncle, his child, John Duta, was a young man [at the time of World War I], here at ninety, ninety-two, ninety-eight, I think, he died about four years ago.

Hehaŋyaŋ nihdi, uŋkaŋ he iŋyaŋnak he waŋżi stepmother tawa uŋ he he yuha yakiya ded ihunniyaŋ yuha uŋ.
He came back alive to live that long and so one of the stones his stepmother had, she sent him with that and he had it with him all the way through.

Haw uŋkaŋ haw ḣtanihaŋ he ehan ḣtani he ehan iŋyaŋ nawaḣ'uŋ de miciŋkśi oyake.
And so yesterday, at that time yesterday, I heard the stone, my son told this.

Taża waŋ kokipapi Tak Wakaŋ wicadapa ob um hena wowicada iyehaŋyaŋ yuhap śni ka kokipap.
Those who believe in Tak Wakaŋ were afraid of a wave, those who are with them do not have the belief as much and are afraid.

Haw he oyake, haw he wanna he Dakota eciyataŋhaŋ nakuŋ nawaḣ'uŋ he.
He told this, yes now I have heard already from the Dakota side.

Iŋyaŋna de waŋżi yuha ye ka mniwaŋca opta de watataŋka ohna yapi uŋkaŋ taża taŋka u.
He had the little stone and they were going across the ocean in a ship and here a big wave was coming.

Wakaŋtuya ka watataŋka seececak kaeś he opawiŋġe, kiktopa heced oyawapi.
It was high and seemed like a large ship about a hundred, thousand they counted.

Haw he taża iwuŋkam hiyu kte.
The wave will come above that.

Wicaniic'iye owas mahed toki eya ka ewicaŋatakap iwohdakapi eciŋ ka owas uk wayakap.
To save themselves they all went inside, where they talked about locking them in because they all saw it coming.

Ye ka wapaha inażiŋ ka wacekiya ka mnik de waḣbadakekta omakiya wode tokiya taku uŋyapi heca katinya ekta uŋkipte do, eya.
He went and stood at the bow and prayed that the waters would be gentle, "Help me, so that we will continue and arrive at our destination," he said.

Ṭaku Wakaŋ iwaŋġapṭa mni kud iyaye he he iŋyaŋ de he he haw heciya ipa hehan heciya yak̲uŋpi.

They asked Ṭaku Wakaŋ that the waters calm down, and it was because of the stone that they arrived over there and they stayed there.

Haw he iŋyaŋnak̲ yuha ik̲ heciya.

He arrived over there with the stone.

Uŋkaŋ ihnunaḣ hena de wohdak̲a yak̲api k̲epçe.

And so, sometimes they sat around talking about those.

After waniyeṭu yamni eceṭuk̲ hehan ihnunaḣ wiŋyaŋ de išṭimma.

After [they had been gone] about three years, then this woman went to sleep.

Išṭimma uŋkaŋ wi haŋbda

When she slept she dreamed.

Uŋkaŋ k̲akiya wopiyeda heci uŋmayamni hena ihduha uŋpi iża hena ake tok̲ iyayapi ake hdip çee de he waŋżi hdi śni heciya da uŋ.

And so the other three kept themselves in the place where they were kept, they too would go somewhere and come back again, one didn't return, it stayed over there.

He hece ope k̲a hdi heced wożuhadak̲ ṭop ohna uŋ.

And here he came back and joined them, and so there were four in the little pouch.

Hehan heciya de nihaŋḣ John Duṭa he uŋ.

Then John Duṭa, he was still over there.

Haḣ'aŋna k̲a kikṭa heca hena hihnaku okiyak̲e.

As soon as she woke up in the morning, she told her husband.

Uŋkaŋ ṭop hena uŋ, yamni uŋ, he waŋżi k̲aki uŋ hdi.

And so those four were there, three were there, [then] the one that was over there came back later.

Haw heced icaŋṭe śiçapi ṭok̲ed hiŋhdap taŋiŋ śni, don't know what.

And so they were sad, they didn't know what happened to them, don't know what.

Woyuṭe ehdep k̲a altar k̲aġapa maka mibe k̲aġapi wizica ehnakapa ṭak̲ owas izidyapa woyuṭe ehdepi k̲a wacek̲iyapa wiŋyaŋ de wacek̲iyapi ṭok̲eca etaŋhaŋ ihnunaḣ okiyak̲e.

They set food and made an altar, they put the wizica[9] in the earth circle they made, they smudged everything, they set out the food and prayed, the woman prayed wanting to know why, suddenly it told her.

---

9. This could be a reference to sage, sweetgrass, or even cedar that is burned and offered with prayers.

"Haw heciya wokokipe waŋ ekta de, haw he, takoża awaŋyak wauŋ kaeś waŋna wokipek he wanice do.

> "Over there where there was something to fear, I watched over this grandchild, but now there is nothing to fear.

"Waŋna okicizek inażiŋ do.

> "Now the war has ended.

"Haw heced aku kaŋhaŋ haw he ope kuktek miye icomamni do.

> "And so when they return, he will come back with them, [as for] me, I was homesick.

"Tiyata waku waciŋ heced de miye ka wahdiyaku do.

> "So I wanted to come home, [as for] me, I returned to where I started from.

"Tokśtake hena ahdi kaŋhaŋ iża wicopeya hdi kte do eya okiyake winuḣca."

> "When they all return, he too will be amongst them."

Ho hehan he okiyake atkuku okiyake, "Haw he miciŋkśi heciya waŋna etaŋ-haś wokipe wanice.

> And then he told his [the young man's] father, "Yes, my son, there is nothing to fear over there anymore.

"Okicize waŋna inażiŋ," he ehan taku deced TV, radio, taku wanice.

> "The war has now ended," and then at that time there was no TV or radio.

Haw he de hdi ka iyohakap tona caŋ hehan wanaḣuŋpta uŋkaŋ okicize inażiŋ.

> So many days after it returned they heard the war had ended.

Haw heced waŋna taku wokokipek wanice, iyohakap waŋna two or three months hehaŋyaŋ aku ka ahdik wicopeya ahdi.

> And so there was nothing to fear, after two or three months of its [the stone's] returning, he came back amongst them.

Iŋyaŋg he uŋ awaŋyaŋke do haw he, First World War haw hecetu.

> The stone looked after him there at the First World War, indeed.

Ehaŋna Woyakapi Inapçiŋwaŋka (The Ninth Historical Narrative)

Uŋkaŋ haw he wiŋyaŋ naŋka ociciyake he Dekśi Duta he wiŋyaŋ he he yuza ka iŋyaŋna hena yuhace epek uŋ he kakiya John Duta yuhe iuŋkaŋ.

> And here I told you about that woman a while ago, Uncle Duta, he married that woman, and I told you John Duta went over there with the little stone that she had.

Hed i ka icomni ka deci hdi.

He went over there and after he got there he was lonely and came back over here.¹⁰

Haw he ake, iṡto Second World War he Dekṡi Duta iye tawicuḳ he he grandson tawa Peter White Cloud eciyapi, haw he iṡto ake yuhe iyaye.

Again, next, in the Second World War, Uncle Duta's wife, her grandson, whose name is Peter White Cloud, he took [the stone] next and left.¹¹

He awaŋyaŋḳe kṭe ḳa yuha iyaye tiyaṭa wacekiyapi ṭohaŋtu ca ake wacekiyapi ake wohamake wacekiyapi.

He brought it along to take care of it, they would pray at home and every now and then they would pray again, they prayed amongst themselves.

Haw heciya, ihnunah woyaḳapi uŋkaŋ Waṡicu woyaḳapi wonah'uŋ uŋkaŋ he ṭaḳu wowakipa White Cloud ed uŋ ḳeyapi, casualty eyapi.

Yes, over there the word was, the Waṡicu word that was heard was that something happened to White Cloud, they said, casualty, they say.

Heca wowapi hi.

A letter about that came.

So then, toṭaḳuya hena owas icaŋṭe ṡicapi.

So then, all his relatives were sick at heart.

Haw heced woyuṭe ṡpaŋyaŋ hehan maka omni ḳaġapi, altar kaġap.

And so they cooked food and then made a circle in the earth and made an altar.

Oizedyapa hehan waḳaŋḳada he wapiye ḳa dowaŋ hehan ṭaḳ ṡkaŋ ṡkaŋna haw he ṭokeca haw heciya ṭaŋhaŋ ayupṭe.

They smudged and then the elderly woman did her medicine and sang, then something happened with the ṭaḳ ṡkaŋ ṡkaŋna¹² and from over there it answered.

"Hiya, he etaŋhaṡ he he ṭaḳu woikope ṡni do.

"No, there is nothing to fear.

"Ikiyeda ṭaḳu anapoyapi hiŋpaye ḳa wicota shell shock eyap heca uŋ heced shocked tḳa they are all coming back, waŋna waṡṭeyapi hed ope do.

"Something that explodes fell close by and many suffered shell shock they say, he was that way, shocked, but they are all coming back, now they are getting better and he is among them.

"Hed White Cloud opeya uŋ do ṭokṡta ṭaŋyaŋ tiyata ki kṭe do," eya, de iŋyaŋna de deci owicakiyake waḳaŋḳada okiyaḳe.

---

10. Uŋkaŋna is talking about the stone here, not John Duta.

11. Uŋkaŋna would have been a cousin to John Duta, and Peter White Cloud, in the Dakoṭa way, would have been a nephew to John Duta.

12. In this case *ṭaḳ ṡkaŋ ṡkaŋna* refers to the *traveling stones or moving stones*.

"There White Cloud is among them, he will return safely home," it said, the little stone told them, told the elderly woman.

So then mahed iyekiyapa — they were looking for him ku kte he akipap.

So then they put it away and they were looking for him, they were waiting for him to return.

Sure enough, ihnunah heced White Cloud hdi.

Sure enough, then White Cloud arrived home.

In that case I don't know whether iŋyaŋ he tokaya hdi iś ka yuha hdi toketu heced nawahuŋ śni.

In that case, I don't know whether, I didn't hear if the stone returned first or if he brought it back with him.[13]

Tka ka umang he de he he communication he he wanica takuda śni hena.

But the other one, there was no communication, nothing there.

Haw ded de Second World War de kakiya ed armistice heced ayustaŋp hehan waŋna dena taku u ka hena nauŋh'uŋpi.

Here there was an armistice over there at the Second World War, it [the war] was finished, then these things were coming now and we all heard.

He kaehaŋ heced wanice.

There was nothing before that.

Those are some of the things that hena Dakota language uŋkitawap he ka, the way of life uŋkitawap hena hena Tak Wakaŋ uŋk'upi hena.

Those are some of the things that are in our Dakota language and our way of life, those things Tak Wakaŋ gave to us.

Haw heced uŋśika de upte dena waŋna eca miyekśe he uŋmaspe macistiŋna he taŋhaŋ uŋmaspe Dakotak, hena kaŋp hena ob wauŋ naka dena taku nah'uŋ wauŋ.

Poor things, the ones who are coming now, as for me, I learned these Dakota things from the time I was little, because I was among the elders I heard these things.[14]

Haw hena he de naka hah'aŋna Tak Wakaŋ wayakapi se ecece keyapi.

Just this morning it seems they thought they saw Tak Wakaŋ, they said.[15]

---

13. Our understanding here is that the message about his safety came from a stone White Cloud's grandmother had at home, not the stone that was with White Cloud during the war. In the next sentence he says there was no communication with that one. Perhaps it also was shell-shocked.

14. Again, the phrase *nah'uŋ wauŋ* is used here, indicating that he didn't just hear these things once, but that he heard them as he was growing up and they became a part of his being.

15. This may be a reference to a news report about some contemporary people seeing Jesus or some other sacred being.

Haw he heuŋ etaŋhaŋ he he he wowaciŋyek[16] **he dena ikoyake he iża wa-śicu ekta hena.**

For that reason, all those beliefs are connected, even with the Waśicu.

He iża Dakota iyeced itokcab śni.

There is no difference with the Dakota.

Haw he heuŋ tokaheya ociciyakapi hehan iyohakab dena ociciyakapta kaŋ-haŋ hena ekta ikoyakapta, put the two and two together kiŋhaŋ you can come up with your own idea and that's why first thing this morning de Dakotak tak owas haw he ociciyakapte.

That is why I told you this first and then after, so these things I tell you will connect, if you put the two and two together you can come up with your own idea, and that's why first thing this morning I will tell you everything in Dakota.[17]

Haw he he de tak śkaŋśkaŋna hena uŋ he he.

Yes, this is why tak śkaŋ śkaŋna exist.

CMN: There used to be this guy, maybe you remember who that was, this one Indian guy, he'd always get up and say to the white people, he says, "The white man had radio, but long before the white man had radio, the Dakota had radio." He was talking about the iŋyaŋ śkaŋśkaŋ. He meant that was our radio.[18]

Yeah, those are our messengers.

CMN: Do you remember who that was?

CCS: The first time I heard that was from your mother—she said that.

---

16. This word was translated as "beliefs" in this instance, but in Dakota it implies something deeply believed in and depended upon.

17. With this comment, Uŋkaŋna is making it clear that we are not passive listeners, rather he encourages us to think about these things on our own and to draw our own conclusions.

18. With this comment my father is referring to a story my Kuŋśi Elsie Cavender used to tell. It was included as part of an oral-history project I conducted with her in the fall of 1990. In reference to these sacred messengers of the Dakota she stated: "Reverend Heminger one time was invited to the United Church of Christ in town. They asked him to preach a sermon in Indian if he could. He talked pretty good English [but] . . . 'I'd rather say it in Indian,' he told them. The choir was invited from Flandreau [South Dakota], so they all went. In the sermon he said, 'You know we Indian people invented the telephone and the radio which is just now coming around. We invented them before you white men ever did . . . a long time ago those Indians had these little rocks. They used to send messages with those little rocks and pretty soon a message would come back.' They [the white people in the church] just didn't believe that at all." I often wonder if Reverend Heminger was ever asked back to speak again at the church!

Haw hena messengers hecapi hena danger kiŋhaŋ.
　Yes, those are messengers when there is danger.
De heciya taŋhaŋ okicize kupte hehan tukted yapte hena wicaṡta wapiya waŋ hena owicakiyake.
　When they were coming back from the war over there, the medicine man told them where they were to go.
He himself was ehaeṡ wicaḣcak waŋna ope okihi kte ṡni.
　He himself was an old man, and now he was unable to be with them.
Haw ciŋca ka takożakpaku hena upte he hena owicakiyake tukte ohna up kaŋhaŋ he Winnipeg ed upte.
　He told them his children and grandchildren will come and which direction they will come, at Winnipeg they will come.
"Red Lake kahda Red River kahdaya up kaŋhaŋ another river deciya taŋhaŋ ye ka he ye.
　"Along Red Lake and along Red River they will come, and then another river from over here goes and goes.
"Haw hena akasampataŋ tipi wataŋka he akan cross heca waŋ he dapi kiŋhaŋ yanipte do.
　"Across [the river] there is a large house with a cross on top, if you go there you will survive.
Haw iyehaŋtudaḣ ed waŋżi do, he ehe.
　And right there, there was one there [a building].

CMN: Was this Brandon?

Hiya, Winnipeg heciya, Winnipeg he kakiyap bdote ed where Y heced eyayaŋkapi.
　No, over there in Winnipeg, over there in Winnipeg at the juncture, where they call it Y.
Hed hed akasampataŋ heciya Red River he kahdaya uŋpi de Winnipeg hed de deced iyopta, akasampataŋ hed.
　Across from there they came along the Red River, past Winnipeg and across from there.
He tokaya waŋżi makipazo de wicaoġa Bob, Joyce hihnaku tka he kakiya wapa he I wasn't happy with it though, haw takuda ṡni do hed.
　It [the actual site] was further on over there from the first one that son-in-law Bob, Joyce's husband, pointed out to me, I wasn't happy with it [the first one pointed out] though, there was nothing there.
So then iyohakab hehan ded ake about a month afterward de, well just about two weeks ago he ehan heci uŋkipa him and his adopted brother, the three of us went out looking for this place again.

So then afterward, then again about a month afterward, well, just about two weeks ago, at that time we went over there, him and his adopted brother, the three of us went out looking for this place again.

Uŋkaŋ he, the one he showed me before, was about a quarter of a mile beyond the fork there.

And so that, the one he showed me before, was about a quarter mile beyond the fork there.

But the one we found is right across from the, hed hed, the old, old buildings that were ed owa he 1840 ṭonakça hena ḳaġapi.

But the one we found is right across from the, there, there the old, old buildings that were built in the 1840s, it was written.

Hehan the flag heca waŋ ikoyaḳyapi.

So then they hung that flag.

That's where they take in orphans and people that have no place to go.

Ecehena iś iwicacupi, it was a place for those people.

They took them right in, it was a place for those people.

Ecan deciya ṭaŋhaŋ upi ḳa hipa uŋġe ḳaŋpi śiceca wabdenicapi huŋḳaḳe wicaḳṭepi ḳakiya.

In the meantime, they came from here and some elderly and orphan children and their parents were killed over there.

Haw hena awicacupi hena he de u, Dakoṭa cażeḳ hena uŋḳodepi.

They took them for that reason, we searched for the Dakoṭa names.

Odepi dehan right now they are looking for it.

They are searching at this time, right now they are looking for it.

Haw heced nakaeś I was satisfied because de wapiya uŋḳaki heye ḳa he okiŋni iŋyaŋ isam wicayuha he okiyaḳa nacece haw hed yapo he aḳaspataŋ tipi waŋ hed hdiçupṭa[19] do, he okiyaḳa nacece.

Finally now I was satisfied[20] because the medicine man over there said that and iŋyaŋ probably told him, "You all go there, there is a building across from there that they will come back to," he probably told him that. There must be something that prompted him to say that.

"Hed yapo, hed yanipṭa do," ḳeyapi do.

"You all go there, they will survive there," they said.

---

19. This is a contraction of the phrase *hdiçupi kṭe* or *they will start out to come home*. Many of the single-word verbs for coming and going require multiple word English translations: e.g., *hda* (*to go home*), *hi* (*to arrive at or come to*), *hdi* (*to return home here*), *i* (*arrive there*), *ki* (*to arrive back where one started*), *ḳu* (*to come home*).

20. For Uŋḳaŋna this was a validation of the story he had heard about this place.

Heced ed ip, hed nipi uŋġe he uŋġe ḳaŋpi ḳa hed t'api ḳa wicaḣapi hetaŋhaŋ waŋna decitḳiya uŋġe ahi from here ḳaked uŋġe Beulah hed uŋpa uŋġe ḳakiya bde taŋkak heciya, heciya uŋġe ḳakiya Waḣpetuŋwaŋ Reserve, Prince Albert heciya.

Some elderly lived and died there and were buried there, and from over this way some came from here, in that direction some stayed in Beulah there, some over there at Big Lake over there, and some further over at the Wahpeton Reserve, in Prince Albert.

Heced yek he ecan uŋḳiś ded reserve uŋḳitawap de ḳaki yapa ecan hena maka yucistiŋna aup, eced reserve cistiŋna hed haw heced Portage hed ye.

That's the way it was going, in the meantime, as for us, our reserve was getting smaller because of the ones who were coming in, so they went to Portage then.

Haw hena hena he takomni yuha yahda waciŋ ke, haw hena yuha yahde kte.

I really think you must take these with you, take these with you.[21]

Haw yahde ḳa hena ṭaku, for what you think it's worth, hena hena iyacu ḳte, what you think you'll be able to get across.

You go back and for what you think it's worth, you will take those things, what you think you'll be able to get across.

Because waniyetu waŋna wikćemna zaptaŋ sampa śahdoġaŋ, hehaŋyaŋ Chief of Indian Affairs, Indian Brotherhood, outside and different organizations hena ob Indian Affairs opapi, I could not get nothing into their head, because their way is the only way.

Because it has been fifty-eight years now, that long since Chief of Indian Affairs, Indian Brotherhood, outside and different organizations, those joined with Indian Affairs, I could get nothing into their head because their way is the only way.

Ehaŋna Woyakapi Iwikćemna (The Tenth Historical Narrative)
WAEHDEPI (THE DEDICATION OF FOOD)

Ṭaku haḣ'aŋna de iwouŋhdaḳapṭa hecihaŋ aŋpetu de ṭoḳaheya iwouŋhdaḳapṭa hecihan nu ṭaku obdaḳe ḳte he waehdepi eyapi, waehdepi eyapi he de woyuṭe ewicakihdepi hena ṭoḳed uŋ heced ecuŋpi hecihan.

This morning what we are going to talk about today first, what we will talk

---

21. He is now directing this advice to us, his audience, saying he really thinks we should take this information home with us.

about is the saying waehdepi, why it is they call it waehdepi if they set food for them in such a way.²²

Haw hena ociciyak̇apa hena hena iża ok̇iŋni uŋśik̇a de ṭok̇etaŋ yahip heciya ikce wicaśta yakum k̇a iża ok̇iŋni dena waŋna uŋġe akik̇tuŋżapi nacece.

I will tell you those, those, they too poor things, those that are where you come from over there, maybe some of these things they too have probably now forgotten.

Haw hena ihnuhanaḣ k̇iksuya wicaweċiċiye k̇aŋhaŋ haw otaŋkada k̇a hed yakuŋp hena okiciyak̇apa uŋ etaŋhaŋ iwohdak̇ wicotaŋ waŋżidak̇ Ṭak̇ Wakaŋ itohiya manipṭa.

Yes, possibly I will get them to remember, those elders and those that are there to tell one another, from that talking they will walk in the direction of Ṭak̇ Wakaŋ with one mind.

Heced awacanmi uŋ etaŋhaŋ he de waehdep eyap he de he ṭok̇ed uŋ heyap he obdak̇e kṭa ṭok̇aheya.

I have this thought, for that reason first I will tell why they say waehdepi.

Uŋkaŋ kośk̇a num icaġap k̇eyapi tok̇aheya.

And so first they say two young men grew up together.

He obdak̇e kṭa kośk̇a num etaŋhaŋ nażiŋ icaġap.

I will tell that two young men grew up together from the beginning.

He tohaŋya eśta kodakiciyapa sakib yak̇uŋpi sakib yak̇uŋp heced iyokpiya yak̇uŋpi k̇a awihnip k̇aŋhaŋ hena iyokpi yak̇uŋp.

They were friends for a long time, they were at each other's side, beside one another, they were happy together and when hunting they were happy.

Uŋkaŋ he waŋna tawicu tuŋpi, hehan he iś bde waŋ iyaṭayada hed, he hekṭa hena ṭak̇u uŋ owoohoda ṭuk̇ṭed ṭuwe wihni k̇iŋhaŋ hena ṭuweda tokċa ed yap śni.

And so now they took wives, then there was a lake by itself there, way back then some things were respected, when someone hunted somewhere, those different ones never went there.

"Waŋ hena iś wihni hena tawapi do," eyapa uŋ inaġi yewicayapa ok̇iciża waciŋ okċiġa wicaŋśk̇aŋ śni ṭak̇uda śni.

"Those are theirs to hunt there," they said, and they did not bother them, trying to fight, argue, there was nothing.

---

22. *Waehdepi* might literally be translated as *an act in which it is set*, coming from the verb form *ehdepi*, meaning *they place or set* with the *wa* prefix indicating the change to a noun. In this context, it might better be translated as *the setting of food*, or *the dedication of food*, as food is implied.

Haw iš he hed yapa he ḣtayetu can ipa ake wetu ça nakuŋ ipa heced.

As for them, they went there when evening came and in the spring they also went again.

Uŋkaŋ he wetu wahmuŋ ip ḳaŋhaŋ uŋġe ihnuḣ umaŋ ṭaku woyute wašte okiŋni ḳiŋhaŋ haw he wakeya iciḳiyeda yaḳapi naka tawicu ṭaku ahdik he špaŋye ši "Deci ḣtayetu eciŋ wahdik ḳaŋhaŋ koda kçi wate kta çe."

And so in the spring when they went trapping, if the other may have some good food, because the tents were close together then, he told his wife to cook what he brought back, "When I return this evening, I will eat it with my friend."

Haw heced, "Špaŋya ehde wo," eya ca tawicu he špaŋye.

And so, "Set it to cook," when he says that his wife cooks it.

Hehan oyokihe wihni yakuŋp.

Then in the meantime they were out hunting.

Waŋna ḣtayetu hdi ḳaŋhaŋ he ecaŋ waŋna wotapte ciŋhaŋ haw wotap, "Waŋ ka waŋżi ehde wo."

Now about that time he returned in the evening when they were about ready to eat. "Set another place."

Ṭakodakup he kco.

He invited his friend.

"Koda u wo ded ded wauŋ de kte do.

"Come friend, we are going to eat here.

"De woyute de špaŋya ehde de wauŋyapte."

"She put this food on to cook, we are going to eat."

"Haw, haw," eyek heced ekta i ekta i ḳa heced he woyute ekihde, hena haw kçi iyokpiya yute.

"Yes, yes," he said and so he went there, he went there, and so he set the food for him, those yes, he happily ate it with him.

Ihnunaḣ maġaksicak waŋżi maġaksica ahdi ḳa paġuŋta waŋżi wašte kte siŋkpe waŋżi wašte cepa kte ḳiŋhaŋ he woyute wašte Dakotak etuk inaġi ikicicopa heced.

If by chance, the duck, a duck, he brings home a nice mallard kill, a nice fat muskrat kill, among the Dakota that is good food, they invite the spirit for these things.

Haw iża ḳakiyak he umaŋ eciyataŋhaŋ yaŋkek he iża haw ṭohan ṭakun woyute wašte waŋżi oḳi ni ḳiŋhaŋ haw iża tawicu okiyake ḳa "Haw de koda ḣtayetu ḳaŋhaŋ kci wate kta špaŋyaŋ wo," eya okiyake.

And so, as for that one who sits over there on the other side, as for him, yes, when he is able to have some type of good food, "Yes, when it is evening I will eat this with koda, cook it," he said telling her.

Haw hece špaŋyaŋ ekcihde hde ca hdipa waŋna ȟtayetu kiŋ.
> She sets on to cook when they return, and it is the evening now.

Haŋpa ṭaku spayak hena ṭaku hena hdušdokapi hehan, hehan "Koda u wo, dena uŋte²³ kta do.
> Then they took off those moccasins and whatever things were wet, then, "Friend, come over, we are going to eat these."

Haw haw hi ka iža kçi woṭe çe.
> Yes, yes, he too will come and eat with him.

Heced waniyetu opṭa upa ake bdokeṭu opṭayapi ihnuȟ umaŋ wayazaŋ hda.
> And so they came through the winter and again went through the summer, suddenly the other one became sick.

Wayazaŋ hda ka heced nina kuwapaš²⁴ heced ocib u ka heced wanice.
> He felt sick and so they treated him a lot and so after coming a while, he was no more.

Wanice ka heced ehnakap hehan nina wocaŋṭe šica iyahde tawicu kçi ka haŋkaku hena nakuŋ koya nakuŋ wocaŋṭe šica.
> He was no more and so they put him away, then very much heartache fell on him, with his wife and sister-in-law also included in the heartache.

Uŋkaŋ ihnunaȟ heyap keyapi heced dena wihni uŋyaŋ çek uŋ de heciya tawat'e ed waye šni tka hed eceyeda uŋ kiš he wiuŋhnip çe.
> And so, and here they said that they said these hunting places we used to go to over there, I am not willing to do that but that is the only place that is ours to hunt.

"Ṭoked icuŋkuŋ kta wo?" tawicu kçi iyukça
> "What shall we do?" he thought with his wife.

"Haŋ, ekṭa uŋye kṭe ye, heciya wadita ka ekṭa uŋye ka heciya wiyahni kṭa."
> "Yes, we will go over there, be brave, and we will go there and over there you will hunt."

Haw haw heced wakic'im ipa heced ekṭa etipa išnana etipi.
> Yes, and so they put packs on their backs and they camped over there, they camped alone.

Waŋna wakeya waŋžida waŋna ed tipi.
> Now there was only one tent where they camped now.

Heçeçe ktukiŋ ihnunaȟ ihnunaȟ paġuŋṭa he nakaha ahdi ka nina wašṭe.
> Just as one would have it, immediately a mallard he just brought home and it was very good.

---

23. This is a contraction of uŋyuṭe.
24. A contraction of kuwapi kaeš.

Paġuŋta he de mallard eyapi çe ḳa haw heca he, haw heca eḳeś hena sdodyaya.
Paġuŋta, they call that a mallard and, yes, you know those already.
Haw hena he nina waśte cepa.
Yes, those are very good fat.
Iwanu kṭa śni he maza nahpe ḳa ahdi ḳa kte.
By accident he stepped on and tripped the trap and was killed.
Haw, "Ded de śpaŋya wo eyaḳe ḳa eciŋ htayetu ḳaŋhaŋ wahdi ḳaŋhaŋ he waṭe kṭe do."
Yes, "Cook this here and later when it is evening when I return, I will eat that."
"Haŋ," eyaḳe.
"Yes," she said.
Haw heced śpaŋye ehde waŋna hdi ḳa hehan waŋna ṭaŋyaŋ śpaŋ, de ihduśṭoḳe, pusic'iye ḳa haw ehan wakśica ohna woṭe kṭa ehde ḳa, "Waŋżi ehde wo," uŋkaŋ eya ḳeyapi.
Yes, and so she put it on to cook now, he returned and then it was cooked well now, he undressed, dried himself and then she put a plate for him to eat in and, "Set [another] one there," they say he said.
Haw hekṭa takodaḳu ḳci woṭa çee heuŋ iyeced waŋżi akab ehde śi.
Yes, back then he used to eat with the one who was his friend, for that reason he told her to set an extra one.
Heced ṭaḳu itḳop wawiwaŋġe, "He ṭoḳed ewahde kṭa?" iś ṭaḳuda uŋ eye śni.
She did not question him, "Why should I set one?" or she did not say anything.
Iża ake hed waŋżi ehde.
Again, she set another one.
Maġaksica uŋśpa okihnaḳe ṭaḳu iś oyatḳeda çeeḳ wahaŋpi nakuŋ ohna ehnaḳa.
She put in a portion of duck for him, also she put soup in whatever he used to drink from.
Haw he de iś de iyoṭaŋḳe ḳa tawicu iża iyoṭaŋḳe, eya ḳeyapi.
Yes, as for him he sat down and his wife, she sat too, they say he said.
"Haw haw koda ṭoḳiya yauŋ hecihaŋ, haw de woyuṭe ewahdeḳ de ed uwa ececi hde do eya.
"Hello friend, wherever you are, yes, I have set this food for you, come to it, I set it for you," he said.
"Uŋkaŋ uwa wauŋṭe kṭe do."
"And so, come, we will eat."
"Haw," eya ḳeyapi taŋkad tiyopa ed.
"Yes," they say he said outside the door.

"Ho," eya ḳa hece timahed hiyu.
> "Yes," he said and so he came in.

Taŋcaŋ hee takodaḳu he timahed hiyu.
> That was his body, the one who was his friend who came in.

Ḳaeś heced de inihaŋpa iś kokipapa ṭakuda śni.
> Even so, they were not anxious or afraid, and nothing.[25]

He woyuṭe ehdeḳ wahaŋpi iś hena u ḳa hed hiyu taŋḳe ḳa he u ia oḳihi śni tḳa hehan ḳicopa, "Haw," iye ḳa hiḳ he.
> She set the food and soup as well, he came and there he sat down here, that is the way he came but he could not speak but they invited him and, "Yes," he said when he came.

Tawicu de iźa kċi woṭe ekṭa wayaḳapa tado hena owa ṭaŋyaŋ yasmi ḳa huhu hena eċa wakśica ḳa ohnaḳe wahaŋpi iś iyokpiyah yatḳe ḳa he wahaŋpi yahepe.
> His wife she too ate with him, they looked over there at the meat, he ate it well down to the bone, those bones he put them in that dish, as for the soup he drank it happily and that soup he drank up.

Haw hehan waŋna tebye ḳa waŋna ayahepa uŋkaŋ heya ḳeyapi, "Koda pidamayayekiya do," eya ḳeyapi.
> Then now he ate it all and drank it up and here they say he said, "Friend, I am grateful to you," they say he said.

"Ṭoḳiya waiḳ ekṭa he woyuṭe ḳa ṭaku yuke ḳaeś uŋġe woṭehda yakuŋpi do."
> "Where I went to, there are food and some things to be had, even so some go hungry."

"De woṭehda wauŋ ecaŋtudah de haw de woyuṭe emayaḳihde, haw iyomakpiya, ṭuwe eya ob wahi ḳa uŋhduṭapi do.
> "I was hungry, just about then you set food for me, yes I am happy and I came with some others and we all ate it.

"Iźa hena woṭehdapi," eya ḳeyapi.
> "They too are hungry," they say he said.

"Haw de wakiyeda[26] wakinawape ḳaŋhaŋ he inuŋpada he ṭohnina wamayadaḳapṭe śni do.
> "Yes, when I leave here and step out there you will never see me a second time.

---

25. It makes more sense in English to say, "Even so, they were not anxious or afraid, or anything."

26. We think this is a form of wakiahde.

"Tka deced woyute eyahde kiŋhaŋ ed wau ka he wate kte tka wamayada kte śni ka nakuŋ namayah'uŋ kte śni do tawaciŋ eçeedahiŋ, eya keyapi."

"But when you set food out like this I will come to it and I will eat that, but you will not see me and also you will not hear me, just with the mind alone," they say he said.

"De yaki kaŋhaŋ tiyata awicakiyaka wo.

"When you get home, tell them this at home.

"Wotap kaŋhaŋ wokitaŋyaŋ kaeś ehdep kaŋhaŋ hena içakiś hiyeye do heciya okiçic'u wotapi do," eya kiŋhdakeye.

"When they eat set out even a small portion, when they are in need over there, they share what they eat," he left saying that he said.

Haw heced waŋna ayaśtaŋ ka hehan tawicu de kaŋhaŋ wakśica hena ikicic'u to hena eś taŋyaŋ huhu yasmi heced he heced kaeś conica ikoyake.

They had finished eating and then his wife, she went to get her dishes, those he had eaten down to the bone, and here the meat was still hanging on.

Wahaŋpek yahepe uŋ hna heced ohna he.

The soup that he drank up was still in it.

Haw hecehna deciya ahdihde çe hece etaŋhaś hena waŋna oyapte heced hihnaku kçi akipta yutapi.[27]

Yes, so right away she brought them right back over here and set them down, now they were already left over and so she and her husband ate it together.

"Haw, he he heced oyak ki wo," eye.

"Take this home and tell this as it is," he said.

Yuhahdik oyake.

He told what he brought back.

He etaŋhaŋ de waekihdep hi.

From that time forward, the setting out of one came to be.

Uŋkaŋ waekihdepi eyapa de obek nuŋpa do.

And so they call it waekihdepi[28] and there are two different ones.

Niś htaŋyetu iyohi nihuŋ de waekihdepi.

As for you, every evening for your mother they set out for her.

Waekihdep ka heced hah'aŋna kaŋhaŋ wekte kaŋhaŋ hena wowacekiya epe

---

27. "Akipta yutapi" refers to eating out of the same bowl one right after the other.

28. *Waehdepi* would mean *they set out [something]* and *Waekihdepi* (with the *ki* in the middle) would mean *they set out for [someone]*.

ka dena nuske... ka aŋpetu opta toked uŋkaya hena wopida epe ka taku wa-ciŋwaye hecihaŋ mitakuya ob wicahduha, hoyewaye.

They set for her and so when it is morning when I awake I say a prayer for those and, these nuske... and I say thanks for how those take us through the day, what it is that I depend on, with my relatives gathered around, I cry out.

Haw wahinawape kaŋhaŋ hehan ho ka woyute itokab mihduźaźa mihduśtaŋ ka hehan he woyute iwacu deciya awaku ded ahiwahde.

When I appear, then yes, over there before the food I finish washing myself, then I take the food over here and I set it down here.

Haw ka hece hena waekihdepi hena wośnapi hena taku he dedication eyap hena hena tokiya hena.

And so those are waekihdepi, those things are gifts, somewhere they call those "dedication."

Haw he waehdepi eyap he he hehan ahake wotapi eyapi nakuŋ waŋżi.

Yes, that is what they call waehdepi, then there is also another one they call the last feast.

Haw he kitaŋna taŋkaya ecuŋpi he kitaŋna taŋka oyate taŋka wowicak'upi wicakcoba.

They do it in a bigger way, a little bigger, they invite and feed a larger group.

Ate, Ina, de miciŋkśi, micuŋkśi, ahpeimaye he de haw de oyate he ahake kći wayatapta ka de uŋp śni.

My father, my mother, my son, my daughter, they left me, you the people will eat with them for the last time and they are not here.

Haw he, that's the last meal with them, but that doesn't, śta he wayakihde kte he he iś itokca he.

Yes, that's the last meal with them, but that doesn't, that wayakihde,[29] it is different from that.

Ahake wotap he iś he he de waśpaŋyapa oyate wicakcob ob wotapi.

That last feast, that one they cook and they invite people, they eat with them.

He ahake wotap heca hehan waekihdep de ekśed tohaŋyaŋ kaŋhaŋ eśta tuktedtukaśta.

That is what the last feast is then, the waekihdep, with this one here [it can be done] for any length of time, anyplace, anywhere.

---

29. *Wayakihde is what you set for one.*

Miš hockey wai ḳaiš baseball ṭoki wai ḳaŋhaŋ ṭuwe ob wai çeeḳ hena waŋżi wabdaḳe šni ḳa taŋhaŋ wicawayeḳ uŋġe iš taŋhaŋši wicawaye ṭuwe...

As for me, when I go to hockey or baseball or somewhere, if I do not see one of them who I usually go with, and some who are my brothers-in-law, as for those who are my cousins, someone . . .

Ho uŋyaŋḳapa ḳaŋyaŋhaŋ popcorn uŋṭapi ḳaiš hot dog ḳaiš coke uŋyatḳaŋpi.

We sit and cheer, meanwhile, we eat popcorn or a hot dog, or else we drink coke.

Ḳaŋhaŋ he num, num opewatuŋ haw heced.

Then, yes that way two I buy two.

Ṭuwe ihnunaḣ eye, "Ho de ed de taŋhaŋ u," ḳa de ewahde taŋhaŋši uŋ de.

Someone suddenly says, "Brother-in-law is coming," and this I set for my cousin.

Haw sdodyapi upa hiyotaŋḳapi, "Heced niye waŋna ṭaḳ wakaŋ ikiyeda yauŋ uŋšiuŋkidaṗ po okiçic'upo heced eha iyeced."

Yes, and they know and so they come and sit down, "And so now you are closer to the Creator, have pity on us, share with one another like you said." 30

Haw he he ekše ṭohnina inażiŋ šni do wayeḳihde eyaṗ.

As for that, that never ends, wayeḳihde, they say.

De ahaḳe woṭaṗ he he waŋcada he iš he ecuŋpi he ahaḳe woṭapi he.

This last feast, that last feast there, they do just once.

He iš waŋcada he woḳiḳsuye uŋ oyate woṭ wicayapi.

For that feast there, they feed the people in the memory of [someone] just once.

Haw he he ohnaya hena oskiya uŋ.

Those two are in that way.

Uŋkaŋ he de ṭaḳu woiwaŋġa waŋ eṭaŋhaŋ nawaḣ'uŋ he woiwaŋġa he hec'ic'upa ded amayadepṭe šni šta.

And so, a question of some kind from this I heard, that question I will give to you all even if you don't answer me here.

Iwoyahdaḳe ḳa nakuŋ ded yauŋḳ ded amayadupṭe ḳa ṭoḳed he ḳapi hecihaŋ.

You talk about it and also while you are here give me an answer [about] what it means if it is so.

He de mitakoda[31] **hena imuŋġe omakiyaḳa ciŋ šni.**

---

30. It sounds here as if this is what people would say to the spirits as they were invited to partake in the offering.

31. He mentions the man's name here, but we felt it best to delete that.

I asked my friend those, he doesn't want to tell me.

Uŋkaŋ hekta tipi wakaŋ ed uŋyaŋp çek he ehaŋ hena waŋna osni ka teȟika uŋkaŋp hena tiyata uŋyakaŋp.

And back when we used to go to church, at that time it was cold now and difficult, those, us elders, we stayed at home.

Uŋkaŋ he ehaŋ wowicada uŋkeyap kaŋhaŋ wowicada uŋkeyap kaŋhaŋ hed uŋkeyap, "I believe in the Holy Ghost, the Holy Catholic Church, the Communion of Saints, the Resurrection," hena uŋkeyapi.

And so at that time we said the creed, when we said the creed, when we said those, "I believe in the Holy Ghost, the Holy Catholic Church, the Communion of Saints, the Resurrection," we said those.

He iś śina sapa Waśicu wakaŋ ded hi tohiŋni wicaȟapi piuŋyaŋpi de waŋkan waŋbdi uŋkiya hiyaye ka uŋkaŋ he Waśicu wakaŋ he heye omakiyake.

As for them, the black-robed holy whites[32] came here one time, we were fixing the cemetery above, the eagles were flying around this, and here that priest he said that, he told me.

"Haw de wocekiya ecanuŋ de waŋkan wapa do."

"Yes, this prayer that you do is above all."

"He wocekiyak he uŋk'uŋpi uŋkiża," eye.

"That prayer we too use that," he said.

"Uŋk'uŋp he iyeced ded niye ecanuŋpi do."

"The way we do it, you also do that the same way here."

"Uŋkiye uŋkeyap iyeced ecuŋk'uŋpi[33] śni do."

"We, we do not do like we say."

"The Communion of Saints uŋkeyap he de wicanaġi hena ob wayatapa de ob iyokpiya hoiyewicakiya ob wayatapi do."

"The Communion of Saints that we say, you eat with those spirits and happily you send your voice to them and eat with them."

"He ecuŋk'uŋp śni ded taku nakaha waśte wabdake do."

"We do not do that, I just saw something good here now."

"Niye ekśe ecanuŋpi do hecehehaŋya yapo," eya omakiyake.

"You, you just keep on doing this that way," he said, he told me.

He eca hecetu kaiś toketu he iś he tak nawaȟ'uŋ ça he he wawimuŋġe ka tukte ohna ka ciŋp kaŋhaŋ he iś omakiyakapi.

When I hear something I ask questions, if that is right, and whichever way they want, as for that, they will tell me.

---

32. This refers to the Catholic priests.
33. This is a contraction of eca uŋk'uŋpi.

Mitakoda imuŋǵe ḳaeś iża answer yuha nacece ḳaiś omakiyaḳe śni.
I asked my friend, even though he also probably has an answer, or he doesn't want to tell me.

Ṭokśta iye ekṭe ṭohan akiṗ he wauŋ kṭa.
For sure he will find it sometime, I will wait around for that.

9. Ṭaku Wakaŋ (*That Which Is Mysterious*)

In transmitting these stories from our oral tradition, Uŋkaŋna Eli Taylor carefully and consciously conveyed the legitimacy and authority of Dakota oral tradition while at the same time emphasizing the centrality of the stories in the shaping of our historical consciousness. In doing this Uŋkaŋna demonstrated that Dakota perceptions of history fundamentally challenge much of what Western academic historians consider standard procedures for historical inquiry and acceptable products of research. Immediately apparent are issues of verifiability and credibility, topics that still garner much debate regarding oral tradition in academic circles. While these areas of contention certainly stem from the divergent worldviews of Indigenous tribal historians versus Western academic historians, the issue goes much deeper. His stories, as do many others, challenge basic understandings and beliefs about truth and reality. This chapter will address the value of these stories as they pertain to the Dakota sense of history, identity, and belonging for contemporary Dakota people.

Because academic historians have often been dismissive of any information deemed scientifically unexplainable or unverifiable, these types of accounts have rarely made it into the written historical record. Or, even when our less controversial voices have been included in written histories, they appear as supplements to the "real story" or as colorful additions to support and validate the written sources. Rarely have they taken a primary position in historical works, as oral histories are believed to provide fragmented or incomplete versions of the past, replete with unverifiable, inaccurate, or irrelevant information. Furthermore, though rarely acknowledged by colonialist historians, our accounts have been dangerous because they relate a different reality—one that reveals the expansiveness of Dakota intellectual and spiritual capacities. This serves to undermine the justification for the invasion of our lands and the continued oppression of our people based on an assumed inferiority.

From the moment Europeans stumbled upon our shores, we were a cause for bafflement, defying Western categorization even in regard to our own humanity. Little has changed in five hundred years. Historians and academics today remain baffled about our conceptions of history, because they defy Western categorization. Consequently, we as Native peoples have had our pasts defined (as well as diminished, trampled, and misinterpreted) by those who have insisted that their sources, ways of knowing, and objectivity provide a superior vantage point from which to view and write about our past. Obviously, this has meant that the colonizer's notions of truth and reality have dominated the record, while valuable information regarding Indigenous interpretations of history have been suppressed and denied. History, then, has been a powerful oppressive influence, a conduit of colonization.

When I think about why Uŋkaŋna chose to relate these stories, two major reasons come to mind—the first being that in providing these narratives he was attempting to preserve and transmit aspects of a worldview often at odds with American and Canadian society. He was bringing elements of the wakaŋ into Dakota daily life, a concept quite separate from the daily realities of many non-Indigenous people. The second reason is that in offering this account, Uŋkaŋna was legitimizing this worldview by demonstrating its effectiveness and appropriateness for Dakota people. He understood well the connection between teachings and a sense of identity, as well as how important these are in the struggle for cultural survival.

The primary difference in worldview conveyed here is evident in the interaction with and acknowledgment of nonhuman spiritual beings. Dakota worldview recognizes a spiritual essence in all of creation, and much time and energy is dedicated to developing positive interactions with these spiritual beings. Presence, or existence of a spiritual being in the world, suggests importance in itself, or a reason for being, certainly worthy of Dakota respect. This basic belief about the nature of the world has implications for what constitutes an acceptable reality or an acceptable truth. Dakota people can immediately place the stories of the iŋyaŋ śkaŋ śkaŋ, for example, in a broader context, one that reflects the relationship Dakota people have with the broader cosmos. However, for Western thinkers who consider rocks to be inanimate objects, understanding the importance and meaning of the iŋyaŋ śkaŋ śkaŋ, or including them in a historical discussion, is difficult at best.

The first story of this nature Uŋkaŋna relayed was a personal one regarding his wife, Kuŋśi Edna, and her illness. One day Uŋkaŋna and Kuŋśi received a visit from Willie Little Crow, her older brother according to Dakota kinship principles. He was a medicine man from Saskatoon and had arrived to offer medicine to Kuŋśi for her arthritic condition. She was in pain and had reached the point where she was unable to open doors or make bread with her pained hands. Willie Little Crow had not been summoned by them, however. Instead, he had been told by the iŋyaŋ śkaŋ śkaŋ in his possession that she was having difficulty, what kind of difficulty, and what medicine to bring to help her. Indeed, they had instructed him correctly, and after following through on her brother's recommendations, Kuŋśi Edna was healed.

Within this first story of sickness and healing, in contrast to most practitioners of Western medicine, the healer is assisted by something that defies Western scientific definitions. In reference to his brother-in-law, Uŋkaŋna tells us:

> Uŋkaŋ okpaza iwaŋka uŋkaŋ he ṭaku messengers wicayuheḳ he, "ṭaḳ śkaŋ śkaŋ" eyap çe. . . . Waŋżi iśṭimmaḳ ecan i k'a heya ḳeyapi, "Waŋ, de niṭankci de ṭokiya iyoṭaŋhaŋ iyekiya do," eya ḳeyapi.
>
> And when it got dark he laid down, and here what messengers he had "that which moves" they say. . . . While he slept one went and said, they said, "Oh, your younger sister is suffering somewhere," he said they said.

In this instance, the ṭaḳ śkaŋ śkaŋ refers to traveling stones or moving stones. They are also commonly referred to in Dakota as iŋyaŋ śkaŋ śkaŋ or stones that move, or even spirit stones. Because all of creation is believed to have a spiritual essence, mutually beneficial relationships are created and nurtured with all aspects of creation. Within Dakoṭa culture, this includes stones or rocks, which are classified as "inanimate objects" in Western culture. From a Dakoṭa perspective stones are not only fully animate (they travel very great distances on occasion, either by themselves or in the company of humans), but they also consciously act to bring about a desired response.

In this and the following section Uŋkaŋna illustrates how these spiritual beings have their own personalities, and this becomes apparent when the medicine man is chastised by the stones for not taking care of his sister. He is told by one stone:

> Wayazaŋḳe tehiya iyoṭaŋ iyekiya ecan de ṭakce śni ded nakanakahe de. Waŋ, ekṭa ye ḳa ed etuŋwaŋ wo.
>
> She's sick and really suffering while here you sit without a care. Go there and look after her.

While Willie Little Crow had the stones in his possession and was thus in a sense their "keeper," they in turn provided him guidance and information and prompted him to fulfill his kinship and healing responsibilities. It is important that the stones be treated with respect, because they have been known to leave their keepers if not shown proper respect; even the use of harsh language around them could be offensive enough for them to leave. Thus, while it is an honor to host them, it is also a responsibility.

In this case, not only did the stones alert him to his sister's health condition, they also told him what he should bring to help her. Willie Little Crow revealed to his sister and her husband why he has come, saying:

> Uŋkaŋ woyazaŋ nitawa de, de uŋ ṭaku uŋ oniciya kṭa he au maśi hece he de awahi do. Hecic'u kṭe do.

> And so, he told me to bring something to help you for this sickness, and so for that I brought it. I will give that to you.

Unlike Western medicine, in this example there was no human diagnosis based on years of medical training and experience. The diagnosis came from spiritual entities working in concert with someone who could then provide a treatment. This *is* Dakota reality.

Another interesting aspect to this story is the use of store-purchased medicine for treatment. Little Crow relays to Uŋkaŋna and Kuŋśi:

> **Haw he de kokadak̇ de de Dakoṭa peźihuṭa de wicak'upi ķin de ka de heca de eṭaŋhaŋ icahi de Waśicu ecupa uŋkaġapi do. Hena alfalfa tablets heca.**

> This little box, they gave this medicine to the Dakoṭa, and from that the Waśicu took and mixed it and made it. Those are alfalfa tablets.

Little Crow acknowledges that knowledge of this particular medicine was originally given to Dakota people, but also that there exists a contemporary form that is more convenient to use, although it also required driving some distance to obtain. This exemplifies the Dakota ability to adapt modern technology to traditional purposes.

In the next section Uŋkaŋna begins to relay a story about his own encounter with being healed by traditional means. In this case, after having his leg broken, his uncle set his leg, and within a very short time it was healed. In both of these stories traditional healing practices were successful and, in the case of his broken leg, probably a lot more quickly than if Waśicu doctors had been called upon.

The next story communicates clearly differences in Dakota/Waśicu approaches to sickness, healing, and the obligations of the healer, which would be humorous if a life had not been at stake. In this case, the Indian agent, almost as a last resort, seeks the help of a Dakota medicine woman for his wife, who doesn't seem to be getting better using more conventional Canadian doctors. Uŋkaŋna was placed in the position of serving as a mediator between the English-speaking agent, who was quite unfamiliar with Dakota protocols associated with seeking traditional doctoring services, and the Dakota-speaking healer. At the center of the differing worldviews presented here is a fundamental contrast about the nature of healing. Uŋkaŋna reveals this at the end of the story when he is saddened and frustrated with the agent's ignorance. When he learns that the agent did not return to the medicine woman's home to receive the next three doses of medicine for his wife's illness because of a disagreement he had with her over her grandchild, Uŋkaŋna tells the man from Ottawa:

> It does not matter, it's a gift that she's got from up above. And you didn't finish what she'd asked you and told you that you had to do, violated some of the rights that she's supposed to have. Maybe you think it will cost too much. I don't know, but you should come. They don't charge, she's going to give you those other three to complete, complete what she's working for is to cure that lady.

Although hearing this message, the Indian agent obviously did not internalize the lesson, as he returned to Ottawa and never refilled the prescription given by the medicine woman.

From the Dakota perspective, the power to heal is given by Wakaŋtaŋka and is heavily reliant on the assistance of other spiritual beings. Along with this privilege, the practitioner is obligated to help anyone in need. This is a sacred obligation, far exceeding the importance of any differences of opinion, personality conflicts, political issues, and/or cultural barriers. Healing, then, is not something that occurs just because someone has received a certain kind of training or because they as individuals have the power to make themselves doctors; it occurs in general because an individual receives a spiritual calling and develops their skills, all the while working in cooperation with spiritual forces who assist in the curing. Dakota healers are able to diagnose and offer medicines to heal an individual they are working with, but because there are other forces at work, these same medicines might be ineffective with another individual suffering the same illness. Uŋkaŋna illustrates this when he relates that the alfalfa tablets did not heal his son's arthritis.

Furthermore, because money and materialism are conceptualized quite differently within Dakota culture, the whole issue about what the woman is going to charge is a source of frustration to any Dakota hearing this story. The notion that someone would be denied treatment because of lack of money is completely foreign to the Dakota way of thinking. Although this happens on a daily basis in the United States, where people are denied medical help because they have no means to pay, within Dakota culture this is a violation of humanity. While some Americans may harbor romanticized images of Indian medicine men, the reality is that medicine people have particularly difficult lives, as do all those within Dakota society who are fulfilling sacred obligations. They may be called upon at any time and, therefore, lead lives with little privacy and are allowed to ask for nothing in return.

Dakota notions of reciprocity and generosity, however, manifest themselves in these situations to ensure the well-being of a valued member of the community. Healers typically do not become wealthy, especially in contemporary society. Generally speaking, permanent employment opportunities are scarce for those who practice medicine because of the frequency with which they are called away and depended upon by those whom they are obligated to serve. Cultural values dictate that those who require their services, along with their families, generously demonstrate their appreciation. This is in accordance with Dakota gift-giving etiquette. A note must be made about this, as it differs from that of the dominant society. On this topic Ella Deloria wrote: "Giving was glorified. The formal 'give-away' was a bonafide Dakota institution. Naturally it followed that things changed hands with readiness when the occasion demanded, since the best teaching said things were less important than people; that pride lay in honoring relatives, rather than amassing goods for oneself; that a man who failed to participate in the giving customs was a suspicious character, something less than a human being."[1]

Rather than giving directly to someone in an attempt to show honor to them, as is the case in Western culture, gifts are given to others in the honoree's name. For example, if a family today wished to show honor to a loved one graduating from high school, receiving a name, winning an award, accomplishing something difficult, or even in the memory of someone deceased, an ituḣ'aŋ, or gift-giving ceremony, would be sponsored by the family of the individual. At that time, gifts, usually as many as the family could manage, would be given to those in attendance—most abundantly to the aged, poor, and to those traveling great distances, in honor of the individual. While a great number of goods are collected by the families in preparation for an ituḣ'aŋ, during the ceremony they are redistributed to people most in need. Prestige is gained for the individual and the family, and others are made happy in the process.

As a Dakota cardinal virtue, generosity, along with the acts of giving and receiving, are taught early in childhood and reinforced thoughout life. The term waṡtecake is used to describe someone of a *generous* nature, and this can also mean *good or well-disposed*, generosity being synonymous with goodness. Oḣ'aŋṡice, however, is a reference to being *stingy and ungenerous* and is also synonymous with being *bad, ill-behaved, or mean*. Referring to someone in this manner is highly insulting and tantamount to questioning his or her status as a Dakota. While frugality is a trait praised by some within mainstream society, it is looked down upon within Dakota culture. Those who are seen to cling too tightly to money or possessions, who have difficulty giving freely, or who carefully measure their losses are viewed as pitiable with serious character flaws.

In light of Dakota ideas about money and healing, the repeated questions about the cost of the treatment by the Indian agent in this story are frustrating and reinforce Dakota perceptions about the Wašicu obsession with money. As Uŋkaŋna finally points out to the agent, "Man, you're worrying about the money, worry about your wife for a change, hope that and pray that she gets better." A Dakota man who seemed more concerned with how much healing might cost rather than the well-being of his wife would be considered a very poor husband, indeed! Even when the agent finally pays the medicine woman, he seems to do it haltingly and illiberally, as though his wife's improved life were of little concern. Although non-Natives are not expected to adhere to Dakota beliefs, this story reinforces the cultural contrasts and the expectations of participants in Dakota life.

Another aspect of this story strengthens the importance of kinship, illustrating another situation in which the making of relatives is a necessity. When the medicine woman met the agent's wife whom she has been asked to help, she explained to Uŋkaŋna: "We as Indian people don't go by names. We commute to one another through our relations." As such, before beginning her doctoring, she first made the agent's wife a relative:

So now, sic'e, this Wašicu winuhca de içepaŋši owaye kte.

So now, brother-in-law, I will take this Wašicu woman as a cousin.

By so doing, she solidified her obligations to the woman, because kinship also requires responsibility. She then refers to her as içepaŋši, a term used by females in reference to a cousin of the same gender. Her spiritual commitment was reinforced with duty to help her newly made relative. About this making of relatives with "strangers," Ella Deloria writes: "The dictates of kinship demanded of relatives that they not harm each other; so it was necessary first to make relatives of erstwhile strangers, thus putting them 'on the spot,' and then deal with them on that basis. You assumed that as relatives they would be trustworthy, and by the same token you obligated yourself."[2]

In the next story, Uŋkaŋna returns to the topic of the iŋyaŋ škaŋ škaŋ, the moving or traveling stones. The stones also represent what is wakaŋ, in the sense of being mysterious and sacred. Dakota philosophical understandings about the nature of the world as articulated in the oral tradition emphasize those things that are mysterious. Rather than a fundamental interest in the truth about nature such as that which drives Western scientific studies, Dakota beliefs relegate the unknown to the category of wakaŋ. Empirical knowledge derived from experience with nonhuman spiritual forces suggests to Dakota people that Western scientific principles, laws, and theories are not hard and steadfast, as they can all be challenged under certain circumstances.[3] Dakota efforts are not directed toward finding answers to questions perceived to be beyond human understanding; rather, efforts are directed toward developing positive relationships with all spiritual beings. Uŋkaŋna related these concepts when he said:

> Wicaśta wayukcaŋ ṭuwe sdoduŋyapṭe śni iye ṭak śkaŋ śkaŋ hena, iye hena heca, sdodyapi hena.
>
> As a man [human] we would never understand, but the ṭak śkaŋ śkaŋ, as for them, they understand.

From the Dakoṭa perspective, even the ṭak śkaŋ śkaŋ are capable of understanding more than we as humans would even be able to comprehend. The Dakoṭa task, then, is to work with the ṭak śkaŋ śkaŋ so that they can help us when we are in need.

The next two accounts relay incidents in which stones were used to watch over men participating in World War I and World War II. In the first instance, when encountering rough waters with tall waves, John Duṭa prayed with the rock and attributes their safe arrival to the spiritual help he received. Uŋkaŋna told us:

> Ṭaku Wakaŋ iwaŋġapṭa mni kud iyaye he he iŋyaŋ de he he haw heciya ipa hehan heciya yakuŋpi.
>
> They asked Ṭaku Wakaŋ that the waters calm down, and it was because of the stone that they arrived over there and they stayed there.

While *Ṭaku Wakaŋ* is a term that may at times be used interchangeably with *iŋyaŋ śkaŋ śkaŋ* (moving stones), it is also used to refer to *Wakaŋtaŋka* (*The Great Mystery*). This suggests a connectedness of all things wakaŋ because they all ultimately stem from the same source. However, it appears in this instance that the term *Ṭaku Wakaŋ* is used to refer to *The Great Mystery* and that John Duṭa, with the assistance of the iŋyaŋ śkaŋ śkaŋ, was praying for help from that source. John Duṭa's stepmother then learns he will return safely when the stone who had traveled with him returned to the place where she kept her rocks.

In addition to helping calm the waters during the ocean storm, the stone helped protect him for nearly three years. However, one night when the woman was dreaming, she became aware of the return of her fourth stone, the one that had been with John Duṭa. To find out what had happened to her stepson and why the stone had returned alone, she set out food, made an altar, and prayed, requesting information from the stone.

As she was doing this, suddenly he informed her that there was no longer anything to fear regarding John Duta, the war had ended. On their Canadian Reserve, they had not yet received word about the war's end from any other source. Similar to the stones in the previous story, in the following passage we gain a glimpse into the personality of this stone as it told the elderly woman:

> Haw heced aku kaŋhaŋ haw he ope kuktek miye icomamni do. Tiyata waku waciŋ heced de miye ka wahdiyaku do.
>
> And so when they return, he will come back with them, [as for] me, I was homesick. So I wanted to come home, [as for] me, I returned to where I started from.

Because the stone was tired of being away and knew John Duta would be returning safely with the other men, he returned home on his own. Alone across the ocean he came, too impatient to wait to accompany the stepson.

The statement above also reflects more than simple homesickness; the stone is exhibiting a strong sense of indigenousness to the land from which he came. This notion is one that unites the stones with the Dakota people with whom they share the land. It also reinforces the importance of the reciprocal relationship enjoyed because of this interconnectedness with the environment.

Dakota men continued their service in the armed forces during World War II. Uŋkaŋna then provided the account of Peter White Cloud's participation with an iŋyaŋ śkaŋ śkaŋ, similar to the experience of John Duta. However, in this story, communication had stopped and the stone accompanying him was relaying no information about his safety or injury. After receiving notice that Peter White Cloud was a casualty, his grandmother, the keeper of the stones, conducted a ceremony to find out what transpired. A stone from home responded to her request for information, and they learned that he had suffered shell shock but would return safely. In this instance, the stone sent to look after White Cloud was not responding, but they were able to obtain the information they were seeking from the stones kept at home.

Stories about the iŋyaŋ śkaŋ śkaŋ are abundant in Dakota culture, and most people, if educated at all in the traditional teachings, are aware of their presence and use. However, the number of stone caretakers has significantly diminished in the last century. Numerous stories exist about individuals who kept stones for years, but then lost custodial care of them. Within my own family, a couple of accounts were provided about these traveling stones. My kuŋśi, Naomi Cavender, a Bdewakaŋtuŋwaŋ Dakota from Santee, Nebraska, provided the following account about the use of these in order to find a young man who had disappeared:

This medicine man came from Rosebud, South Dakota; I believe his name was Poor Dog. He was a medicine man and healer. A young man had disappeared from Santee, Nebraska. They waited for him to come, but he never showed up. This was almost six months later that the mother contacted this medicine man from Rosebud. So he came to Santee and he got his information about what they wanted him to find so they would know where her son was. They had a special night set for this occasion. It was in the young man's home, where he disappeared from. The night that he left his home he went to Springfield, South Dakota, to be with some friends that live there. I imagine they visited for a while, then he never came back. The boat that he went across in was found in the place that he got out from where he took it from the Nebraska side. His mother was very worried so she asked Mr. Poor Dog to perform a ceremony to see if he could contact her son and find some answer to why he isn't home.

This very night he invited a few members of the Santee village and they were there. My brother, John Mato, was one of them. He said he sat on the floor because that's where he wanted them to sit. And they had a blanket in the middle of the floor where the medicine man sat with his helper.... He talked to his little iŋyaŋ śkaŋ śkaŋ, his little spirit stone, and he told them about the tragedy, or the missing of this young man, to see if he could go out and follow in the trail that he left on his way to Springfield, which was across from Santee.

So the little stone left and he was gone for one hour, two hours, and about the third hour they heard a rustling, and it seemed like it was from the window where he came through. With him, he brought a handkerchief, a farmer's handkerchief, and it was red. It was all soaked with water and it had sand mixed in and so the handkerchief was all covered with sand. They heard this thump and the medicine man said, "There, he is back." So they asked him, "What did you find?" The little spirit stone gave the message that the young man was in the river and he is dead, and to tell the mother that was all he could find. There were no more signs of him anyplace. So the mother was contented then that she at least knew her son would never come back and that he passed on. Then she thanked the medicine man for his efforts and the message that the little spirit stone brought back. This is the extent of this ceremony. My brother experienced this and all the noise and sounds. He heard a whirling sound, so he thought maybe it was the little spirit stone that was making that sound as he entered the room.

My grandmother's mother had one of these little spirit stones. You have to take care of them, at least handle them every now and then and put it in a nice container or something. Otherwise they are fussy little stones, and if you mistreat them, they will leave. Here, she had forgotten to take care of her little stone. This was a family stone; we had it in our family for years. It was up to her to take care of it because she was the last of the family, but she forgot and when she did remember she went to look and the little stone was gone. She told her husband and her father and all of the family members, so they all went looking to all the different places they thought he might be, to someone's grave or something. In Peever, South Dakota, there is a hill. It's almost like a mountain. I think his name is Chief Renville, [who] is buried up there on that hill. There are other members of the tribe, some notables that are buried up there. They went up there and they looked and they found the little stone at somebody's grave. So, they recognized him because they had him for so long, and they brought him home. My dad said he doesn't remember what happened to the little stone after the grandmother died. They might have buried him someplace. That is what you are supposed to do if you can't take care of him. The one that grandmother had, his features were just like a human's. I guess it is just once in a lifetime that anyone finds one. It's like a gift or something because it carries you through any kind of problems or troubles. It is like a guardian.[4]

Kuŋśi Naomi's account reinforces the widespread belief in and experience with these stones and emphasizes the respect that must be shown to them.

My grandmother's grandparents, John and Isabel Roberts, also had iŋyaŋ śkaŋ śkaŋ in their possession. Growing up I heard numerous stories about them from Kuŋśi Elsie (Two Bear) Cavender. One story was of particular interest to me because it relayed how the moving stones contributed to the migration of Dakota people from Canada back to Minnesota years after the U.S.-Dakota War of 1862. She relayed to me that Lazarus Skyman, the son of Maḣpiya Wicaṡta, or Chief Cloudman, told his relatives in Canada that he wanted to return to Minnesota about twenty-five years after 1862. However, at that time bounties for Dakota scalps were still in effect in Minnesota, and his brothers warned him that if he returned he might be killed for the bounty. He responded to them that he was lonesome for his homeland, and even if he might be killed he was going to go. He told them if nothing happened, he would get word to them. My grandmother believed it was through the iŋyaŋ śkaŋ śkaŋ that Lazarus's relatives learned of his safety in Minnesota.[5]

When she was a child, my grandmother said she used to play with the four stones her grandparents had. She talked about her grandmother getting very upset when she would catch them because of their wakaŋ quality, and so she would then hide them away. Similar to the stones in Kuŋśi Naomi's story, she was not aware of what happened to them in more recent years.

The last story included in this section details the origin of the waehdepi or the "setting of food." In this account we learn about the very close bond between two men who were raised together from childhood. Even when they married, the men continued to hunt together and were a daily presence in one another's life. In their experiences together, they often demonstrated their care for one another in the sharing of meals. So when one died prematurely, the other was so distressed that this bereaved friend continued to set a place for him to eat. At this invitation, his friend returned to enjoy this gift of a meal. In this manner a way was created to ease the sorrow of the grief-stricken friend while the spirit of his koda was fed.

The close friendship that sometimes formed between Dakota men was one discussed by Ella Deloria in *Waterlily*. When discussing the relationship between Rainbow and Palani, Deloria states:

> A *kola* was someone special; his wishes and needs could not be ignored, for that was the basis of the relationship. . . . "Fellows" were men of comparable standing and ability who were drawn together by like tastes and by a mutual respect and admiration for each other's character and personal charm. "The best I have is for my fellow" was their code from the time they pledged eternal loyalty. In line with that, one's best horse automatically went to the other whenever they met after a prolonged separation. When possible, they went on the warpath together in order to protect each other. In every phase of life they must act without thought of self, in defense of and to the advantage of the other. One must give one's life to save the other. Fellowhood was a compelling association whose obligations were a pleasure.[6]

While Uŋkaŋna never stated that these men joined a pact of "fellowhood," certainly many of these qualities were present in the story, and the closeness of their relationship is evident.

Again, this is a story that cannot be validated by standard historical methods, and exactly when this story occurred is irrelevant. What is important is that a tradition was started between these two men, one that is reliant on the notion of spirit and a belief in the wakaŋ. Through this story Dakota people are taught about the connection of people in this world to those who have passed on. A messenger was required to relay that other spirits are hungry:

> "Wotaŋ kaŋhaŋ wokitaŋyaŋ kaeš ehdeŋ kaŋhaŋ hena içakiš hiyeye do heciya okiçic'u wotapi do," eya kiŋhdakeye.

> "When they eat set out even a small portion, when they are in need over there, they share what they eat," he left saying that he said.

To feed these spirits, then, only small portions are needed, and as is the case here, the Dakota of the spirit world share whatever they have.

As Uŋkaŋna points out, the practice of setting out food for deceased loved ones is still practiced today by many Dakota. He also mentions what he refers to as ahake wotapi or the last feast. This is a public event that occurs one year after the death of a loved one, and this large feast is usually accompanied by an ituḣ'aŋ or gift-giving ceremony. This, Uŋkaŋna relates, is different from the more personal and private waehdepi, which he tells us he practices daily for his relatives who have gone on. This story offers one of those poignant glimpses into how we as Dakota people can maintain our identities and proper relationships in the twenty-first century. Very much a man of the modern world, Uŋkaŋna relates how when going to a hockey or baseball game, he continues feeding his relatives by buying an extra popcorn, hot dog, or soda. These can then be shared with his living loved ones, while he honors and remembers the deceased loved ones.

These stories are important not only for the teachings they provide about how to live and interact with other spiritual beings; they also demonstrate a couple of important points about the Dakota oral tradition. The first is that the oral tradition is not something that begins several generations after an event has happened (as many academic historians have contended); rather, it is a dynamic, ever-changing process of interpretation carried on by those who have had specialized training. These stories do not have to wait generations before they become a part of the oral tradition. They become stories from the oral tradition the moment they are conveyed to an audience by someone charged with that responsibility. The second important point about the modernity of these stories is that they demonstrate the sustainability and adherence to a worldview that is often associated with Indigenous Peoples of the nineteenth century or earlier. Presumably, after being shown the self-proclaimed superiority of the colonizer's science and technology, Indigenous Peoples would have shed these "primitive" ways and beliefs and gratefully accepted "reality" according to the dominant society's oppressive culture. While certainly many Native people have been converted intellectually by colonizing forces, in every generation there have existed Dakota individuals and families who have resisted these colonizing forces. When we accept and transmit stories embodying our culturally defined historical reality, stories that defy Western scientific principles and epistemological foundations, we are resisting.

Because of the importance of history in the formation of contemporary identity, the supplanting of Dakota voices and worldview with that of Western academic "Indian" history has had a devastating impact on how Indigenous Peoples see themselves. While ethnohistorians and anthropologists might make use of stories such as these to demonstrate Native "beliefs," they have been relegated to a place outside the historical realm. One prominent historian summarily dismissed these kinds of stories as unacceptable historical sources because they are based on what he referred to as "privileged information."[7] The consequence of this is that many Native peoples have come to accept Native accounts about the past as inferior to white written sources. Scholars like myself who are working at re-legitimizing traditional knowledge are doubly challenged. Not only must we educate non-Native academics and popular culture, we must also attempt to undo the damage done to those Native people who have internalized this intellectual racism and oppression.

However, the documentation of these stories and their addition to the historical record requires answering some specific questions: What role should stories such as these play in the written interpretation of Dakota history or Indigenous history in general? What about tenets of historical inquiry that demand validation and verification by other sources, preferably written? Historians have not known what to do with stories that seem to be impossibilities by their standards, so they have ignored them or handed them over to anthropologists to be dealt with as myths or folklore. I would suggest that history does not need to be the place where the unexplainable is explained. Nowhere in my grandfather's accounts does he attempt to explain how the iŋyaŋ śkaŋ śkaŋ actually move from one place to another or how they convey their messages—stones are without legs, mouths, and vocal cords, after all. From our historical perspective, the *how* does not really matter, the reality is they *do*. Many of the stories dealing with such unexplainable mysteries as the iŋyaŋ śkaŋ śkaŋ, the tak śkaŋ śkaŋ, or the spirit that came forth to partake in the waehdepi are still part of the Dakota historical record. They are impossible to verify according to standard historical practices, but they are no less significant in shaping our sense of the past and the place we, as contemporary Dakota people, have in that past. To deny their legitimacy is to deny the legitimacy of Dakota human experience.[8]

Our oral traditions have survived thousands of years, and my elders fluent in our languages and traditions have conveyed a complete confidence in our oral traditions. They also view our stories as essential to the cultural survival of our people, but they see them as being severely threatened in the face of cultural domination and oppression. At the end of the second section, Uŋkaŋna Eli Taylor closes by saying: "You go back and for what you think it's worth, you will take those things, what you think you'll be able to get across. Because it has been fifty-eight years now, that long since Chief of Indian Affairs, Indian Brotherhood, outside and different organizations, those joined with Indian Affairs, I could get nothing into their head because their way is the only way." For ninety-one years Uŋkaŋna saw how differences in worldview affected Indigenous-white relations, and in all of his positions he constantly attempted to educate those who would listen. He hoped that by sharing these stories, by having them documented, that more success might be achieved. Are non-Indigenous Peoples ready to listen?

10. Akicitapi (They Are Warriors)

The narratives contained within this chapter were grouped together because they all deal with some aspect of war but demonstrate a definite range in content, format, and style. The first story begins with a brief discussion of languages and the establishment of the U.S.-Canadian border. Then as he talks about love of land, Uŋkaŋna relays his thoughts about the thirty-eight Dakota men who were hanged in Mankato, Minnesota, in the winter of 1862. Much of this serves as a conversational lead into the story about the vanity of four young men. This story has clearly survived through the years and is repeated through the generations because of the lesson it teaches about the importance of humility. Within this story is something Uŋkaŋna refers to as a wapetokca, a miracle.

The second story is what may be termed an okicize story, or story of war. Uŋkaŋna relays an account of Herb Hapa and George Blackface serving as Dakota code-talkers during World War I. While some nations have received much publicity around their formal service as code-talkers, particularly the Diné during World War II, there are many examples of Indigenous servicemen from other nations using their langauges for code-talking less formally in situations similar to the one described here with these two Dakota men.[1] They differ from the Navajo code-talkers in that they used their regular conversational language as code rather than a code within the language as did the Diné.

Ehaŋna Woyakapi Iakewaŋźi (The Eleventh Historical Narrative)

Hehan deciya wauŋ ded imacaġe, hehan ihaŋktuŋwaŋnak wicope wauŋ iapi iś tokça.

This is where I was born, I was amongst the Ihaŋktuŋwaŋna at that time, they speak differently.

Ihnuna toketaŋ tuwe hip nakuŋ, "Haw kola," he iap tokça, "Haw, dina osni yedo," he Ihaŋktuŋwaŋ.

Also those who came from elsewhere, "Hello friend," speaking differently, "Hello, it is very cold," that's Ihaŋktuŋwaŋ.

---

1. See Margaret Bixler, *Winds of Freedom: The Story of the Navajo Code Talkers of World War II* (Darien CT: Two Bytes, 1992); Doris A. Paul, *The Navajo Code Talkers* (Pittsburgh PA: Dorrance, 1998); and Kanji Kawano, *Warriors: Navajo Code-Talkers* (Flagstaff AZ: Northland, 1990).

Haw ṭukṭe ed hena nawicahuŋ śni, ṭohan heciya uŋyaŋpṭe wokokpe he ehan haw dena owicaġu ḳahab, haw hena he Isaŋtaŋḳa heca.

Those places where they don't hear this language, at that time it was dangerous to go over there because of this border line the Big Knives made.

Haw hena uŋkiś deciya taŋhaŋ dena uŋciyapi uŋ wicaśta he uŋcapi.

Those of us here, for our grandmother,[2] we are men.

Haw heuŋ eṭaŋhaŋ, ḳana Waśicu tawaciŋ dena ṭaḳu ed ohnihnakaba.

Therefore, for that reason those Waśicu put these things into your mind.

Haw hed ocistiyeda hed yutokca, haw de uŋḳiża Canada hed Isaŋtaŋḳa he wokokpeḳapi kuwa uŋḳaupa pabaksa uŋḳaupi śicecaḳ.

So there was a change for a little while, yes, as for us there in Canada, the Big Knives were dangerous, they chased after us, cutting our heads as they came, the children.

Haw heced, ṭaḳuwicayeḳ iś Ina heci deciya iś ihihnatuŋ deci imacaġe owicaġu de opṭa.

Yes, those who are the relatives, as for Ina over here, as for her, she took a husband, I was born over here across the border.

Wokokcikpapi he Dakoṭak eḳaś tka he Ṭaḳ Wakaŋ ed euŋkcituwaŋpapa dehan aŋpeṭu de oyaṭek hena uŋhdu uŋkaŋpi uŋśipi akṭa wicaśkan.

Even the Dakota were afraid of each other, but something sacred watched over us, and now today those people are telling us to rid ourselves of things and start over.

Haw he wiṭaya uŋḳinażiŋpi kiŋhaŋ, haw he kopawahdaḳek he he hehaŋyaŋ inażiŋ Dakoṭak de uŋwiṭayapi uŋwaŋżipina kaŋhaŋ.

Yes, if we should all stand together, the fear I have, it will stop there, if we the Dakota stand together as one.

Tokaṭakiya ihnunah owitaŋcan ḳa maka akinicapi, wicakizapa śkaŋpi, kicazaba wicaza wicota wicaśta ota awihnunapi.

Sometime in the future, maybe the leaders and the people fighting over the land, fighting each other, they will destroy masses of people for nothing.

Dauŋkoṭap uŋġe heciya uŋ.

Some of the Dakota people are over there.

Miś ciŋye waye heciya waŋke, First World War ed.

As for me, my older brother lies over there, from the First World War.

Haw, he he hena wocaŋṭe śice hena eṭanś ṭoḳed dehan ekṭa ṭoḳed uŋ hena heced waŋḳap maka tehiŋda.

---

2. Grandmother here most likely refers to Canada and Queen Victoria of England.

Yes, those are heartaches, but in these times the reason why they are lying there is because of the love of their land.

Wicaḣcadakiya otke wicayapi, hena maka teḣiŋdapi.
They hanged some old men, those who cherished the earth.

Tokaṭakiya takoźakpaku ciŋcap hena ṭak saŋpa hena makaḳ teḣiŋdapi.
Their future grandchildren's children will cherish the earth even more.

Hena otke wicayapi.
They hanged them.

Eṭaŋhaŋ tokaṭakiya waŋna hena wowaṡṭe ecuŋpi hena.
They have blessed the future now.

Hena ṭaḳ śica ecuŋpa otke wicayapi śni.
They were not hanged for doing anything bad.

Hena ṭaku wowaṡṭe uŋ t'api he wowaṡṭeḳ he ṭuweda ḳapeya śni.
They died for doing good, no one can compare to what they died for.

Wowaṡṭe uŋ hena otkewicayapi.
For that righteousness they were hanged.

Okicize ekṭa yeḳ hena wowaṡṭeḳ uŋ hena wicakṭepi.
They killed the ones who went to war for that righteousness.

Heced owas okiciyakapi ḳa nakuŋ heced uŋḳokiyaḳapi Dakoṭaḳ hena.
They all told this to each other and also, they told us, the Dakota.

Wowapi wakaŋ de wakaŋṭuya deced wohdake Dakoṭa ia ḳaġapi, yega wadake kte.
This is the way it reads in the great holy book they made into Dakota, go and see it.³

He ḳiciyuhap he ahakeḣ ciŋye George Willard he he mak'u.
The last one who had it was older brother George Willard, he gave me that.

Hed wahnake, ṭohanṭu ca bdu, bduġaŋ ḳa bdawa ce.
I have it there, sometimes I open it and I read it.

Yawa abde ḳiŋhaŋ ṭohaŋya bdawa ḳaŋhaŋ haw hed imayuḣica.
As I read along, when I read it so far, indeed, it revives me.

Ḳakiya hehan Dekśi wicawayeḳ ateda wicawayeḳ hinaḣ wahokumaḳiyapi he hena oṭa owa, ṭaku commandments heced hena owas.
The uncles I have over there are like fathers, the ones who still advise me write a lot of it, like the way all of those commandments were written.

---

3. Here he may be referring to a Bible that has Dakota accounts written by hand in it, where people used to keep treasured writings or record important personal data such as births, deaths, and marriages.

Tid wica kṭe śni.[4]

Thou shalt not kill.

Nihuŋkake uŋśiwicakidake, wamanu śni wo, ṭaku yaciŋ ke kiŋhaŋ, ṭak he yuha wo.

Have love and compassion for your parents, do not steal, if there is something you need, have what it is you need.[5]

Ṭakuda kuŋ śni wo.

Don't covet things.

Hena ded owa hed ded oyaŋke hena waŋna itokab kaki dena wabdake uŋmaspe śni, hena waŋna naȟ'uŋ wauŋ.

He wrote those here in this community, over there he's already heard that before, I didn't learn from seeing,[6] I grew up hearing those.

Haw heced, ṭaku oṭa.

And so, there are many thoughts.

Ḣtanihaŋ uŋġe wociciyakap hena nakuŋ uŋġe iyaçupi nacece.

Some of the things I told you yesterday, you all probably took in some of those.[7]

Uŋkaŋ, mni waŋ opṭa hdiçupi de iś kat'a awicaupi uŋkaŋ, okpaze . . . hena ȟtanihaŋ iyacupi, nacece.

And so, it got dark when they [Europeans] came back across the waters and they [Indians] were being knocked down unconscious . . . you probably got those yesterday.

Iyacup śni ka ṭośṭa nayakiȟuŋpi ake ṭośṭake, akṭa ociciyakapṭe.

If you didn't get them you will hear it over again, I will tell it to you all over again.

Ṭaku oṭa, ṭaku wapetokça oṭa naȟ'uŋ wauŋ.

I grew up hearing many of these miracles.

Hena waśicuŋta kaki mniwaŋca akasam heciya hena ṭaku wapetokça.

Amongst the Waśicu over there, over the ocean, those things are miracles.

Ded iża deciya Dakoṭak uŋġe iża ṭaku oṭa ṭokça heca, heca oṭa.

Over here some Dakoṭa also have many different things happen.

Ito, waŋżi ociciyakapṭe he heca kecanmi.

---

4. Interestingly, the Dakoṭa translation more literally refers to not killing anyone in the house—a differentiation the Dakoṭa make between murdering someone domestically and killing that might be done outside the house (as in wartime, which would not be considered unethical).

5. You should have what you need so you don't have to steal.

6. This is a reference to reading, "seeing" writing on paper.

7. His expectation here is that we not only heard what he told us the previous day but that we took the information in, internalizing it and making it a part of ourselves.

I will tell you about one that is [a miracle], I think.

Ṭaku waśicu ḳa wau uŋkiś Dakoṭaḳ wapetokça uŋkeyapi de miracle heca he uŋkapi do, wapetokça.

For us, the Dakota, when we say wapetokça what we mean is the Waśicu's miracle, wapetokça.

Uŋkaŋ, waŋna hed de waŋna de oyaṭek uŋġe iciman kciyuzapi.

And so, now the different tribes are marrying into each other.

Oyaṭe ṭokça uŋġe Ḣaḣatuŋwaŋ, Śaiya, iś Maśṭiŋca Oyaṭe, ḳaiś Sihasapa ḳa Ḣewa, Oohe, ṭaku oṭa uŋyaŋpi icicahi several uŋkitawapi.

Ours are some different nations, Anishinaabe, Cheyenne, Cree, also Blackfeet and Hidatsa, Assiniboine, there are many mixed cultures, several are ours.

He ṭaku oṭa ikoyaḳe haw wicotawaciŋ hena owas mitakoźa he eya uŋġe Ḣewapa uŋġe, Ḣaḣatuŋwaŋ, naḳuŋ uŋġe can Ḣaḣatuŋwaŋ.

There are many ways their thoughts are all connected, some of my grandchildren are Hidatsa, Anishinaabe, and also some woodland Anishinaabe.

Hena waŋźida iyececa dehan wicotawaciŋ yuke.

From their being one, there are some thoughts from that.

He uŋ he ehan kośkaḳ eya ṭonakça nuŋpa yamni ced, heyapi, "Waŋ! Ḳa ye waŋ wiyaka aopaza yeda waŋ he ṭoḳed."

So many young men, two or three they said, "Wow! Look at that little one going with a feather in his hair."

"Hohe, toka kṭe da waŋ."

"Hohe, he has killed an enemy."

"He toka kṭe he uŋ etaŋ waḳan opeya woyuonihaŋ ikoyake do."

"Because he killed an enemy, for that reason he's elevated with honors."

"He ṭaku aokpani."

"He's still lacking."

"Uŋkaŋ, waŋźi wiyaka wapaha uŋ he iś ṭokeca?"

"And so, the one who wears a war bonnet, how is it with him?"

"Haw he waŋna wiyaka iyenakca ic'iye toka ṭop wica kṭe wiyaka wapaha he uŋ kta he, ihdamna do."

"Yes, now he has completed the feathers that he should have because he killed four of the enemy, he earned that."

Kośka ṭopap ṭukṭed uŋpi uŋkaŋ wohdaka yaŋkapi.

Four young men were sitting around someplace talking.

"Waŋ! Eś uŋkiźa ṭoḳiya zuya uŋyaŋpa."

"Waŋ! We could go on the warpath."

"Toka etaŋhaŋ paḳ pauŋśta ḳaba uŋkahdiṗ ḳiŋhaŋ uŋkiźa wiyaka aopaza uŋk'uŋpta uŋkiźa dena wicaśṭapi."

"We'll take the scalp of the enemy and bring it back, we too will wear a feather on our head, we are men also."

"Haw, hecetu kte do."

"Yes, it will be so."

"Haw he taŋyaŋna," eyap keyapi.

"Yes, that would be well," they say they said.

Haw heced nahmana tokitkiya zuyayapte.

Yes, without being seen they left to go on the warpath.

Toka etaŋhaŋ tukted tipta de yapta.

They went where the enemy lived.

Ihnuh koškak hena toki iyayapi.

Suddenly, the young men went somewhere.

Toki wihni iyayap šta kup šni ecinpi.

They thought they went hunting somewhere but didn't come back.

Haw, iš de yap he waŋna nuŋpa ced yamni ce yaba.

They were going for two [days] and then they were going three.

Itopa iwaŋkapi.

The fourth [day] they laid down.

Hah'aŋna deced kaowotaŋyaŋ ayek hecan koškak waŋži kikta ka taŋkad ye kta hca heced taŋkad iyaye.

At the break of day one of the men woke up and really had to go outside, so he went outside.[8]

Cehnake de iyut'iŋse iyekiya iheye kte secece uŋkaŋ takuda šni.

He reached in where his breechcloth was tied to go to the bathroom, but there wasn't anything there.

Saŋpa yutaŋtaŋ kta uŋkaŋ wiŋyaŋ.

He felt further and he was a woman.

Haw heced ceya, ceya uŋ umaŋg dena iš uŋpi dena iš, "He de wiuŋcap uŋkohitikapi dena zuya uŋyaŋpi."

And so he cried—he was crying around—the others said, "We are men, we are brave, as for us, we are going to war."

"Canwaŋka ka ikopa heced u kte šni tka tak ode u he?"

"He's scared and he's afraid, he shouldn't have come, what did he come looking for anyway?"

Iža eyapi taŋkad yaŋkap waŋži he eyaya ye ka inažiŋ ka iža iheye kta uŋkaŋ hehan takuda šni, wiŋyaŋ.

---

8. Taŋkad ye kte (she or he is going outside) is how the Dakota would say, "She [or he] is going out to the bathroom."

One was saying that as they walked out and he stood to go to the bathroom and there was nothing, he was a woman.

"Haw iża de wayaka de uŋśika awacinye nakaha iża ceya do," eyaba umaŋ iża hena.

"Well look at him, poor thing, he [meaning the first man turned to woman] made him think about it because he's also crying," those others said.

Iża ipta nakuŋ hena heced topa owas nażiŋpa ceyayakapi, owas wiŋyaŋpi.

The others went out and they were all four standing there crying, they were all women.

"Tokedked uŋyaŋkupta," eyapi.

"How are we going to live?" they said.

"Tiyata uŋhdap śta woiśteca wiŋyaŋ uŋkipte do."

"We will go home, shamefully, as women."

"Hehan iś uŋkic'ikepta uŋkaŋ he, iye uŋyaŋp kaŋhaŋ uŋwiŋyaŋpi iyeuŋyaŋpta."

"And if we should kill ourselves, when they found us, they would find us as women."

"Tukted aya pica śni do."

"There is nowhere to turn."

Iyukcapi uŋkaŋ haw he iś heye hecetu śta, "Uŋhdapta de uŋ topap tuweda awicuŋ uŋkiyapte śni do."

They thought and they said they made a decision, "We will go back, but the four of us, none of us will say a word."

"Tuweda takiye kte śni do."

"No one will say anything."

"Heced hehan nakuŋ wiŋyaŋ uŋyaŋkupte do."

"So then, also, we will be as women."

Haw heced hdapa kiwuŋkapi ake hdapa ake kiwuŋkapa.

And so they went on their way home and they laid down to sleep and again they laid down.

Waŋna hah'aŋna kihuŋni nipta aeś hena woiyukcaŋ toked iyukcaŋp taŋ iś śni.

Now they were going to arrive at home tomorrow, indeed it was something to think about, but they didn't know what to think.

Hah'aŋna hehan hah'aŋnah waŋżi he kikta ka taŋkad i kta uŋkaŋ waŋna ake wica.

The next day, when it was very early in the morning, one woke, went outside, and he was a man again.

Ake waŋżi iża i kta uŋkaŋ iża waŋna ake wica.

Again, one went out to go and here he too was now a man again and he gave a cry.

Uŋkaŋ ka iża hehan ṭopa owas ake wicapi.

And so, they also were all four men again.

Uŋkaŋ, he ecan waŋna tawacin ṭuwe tid wicakṭepa wiyaka keya aopazo uŋpṭe, wakantuya ecidapta wicoṭawaciŋ . . . wakantuya wica waciŋwicakiyuzapi ciŋpi hena ṭakuda ed uŋp śni.

And so, already in their minds [before], were thoughts of those they killed and that they would wear some feathers, thinking highly of themselves were their thoughts . . . [now,] that they would want them to think highly of them was not even in their minds.

Kipi ka uŋśiic'iya oyaṭek hed wicopeya.

They went home in all humbleness there amongst the people.

Uŋkaŋ he, he de ṭaku wapetokça ṭokiki pazo.

And so, this is something showing a miracle some place.

Haw he heca nacece wakiye—sdodwaye śni ka hehan, heca okihi he, uŋkis uŋkiyepi he.

Yes, I believe that is probably what it was—I don't know, and then, that is what it could be, for us that is what it could be.

Wicoṭawaciŋ hena yuwaśṭe ka hena śica hena ṭaku hececa ḣçe oṭa do, he ṭaku he oṭa.

It makes for those good thoughts and those bad, there are many things like that, many things like that.

Woyake Okicize Ṭokaheya (The First War Story)

Uŋkaŋ hehan heciya ṭaŋhaŋ First World War ahdip hena wohdaka yaŋkaŋpi hed nakuŋ ṭakuwaŋ nawahuŋ.

And so then the ones who returned from the First World War over there, they sat around talking, there I also heard something.

Ḣṭayeṭu ca pika kic'uŋpi returned men ciŋ ṭaku ṭokça icuŋpte yuhapṭe śni heced akicita wicaśṭa ḣṭayeṭu tukṭed pika kic'uŋpi iś ṭoki wawaŋyaŋkapi iś waciŋ ṭaku.

In the evenings the returned men played cards, they didn't have anything different to do, and so the veterans in the evening they played cards someplace or went to the movies or to a dance or something.

Haw pika kic'uŋpa ecewakṭapi hena.

They got used to playing cards.

Heced hdipi nakaha de ṭaŋhaŋ wayek akicita hdi he iża heciya ṭaŋke kci uŋ.

And so that is how they came back, my brother-in-law returned as a veteran, he too stayed with older sister over there.

Hed hipa piḳa ḳic'uŋpi he iża wohdaka yaŋḳapce ihnunaḣ he de detaŋhaŋ, Herb Hapa eciyapi, wicaṡta he iża First World War ekta i.

They would go there and play cards, they too would sit talking, and here a man from here called Herb Hapa, he had gone to the First World War.

Iŋkpaduta eciyapi.

His name was Scarlet Point.

Uŋkaŋ he, Beulah heciya taŋhaŋ koṡka waŋ George Blackface eciyapi.

And so, there was a young man named George Blackface from Beulah.

He kci detaŋhaŋ iyaye deda hed trained iyeyapa he kci tohaŋya eṡta ouŋye⁹ kci sakib ouŋya ḳa haw heced heciya iyayapi.

He left with him from here and trained with him right here, he was with him and by his side for a while and so they left for over there.

Tohan eṡta tuktetu kci ouŋye ḳa maka makokeḳ hena kci ouŋye.

For a while he was with him in different parts of the land, he was with him.

Iyokpiya kci yauŋ ihnunaḣ, ihnunaḣ ob akicita optayeḳ de kiwica yaṡpupi, division num ḳaġapi.

They were happy together, and all of a sudden the military troop separated them to make two divisions.

Uma eciyataŋhaŋ Herb Hapa opeḳ uma eciyataŋhaŋ iṡ de George Blackface opa.

Herb Hapa joined the other division, as for George Blackface, he joined the other side.

Haw heced commanders iṡ hena toktokçapi wicayuhapi.

So they had different commanders.

Haw heced George Blackface ed ope ded de ḳakiya German front lines heci ikiyeda iża de front line de aba haw ḳa sutaya yaŋḳapi, they have a strong hold on Germany hena haw de heci yaŋḳapi.

And so George Blackface, the one that joined over there close to the German front lines, as for them they went to the frontlines, they were in a stronghold, they have a stronghold on those Germans, yes, they were over there.

Hehan deciya iḣayata hed iṡ Herb Hapa de opa hed ope yaŋḳe.

And then over here in the rear, Herb Hapa was amongst the ones that he joined.

---

9. *Ouŋye* might also be translated as *roaming around together*, or *hanging around together*, but indicates they spent a lot of time together in friendship.

Ṭaku nina kapi uŋkaŋ haw ka haḣaŋna kaŋhaŋ wihiyayeda oape ṭohan ṭuŋ-waŋ they were going to attack ka German sutaya yaŋkap he tawicak pepṭa kiŋhaŋ he ecan de oape iyehan de iża iyayapṭa kaŋhaŋ wicota kṭe.

They were really discussing something and at some hour of the morning, they were going to attack, the German stronghold they were going to attack, and if they all left at the same time there would be many of them.

He wicakipṭe the stronghold heced iwohdakapi.

They would take over the stronghold, that's what they were talking about.

Haw he waŋna ṭohan ṭukṭa keyapi.

They had said when it was going to be.

Wihiyayeda oape ṭohan ṭukṭe keyapi yuṡṭaŋpi uŋkaŋ deciya he ṭaku eyeceṭu ṡni keyapi.

They had agreed on the time and here something wasn't right over here, they said.

Ḳaya waŋna kakiya hena naḣ'uŋpa hehan hena deciya ekṭa iyehan iyayapi okihip ṡni.

The ones that were on their way now over there heard, but over here they could not leave on time.

"Haw heced ka owicauŋkiyakapi iyehaŋ uŋkiyapi uŋkokihip ṡni," eya. "Commanders hena okiciyakapṭa kaeṡ iaṡicak hena wires hena tap iyayap heced."

"And so we told them we could not leave in time," he said. "Those commanders were going to tell each other but the Iaṡica[10] had tapped the wires."

Ṭaku iapi ṭokça hena iaṡica ka ṭaku oyaṭe obe hena naḣ'uŋ yakapi ṭaku ṭuwe iyek kaeṡ ṭuwe oyake kaeṡ hena owas okaḣniġapi.

The different languages, the Iaṡica and different nationalities, they were listening, they understood all of whatever anyone said.

Uŋkaŋ de he Herb Hapa he wicaṡṭak de hececa waeyayeke ka nakuŋ ṭak owas nakuŋ ṭakudaṡ ṭokça dake ṡni.

And here this Herb Hapa, that man is someone who speaks his mind and also he doesn't really care.[11]

---

10. *Iaṡica* is the Dakoṭa word for the *Germans*. Literally translated it means *bad speakers*. Common knowledge among the Dakoṭa states that this was a reference to the tremendous amount of swearing done by the Germans encountered by the Dakoṭa. Within Minnesota a large number of German immigrants had settled in Minnesota, and Dakoṭa people were shocked that German people would take the name of their God in vain, something inconceivable to Dakoṭa people, even today.

11. While the phrase *ṭakudaṡ ṭokça dake ṡni* can be translated as *he doesn't really have an opinion or care*, another aspect of its meaning can be *he really wasn't afraid of anything*.

Commander heceḳ de okiyaḳe, "My partner George Blackface heciya uŋ do."
    And so he told the commander, "My partner, George Blackface, is over there."
Commander tawaḳ he, "You tell him I want to talk to him," eya.
    His commander said, "You tell him I want to talk to him."
"Oh it's never going to work because the wires are all tapped ḳa owicayakidaka ḳa de sdodyap ḳaŋhaŋ, they are going to come out and attack ours instead."
    "Oh, it's never going to work because the wires are all tapped and if you tell them and they know this, they are going to come out and attack ours instead."
Heced either way there was danger ḳakiya hena.
    And so, either way there was danger over there.
Heced de Herb Hapa he commander he, "Look here, he George Blackface kci wowahdaḳe ḳaŋhaŋ ṭohniŋna Iaśicaḳ hena sdodyapṭe śni do ḳa oḳahniġapṭe śni do."
    And so this Herb Hapa [told] the commander, "Look here, if I talk with George Blackface the Iaśica will never know those and they will not understand."
"What did you say? What are you talking about?"
Haw he Dakoṭa iwaye ḳa he he sdodyaye hecihan owicakiyaḳe kṭe do.
    I speak Dakoṭa and if you know this, he will tell them.[12]
"What are you saying?"
"He's an Indian and I'm an Indian, same tribe, what I tell him only the two of us can understand.
"No Germans, nor any English, Irish, or whatever know what's going on or understand.
"Well, it's worth a try, we are desperate now."
Commander he hecaḳ he, "George Blackface around?"
    The one that is the commander said, "George Blackface around?"
"Yes, well get him around, we want to talk to him."
Haw heced icipaś ihnunaḣ ihnunaḣ answer he hi.
    And so suddenly it came back, the answer came back.
Haw he k'up, "George he niye he? George Blackface he niye he?"
    They gave it to him, "George is that you? Are you George Blackface?"
"Yes, Herb Hapa wants to talk to you, hear him."

---

    12. George Blackface will tell his commander.

"Haw he niye? Ṭokedked niś yauŋ he?" sort of a visit before they got into it.

"Hello is that you? And as for you how are you?" sort of a visit before they got into it.

"Haw ṭaŋyaŋ de uŋyaŋkapi do."

"Hello, we are all doing fine."

"Hah'aŋna ḳaŋhaŋ hah'aŋna ḳaŋhaŋ naṭaŋ idadapṭa he yapi śni po.

"Tomorrow, tomorrow when you go to charge, don't go.

"Nihakab uŋhiyapṭeḳ he uŋkokihiṗ śni do ṭaḳṭoḳeṭu haw heced uŋhiyaṗ ḳaŋhaŋ ecan nicasota uŋkokihiṗ śni he ecan idadaṗ ḳaŋhaŋ nicasotapṭa do.

"We can't follow after you, something is wrong, and so if we start out when we can't, if you go they will wipe you out.

"Haw he uŋ eṭaŋhaŋ de wireḳ de nu mazapsupsuna dena ṭuwe oyaṭe ṭoḳca nah'uŋpi do, ociciyaka ca.

"For that reason this wire, the phone, these different nationalities are listening, I am telling you this.

"Itaŋcaŋ nitawaḳ he okiyake wo, haw ṭuweda ṭoḳca okiyaḳe śni wo."

"Tell your commander, don't tell anyone else."

Haw, haw heced, hah'aŋna hehan oape iyehaŋṭuŋhaŋ ḳa yapṭa keciŋma, "They were expecting us, heced ṭuweda ie śni."

And so, when it was morning it was the time they thought they were going, "They were expecting us, but no one went."

They helped because they heard through the wires that they were going to attack and they didn't attack.

Hah'aŋna hehan naḳaeś hehan, hehan yapṭeḳ iyehan iyayapi heced, stronghold icup ḳeyapi.

Tomorrow was when they were to go, they went on schedule and so they took the stronghold they said.

John Duṭa ded yaŋka uŋkaŋ heye, "Herb?"

John Duṭa was here and he said, "Herb?"

"Ṭaḳu?" eya.

"What?" he said.

Ciŋś he hecanum he eṭaŋhaś he hecanum he he ṭaŋyaŋ ecanuŋ wicaśṭa oṭa niwicayapi commander iś hena medals waśṭeśṭe ohiyaṗ ḳeyapi," eyaḳe ihapi.

"My son, what you did, even so you did that and you did well, a lot of men you saved, but as for the commander, they say he won all the nice medals," he said and they laughed.

That language means that much to us as Indian people.

Haw he he naŋḳa de miciŋkśi owikiyaḳe he.

Yes, that is what I told my son a while ago.

CMN: They always talk about Navajos doing that during World War II, but here are examples of Dakȟóta people doing that, exchanging intelligence like that.

Haw hehan ake, haw hehan ake, World War II de ake hiŋhuŋni, hiŋhuŋni.
Yes, then again, then again this again happened in World War II.

11. Wicotawaciŋ Yuwaṡte
(It Makes for Good Thoughts)

Historical consciousness is very closely related to feelings of self-worth and pride and is greatly affected by historical interpretation. A problem faced by many First Nations people is the discrepancy between how Indigenous history is interpreted in written texts, most often written by the colonizers and oppressors of Indigenous people, and how Indigenous history is interpreted within our oral traditions. This becomes even more obvious in accounts written about events in which direct conflict occurred between Indigenous people and whites. For the Eastern Dakota, this is nowhere more evident than in accounts surrounding the U.S.-Dakota War of 1862.

While many of the more recent texts depict a more sympathetic portrait of Dakota attacks on white settlers, highlighting the circumstances leading up to the war and the wrongs committed upon the Dakota, they still differ from many Dakota accounts. Dakota and Waṡicu beliefs and ideas about heroism and martyrdom are often at odds. However, in his book *History of the Santee Sioux*, Roy Meyer illustrates his understanding of this kind of discrepancy while discussing those typically depicted as "good Indians" during the U.S.-Dakota War of 1862:

> Noble deeds were performed by many of the participants in the conflict.... Among the Indians there were John Other Day, Lorenzo Lawrence, Paul Mazakutemani, Simon Anawangmani, and others, who took very real risks to help their white friends. They were praised in the newspapers and from the pulpits, and some of them received a more tangible reward through a congressional appropriation for their benefit a few years later. But no amount of praise for their courage can disguise the fact that they were betrayers of their people.[1]

Thus, "noble deeds" performed by some may be construed as acts of betrayal by others, depending on which side the observer is standing.

Yet on December 26, 1862, when thirty-eight Dakota men were hanged in the largest mass execution in United States history, historians (including Meyer) still present a very different picture of those men than do stories in the oral tradition. In many of the Waṡicu accounts, the thirty-eight are either written about as murderers, thieves, and rapists or, in the more sympathetic histories, as simply disorganized and rather pitiful warriors. Despite an increased awareness of racism and oppression in the twenty-first century, the colonialist interpretations of 1862 are alive and well. For example, though there have been a number of efforts in Minnesota within the last few decades to educate the public about the U.S.-Dakota War of 1862 (including events during the governor-declared "Year of Reconciliation" in 1987), many attitudes about Dakota involvement in the war remain extremely negative. This became apparent in a late 1997–early 1998 newspaper exchange that began when Dave Gonzales wrote an excellent editorial that appeared in the *Minneapolis Star Tribune* on Thursday, December 25, 1997, about the spiritual run held every Christmas night from Fort Snelling to Mankato to honor the thirty-eight Dakota who were hanged. On January 5, 1998, a counterpoint to Gonzales's article, written by two Minneapolis attorneys, John H. Hinderaker and Scott W. Johnson, appeared with the title, "Were Sioux hanged in 1862 patriots, or murderers and rapists?" According to the writers of this editorial, the thirty-eight hanged at Mankato were murderers and rapists, and President Lincoln, who signed the executive order, was a "combination of genius and compassion."

It was astounding that such an editorial would be published in a reputable newspaper, but given the apparent blindness to the need for a critical interrogation of Manifest Destiny ideology by most Americans, it is not surprising. Colonialist history is always about justifying the actions of the colonizer or, in this case, the invasion, conquest, genocide, removal, and colonization of Dakota people. A necessary component in this justification is an accompanying vilification of the colonized. Gonzales was aware of the conflicting narratives that emerge when the colonized voice is heard. In his article, he rightly stated: "There are two historical interpretations of the Dakota Conflict. The Dakota people interpreted the conflict as patriotic resistance to the unlawful peopling of their ancestral lands; the settlers interpreted the conflict as their right to farm and build towns and cities west of the Mississippi River."

Another disturbing article by Annette Atkins appeared in 2002, demonstrating that even the more "sympathetic" non-Indigenous historians have not been able to shed their colonialist perspective. Her article, printed in the *Minneapolis Star Tribune* on August 18, 2002, stated that Henry Sibley, the man responsible for setting up the shameful war trials, was in some sense "really their [the Dakota people's] friend and castigated for it" because "others would have skipped trials entirely and gone directly to execution."[2] With Atkins's twisted logic, the Dakota people should actually be grateful to Sibley for sentencing over three hundred Dakota men to death through trials that in some cases lasted as little as five minutes. With the equally twisted logic of Hinderaker and Johnson, we should also be grateful to Lincoln for "only" hanging thirty-eight of our men. Ngũgĩ wa Thiong'o, in reference to colonialist ideas about Africans writing in their own languages, describes the mythmaking phenomenon that occurs among the colonizing class, stating: "Once reality is perverted so totally, everyone begins to see things upside-down."[3] Indeed, the colonialist myth regarding 1862 has become so pervasive, Indigenous Peoples defending their land and way of life against invasion have become the villains.

Dakota portraits are markedly different and characterize the Dakota men hanged at Mankato as heroes, patriots, and martyrs who died defending their people, their way of life, and their land. These are the stories essential to the decolonization project, as they subvert the colonialist interpretation of events that have come to be identified as unchallenged "truth." This is why, in reference to the history of the oppressed, Ngũgĩ states: "History is subversive."[4] Uŋkaŋna Eli Taylor's powerful description of these men offers an exemplary subversion of the master narrative in some brief comments after his first story. While the remarks were offered casually, as commentary between two stories, they are profound in meaning. About the thirty-eight Dakota, he said:

> Wicaḣcadakiya otke wicayapi hena maka teḣindapi. Tokatakiya takoża-kpaku cincap hena ṭak saŋpa hena makak teḣindapi. Hena otke wicayapi. Etaŋhaŋ tokatakiya waŋna hena wowaṡte ecuŋpi hena. Hena ṭak śica ecuŋpa otke wicayapi śni. Hena ṭaku wowaṡte uŋt'api he wowaṡtek he ṭuweda kapeya śni. Wowaṡte uŋ hena otkewicayapi.

> They hanged some elder men, those who cherished the earth. Their future grandchildren's children will cherish the earth even more. They hanged them. They have blessed the future now. They were not hanged for doing anything bad. They died for doing good, no one can compare to what they died for. For that righteousness they were hanged.

Not only does this account differ dramatically from accounts relayed in written texts and the perspectives of many white Minnesotans today, it relates Indigenous agency and resiliency in a way that no existing written text on the topic does.[5] When knowledge of this Dakota account is transmitted from generation to generation, not only is a sense of pride instilled in the young listener, but a worldview is shaped that begins to inform future actions and thoughts. As the recipients of the Dakota oral accounts learn about the sacrifices made for them, in this instance the thirty-eight hanged in Mankato for cherishing their land and fighting, with each telling the attachment to land and place becomes strengthened, and the message of their sacrifice becomes deeply embedded in contemporary identity.[6] Unfortunately, many of our Dakota young people have not been exposed to perspectives such as Uŋkaŋna's but have become thoroughly familiar with the myth of the colonizers instead. Thus, this alternative knowledge has revolutionary potential. As we engage in the process of decolonization, we will restore those Dakota who were our fiercest resisters to the status of heroes. Our children will carry these heroes with a culture of resistance into the future.

Following his commentary, Uŋkaŋna then relayed a story that addresses the importance of humility within Dakota culture. The story begins with four young men admiring the feather worn in the hair of another warrior and his accompanying elevated status. They resolve to go out on the warpath in order to gain the honors necessary for them to join the ranks of those men wearing feathers. The wearing of feathers among the Dakota has always been a privilege rich in symbolism and detail. Charles Eastman wrote an explicit explanation of meanings associated with some of the various feathers. While eagle feathers, he said, were worn to represent a count of coup in battle, other animal feathers and eagle feathers that were specially marked were also worn.[7] All of them relayed a specific war chronicle:

> For instance, a group of raven or of Canadian goose feathers trimmed on the sides indicates that the wearer has been wounded in battle more than once. A single goose feather dyed red and trimmed, means that the wearer was severely wounded in battle. Sometimes a man wears an eagle feather dyed or trimmed, meaning that he was wounded at the time he counted the *coup*. An eagle feather notched and the cut dyed red, means that the wearer counted the *coup* and took the scalp also, but was wounded while so doing.
>
> He may have the feather cut off at the tip, showing that he killed his foe and counted the *coup* on the same enemy. If he fought a desperate battle, with the odds against him, in which he came off victor, he may tip his eagle's feather with buffalo hair; and if he counted *coup* in a charge on horseback in the face of imminent danger, he may tip it with hair from a horse's tail.[8]

Thus, the wearing of an eagle feather, or any other feather, provided a visible public display of each man's war history and exemplified his bravery and courage. However, because the young men in this story were intent on going to war for the wrong reason, to feed their vanity, a miracle occurred and the men discovered one by one that they had become women.

As the men began crying and pondering their condition, they made the following statements to one another:

> "Ṭokedked uŋyaŋkupṭa?" eyapi.
> "Tiyaṭa uŋhdap šta woišteca wiŋyaŋ uŋkipte do."
> "Hehan iš uŋkic'ikepṭa uŋkaŋ he, iye uŋyaŋp kaŋhaŋ uŋwiŋyaŋpi iye-uŋyaŋpṭa."
> "Ṭukṭed aya pica šni do."

"How are we going to live?" they said.
"We will go home, shamefully, as women."
"And if we should kill ourselves, when they found us, they would find us as women."
"There is nowhere to turn."

This raises an important and often misconstrued point about the status of women within Dakota culture. Among Dakota people listening to the story, there exists an implicit understanding that an exchange such as this has no negative implications about the value of women within Dakota society. Rather, the "shame" indicated here would reflect the problem with changing genders in adulthood and having to be accountable to the people about the reason they were turned into women. The men decide they will return to their homes and agree they will not say a word to others about what happened, but they would simply be as women.

The use of the term "shamefully" in this context may provide a temptation for others outside of Dakota culture to make negative assumptions about the value placed on women and their roles. One of the founding mothers of feminist archeology, M. Z. Rosaldo, in her essay entitled "The Use and Abuse of Anthropology: Reflections of Feminism and Cross-cultural Understanding," wrote: "Could I cite a single instance of a truly matriarchal—or, for that matter, sexually egalitarian—social form, I could go on to claim that all appeals to universal 'nature' in explaining women's place are, simply, wrong. But instead, I must begin by making clear that, unlike many anthropologists who argue for the privileged place of women here or there, my reading of the anthropological record leads me to conclude that human cultural and social forms have always been male-dominated."[9] However, a universal model such as this seems seriously flawed when applied to many Indigenous cultures and can be dangerous if it is allowed to define gender relations in societies worldwide. Because the issue of women's rights is one being confronted on a global scale, often led by Western women, it is important for non-Western women, and especially Indigenous women, to articulate internally their perceptions of their own status within their respective cultures.

Ella Deloria addresses the issue of gender roles in *Speaking of Indians*, saying: "Outsiders seeing women keep to themselves have frequently expressed a snap judgment that they were regarded as inferior to the noble male. The simple fact is that woman had her own place and man had his; they were not the same and neither inferior nor superior."[10] As mentioned previously, among the Dakota, the difference between traditional male and female gender roles was not an indication of gender hierarchy but rather a practical division of labor.

In this story the men learned their lesson and were restored to manhood. They were then able to return to the people with their newly found humility. In a society that depended heavily on cooperation and positive familial relationships for survival, individual pride and envy were not traits conducive to the well-being of the community. While men might receive special recognition for feats in war and in hunting, it was because of the protection and food they provided for the people. The wearing of certain feathers was also an indication that a man was ready to support and defend a family. Typically men were encouraged not to marry until they had proven abilities in war and in hunting, and parents would be reluctant to have their daughters marry men who had not yet attained such honors.[11]

With the recitation of this story, the audience is reminded of Dakota virtues and a code of ethics to be abided by, not just because of fear of reproach from the people but also because there are powers greater than ourselves capable of performing miracles. The desired qualities associated with manhood, as Eastman asserts in *Indian Boyhood*, are found in self-control: "The truly brave man we contend, yields neither to fear nor anger, desire nor agony; he is at all times master of himself."[12] By mastering their envy and vanity, those in Uŋkaŋna's story become men by Dakota standards.

The modern okicize account offered next is the story of Dakota code-talkers Herb Hapa and George Blackface. Until hearing this story, although I was well familiar with stories of other celebrated code-talkers, I was unaware that the Dakota had also been successful in this context. Stories such as this are rarely heard within the dominant society or mainstream educational institutions, or if they are discussed, Indigenous veterans are often portrayed as good, patriotic citizens. In this instance their contributions were not even recognized by the military, as it was their commanders who received the medals rather than the men who were largely responsible for their success. Within decades of military resistance against the invaders to our homelands, our people began serving on the side of our colonizers in their wars. This story illuminates how there is little reward for the Dakota for this participation. Our warriors and warrior traditions have been appropriated and used by the dominant societies for their own purposes to fight in wars that achieve their ends, while we struggle for basic human rights in our own lands.

However, this story is another testimony to the importance of language. At the end of this story, Uŋkaŋna concluded: "That language means that much to us as Indian people." Ironically, while World War I was being fought across the ocean and Indigenous people were helping the United States and Canada by utilizing their Indigenous language skills, at home our languages were being systematically destroyed and supplanted with English. This is one of the painful ironies of colonization.

Okicize stories, or war stories, may encompass a whole range of accounts, and the one exemplified here is set in a more recent, twentieth-century context. The first section, with its beginning commentary, offered a glimpse into Dakota attitudes toward important historical figures, namely the thirty-eight hanged in 1862, who were involved in the most significant war in Dakota history. The story about the four men in search of glory is not an okicize story but would be categorized as an ehaŋna woyakapi, in spite of the element of the wakaŋ within it. It was included in this section because it also demonstrates a Dakota belief about the importance of humility and the danger of vanity, especially for those who risk their own lives and threaten others while in battle. The story provides a lesson for all future warriors about keeping properly focused. When killing is involved, glory for glory's sake should not be sought. The final story included in this section on Dakota code-talkers Herb Hapa and George Blackface offers recognition to those forgotten in other contexts. In this case, it was the men who used our language for an important task. These contributions provide the opportunity for Dakota heroes to be celebrated by Dakota people.

12. Ṭoked Ḳapi Oyaḳapi (Commentary)

This next section is more conversational in nature. Uŋkaŋna is expressing some of his concerns about the future, beginning with a discussion over the possibility of a future war and who would fight to protect the people and the land here in North America. His views are clearly indicative of the deep connection to the land felt by Indigenous Peoples, in contrast to those considered by First Nations people to be newcomers or those with connections to other parts of the world. He also speaks of the sense of failure he feels toward the young people, because many young people have not received the teachings that will help carry our people into the future. More positively, he finishes this first section by discussing how knowledge can be gained and the teachings internalized.

Uŋkaŋna's good sense of humor is apparent in the second commentary, as it simply consists of a short anecdote about brother-in-law relationships. The third commentary is more serious and addresses how the traveling stones should be taken care of and a little bit about what will be expected of us when we enter the spirit world. Finally, the fourth commentary begins with an amusing story about a heyoḳa, or contrary, which serves as a lead-in to the story about how he received his Dakoṭa name and the kind of singing he has done. He then describes how non-Indians tend to disbelieve Dakoṭa traditions, ending with another humorous anecdote that draws on the similarities between cultures. Because Uŋkaŋna's message requires little explanation, rather than provide a separate chapter for commentary, my notes will appear at the end of this chapter.

Ṭoked Ḳapi Oyaḳapi Ṭokaheya (The First Commentary)

Ihnunaḣ ake naḳuŋ, okicize ḳiŋhaŋ. . . . Haw oyaṭe obe oṭa ahip dena.[1]
    Also, if there should suddenly be another war. . . . Many different nations have come here.
Wicaḳeya akicita opapa tiyaṭa kiya hadapa tuŋḳaśitkupa, atḳuku, huŋku hena, hena wicakuṭepṭe śni, kecaŋmi do.
    They would never go back to their homeland, joining forces with all their

---

1. The [. . .] here does not indicate that material was left out in this place, rather it indicates that Uŋkaŋna has shifted topics. The first sentence trails off and he begins a new sentence.

heart, and shoot their grandparents, their fathers, their mothers, that is what I believe.

Ķiŋhaŋ hed nakaha hehan Dakoṭaḳ ded uŋpi ḳiŋ haw, "Dakoṭaḳ hiyupo," eyap ḳa hehan Dakoṭa oyaṭe de eceyeda wicakehaŋ Canada de teȟiŋda.

If so, they would say, "Come all you Dakoṭa," expecting the Dakoṭa who are here—because the Dakoṭa nation alone cherishes this Canada with all their heart.

Iaṡica ḳa ṭaḳu oyaṭe wicakiza ḳaŋ he hduhe waciŋ hed wicakizapi kṭe hehan oyaṭe ṭokça hena hena wicakeya tawacin caŋṭe ocowas, uŋ woohiye.

Germans and other nations, they [Dakoṭas] will fight them to hold on, and then the different nations they will with all their minds and hearts win.

Awacin ṡḳaŋpte ṡni nacece kecaŋmi çe wakida naḳuŋ, I could be wrong though.

They would not think that way, also I feel they would not, I could be wrong though.

He woiye he iyukça wauŋ he.

I think about that a lot.

Ṭoḳed wakeḳ oyakaȟniġa he?

Do you understand?

CMN: I don't understand.

There are so many different nationalities that came in this country, migrated into this country and, to start with there was the English people and then there's the French, and now they are arguing about who the distinct people are, forgetting about the Indians. They don't include them in that new agreement that they're working on.

Haw he uŋ eṭaŋhaŋ Dakoṭaḳ[2] waŋżidaȟ hed government ed opa provincial wiyaka yuha inażiŋ ḳa iṭe owapi wowapi ed owapa ehnakapi wiçada ṡni.

For that reason, he is the only Indian who is in the provincial government and he took his place with an eagle feather, and that photo with his picture was in the newspaper, they wrote in there that he did not agree.[3]

CMN: Is he from Manitoba?

---

2. While Dakoṭa usually refers to Dakoṭa people, it may also be used, as it is in this context, as a general term for Indian people.

3. Uŋḳaŋna is referring to Elijah Harper, the man responsible for stopping the Meech Lake Accord in 1990.

Haŋ, heced okihip śni.
>Yes [he's from Manitoba], so they weren't able to do that.

Hed de kad, tokeh Meech Lake Accord he kakse.
>Over there he broke how that Meech Lake Accord was.

One province okiya Newfoundland heciyataŋhaŋ.
>One province helped from over there, Newfoundland.

Ho hena hena he wicawake hena, nihaŋh de makoce otaŋkaya ka taku waśte ota waŋke do deciya taŋhaŋ.
>Those are the things I mean, there are still many good things all around the country on this side.

North America de, hena oyate obe ota there are so many different kinds of people who had full stake down there and come down through the years so they can have a quiet life, taŋyaŋ iyokpiya uŋpta.
>There are many different kinds of people in North America, so many different kinds of people who had full stake down there and come down through the years so they can have a quiet life, they will be well and happy.

Haw hena heciya—they got grandfathers and grandmothers and they got their uncles and aunties and they got a lot of those French people back there.
>Those over there—they got grandfathers and grandmothers and they got their uncles and aunties and they got a lot of those French people back there.

The Germans, they've got lots. Ukranians, they've got lots of parents over there. Deciya taŋhaŋ de hena owas population of different nationalities are increasing.
>From over here, all of the populations of different nationalities are increasing.

Haw hena, if ever a war comes about, only the Indian people will be fighting for Canada and the United States, with full intent of trying to save it, save their country.
>Yes, those, if ever a war comes about, only the Indian people will be fighting for Canada and the United States, with full intent of trying to save it, save their country.

What I'm scared of is that other people, such as the English, French, and other minor nationalities that come across here, that migrated across, may not put full heart and soul into that fight and go and shoot their grandfathers and their grandmothers. That's the thing that I'm scared of.

Kiŋhaŋ, we are going to lose a lot of our Indian people down there.
>If so, we are going to lose a lot of our Indian people down there.

Hecetu tukte he kowakipe he.
>I'm afraid of that happening.

I won't be around to maybe see it, and maybe it may never happen, but that kind of bothers me, you understand now what I'm trying to say? But I know if there is Indian people down there that come up here and start fighting, United States and Canada, the Indians will hesitate to shoot their own people here. Likewise, these people [non-Indians] will hesitate and they won't put full force, honest to goodness force, into trying to save Canada and the United States. You understand what I'm trying to say?

He kowakipe he.
  That is what I'm afraid of.

Hena ekśe uŋ hena wocekiya uŋkeyapi tokśta hena wocekiya uŋkeyap kaŋhaŋ hena Ṭak Wakaŋ naḣ'uŋ sdodye keya omakiyakapi dowapiya wicaśta hena.
  At least for those that we say our prayers for, certainly if we say the prayers for those, it is said Ṭak Wakaŋ he hears and understands, those medicine men told me so.

Haw he he he nakuŋ he, wicaśta keya tokca tuwep eya uba.
  That, and also that some men who are different will come.[4]

"Haw he wahokuŋniciyapta çe."
  "They will preach to you."[5]

Eyap he, haw he de Ṭak Wakaŋ, ciŋca he hiyuyek he.
  What they said was that Ṭak Wakaŋ sent his son.

Haw he he wouŋkiyakapi ake u kte tka ktepi ekta.
  That is what they told us, he was to come again but was killed over there.

Haw hetaŋhaŋna heciyataŋ wakan iyaye.
  From that place over there he went up.[6]

Spirit heca waŋna hehanyaŋ, spiritually Dakoṭak oyaṭe detkiya u ka ake bodily wowicakiyake kte okihi śni.
  He was already a spirit then, spiritually he came to the Dakoṭa people over here this way, but he couldn't come again bodily to tell them things.

Heuŋ etaŋhaŋ ṭuwe wowicakiyake kte hena iśtimma hehan ekta wowicakiyaka Dakoṭa awaŋkciyakapta zanipta.
  For that reason, while they are asleep someone will tell them, there he tells the Dakoṭa to take care of each other and to be in good health.[7]

---

4. He is referring back to the first story and the message given to the Dakoṭa by the different man they encountered.

5. Uŋkaŋna is referring to teachings of the missionaries who came among the Dakoṭa to teach about Ṭak Wakaŋ.

6. "Ascended upward" would be another translation, in a reference to Jesus.

7. This is a reference to how Dakoṭa people are told things in their dreams. Messages are often given to Dakoṭa people in this manner.

Hena, hena he u wicay.
    Those things he sent to them.

Haw hena Dakoṭak dena suṭaya nauŋżiŋpa hena okinic'iyaŋpṭa ḳa uŋkup ḳiŋhaŋ, ḳiŋhaŋ hena wicadapṭa opiniyec'iyapṭa tḳa heced we failed you people.
    If we the Dakoṭa would stand firm and if we told all of you, you would have believed and you would have lived accordingly, but we failed you people.[8]

Owas euŋyaḳupa, we didn't get that chance.
    They took us all and we didn't get that chance.

Ṭokiya inicupa anikiyahdapa tiyaṭa two months yahdip ḳa hehan ṭaḳu šuŋkciŋcadaḳ ḳa ṭukṭed kaḣap iyeyap iyeced hena iyokpiyapi.
    They take you from somewhere and take you on home two months, you are home and then you are like little puppies happily being driven out somewhere.

Parents don't get a chance wahoḳuniciyapi deciya taŋcaŋ iyoḣpeyapṭa hena oiyociŋyaŋ Ṭaḳu Wakaŋ uŋḳaġapi hena tamahed iyaye kṭe.
    Parents don't get a chance to instruct in teachings over here, within our body, trustingly, Ṭaḳu Wakaŋ made us so that everything that is told to us is taken within our body.

Tḳa heced, iapi uŋ ṭokca wahoḳuŋciŋyapa de uŋġe ded wayawapa ... ded de mitaḳożaḳ de okiŋni wayawa de Ṭaḳ Wakaŋ wicadaya tawacin yuha wayawa nacece.
    But so, some of them here study teachings with a different language ... perhaps this one, my grandchild who studies, believes in Ṭaḳ Wakaŋ, and she studies with that belief in her mind.[9]

Heuŋ etaŋhaŋ okiye ḳa wouŋspe hena ṭaŋyaŋ k'u hed ihaḳabya niża wauŋspe kṭe hena yada he.
    Therefore he helps her, he gives her knowledge in a good way; you also asked that she would gain knowledge.

Ho heced iyeced wouŋspe hena k'upa toḳaṭakiya waciŋyaye, waciŋwayeḳ, waciŋuŋyaŋpṭa, heceṭu kecanmi do.
    For that reason she was given that knowledge and in the future you will

---

    8. He is talking about failing the younger generations by not passing on the teachings.

    9. This is a reference to me and my education. Here, and for the next several sentences he is speaking directly to my father, Chris Mato Nunpa. When we did this recording I was a senior at the University of Minnesota, but he knew my plans for graduate school and realized that I had a great deal more work to do.

depend, I will depend, we will all depend on that, that is how I think it will be.

Hehan de ḳa haŋhiya ḳa hed de hepa.
Then I say this with difficulty.¹⁰

Ṭoked Ḳapi Oyaḳapi Inuŋpa (The Second Commentary)

This Indian agent laughed and I said Indian people only joke with their brothers-in-law. They don't joke with no other person. They're serious with the other people, but they joke with the brothers-in-law. "Oh that's a good idea." And we went, he took us to Oak Lake. I got ahead of him and got back to the café in Griswold, and here that Indian agent came from Brandon and he was sitting at the counter there having coffee. As soon as I walked in the door, he said, "Come on and have coffee with me."

So I said, "Okay," so I went and sat down beside him. I knew Don was behind me. So, Charlie brought that coffee, and he brought that coffee and set it.

"Thanks," and the door opened, and I looked up and there was Donald. I said, "Donald, come on sit down here and have coffee with us, have a cup of coffee with us."

He says, "No thanks, makes me sick when I drink coffee."

I says, "Charlie, bring him two cups, make him good and sick." The Indian agent looked at me and said, "Is he your brother-in-law?" He didn't forget that only brothers-in-law joke.

Ṭoked Ḳapi Oyaḳapi Iyamni (The Third Commentary)

Okpaza ca heced nażiŋ heced de iye ed ipa yukçapa heced iyayapi.
When it got dark it [the horse] stood there and so they went and untied it, and they were gone a long time but they said they would bring it back to you.¹¹

Tehan u do tḳa tokśta, tokśta nicicaḳupta ḳeyapi do.
He was a long time coming, but they said for sure they would bring it back to you.

---

10. We believe he is referring to all the "difficult things" he discussed, particularly the way the young people have been failed because of their lack of traditional teachings.

11. It is unclear exactly who or what Uŋkaŋna is referring to here. He began talking about these things during a break and then recording began, catching him later in this story. This section is used as a lead-in to the next story about the taḳ śkaŋ śkaŋ.

Haw heced ṭokiya akipa haw he de wapiya ka ayuśtaŋ ka canuŋpa ka ake wacekiya.
> They took it back somewhere, the medicine man finished and smoked and prayed again.

Haw wohdakek ayuśtaŋ wohdake yaŋka ihnunah, haw, haw.
> Yes, he finished talking, he kept on talking, and suddenly, yes, yes.

Haw waŋna nicicahdip keyapi do.
> Yes, now they brought it back for you, they said.

Taŋkad inape kṭa uŋkaŋ hed iyakaśkaŋ nażiŋ he śuŋwakaŋ ahdipi.
> He stepped outside and here they brought the horse back and he stood there tied up.

Ṭokedked ahdip he ṭuweda, ṭuweda he sdodye śni.
> How they brought him back, no one, no one understood.

Wicaśta wayukcaŋ ṭuwe sdoduŋyapṭe śni iye ṭak śkaŋ śkaŋ hena, iye hena heca, sdodyapi hena.
> As a man [human] we would never understand but the ṭak śkaŋ śkaŋ, as for them, they understand.

Hena he ṭaku iŋyaŋna hena heca hena.
> So those little rocks, that is what they are.

Hena ṭaŋyaŋ awaŋyaŋkap ohodapṭa kiŋnihaŋ ṭaŋyaŋ awaŋwicayaŋkapṭa kiŋhaŋ hena ṭuwe sdodye kiŋ hena waciŋwicayapṭa.
> Take good care of them, respect and honor them, take good care of them, whoever understands this will depend on them.

Haw hehan iŋyaŋ hena ṭuwe waŋżi yuhaśṭa ed uŋ śni kaŋhaŋ kokak hed ohnakapṭe śni hena deci akab, ṭaŋcaŋ eceyeda wicakap.
> Whoever has the stones, if they should die, they are not put in the box [coffin] with them, they are kept outside, the body alone they bury.

Haw he ṭaku waŋżi iyamauŋpe—ṭuwe ed uŋ śni ka ṭaku wanbdi wiyaka ṭaku yuha waceuŋkiyapṭa çe hecihaŋ kokak hed hed ohna kap kaŋhaŋ haw hed ṭokeda ye śni.
> He left me with that—when someone dies, if we are to pray with the eagle feather and whatever else, if they are placed in the box, it doesn't go anywhere.[12]

Heced wicauŋdapi.
> That is how we believe.

Haw he uŋ eṭaŋhaŋ wiyaka ka canuŋpa ka iŋyaŋ hena ṭaku hena ṭohni hena hed a hed naġi hed yus'uŋ hena ṭopa caŋ kaŋhaŋ hena ṭoki iyaye kṭe.

---

12. It would be dangerous to bury sacred objects with a body, as the spirit of the person would hold on to those objects, never departing.

For that reason, the feather and the pipe and the stones, the spirit hangs on to those things there, on the fourth day they will leave somewhere.

Ḳaeš heca canuŋpa ḳa waŋbdi ḳa ṭaḳu ḣupa huḳ hena ṭaḳ šḳaŋ šḳaŋ hena naġi heda yus'uŋ ce iwaŋḳap opiic'iye uŋyaḳuŋpṭa.

The pipe and the eagle and the winged, all those things ṭaḳ šḳaŋ šḳaŋ holds the spirit there, hovering above and going nowhere.

Heced naḳuŋ sdoduŋyapi okiciyaḳ uŋyapi ṭuwe ehnaḳapṭa ce ḳaŋhaŋ hena ṭaḳu ed ohnaḳapṭa šni tokan.

So we also understand this, we tell each other, when someone is buried they don't put those things in with them, [they put them] elsewhere.

Dakoṭa haŋpa waŋżi ṭuwe heced ed uŋ šni ḳiŋhaŋ he ṭuwe Dakoṭa wica caże waŋżi yuhe kṭe, ḳaŋhaŋ odowaŋ waŋżi yuhe kṭe.

When someone passes on that person will have a pair of Dakota moccasins and a Dakota name, and then he will also have a song.

Haŋpa ḳa Dakoṭa heyake he yuhe kṭe, haw hehan wicoṭawaciŋ wašṭe.

He will have moccasins and Dakota clothing and then a good disposition.

Hena akiciyuhapṭe, hena yuhapṭe ḳiŋhaŋ aŋpeṭu ed naġi iye ḳiŋhaŋ inażiŋ ḳiŋhaŋ, "He niṭuwe he?"

They will keep these for each other, they will have these so that one day when the spirit is standing, "Who are you?"

Haw hena bduhe kokaḳ ed muke šni ḳiŋhaŋ naġi bduhe ṭukṭe ed inaważiŋ ṭuwewe Dakoṭa waŋżi heca iża naḳuŋ wicomani hena owaŋyaŋḳe.

Yes, I have them, I'm not laying in the box, as a spirit I stand somewhere, some who are Dakota, they also take care of the path that everyone takes.

Ṭoki iš he de St. Peter ṭuwe awaŋyaŋḳa ce eyapi he iyeced Dakoṭa uŋyaŋp hena awaŋyaŋḳa.

They say that somewhere St. Peter takes care of someone in the same way the Dakota that we have takes care of them.

Hed ikaŋyaŋ inaważiŋ, "Haw de niṭuwe?"

If I were to stand along there, "Hello, who are you?" [he would say].

"Haw de Eli Taylor miye do."

"Hello, I am Eli Taylor."

"Ṭoked ṭaḳu he Eli Taylor?"

"Exactly what is Eli Taylor?"

"He ṭaḳu iapi he?"

"What language is that?"

"Haw de Oṭa Kuṭeda he miye do."

"Yes, I am Many Shots."

"Haw de Oṭa Kuṭeda, he tḳa heced ṭoked de caŋhaŋpa ohaŋ yauŋ he?"

"Yes, this is Many Shots, but why are you wearing these shoes?"

"De dena Dakoṭa nihduza yaupṭa tka do."
"You should come dressed as a Dakoṭa."

Haw hececa waŋ hed awakipe kṭa.
I'll come up against that.

Haw heuŋ eṭanhan, hena ṭakuk he uŋkaihduhapṭa keyapi heced amihduhe ka de wiyaya wauŋ.
For that reason, they say we are supposed to have those things ready for ourselves, and so I have these ready for myself.

Miciŋca ka miṭakuye hena haŋpa ka ṭaku hena mak'upa yuwiya hena yuhawa uŋ.
Those moccasins and the things my children and my relatives gave me, I have them ready.

Waśicu iś ekṭa iś inaźiŋpa he wowapi yuieska.
For the Waśicu, they stand and interpret the book.

Ṭoked Ḳapi Oyaḳapi Iṭopa (The Fourth Commentary)

[The heyoḳa said,] "Śuŋka iċupṭe śni iyeced he ehnak maya śni caŋpahmiyaŋ hed ohdateya ohdoka taŋka yaŋke.
[The heyoḳa said,] "You told me to put it where the dogs won't get at it, underneath the wagon there is a large hole there.[13]

"Owakaśtaŋ hehan awakahpe śuŋka icupṭe śni."
"I poured it then covered it, the dogs won't get at it."

So she takes it outside and brings the pan back empty.

"Oh my, what did you do, what have you done with all my grease?"

"Well, you told me to put it where the dogs won't get at it, and there's a hole at the bottom under that wagon out there. I poured it down there and I covered it up so the dogs won't get it."

After all the work she did. Those are the contraries. Oh, he does a lot of things like that. He's the guy that gave me a name, my name. When you name something or somebody, I mean, it has to be done through some of his deeds. He just don't give you a name any way you want, it has to be their deeds. So he gave me the name Oṭa Kuṭeda.[14]

---

13. The heyoḳa is a "contrary" in Dakoṭa culture, a bit of a clown, someone who does things backward compared to what most of the people do. For example, in winter he might dress lightly and in summer dress warmly. There are those individuals in every culture who are inclined to be in opposition to the "norms" and who go against what the rest of society is doing. That behavior is expected of a heyoḳa, and they have a revered status within Dakoṭa culture.

14. He translated this name as "Many Shots."

One of the medicine men from the South came here. He gave me that name because some enemy men came into their camp one night, and he was camped closest to the creek that the enemy came up and he held them at bay by shooting lots at them before the others came along. So, that's why he's named lots of shots, he put in a lot of shots before, held them at bay before. You understand? So he gave me that name.

And then after he gave me the name, after that I broke my leg and he fixed it all up for me and even when I was a baby, in a bundle, I took sick and mom took me down there and my brother [said], "I want you to help him." So he helped me, pulled me through that sickness and then he pulled me through that broken leg, and he pulled me through when I was a small baby.

My mom said, "Han, he uŋśiyakidaka, yupiya my child, you cured him, I wish you would also give him a name, too."

My mom said, "Yes, you have a heart for him, you healed my child, you cured him, I wish you would also give him a name, too."
"Haw, tośta ake Taŋkśi wicacaże wanżi, I'll give him a name."
"Yes, Taŋkśi,¹⁵ for sure a title, I'll give him a name."
So, he gave me that name and he had me under his thumb.

"This name, you are going to bear this name for the rest of your life, and you are going to live for a long, long time. You are going to be old and your hair is going to be gray. You are going to live a long time." That's what he was telling me and my mom was sitting there.

She told me afterward he wrote me not long after. I said I told one of my nephews in Pipestone, that's what uncle said when he gave me my name. "There's one mistake though, he should have said you are going to live for a long, long time, you are going to be an old man and your hair is still going to be black."

My nephew says, "I thought you were going to say, I thought he was wrong too, he should have said that you are going to grow to be an old, old man and you won't have no hair, just like a billiard ball."

So he was right and I'm still around. Oh, there's lots of things.
CMN: **What was this heyoka, he ṭoked eciyapi he?**
What was this heyoka, what was his name?
Waŋ Duta eciyapi.
They called him Red Arrow.
Waŋ Duta eya caże yatapi, Red Arrow, isn't that the way you translate it?

---

15. *Taŋkśi* is the kinship term a man uses to refer to his younger sister.

> Red Arrow, that's how they called him, Red Arrow, isn't that the way you translate it?

Waŋ Duta, waŋka is the arrows, duta is red or scarlet, or one of the others.

Haw hena he ṭaku, ṭaku waśte oṭa ŋu ŋawaḣ'uŋ ḣeŋa.

> Yes, many good things, those I heard.

Ṭukṭed imacageḣ hetaŋhaŋ, I sang, like I told you before, I sang since I was about thirteen, fourteen years old.

> From the time I was born I sang, like I told you before, I sang since I was about thirteen, fourteen years old.

So people knew that I can sing, eh? Some of them went as far as to like my singing. So, and they think that I have a good memory and that when they want to, when they run across something like I told you the other day, this boy, he was having these dreams and he was scared and he had to have a pipe and he had to have four stones.

When they start doing these things, a song, they have to have a song. And that song is their song, it's different from everybody else's song and it's a sacred song.

So therefore, they teach me that song, just like this śake haŋska was teaching this, his friend, that first song, and the second song and the third song, he uŋspemakiyapi, their main song.

> So therefore, they teach me that song, just like this grizzly bear was teaching this, his friend, that first song, and the second song and the third song they taught that to me, their main song.

So when they start doing their research and doing their?, and living out what is gifted to them, I have to sing for them. And I have to sing for that heyoka too. I sang for one, I sang his main song. And other ones, and the buffalo dancing, which I don't want to sing this time because you have to have somebody that knows buffalo are around to be able to sing that buffalo song.

But it's on tape, the Goodwill's, but it's already there on some tapes and so I don't have to sing because if I, like I'll tell you an example. I went down to Joyce's house one night and my son-in-law, and it was in the wintertime a nice evening we went down and we all had supper and we talked there for a while. My son-in-law got talking to me and started asking me questions about what kind of songs I could sing.

I said, I told him I could sing those woktehdi[16] songs and old songs, some I don't know too many of them, but I can sing them, the old songs.

---

16. Although we weren't sure about the meaning of these, Kuŋśi Carrie suggested that it was a reference to the songs sung by men when returned from the hunt.

He said do you know any buffalo songs?

Yeah, I says, but you don't sing them any old place, I says. If you sing it brings on bad weather if you don't know nothing about it, so I don't want to sing.

"Ah Dad, that's, nothing's going to happen, sing it."

Just like drinking beer, one wouldn't hurt, so I went and I sang one.

"Oh, that's the way it's done."

When he was all ready to come out, we went out and here the snow was blowing and the wind blowing. "Oh boy," he said. But we didn't have very far to come home.

So those are some of the things that we have to revere these, those people's gifts. We don't just go and, it's a little bit different to the Waśicu, white people's way. So I don't sing those sacred songs, but the other powwow songs and all these like the New Year's song and the ośkaṭe[17] songs, welcome songs, and farewell songs and honorings songs, I can sing them anywhere.

Now I sing with the sundance, sundance songs because they gave me that privilege. Took me out to that center pole and they gave me that privilege to be able to sing those songs. So I sing them.

So a lot of people don't believe in those things. Even the younger generation now, mitakożas[18] and a lot of them, not in the immediate family, they all know it and respect the Indian way.

Waehdepi that, waehdepi he uŋġe wicadap śni Waśicu he he ṭakuda wicadap śni Dakoṭak etkiya.

> Waehdepi,[19] that waehdepi, some do not believe in that, the Waśicu don't believe anything in the Dakota way.

Heced wanawaḣ'uŋ uŋkaŋ he ṭukṭed Mankato hed ob ṭaku waecanunp ob okiciya yaśkaŋp.

> And I heard that somewhere at Mankato you helped them with their activities.[20]

Haw heced niża Dakoṭak ekta ṭaku owohdaka ṭukṭe wohdak ecanuŋ yai owicakiyake ḵaeś wicanidap śni.

> And you, you also had gone to the Dakota to give a talk, you shared with them but they didn't believe you.

Haw heuŋ heṭaŋhaŋ hehaŋyeda inayażiŋ tokan idada ḵeyapi, omakiyaḵapi heced nawaḣ'uŋ.

---

17. *Ośkaṭe* refers to *play or games*, so these would be songs used for games.
18. He is using the English plural for the Dakota word Mitakoża, meaning "my grandchild."
19. *Waehdepi* refers to the dedication of food, a tradition carried on by the Dakota in which food is set out for the spirits of loved ones.
20. He is directing this comment to my father, Chris Mato Nunpa.

For that reason they said you stopped right there and stepped aside, what I heard is what they told me.

Ake miś owicawakiyeķe, "Ṭaku hena niye niśnana wicayake nic'iyedapa hena uŋkiża, we have our own, we have our own beliefs."

As for me, I told them again, "There are things that you yourself have yourself believing and as for ourselves, we have our own, we have our own beliefs."

Haw hed waekihdepi he haĥ'aŋna ķaŋhaŋ Amos Owens owakiyake ṭohan heci uŋkip two years heci uŋkipi.

When it was morning they set up, and I told Amos Owens when we were there, two years we went there.[21]

We must remember that . . . he ehan heciya waŋna two years maġażu ake hed uŋkokihip śni . . . çe cistiyeda ake wacipa ake he ehan ho.

We must remember that . . . at that time over there it rained again for two years and again we weren't able to . . . they danced for a little while again.

Ociciyakeķ ķaeś ṭuwe owakiyake çe ķaeś ķośka Goldtooth eciyapi he owakiyaka nacece uŋkaŋ Amos Owens haĥ'aŋna ķiŋhaŋ waekihde aŋpetu waśṭe da kṭe do, wicaĥca hena.

I told you, or I wonder who it was I told, a young man named Goldtooth, I probably told him, and so when it was morning, Amos Owens set up and he will ask for a good day [with] the elderly men.

Ķiŋhaŋ aŋpetu waśṭe miża ito wawaŋbdake waciŋ ķa heced omaka nuŋpa owicahaŋ he Amos Owens haĥ'aŋna ca hed wotap ķaŋhaŋ he inima ayuśṭap wotap hed aŋpetu waśṭe da çe ķa oiyokpiya waśṭeya wawaŋuŋyakapi.

If it was a good day I also wanted to watch, and for two years in a row at the morning meal, at the feast after they finished their inipi[22] there, he asked for a good day and we were able to watch very happily.

Haw heced uŋkit'api he haw heced last year he ehan heci uŋkibaś iża waniyetu ded taŋķad osni awohececa ķaŋhaŋ teĥike heciya wo.

All that didn't happen for us, and when it was last year we went over there but it too was winter here, it was cold out, just like here and then it was difficult.

Wacipa waktaķ uŋyaŋķaŋpi hena owas uŋkokihip śni.

---

21. Amos Owen was a well-respected spiritual leader from the Prairie Island Reservation near Red Wing, Minnesota. The "setting up" here is most likely a reference to ceremonies held before the powwow to make sure things are started in the right way, in this case the Mankato powwow, which was a favorite of Uŋķaŋna's.

22. The *inipi* refers to the Dakota sweat lodge, a purification ceremony.

We were all sitting there waiting in anticipation to dance, but were unable to.

He de ṭaku hena owicayakiyaķe ķa, hena owicayakiyaķa ķaeṡ cet'unihdapi heced uŋ hena that ķeyapi nawah'uŋ, I don't know how true that is.

These things you told them and these you told them, but still they doubt you, I heard they said that, I don't know how true that is.

That reminds me, he de Dakoṭa waŋ cemetery ekṭa i ķeyapi.

That reminds me, a Dakoṭa went to a cemetery they say.

He went to the cemetery, haw cemetery ekṭa ķa, hey they have the same traditions we've got, I guess, so he took an orange and a little, some grapes and some like that.

He went to the cemetery, and at the cemetery, [he thought] hey they have the same traditions we've got I guess, so he took an orange and a little, some grapes and some like that.[23]

He even took a little bottle of pop and set it up and then wacekiya.

He even took a little bottle of pop and set it up, and then he prayed.

Along came a Waṡicu next, gray head of hair, the white people. He had his friend there.

All he brought along was a flower heced, hed ehde.

All he brought along was a flower so he set it there.

He thought that, the Waṡicu thought that this man was doing something funny, you know, by putting food over there. So he asked him, "Charlie?"

"What?"

"When is your friend [going to] come up and eat that food?"

"Oh, same time your friend come up and smell that flower," eye.

"Oh, same time your friend come up and smell that flower," he said. There is no difference there.

Iwaa (I Speak)

While actual stories did not comprise the last chapter, it was important to include Uŋķaŋna's commentary because of the insights he provides into Dakoṭa ways of thinking about the world. His topics ranged from the possibility of future war, some instruction on how to take care of the iŋyaŋ ṡķaŋ ṡķaŋ, how our spirits will be recognized in the next world, the heyoķa, how he got his Dakoṭa name, singing, and even an anecdote about cemetery practices. Most of his dis-

---

23. It is a tradition of Dakoṭa people to set out food for the spirits of those deceased, so often at the cemeteries there will be fruit baskets laid out by graves. It is a dedication of food, to feed the spirits. In this case, even pop was set out.

cussion is descriptive and requires little commentary, especially since sections were in English; however, there were some points that will be expounded upon here.

In his commentary on the possibilities of future war and the different nationalities currently residing in Canada, Uŋkaŋna described Elijah Harper and his connection to the importance of remembering Indigenous people as the distinct people of Canada, saying:

> Haw he uŋ etaŋhaŋ Dakotaḳ waŋżidaḣ hed government ed opa provincial wiyaka yuha inażiŋ ḳa ite owapi wowapi ed owapa ehnakapi wiçada śni.

> For that reason, he is the only Indian who is in the provincial government, and he took his place with an eagle feather, and that photo with his picture was in the newspaper, they wrote in there that he did not agree.

Elijah Harper is credited for being the sole person responsible for killing the Meech Lake Accord in 1990 and for his actions remains a celebrated hero to the people of Canada's First Nations. Under the terms of the accord, Quebec would have gained recognition as a distinct society under the Canadian constitution, a designation still not constitutionally recognized for the Indigenous people of Canada. During the process in which provincial legislatures had to ratify the agreement with a unanimous vote, "Elijah Harper, an Oji-Cree chief from Red Sucker Lake and the only Native member of the Manitoba legislature, withheld his vote, on the grounds that procedural rules were not being followed."[24] Because the ratification of the agreement was introduced late into the legislature, Harper's actions killed the accord, which needed to be ratified within a three-year time period after it was signed by conservative prime minister Brian Mulroney and the provincial premiers in 1987.[25]

About the growing Indigenous movement in Canada today, métis scholar Olive Dickason says: "If one were to pinpoint the moment of truth for this cultural momentum, it would be when Elijah Harper said 'No' to the Meech Lake Accord. The occasion could not have been more appropriate: not only was the whole nation watching and listening, but a good part of the world as well. Harper rose to the occasion, withstood the pressures mounted to bring him into line, and spoke for himself and his people."[26]

As he later invokes the memory of the thirty-eight hanged at Mankato in

---

24. Olive Patricia Dickason, *Canada's First Nations: A History of Founding Peoples from Earliest Times* (Toronto: McClelland & Stewart, The Canadian Publishers, 1992), 409.

25. Dickason, *Canada's First Nations*, 408–9.

26. Dickason, *Canada's First Nations*, 420.

1862, Uŋkaŋna here quietly relayed the importance of Indigenous heroism in discussing Harper. Often these heroes run contrary to public views, and the Quebecois certainly would not hold him in high esteem. However, those who continue their resistance, fighting for First Nations people—and who also maintain their attachment to what is viewed as sacred—are elevated to a special status within the memories and stories of Dakoṭa people.

Some of Uŋkaŋna's personal reasons for wanting stories recorded become apparent in this section:

> Haw hena Dakoṭak dena suṭaya nauŋżiŋpa hena okinic'iyaŋpṭa ka uŋ- kup kiŋhaŋ, kiŋhaŋ hena wicadapṭa opiniyec'iyapṭa ṭka heced we failed you people. Owas euŋyakupa, we didn't get that chance. Ṭokiya inicupa anikiyahdapa tiyaṭa two months yahdip ka hehan ṭaku śuŋkciŋcadak ka ṭukṭed kahap iyeyap iyeced hena iyokpiyapi.

> If we the Dakoṭa would stand firm and if we told all of you, you would have believed and you would have lived accordingly, but we failed you people. They took us all and we didn't get that chance. They take you from somewhere and take you on home two months, you are home and then you are like little puppies happily being driven out somewhere.

Because he believed the teachings were necessary for the future survival of Dakoṭa people, Uŋkaŋna clearly faulted the boarding schools for interfering in the transmission of wisdom among the Dakoṭa. His words convey not only the problem with children being taken away from their homes but also with the influence of their boarding-school teachings. His descriptive reference to the children returning home from there as "happy little puppies" suggests he believes they were content with the teachings and experiences that would deny their Dakoṭa identity and destroy their cultural traditions; colonization had taken root and they essentially lost their ability to see.

Because of the boarding schools, Uŋkaŋna stated that the parents no longer had the chance to teach their children. His usage of terminology here is interesting. Similar to the concepts relayed earlier about the internalization of our teachings, in this section Unkaŋŋa expressed this same idea using different language. In reference to directions given to us, he uses the phrases *taŋcaŋ iyoȟpeyapi (cast or planted in the body)* and *tamahed iyaye (to go into the body)* to describe what is taken within or placed within our bodies. The imagery is striking and reinforces the notion that there exists an almost physical aspect to the absorption of teachings. Again, this suggests not only listening to the guidance provided in the teachings but also having them become a part of our bodies. These kinds of teachings or directions cannot be discarded or denied as they become a part of our existence. However, in this instance it is a reference to what the children have not learned, because their traditional teachings have been supplanted with boarding-school teachings.

Uŋkaŋna's frustration with the lack of understanding of the Dakoṭa way of life by Waśicu people comes through in the fourth commentary. He makes reference to the responses of disbelief and doubt Dakoṭa people encounter when attempting to articulate our values, belief systems, and traditions to non-Natives. Most (white) members of the dominant society maintain the privilege of living their lives, assured that most of those around them, if not subscribing to their particular belief system, at least have an understanding of them. However, this is not a privilege experienced by most Indigenous people. This is not to suggest that white people in the United States or Canada never have to defend their personal beliefs, values, or traditions, but rather to recognize the existence of white privilege. Indigenous people, outside of their own communities, can never assume that those around them share a common belief system, way of thinking, value system, or worldview. Because we "deviate" from the norms of the dominant society, we continually face challenges to our worldview, which is almost daily subject to attempts to invalidate, demean, and relegate us to an inferior status. Uŋkaŋna, firmly believing people are not so different, addresses this issue with humor and grace. After outlining his concerns he ended his commentary with the cemetery scenario, and in doing so reminded us that the distance to overcome in recognition of our common humanity is not so far. It is this spiritual essence in all people that may unite us.

13. Ṭaku Ṭokṭokça Iwohdaḳapi
(A Discussion of Different Things)

This chapter first includes answers to questions we posed to Uŋḳaŋna Eli Taylor on our last day of recording and follows a more standard interview format. At this point in time he had accomplished his goal of working through the list of topics he set out for himself in the beginning, and it was our turn to pursue a few questions of our choosing in the bit of remaining time. Probably because the questions were posed in English, his responses were also in English rather than Dakoṭa. Because this entire section is English, his statements will not be in italics or boldface. The question we first asked was about the people we call wiŋkṭa in Dakoṭa. This discussion was followed by questions about the meaning of being Dakoṭa and his hope for the young Dakoṭa people of the future.

This first section presented here is a discussion of the Dakoṭa term *wiŋkṭa*, and though difficult to translate, it would fit within the "two-spirit" category claimed by many contemporary Indigenous gay, lesbian, and transgender people. Wiŋkṭas defy simplistic male/female gender categorization, and within Dakoṭa culture the term is applied only to those who are biologically male. Kuŋši Carrie had requested Uŋḳaŋna's thoughts about wiŋkṭas, because students at the University of Minnesota commonly asked her questions about gays and lesbians within Dakoṭa culture. It is important to note that attitudes about the wiŋkṭa, even within Dakoṭa communities, have been influenced by biases in mainstream American society. The following discussion begins with Chris Mato Nunpa's English interpretation of Uŋḳaŋna Eli Taylor's Dakoṭa comments.[1]

CMN: Let me translate some of the things that I understood and then you can correct. One of the things that I heard him say was that the wiŋkṭa, Wakaŋtaŋka (God) made them and that, if I understood correctly, that just as we have the heyoḳa, whom God made, so we have the wiŋkṭa whom God made as well. And they are in the same kind of category, that is they are wakaŋ, holy, sacred, and

---

1. The Dakoṭa discussion happened to be on a tape that broke and was repaired, but with a small section missing. It was thought it would be better to provide the English interpretation here (one approved by Uŋḳaŋna) rather than an incomplete Dakoṭa transcription and translation. The missing portion is retrievable from the videotape for future purposes, but will require more transcription and translation work.

in the old days, when this wiŋkṭa would say something, it will be like that then. And it was thought that he had powers and his powers were to help. And Wakantanka made very few of them so maybe one would be here and maybe over there and in another village maybe one would be over there, ṭonana k̇age,[2] and then he was saying that he hardly ever hears of any now among Dakoṭa society, hardly ever hears of any wiŋkṭas. He told an anecdote where there was starvation. The family, the children were hungry, needed food, but yet it seemed like he couldn't get it. But he went to this wiŋkṭa for help and the wiŋkṭa said yes, I will help. And so he left, the man left, and then he went hunting and he found game, deer, I think he said taḣica.[3] And so it is believed that that wiŋkṭa helped that starving family, and our attitude toward them is that we should not think of them with contempt and we should not laugh at them, but we should accord them respect as fellow human beings whom God has made as well. Is that close?

Uŋkaŋna: Well, that's not close, it's actually as it is, the way you told.

WAW: I have a question about it still. Does wiŋkṭa mean that they were like women, that they were feminine, or does it mean that they were actually with other men, [as in] homosexuality today?

Uŋkaŋna: No, they were men, but I don't think were, they never married. But sometimes he has the desire to accommodate a man in need. When she has that attitude toward another Indian, she wants his service, to satisfy her desires, or his desires, whichever the case may be. This guy, some of her goodness, and some of her knowledge rubs off on this person, so he can go back and ask for help, or whatever. You understand what I'm trying to say? I can't speak English too well, but that is the understanding that I got. I could be wrong, but if I am giving out the wrong information, well then if the good Lord will forgive me so and create better understanding. After you hear you use your own judgment as to what, you know everything that I, that needs to be known. So what I tell you is what I hear. And what I think about, you don't have to think that's the gospel truth, but you think about it too.

CMN: Oh, one other point he made too, about the ikce wicasta, the common people, they married, male and female, man and woman, so that the wiŋkṭa, like he said "ṭonana k̇aġapi," there were just a few of them, so that was not the norm, it was the exception.

---

2. *Ṭonana k̇aġe* can be translated as *he made few*.
3. *Taḣica* is the Dakoṭa word for *deer*.

Uŋkaŋna: No children ever comes out of those, they are just given that power and they stay single. But the common people are made to multiply, tokaṭakiya.⁴ That's what their one purpose is, just that one, they are going to help people. And he's not to be ridiculed. That's the way I heard it.

waw: Then I have a couple of questions. These are kind of personal questions about how you feel about things. The first one is, what does being Dakoṭa mean to you?

Uŋkaŋna: Well, Dakota means to me that, I don't thinks it's better, any different to what Waṡicu is to a Waṡicu. They believe in their teaching, at the beginning. That's why I told you that first story where they run across this man looking down over the mountain and he was creating something, and then he took them around and showed them all the medicines and all the good things that could be got, and explained everything to them and the way of life that they have to live. And that way they have been teaching as they come along, up to when I was born. And when I can remember they were still teaching some of those. I remember that, and therefore, I don't believe in any of these, tribal, nationality, or what. I believe that we are all one people, we're all one people. But for some reason we have different languages, different ways of life. So therefore I cannot criticize anyone that is not doing things my way, because that is the way they were taught. And that's what they are doing. And I can't understand them, but I can only sit there and if they're praying at the same time, pray in my own way. Because I know that they're praying and then at the same time that's when I pray too for my needs.

While you are here on earth you have to live and learn to pray. Because when that days comes, you're going to have to pray for yourself, pray for your needs and your family and whatever. But then everybody has to pray for their own. Everyone will be judged according to their merit, while they are on earth. Because when you're on earth, when you leave earth, you're not going to get that chance anymore. You're going to go to where all your loved ones are and stay up there, with them for the coming day. The Waṡicus they've got their own, we have our own. I've heard that story too.

We were up there at one of those cultural meetings. We went up there and Saskatchewan came down too, they were Crees. And there were Ojibwes there too, all different tribes, all going together to one place and we were having a meeting. I heard this one guy, a Mohawk Indian, a Mohawk Indian was sitting over there with one of the Crees from Saskatchewan, and I was sitting over here by myself as a Sioux. And I heard these guys talking and we were sitting waiting

---

4. *Tokaṭakiya* means *in the future*.

for a meal, for the bell to ring because we were having a meeting in an old abandoned air base, with lots of buildings. And I was listening to them, I knew when I talked I had talked to them before, and the Mohawk cannot speak his [the Cree] language, but he chooses to speak. So they had to use English. So I went and I stood there and they said, "sit down," and I sat down. He was telling this story, but I didn't hear the beginning, but I heard from there on some of the things that amazed me and surprised me. But before he ended that story, the bell rang and we had to go to supper. So we all got up and, "I'll tell you the rest of it after." We lined up and so I just heard the center of that Mohawk story and it interested me very much because of the fact that what he's saying was something like that story the Dakoṭas tell one another, generation after generation, the one that I told you. Where they are going to see where the end of the world is and they are going and going, and they seen something down there, they go down there and here's what they're going to find, he told them, he advised them and he told them the way of life that they have to live. That's what I heard them bring back, I heard that they brought back. And it was relayed to me and it's what I believe in. That doesn't mean that I don't believe all the others because I know, I know that they were given that way of life to live. Just the same as they gave the Dakoṭa people. So that's why I say regardless of what and how you learn, because more recently in the few years we have neglected our responsibilities very badly. Very much so we have adopted this Waśicu way of life. Boarding schools has brainwashed them and told them that we are all pagans in what we do.

In fact we had, I think I told you that an Indian agent one time advised them, he says, they should build a church here. "It's sad," he said, "I feel sorry for you people, you don't know God, you don't know." And one old man that was in that "General Custer War," that was years after the "Sioux Uprising," he had wandered back into Canada and wandered this way and got married to a woman down here and he was here. He was a very, he was one of those quick-tempered old guys you know. He got up and he said, "Who does this man think he is to be talking to us like that? We as Indian people we have our Creator and we know our Creator right from the beginning and we pray to him, ask him for whatever." And the chief, that was Donald's great-grandfather at that time,[5] he said, "George, sit down. Sit down because I think we're going to have to learn the Waśicu way because, there is going to come a day that we'll be crowded out of our own country, and we wouldn't have a place to go so we better start learning the way of life of these people, go to school, get an education and try and

---

5. A reference to the great-grandfather of Donald Pratt, we believe.

live their way of life." At that time all us Dakoṭa people are living the Dakoṭa way of life, but the younger generation is going to carry on. So he sat down.

So that's the general attitude that they have, back in those days. And I would think that, I'm tempted to think that that attitude toward the Indian people by the Waśicu still carries on today. And what I call this era that we are in now, that the Dakoṭa, educated Dakoṭa people are trying to fight for their rights. Whether they got us up the line, internationally, we should pool our thoughts, our ways, and all come together and stand together, unite and live in harmony. Forget about that line. Because the Waśicus, they're doing it. They go over there and they stay over there and they come back. At universities they are using both sides of the line. Now we got one, I got one grandson going out to Bodnar University there. If the Waśicu can do that, why can't we Indians do it?

The only reason is that they're allocating just enough money to keep us half trained. If you want to run a business and they give you a loan—that's the kind of life that we are living over here—if what you intend to do in setup is going to cost maybe ten thousand dollars, so you go to the Indian Affairs and you say, "I would like to borrow ten thousand dollars. I want to start a business and it's going to cost me that much."

"Oh well, I'm sorry, but there's no money, we haven't got money." Yet there's lots of money there, we know that. That there money was meant for the Indian people to begin with, so they know that they've got lots of money over there. But, "You may need ten thousand dollars, but I can maybe give you five thousand." Mr. Indian, he thinks about it, "Maybe I could make it go on that." So they take that five thousand dollars. And that Indian Affairs guy is standing a double chance of getting a good name out of that loan of five thousand dollars. Because if the Indian is not a very good manager and he goes in the hole because he didn't have enough money, "I told you, I told you that the Indians can't think for themselves," [he would say].

But Mr. Indian happened to be a good Indian and he works and he understands and has the good understanding and with that five thousand dollars he completed that business that he wanted to do and he was making money. That Indian Affairs guy is going to say, "Hey, I lent him money and that's the way he got it because if I didn't lend him that money he wouldn't have it." So, whichever way, the Indian Affairs gets a good name for it, whether he fails or whether he succeeds.

So these are some of the things, and then this is the way we are supposed to work. To top it off, they want to give us some money, but they want to hang on to it, and see how we spend it and what we do with it. They want everything down in detail, where that money went, to what Indian people, but what are they doing in government? Nobody keeps track of that, so these are some of the things.

And when we think, like take for instance, I'm going to tell you something. You could get cattle, you could get a loan to buy cattle. We had cattle at one time, but we cannot do the way we want to do with them. One guy had some cattle, the stipulations and the regulations of Indian Affairs is that that steer has to be three years old before he can sell it. So one of my cousins, Jacob Blacksmith, came down when I was chief and he said, "Tahaŋśi, omiciyaka wo,[6] all my kids come back from," he had about three or four or five girls and two or three boys, "wayawa hdipi do.[7] They come back from the boarding school and the Brandon Fair is coming about. But I was busy on my land all summer following this and I don't get no seasonal, seasonal jobs. So I want to sell a two-year-old steer that I got and to use that money to buy clothes, decent clothes for my kids to go to the Brandon Fair, and a dollar here and there for them to enjoy themselves. I want to sell mine."

Now the Indian Act doesn't say, that steer stays right on the reserve until, you can't sell it until [the three years]. Now that was the Indian's intention, but it's no good for the Indian agent. So he went home and next thing I know he went home and opened the gate and chased all the cattle out. "If I can't use them the way I want to use them then. . . ." Had the Indian Agent [said], "Okay, I'll bend the rules a little bit, here you go and sell that, use it for your children," that Indian would have thought and said, "Oh boy, I used that cattle so therefore I better get up more hay and try to get more cattle and look after them because that was something like, this is something similar to what the blacksmiths say, 'Strike while the iron is hot and then you get results.'"

But that's the way the regulations are. You go and farm and if they buy some seeds for you, you have to pay it back in the fall, which is quite all right, we all do. But when we plow or something, I said, when we want a loan you give us a loan, all you do is hang on to one line. I took, for an example, when we were plowing I said we were plowing with the horses. I said we used two lines, we pull this one and they turn around and they go back in the furrow and they work it smooth. But, you only give us the one line and then when we pull on the other, we can't pull this other one, drives them back and we go around in circles and I think that's what they were doing.

These are some of the things that we were talking about. If the white people can understand the Indian's needs and the way of life and if they knew anything about it, well we might be able to understand that. They say the Indians are not

---

6. "Cousin, help me out."
7. "They arrived home from school."

ready yet, they don't understand the proper and direct way. And I sit back here and I says, the white people don't understand the way of life that was intended for us people. That's where we differ. The sooner we come to an understanding we are going to be able to get together and see all tribes and all nations as one and work together. That's the way I personally, when you asked me what I personally believe in, this is my belief. So, therefore, the new eras that I told you in this age [are] a godsend, awakening, cultural awakening, an awakening from our, spiritual awakening I call it.

We're being, now the government is saying it, since that Meech Lake Accord that didn't pass, you probably saw that picture where Indian Elijah Harper's son was one. He alone and another from the East, Wašicu was there. He couldn't get them all 100 percent, and that Meech Lake deal didn't come through. What is an old Indian with just one feather in the minds of those people? I think that only one person from up above had given this Indian power to be able to control these other people, and that's the way our good Lord wants it done. Our good Lord wants the Indians to be recognized in this country. Not Columbus or any other president or member of Parliament or whatever because the English want distinct society, the French want distinct society and they say they were here first and the other guy says, "No, I'm here first."

That's why I, myself, ever since I was young, I call this English language the working language. That's my second language, the Wašicu. My language is the official language as far as I'm concerned, and that's what I go and live by.

WAW: I have one more question for you. What kind of message would you like to give to young Dakoṭa children?

Uŋkaŋna: Young Dakoṭa children, the message that I want to give them is that I want them to educate themselves because, because, take myself for an example. I did not go to school and therefore [are] a lot of things I would like to have said, but you probably notice now, by this time that you notice sitting here, any, you too miciŋkši,[8] I'm trying to explain myself in English this morning to an extent. But you probably notice that I put the wrong word in some places where it's hard to understand, and therefore, that's why I use the Indian language all the time. But I still trust that the misword in my speech is looked after by my Creator and he's providing me with words now to be able to tell my young children all the days.

Go and get an education. Become lawyers and nurses and doctors and technicians or scientists, or whatever the case may be, and work up there. Just like

---

8. *Miciŋkši* is *my son*.

what the Indian said, there's going to come a time when we are going to be outnumbered and we are going to lose our country and it's heading that way now. So I'm advising my young generation now to get an education. But the money is short now for education. We are not the wealthiest of tribes and money is scarce, and therefore we cannot pay tuition [and] fees, and therefore the federal government is responsible for our education and for our way of life and for our welfare. Like I said, they are holding that money back. The more ignorant we are, the more secure their jobs are. So that's how come we lack life skill. So there's a difference between that side and this side.

So, therefore, our alternative is to educate ourselves and all the time and acting and changing laws and regulations. We can turn around in all three, use their own regulations against them and retain our treaty and make them live up to their treaty. And if they break their own treaty, why we'll hold them to it, we'll have that knowledge. That is my idea. That is why when I was chief, all the children, from grade one, we had the kindergarten here, but from grade one up to about grade four, five, or six, went to the outside schools, some in Griswold, some in Oak Lake, Canton, and in Alexander. We want them to go to that school so they get accustomed to the outside environment and find their own partners and find their own friends amongst the Wašicu people so they can learn off the Wašicu children, and we like our school here. So when they get to the age where they have to go to the high school at grade nine or ten, ten or eleven, they can commute from here to Brandon. But they cannot hack it because of the fact that the teachers, you probably experienced some of that too, because the moment the children know that you are an Indian they harass and they harrass you, skunk-eaters, and what have you and all this. By that time these children had matured, they had already learned the beginning things and way of life at home before they went in there, and that in between there is to get across to them the way of life that they are going to encounter.

So, we've got a lot of dropouts. We got a lot of dropouts because their mind is matured now and they resent those, being called and being harrassed, so they don't want to go to school anymore. That is where we should have a high education with class to twelfth grade, eleventh, twelfth, and qualified teachers here to bring in those dropouts into here and train them there. And then after we train them to come to grade eleven or in those cases when they learn enough to be able to learn a trade, a trade of some kind—if they want to become nurse, or if they want to become secretaries, or if they want to become whatever profession that they choose—they can go back into the university or college. By that time their mind will be resenting those harrassments, they'll be more developed to be able to withstand what harrasssments that are over there, so they will get what they want.

That is my present thinking now. But they don't do that, just for the sake of a few people, making one here, who have some people here. When they drop out, they drop out and that's it. Some of them are too young to have a family, but what other alternative has he got?

So then, I was going to say I'm taking up too much of your time, but this is what you came here for. So I don't believe in taking too much time, but this time I had to come out with these because it's going on a tape, other people are going to listen to it. There may be one or two words in there that might get them to think about doing something. So that is why. I mean I don't want whoever sent you down here, you to go home shorthanded. So that's your grandpa who's talking.

Iwaa (I Speak)

The first question posed to Uŋkaŋna was about the wiŋkta in Dakota society. While male and female gender roles were traditionally very clearly defined, there existed those people who defied those boundaries and traversed freely between and outside of them. Wiŋktapi[9] were such people. The first question posed about the roles of the wiŋkta within Dakota culture, as mentioned earlier, was provoked by questions arising from students Kuŋši Carrie encountered at the University of Minnesota. A common occurence for her, and one that I have experienced frequently enough to prompt the question of clarification I raised within the interview, is the quest for information by those from Western culture about this elusive gender category. Often questions of this nature have been asked by those seeking some validation within Dakota or other Indigenous cultures for their own sexual or gender identity that they are not receiving from mainstream society.

The term *wiŋkta* may linguistically be broken down in a couple of ways. The first would be as *wiŋ*, a contraction of *wiŋyaŋ*, meaning *woman*, and *kta*, an indication of future tense, meaning *shall or will*. The word as a whole, then, might be translated literally as *shall be a woman*, indicating an inclination toward being female. The other possibility is that the last part, the kta, is a contraction of *kte tka*, which translates as *should have*, making the translation *should have been a woman*. While this is a specifically Dakota term, *wiŋkta* has also been encompassed in other non-Dakota terminology.

Although it is inappropriate and offensive, *berdache* has remained an academic term that has been used in the past to refer to the wiŋkta and to other

---

9. *Wiŋktapi* is the Dakota plural of *wiŋkta*.

special gender categories from other cultures, which might include those who identify as "gay," "lesbian," "bisexual," or "transgender."[10] Because of the disparaging and insulting etymology of the term *berdache*, it is now being rejected by a growing group of Indigenous people exerting their right to define themselves.[11] Thus, many contemporary Indigenous people, falling under the anthropologically constructed "berdache" category, are now defining themselves either as two-spirit people or in their own Indigenous language terms. In her discussion of the term *berdache* and the purpose it has played for non-Natives, Sue-Ellen Jacobs writes: "I knew that for many non-Native individuals the 'berdache' had become a liberating icon of possibilities in a society that has often denigrated, and in recent years had begun to trivialize, the hardship of their daily lives (e.g., male-to-female transsexuals, gay males, lesbians, and transgenders and bisexuals within diverse cultural traditions)."[12] However, while it is easy to empathize with the non-Native's desire for sexual and gender identity validation and inclusiveness, for a couple of reasons, Indigenous cultures may not provide the haven they are seeking. The first is that there exist larger cultural responsibilities that have little to do with the gender or sexuality of the wiŋkṭa, in this case; and second, it is questionable whether diverse genders are still accepted by communities of Indigenous people.

A difficulty in defining a term like *wiŋkṭa* cross-culturally stems in part, at least, from the insistence in Western culture on linking gender with biological sex. This has also been true of those who have meant to define two-spirit people within Indigenous culture. Evelyn Blackwood, in her essay "Native American Genders and Sexualities: Beyond Anthropological Models and Misrepresentations," points out that "most non-Native Americans have difficulty perceiving a physical male as a woman or a physical female as a man. The critical importance of biology to Western constructs of gender meant that white scholars were rarely able to separate biology from gender successfully when talking about two-spirit people."[13] Wiŋkṭapi within Dakota society may be biologically male

---

10. An example of "berdache" applied to the Lakota wiŋkṭa may be seen in Raymond J. DeMallie, "Male and Female in Traditional Lakota Culture," in Patricia Albers and Beatrice Medicine, eds., *The Hidden Half: Studies in Plains Indian Women* (Lanham MD: University Press of America, 1983), 243.

11. Sue-Ellen Jacobs, Wesley Thomas and Sabine Lang, eds., *Two-Spirit People: Native American Gender Identity, Sexuality, and Spirituality* (Urbana: University of Illinois Press, 1997), 4.

12. Sue-Ellen Jacobs, "Is the 'North American Berdache' Merely a Phantom in the Imagination of Western Social Scientists?" in *Two-Spirit People*, 21.

13. Evelyn Blackwood, "Native American Genders and Sexualities: Beyond Anthropological Models and Misrepresentations," in *Two-Spirit People*, 285.

but may participate in activities usually associated with women and, consequently, in terms of gender may identify more as women. However, because this is not always the case, meaning they may at times also participate in activities associated with men, defining this term with a singular English explanation is nearly impossible. English has no term for this fluidity in gender, only for sexuality. Interestingly, within the Dakota language there exist no gendered pronouns. Thus when referring to a wiŋkta in Dakota, there would be no designation of she or he as there is in English. However, in the English discussion of Uŋkaŋna's response, he repeatedly referred to the wiŋkta as "she," indicating his recognition of gender rather than biology.

Superseding the importance of sexual preference or even gender identity is the importance of the cultural role traditionally played by wiŋktas within the broader Dakota community. As Uŋkaŋna Eli Taylor points out, they are people who have been accorded special powers, and those powers must be used to help people. In that way they serve a very important function within society, one not to be ridiculed but to be respected. Another important talent of the wiŋkta is the ability to predict the future, "when this wiŋkta would say something, it will be like that then." Thus there was always an element of the wakaŋ in the wiŋkta. Ray DeMallie, in his research on the Lakota, describes this aspect, saying: "*Winkte* in a sense was a mediating category between male and female. . . . Most of the evidence suggests that boys never made a conscious choice to become *winkte*. They were imbued with a supernatural power that made them *wakan* in this special way and marked them off from other members of society."[14]

A general respect and inclusiveness seems to extend to the wiŋkta, or the concept of the wiŋkta, by those who are familiar with the older teachings, typically those we consider more traditional. However, within contemporary Dakota culture it would be erroneous to suggest that there is a general acceptance and respect shown to those outside of male-female gender categories, or that there is even intellectual agreement about the status of the wiŋkta within Dakota society. Christian influences remain so great within communities, even from some of the non-Christian segments, it seems the Judeo-Christian teachings about the "sinfulness" or "innate wrongness" of anything other than male-female sexuality has left a lasting impression. That intolerance has now been widely internalized. Michael Red Earth, a self-identified contemporary wiŋkta, characterizes the duality in attitudes among Dakota people today as assimilationist versus traditional views and sees himself as a living example of someone

---

14. DeMallie, "Male and Female in Traditional Lakota Culture," 245.

subject to these contradictory attitudes. In this section, he offers the following testimony about his own experience:

> The assimilationist view would believe that because I was gay I was bad, but the traditional views of the importance of family and respect for a person's spirit helped them see that "Michael is good." The assimilationist would feel that effeminacy is "bad" for a boy, whereas the traditional way allowed my interest in beadwork and feminine behaviors to be nurtured. One of the feminine behaviors that was nurtured was taking care of children, which conflicted with the assimilationist belief that it is bad to have gays around kids.[15]

In reality, it is no longer safe or comfortable for many contemporary wiŋkta to live openly on the reservation. Uŋkaŋna's assertions that he rarely hears of any today is a reflection of this lack of acceptability. However, perceiving that these negative attitudes exist and are not part of the Dakota worldview, Uŋkaŋna repeatedly relayed to us that those defined as wiŋkta should not be ridiculed or treated badly; rather, they should be shown respect.

Another point must be made about the evolving nature of language. Because of these changing ideas about gender and the influences of Western thinking, the term *wiŋkta* is more loosely used in contemporary Dakota communities as a reference to a gay man. This usage has little to do with gender identity and more to do with sexuality. Some elders I have talked to are uncomfortable about this modern usage as it denies the traditional role the wiŋkta played within Dakota culture and the sacredness of that position. Certainly we still have those who live according to the traditional role of the wiŋkta, but more often now the term is used as a reference to male homosexuality (whether or not they assume any of the characteristics typically associated with the traditional role). It is primarily those who are unfamiliar with the older teachings, or those influenced by Christianity, who use the term in this way.

The next question posed to Uŋkaŋna was on the meaning of being Dakota. Perhaps this section is one of the most revealing about Uŋkaŋna's overall purpose in relaying these stories. In communicating the Dakota language, stories, and values to this audience, he is effectively delineating our distinctiveness as Dakota people, but not with the hope of converting others to the Dakota way of life. Instead, he imparts this knowledge with the hope that the common humanity of all people will eventually be realized. This is quite similar to Ngũgĩ's

---

15. Michael Red Earth, "Traditional Influences on a Contemporary Gay-Identified Sisseton Dakota," in *Two-Spirit People*, 213.

position as an "unrepentant universalist," in that he believes "that while retaining its roots in regional and national individuality, true humanism with its universial reaching out, can flower among the peoples of the earth, rooted as it is in the histories and cultures of the different peoples of the earth."[16] While Uŋkaŋna recognizes the universal commonality, he also seeks the recognition of Dakoṭa humanity by others. He believes our purpose is to fulfill our obligations as Dakoṭa people, just as it is every human being's purpose to carry out his or her responsibilities as outlined to him or her in the beginning. Ultimately, then, our purpose lies in the fulfillment of our divine instructions, as all peoples must follow their own divine instructions.

However, Uŋkaŋna is concerned because he is aware that even as Dakoṭa people, we are currently not complying with the directions given us. The oral tradition is essential here, as one of the fundamental teachings violated today originates with the first story he shared. The instructions from the different man the Dakoṭa men encounter outline that concept:

> Uŋkaŋ eya ḳeyapi "Dena ṭaku ociciyakap dena ṭohaŋya śta tokaṭakiya kiksuya uŋpo ḳa okiciyag yeya po omaka iyohi ḳa wowicaġe iyohi, ḳa saŋpa nitaḳożap ḳa nakuŋ saŋpa nitaḳożap hena okiciyag yeya po," eya ḳeyapi. "Ṭokśta tawacin he suṭa cicaġapi, hena ḳiksuya mayanipṭe do. Ṭuwe wiçakeya ohna manipṭa, hena kiksuyaŋ, ohna manipṭe," eya ḳeyapi.

> And so, they say he said, "These things that I am telling you, always remember these as long as you can in the future, tell each other every year and every generation, and your grandchildren and your great-grandchildren, continue telling each other," they say he said. "For certain, I made your minds strong, you will carry those memories. Those who walk with commitment, they will walk in that path of what they remember," they say he said.

By not transmitting this story and many of the other teachings, Uŋkaŋna is aware that the Dakoṭa ways are being lost. In these wakaŋ instructions, the correlation between the telling, the memory, and the walk was concisely constructed. No Dakoṭa can live according to these directions if the stories have not been shared and the memories internalized.

In this last section he offers more comment on the reasons for the deterioration in the transmission of the teachings. He states, "More recently in the [past] few years we have neglected our responsibilities very badly. Very much so we have adopted this Waśicu way of life. Boarding schools has brainwashed

---

16. Ngũgĩ, *Moving the Centre*, xvii.

them and told them that we are all pagans in what we do." While boarding schools played a powerful role in this, he demonstrates also, with the anecdote about the two men's views on the Indian agent and the building of a church, that assimilationist intent was another underlying factor. One of the men explicitly states, "We better start learning the way of life of these people, go to school, get an education and try and live their way of life." This is a powerful statement about the consciousness of Dakota decision-making and the personal agency involved in the acceptance of the Wašicu way of life, as well as a certain Indigenous complicity in the colonization process.

Cognizant of the fact that the Wašicu way has failed Dakota people, Uŋkaŋna offers another short story that critiques the way Indian Affairs has been administered. In this case another rather tragic illustration of the inability of an Indian agent to understand the needs of the people he was to serve is depicted. When he realized he could not tend to his family the way he wished, the frustration felt by Jacob Blacksmith was so severe that he released all his cattle. About this kind of conflict, Uŋkaŋna concludes: "I sit back here and I says, the white people don't understand the way of life that was intended for us people. That's where we differ. The sooner we come to an understanding we are going to be able to get together and see all tribes and all nations as one and work together."

When Uŋkaŋna was asked about the message he would like delivered to young people, his immediate response was to encourage them to get their education. Recognizing that the non-Native population is not going to go away, Uŋkaŋna was in many ways espousing the same concerns of the man advocating assimilation and again quotes him about being outnumbered and losing our country. His response to this, however, is vastly different in that he promotes becoming educated, learning the laws and regulations of the white world, learning how to operate within that world, so that, ultimately, "we can turn around in all three, use their own regulations against them and retain our treaty and make them live up to their treaty. And if they break their own treaty, why we'll hold them to it, we'll have that knowledge." His hope is that by gaining valuable skills in the white world, educated individuals can then use those skills to further Dakota causes.

He also discusses the difficulty Native students have with achieving educational goals. He attributes much of this to the racism Native students face from non-Native students. As in Canada, dropout rates remain very high among students from the Dakota reservations in Minnesota. There seems to be a general consensus that it is very difficult for our young people to graduate because of the extent of racism in the towns bordering the reservations where most of them attend school. In addition, in Minnesota where per capita gaming profits are distributed to all adults eighteen and older, there is little incentive for young people to further their education, especially in light of the hardships they tend to suffer while in school. Furthermore, at this point in time those who really support education are few in number because many still retain the view that a white man's education means a denial of "Indianness." Until the reservation communities as a whole embrace education as a means of fighting for Dakota sovereignty and helping Dakota people, little is likely to change. If more young people and their parents could hear this message of Uŋkaŋna's, perhaps communities could begin to view education as a means of exerting self-determination rather than as a threat to it.

Conclusion
Oyaṭe Nipi Kṭe (The People Shall Live)

Over breakfast our first morning in Sioux Valley, Uŋkaŋna Eli Taylor commented that he wanted the Waṡicu to realize we were human. Somehow, he hoped by sharing who we were as Dakoṭa people, by sharing his stories with others, our common humanity would be recognized. He cited this as a reason for wanting his stories recorded and disseminated to a larger audience. If it were a possibility that people could see for a moment how we as Dakoṭa people see the world, if some insight could be offered about how we conceptualize our past, present, and future, then maybe a non-Dakoṭa could hear our voices. Not just hear the sounds of our language and our words, but actually take the teachings within, have them implanted within, have them internalized, and we would be seen as fellow human beings. Perhaps it is those who have been denied recognition of humanity who feel the greatest need to convey it.

The stories were not just intended for a Waṡicu audience, however. The most important reason for the documentation of these accounts was internal to Dakoṭa culture; Uŋkaŋna knew many Dakoṭa people had not heard these stories and had not received these teachings. He wanted to ensure some means for modern-day Dakoṭa to find a haven in which our cultural identity is strengthened and our spirits nurtured. From the Dakoṭa perspective, when the stories are remembered and transmitted, past and future are intertwined as the cultural memories are carried forward to future generations. To describe this concept, Uŋkaŋna would tell us, "Hena ḳiksuya mayanipṭe do,"[1] or "You will carry those memories." By doing so, by walking into the future in this manner, as Dakoṭa people we will ensure our cultural survival through an understanding of what it is that makes us a distinct people.

He relayed these accounts with knowledge that young Dakoṭa people have been failed in a very profound way, not intentionally, but with severe consequences. For that reason, in his waning years he wanted to contribute what he could to the future generations. Not everyone has done so. Our parents and grandparents did not always share the teachings with us that they took for granted as children. They allowed our language to begin to slip away. Believing the next generations would be better off living as Waṡicu and that Dakoṭa traditions and ways were no longer useful, the older generations made some conscious and unconscious decisions about what should be passed on and what should be left behind. Whatever the consequences today, it must be remembered that they made these choices out of love for their little ones.

It is obvious, however, to those of us who have lived on our Dakota reservations and reserves, that the attempt to live as white people has failed. Not only are Indigenous people generally not accepted or treated with respect among Wašicu populations, but the loss of the sense of what it means to be a Dakota has led to serious social problems. Many of the problems arriving from chemical addiction and various forms of family violence are symptomatic of such problems. One need only spend a short time in our communities to witness the great sense of despair. The weight of the grief from loss is great and is a heavy burden for the young people to carry.

Many of the stories then are told in fulfillment of an obligation—the obligation of the elders to ensure the continuity of the stories. This is no easy task since elders are competing with the fast-paced world of radio, television, and computers, all of which make it increasingly more difficult to hold the attention of young people who have grown accustomed to instant gratification and multimedia stimuli. The messages within the stories contain an importance far beyond what immediate content might suggest. Uŋkaŋna's gift is timeless in that the messages provided about how we as Dakota people are to behave are intended to last as long as we continue to relate the message and attempt to live our lives accordingly. With the telling of the accounts and by setting his example, Uŋkaŋna sends a message to all present and future Dakota that it is possible to maintain a distinct identity that transcends specific ages and eras. We will win the struggle for survival by remembering who we are and fighting for self-determination from this spiritual and cultural position of strength.

All of us who were present at the recording of Uŋkaŋna's stories have felt a great sense of privilege in being able to hear the stories firsthand and to participate in their documentation. It is difficult to relay what an uplifting experience it was and continues to be even as I reread these stories today. It has affected me deeply in a very personal way. There were others interested in recording Uŋkaŋna's stories, but he chose us to carry out the work. I believe his decision had much to do with kinship; to him, I was a granddaughter who volunteered for this task, seeking his knowledge. Within Dakota culture, it is understood that when you request knowledge or understanding in earnest, you also become obliged to carry out the responsibilities associated with that knowledge. By becoming involved in this project, I was also declaring my commitment to seeing it through to completion and, more important, my commitment to ensuring the continuity of the stories.

Uŋkaŋna and other Dakota people who have filled their roles as tribal historians serve as both an archive of information and as interpreters of our history. The love for what they do reveals that it is far more than a profession—rather it is their charge, and they live their lives with that in mind. When our historians die without passing on their knowledge, the people suffer a great tragedy. Uŋkaŋna wanted to make sure this did not happen with the important stories, lessons, language, and values he carried; rather, he wanted his teachings to persist in the future. In this record, we carry a language and way of speaking from the previous century. Uŋkaŋna used words and phrases no longer well known, especially by the Minnesota Dakota, and now they are preserved. We are extraordinarily thankful we were able to document at least a portion of what he knew, especially since he is no longer here to bless us with his storytelling, singing, and humor. More important, his stories will serve as an important contribution to a body of Dakota literature that, with ongoing language efforts, will continue to grow. His voice and his stories will live on, not only in the continuation of the language and stories he transmitted to us directly but also in the publication of his narratives.

He is missed by a great number of people in Canada and the United States. Thousands of people were touched by the gifts he brought to this world and felt a tremendous sense of loss when he passed away. His obituary in the *Brandon Sun* read:

> Dr. Elijah Taylor 'Ota Kute,' born December 21, 1907, entered into rest peacefully Sunday, January 10, 1999, at the age of 91, in his home on the Sioux Valley Reservation, after a brief illness. He is survived by his wife of 68 years, Edna, and five generations of family members plus countless adopted family members.[2]

Another more personal obituary appeared in the *Free Press* in Mankato, Minnesota, entitled "Pow Wow Fixture 'Eli' Taylor Dies at Home in Canada," and it was reprinted in *Ikce Wicasta: The Common People Journal*. This tribute to a man who had blessed so many lives spoke of the loss of a great teacher and storyteller and highlighted his contributions to the Mahkato Wacipi (Mankato Powwow). For years this wacipi has included an "education day" as part of the powwow as a means of building positive Dakota-Wašicu relationships. Dakota elders, teachers, and skilled artists are brought in to educate children about Dakota history and culture.[3] Literally thousands of children have participated in this part of the powwow over the years, many of them receiving instruction directly from Uŋkaŋna. The author of the *Free Press* article, Peter Passi, quoted Bruce Dowlin about Uŋkaŋna's participation in his last education day, when he told stories to the children: "I recognized it would probably be his last trip to the home land. Taylor made a point of shaking the hand of every student who attended the event." Uŋkaŋna afterward told Dowlin that he loved every one of them.[4] This story signifies, I think, the great hope that Uŋkaŋna carried that education holds the best opportunity for peace and understanding.

The Mahkato Wacipi remained a favorite of his, and he and the family made the drive every year from Canada to attend. In fact, my early memories of him and Kuŋśi Edna are from the Mankato Powwow. After discussions with Uŋkaŋna's family about what we should do with whatever royalties are generated from the sale of this book, it was decided that the money would go toward support of a moccasin game tournament at the annual Mahkato Wacipi. The moccasin game is a very old game among the Dakoṭa; its origins derive from a meeting a long time ago between two men, one Dakoṭa and one from an enemy tribe. Rather than engaging in battle they challenged one another to a game of skill they played by hiding a small object underneath one of their moccasins. A peaceful resolution was found between enemies and a game was born, one that became a lively and exciting pastime among Dakoṭa people, often with much taunting and betting accompanying it. As Uŋkaŋna Eli was an avid fan of the moccasin game and the Mankato Powwow was also a favorite, we believe it would please him to know that the celebration of our culture will be carried on in his name at an event he loved to attend.

These stories and commentary also are significant from an academic perspective. Rarely have historians in their writings and interpretations of Indigenous history utilized Indigenous languages. Furthermore, Indigenous accounts that are less than concise, which don't fit into a neat chronological format, or which deviate from a specific historical "event" have been left to the anthropologists and relegated to the categories of myth and legend. This work represents the first attempt at an examination of Dakoṭa stories and language from a historical perspective. Moreover, in this instance, the academic methodology, terminology, and theory have been filtered through the lens of Dakoṭa eyes. The result is a product that stretches the boundaries of historical scholarship and brings to academic audiences our Dakoṭa history as we perceive it.

This Indigenous-centered project, which examines the past from an Indigenous perspective, challenges others in the area of Indigenous history to grapple with the issue of how they are incorporating Indigenous voices into their history. Though it has been done for centuries, it was never acceptable for our voices and perspectives to be excluded from our own history. It is still unacceptable, and a growing number of us our joining our voices in the academy to speak out against colonialist history, that history which denies our voice in our own story. As more Indigenous and conscientious non-Indigenous historians bring Indigenous perspectives to the forefront of their research and writing efforts, Indigenous history will take on a whole new face. Indeed, American history takes on a whole new meaning when examined from Indigenous perspectives. There are few ideals that will go unchallenged, few events unmarked, few theories uncontested.

However, there is also a swell of voices emerging from our tribal communities that will have an impact on the challenging of the academy from the outside. Those who have lived their lives from a position of struggle, who have led resistance efforts in our own communities, understand clearly how our traditional knowledge and language have been subjugated by the dominant society. As Indigenous communities become more forceful about exerting their own decolonization agenda, new ways will be devised to regain control over our history and language.

Most important, this work is part of a larger struggle, one that challenges the colonial structure, which has silenced and discredited our voices and perspectives. This has been an essential element of the colonial project because for colonialism to be perpetuated, colonizer and colonized alike must subscribe to the superiority of everything belonging to the colonizer, including their language and stories about the past. In the last seven generations, we have waged a struggle amongst ourselves about the extent to which we have subscribed to the colonizer's depiction of our people. As Ngũgĩ wa Thiong'o writes:

> An oppressed class, or nation, that believes in itself, in its history, in its destiny, in its capacity to change the scheme of things, will obviously be stronger in its class and national struggles for political and economic survival. Similarly, an oppressed class or nation that loses faith and belief in itself, in its history, in its capacity to change the scheme of things, becomes weakened in its political and economic struggles for survival. Such a class or nation can only work out its destiny within the boundaries clearly drawn by the dominating class and nation.[5]

By putting forth our stories we are exerting this belief in ourselves, in our history, and our ability to transform the world. While faith in ourselves has faltered among many of our own people over the centuries, as a nation we must struggle to reclaim this faith as part of our larger project to fight those who have dominated us.

This work then stands as a counter to the colonial project. We, as Dakota people, are at the center of the story. Though the colonial forces are present in the background, as is government policy, we are the major players and our voices are prominent. In this recentering of our history for our own purposes, we are sharing with our future generations strategies for resistance and empowerment. We are strengthening ourselves, building our own sense of nationalism, so we can free ourselves from the oppressive forces at work in our daily lives. The stories conveyed here, in the language of our ancestors, will assist us in these decolonizing ambitions.

Currently there is a growing movement among Dakota people, a struggle for rebirth. The seventh generation from those who fought, died, were imprisoned, and exiled in 1862 is now living. Even amid all the problems and negativity among our people today, there exists a swelling of pride in Dakota ways, and there is an expanding number of young people interested in hearing the voices of our people from the past. This is key to our cultural survival. With our seventh generation, we just might spring back more powerful than ever! There is great hope.

Appendix A
Explanation of Dakota Orthography

The Dakota orthography adopted by the Dakota/English Dictionary Project (DEDP) and used for his work is loosely based on the one developed by Stephen Riggs in his *A Dakota-English Dictionary*, though with some distinctions. The DEDP knew the Riggs orthography needed revision, but we struggled with which symbols we should continue to use, which symbols should be eliminated, and which ones should be added. Alan Ominsky then worked with us to create a special computer font that would serve our specific needs. Having worked with several different orthographies over the years, this one has been the easiest to use, though I struggled with distinguishing the aspirates from the others, as making these distinctions in writing was a new experience for me. This is the first publication utilizing this particular orthography.

The following explanation of the writing system was generously provided by Tim Dunnigan, a linguist from the University of Minnesota dedicated to the Dakota language. For about thirty years Dr. Dunnigan has assisted Dakota people in language efforts ranging from the development of University of Minnesota Dakota Language Program curriculum materials to serving as coeditor for the Dakota-English Dictionary Project. I have added comments at the end of some sections in layman's terms to help the nonlinguists among us more easily understand the writing and sound system.

Dakota orthographic or writing symbols are bounded by slash marks in this explanation section to indicate that they function as phonemes, that is, they allow speakers to distinguish units of meaning, such as words and affixes, on the basis of sound contrasts.

The Dakota vowels /a/, /e/, /i/, /o/, and /u/ have close equivalents in English. (See chart below.) Three Dakota vowels are strongly nasalized and, consequently, cannot be adequately illustrated in English. This nasal quality is indicated by writing a vowel followed by an angma (ŋ) symbol to produce /aŋ/, /iŋ/, and /uŋ/. Each digraph represents a single phoneme. For example, the nasalized /iŋ/ sound in Dakota is similar to the /in/ sound found in the English word *drink*.

Although glottal stops occur at the beginning of words before vowels and between adjacent vowels within words, these stops are not marked in written texts. Thus, the Dakota word *aa*, meaning "mold" or "moldy," is pronounced as /'a'a/ and not as a single long vowel.

Most of the Dakota consonant symbols are pronounced like their English counterparts, but there are a number of exceptions. Dakota /c/ is articulated much like the English /ch/ in *church*. An important distinction in Dakota voiceless stop phonemes is whether they have a breathy release called aspiration (/p/, /t/, /k/, and /c/) or lack aspiration (/p̣/, /ṭ/, /ḳ/, and /c̣/). When they occur before vowels at the beginning of words and at the beginning of stressed syllables, English speakers initially tend to hear Dakota voiceless unaspirated stops as being voiced. In other words, a lack of aspiration is heard as vocal cord vibration. For example, Dakota ṭoked (interrogative "how") is usually heard as /doked/ by English speakers. The aspirated consonants are the same as they usually appear in English. For example, the Dakota /p/, /t/, /k/, and /c/ would be pronounced as they are in the English *pea, tea, kite,* and *chair,* with a strong breath release. The unaspirated Dakota sounds (with no breath release) sound flatter. For example, the Dakota /p̣/, /ṭ/, /ḳ/, and /c̣/, to the English-speaking listener, may sound closer to the English sounds of *b, d, g,* and *j,* though the Dakota sounds are actually distinct.

Apostrophes are written after consonant symbols to indicate that a feature of the phoneme class is a glottal closure and release, as in /p'/, /t'/, /k'/, /c'/, /s'/, /ḣ'/. These are more difficult to explain as they represent a sound not present in the English language. Directly following the consonant sound is a breathy release that creates an exploding sound before the next sound in the word is pronounced.

Just as subscript dots are used to indicate a lack of breathy release or aspiration for a series of consonantal stop phonemes, superscript dots are used to distinguish other consonantal phoneme classes. Most have close English equivalents (see chart below), but two do not. Dakota /ḣ/ is a voiceless velar fricative, and Dakota /ġ/ is a voiced velar fricative. These are the gutteral sounds in our language.

The difference between Dakota words can also be marked by stress contrasts. For example, the meaning of the written form wiyaka depends upon whether stress is placed on the first syllable (wíyaḳa = "feather, quill") or on the second syllable (wiyáḳa = "sand").

Dakota Writing Symbols

Character		Dakota Example	English Explanation
A	a	aa (mold, moldy)	has the sound of *a* in *father*
Aŋ	aŋ		
B	b	ba (to blame)	has the common English sound
C	c	icapa (to stick into)	aspirate with the sound of *ch* in *church*
Ç	ç	içapa (to open the mouth)	unaspirated *ch* sound

C'	c'	ic'eši (woman's male cousin)	ch with glottal closure and release
D	d	da (to ask, to demand)	has the common English sound
E	e	hecetu (that's right)	has the sound of e in pet
Ġ	ġ	gi (brown)	voiced velar fricative
H	h	hi (tooth)	has the common English sound
Ḣ	ḣ	ḣa (curl)	voiceless velar fricative
Ḣ'	ḣ'	ḣ'a (gray)	voiceless velar fricative with glottal closure and release
I	i	i (she/he went)	has the sound of i in marine
Iŋ	iŋ		
K	k	ka (mean)	has the common English sound
Ḳ	ḳ	ḳa (there/yonder)	unaspirated k
K'	k'	k'a (to dig)	glottal closure and release
M	m	maġa (field)	has the common English sound
N	n	nica (to lack)	has the common English sound
O	o	o (shoot, hit by shooting)	has the sound of o in note
P	p	pahiŋ (hair of the head)	has the common English sound
Ṗ	ṗ	ṗaha (hill, mound)	unaspirated p
P'	p'	p'o (fog)	glottal closure and release
S	s	sapa (black)	has the sound of s in say
S'	s'	s'a (to hiss)	glottal closure and release
Ś	ś	śa (red)	has the sound of sh in shine
Ś'	ś'	ś'a (to shout)	sh with glottal closure and release
T	t	ite (forehead)	has the common English sound
Ṭ	ṭ	iṭe (face)	unaspirated t
T'	t'	t'a (to die, to faint)	glottal closure and release
U	u	u (to come)	has the sound of u in rule
Uŋ	uŋ		
W	w	wiyaka (quill)	has the common English sound
Y	y	yuṭa (to eat it)	has the common English sound
Z	z	zica (partridge, pheasant)	has the common English sound
Ż	ż	żica (rich)	has the sound of s in pleasure

Appendix B
Upper Sioux Community Resolution

Upper Sioux Community Board of Trustees
Dallas Ross, Chairman
Brad Lerschen, Vice Chairman
L. Alan Olson, Tribal Secretary
Jeanette Marlow, Treasurer
Tom Ross, Member at Large

USC Resolution No. 27-97

WHEREAS, The Upper Sioux Community is a federally recognized Indian Community possessing the powers of self-government and self-determination, and is governed by the Constitution of the Upper Sioux Community; and

WHEREAS, The Upper Sioux Community has an elected governing body called the Upper Sioux Board of Trustees, which is empowered by the Tribal Constitution to act on behalf of the members of the Upper Sioux Community; and

WHEREAS, Angela Cavender Wilson has articulated the following arguments in her essay, "Renegotiating Historical Definitions and Methodologies: An American Indian Perspective on Oral Tradition and History":

> (1) American Indian perspectives are a necessary component in the understanding of American Indian history.
>
> (2) Native oral traditions are some of the most valuable sources for providing American Indian perspectives on history.
>
> (3) Historians have, in the past, defined history narrowly, according to their cultural traditions, and this definition must be expanded to include other, non-Western ways of knowing.
>
> (4) Dakota communities have internal mechanisms which validate and verify their oral accounts and determine who had authority to relate certain stories; therefore, Native stories should

not be tested and evaluated by non-Dakota standards and they should be kept beyond the reach of Western historical analysis.

(5) Native stories must be allowed to stand on their own, without the need for corroboratory evidence.

(6) Oral histories should be obtained in cooperation with and respect for native peoples and their bodies of leadership according to each group's own cultural standards.

(320) 564-3853
PO Box 147, Granite Falls, MN 56241
Fax: (320) 564-2547

USC Resolution No. 27-97
Page 2

THEREFORE BE IT RESOLVED, That the Upper Sioux Board of Trustees supports these arguments Angela Cavender Wilson has made and we encourage her pursuance of these issues in academic circles.

Certification

We, the undersigned members of the Board of Trustees, do hereby certify that the foregoing USC Resolution No. 27-97 was duly adopted and approved on April 30, 1997, by a vote of Five (5) in favor, Zero (0) opposed, and Zero (0) abstentions.

Dallas Ross, Tribal Chairman
Upper Sioux Board of Trustees

L. Alan Olson, Tribal Secretary
Upper Sioux Board of Trustees

Notes

Introduction

1. *Waṡicu* is the Dakota word for white people. Various explanations exist concerning the etymology of the word. While Riggs does not provide an etymological discussion of the word, he does say this: "Frenchmen, in particular; all white men, in general. It is said that this word is nearly synonymous with 'wakaŋ.'" See Stephen R. Riggs, *A Dakota-English Dictionary* (St. Paul: Minnesota Historical Society Press, 1992), 536. Others have similarly suggested this saying might be interpreted as "any person or thing that is wakaŋ wrapped in mystery" and upon contact applied to the whites who came across the ocean. It also might derive from words meaning "one wearing inappropriate clothes." For the last two explanations, see Eugene Beuchel and Paul Manhart, eds., *Lakota Dictionary* (Lincoln: University of Nebraska Press, 2002), 352. Other translations suggest it means *takes the fat*, from the words *waṡiŋ* (fat) and *icu* (to take). However, there is not a consensus about this.
2. *Uŋkaŋna* is the Dakota kinship term for *grandfather*. Unless otherwise specified, whenever Uŋkaŋna appears, it is a reference to Eli Taylor.
3. *Wacipi* is the Dakota word for *dance or powwow*.
4. The making of relatives is a common event among Dakota people. Adoption can occur among all kinds of relationships for both genders. It usually involves a formal ceremony, feasting, and giveaway.
5. *Oyaṭe* is a term meaning *The People* or *The Nation* and may include not only all Dakota but also the Nakota and Lakota as well.
6. Throughout this work I will use *Dakota* to signify both the singular and plural form because, within our language, the term *Dakota* in itself means not *The Ally* or *The Friend* but the plural of those.
7. "The term 'Sioux,' a derivative of the Algonquin 'Naudoweissious,' meaning *enemy*, is consistently used by authors even though the easternmost Sioux called themselves the 'Dakota,' a word that translates as 'league' or 'ally.'" See Gary Clayton Anderson, *Kinsmen of Another Kind: Dakota-White Relations in the Upper Mississippi Valley, 1650–1862* (1984; reprint, St. Paul: Minnesota Historical Society Press, 1997), 284. Although *Sioux* is not a term we use to describe ourselves, it is a term that was used in treaty negotiations with the United States government and is present throughout many of the historical documents.
8. This translation of Minisoṭa Makoce is one used by Chris Mato Nunpa.
9. The infamous "trader's papers" provide an excellent example of the wealth that was gained by Dakota traders at the expense of Dakota people. See Roy W. Meyer, *His-

tory of the Santee Sioux: United States Indian Policy on Trial* (Lincoln: University of Nebraska Press, 1967), 80–87.
10. For an account of the preferential treatment given the "friendlies," see Gary Clayton Anderson and Alan R. Woolworth, *Through Dakota Eyes: Narrative Accounts of the Minnesota Indian War of 1862* (St. Paul: Minnesota Historical Society Press, 1988), 26.
11. Some might argue that land ceded through treaty cannot constitute theft, but all one needs to do is examine the conditions surrounding the negotiation and signing of the treaties, beginning with the treaty of 1805, to understand that the coercion, bribery, bullying, inadequate signatorial representation, etc., mean that most of the treaties should never have been ratified. That they were is an indication of how far the government was willing to go to gain title to lands. Furthermore, each time the government violated the terms of the treaties, the lands should have reverted back to the Dakota, but they were not. This constitutes theft.
12. Paulo Freire, *Pedagogy of the Oppressed* (New York: Continuum, 2001), 55.
13. In 1998 the Minnesota Department of Natural Resources opened a new display at Fort Snelling, using the term *concentration camp* for the first time.
14. This basic information on the U.S.-Dakota War of 1862 may be found in many texts on the Dakota, but perhaps the most detailed account may be found in Kenneth Carley, *The Sioux Uprising of 1862* (St. Paul: Minnesota Historical Society, 1976). For a detailed discussion of circumstances leading up to the U.S.-Dakota War, see Meyer, *History of the Santee Sioux*.
15. See Kenneth Carley, *The Sioux Uprising of 1862*, 76; or Message of Governor Ramsey to the Legislature of Minnesota, Delivered September 9, 1862 (St. Paul: Wm. R. Marshall, State Printer, 1862), 12.
16. The Dakota Summit is an annual meeting of Dakota, Nakota, and Lakota people who are struggling to renew their historic alliance, thereby strengthening the entire Nation. The first gathering of the Dakota Summit occurred in 1989, although the "Articles of Unification Accord" were not passed until 1990. Every year a different community in either Canada or the United States hosts the meeting.
17. *Miaṭe* means *my father*.
18. *Dekši* means *my uncle* in Dakota and *Caske* refers to the *firstborn child in a family if male*.
19. Ngũgĩ wa Thiong'o, *Moving the Centre: The Struggle for Cultural Freedoms* (Oxford: James Curry, 1993), 21.
20. Frantz Fanon, *The Wretched of the Earth* (New York: Grove, 1963), 50.
21. Linda Tuhiwai Smith, *Decolonizing Methodologies: Research and Indigenous People* (London: Zed Books, 1999), 35.
22. Winona Lu-Ann Stevenson, *Decolonizing Tribal Histories* (Ph.D. diss., University of California, Berkeley, 2000), 212. This book is forthcoming from the University of Nebraska Press under the author name Winona Wheeler.
23. Haunani-Kay Trask, *From a Native Daughter: Colonialism and Sovereignty in Hawai'i* (Honolulu: University of Hawai'i Press, 1999), 251.

24. Stevens, *Decolonizing Tribal Histories*, 257.
25. Leslie Marmon Silko, *Storyteller* (New York: Arcade, 1981), 6–7.
26. Albert Memmi, *The Colonizer and the Colonized*, expanded ed. (1965; reprint, Boston: Beacon, 1991), 88–89.
27. Smith, *Decolonizing Methodologies*, 28.

Chapter 1

1. In Dakoṭa history, for example, non-Indian traders, missionaries, and mixed-blood Dakoṭas often served as interpreters during treaty negotiations; land, money, and trade disputes; in government letters, etc., in which they might have a sizable stake in the outcome. It is difficult to ascertain how accurate their translations and interpretations were.
2. See Ramón Gutiérrez, *When Jesus Came, the Corn Mothers Went Away: Marriage, Sexuality, and Power in New Mexico, 1500–1846* (Stanford: Stanford University Press, 1991); Fred Hoxie, *Parading through History: The Making of the Crow Nation in America* (New York: Cambridge University Press, 1995); and Nancy Shoemaker, ed., *Negotiators of Change: Historical Perspectives on Native American Women* (New York: Routledge, 1995).
3. Vine Deloria Jr., *Red Earth White Lies: Native Americans and the Myth of Scientific Fact* (New York: Scribner, 1995), 49.
4. This is not to suggest that all academics are racist. I believe a great number of historians may simply not know how to go about seeking Indigenous perspectives.
5. James Lockhart, *The Nahuas after the Conquest: A Social and Cultural History of the Indians of Central Mexico* (Stanford: Stanford University Press, 1992), 6.
6. Jan Vansina, *Oral Tradition as History* (Madison: University of Wisconsin Press, 1985), 84.
7. Richard White, "Indian Peoples and the Natural World: Asking the Right Questions," in Donald Fixico, ed., *Rethinking American Indian History* (Albuquerque: University of New Mexico Press, 1997), 94.
8. David Henige, *Oral Historiography* (London: Longman, 1982), 2.
9. Vansina, *Oral Tradition as History*, 12.
10. Those who carry on oral traditions in Native cultures are the experts and the authorities, and Henige's reference to them as "informants" reveals a problematic relationship and diminishes the respected and revered place oral historians carry within their own cultures. Vansina is even more forthcoming with his cultural bias through his defining of "hearsay" as a source for oral historians. This reveals a belief held by many outside of an oral culture that oral histories are ultimately not reliable sources of information, much like the "telephone game" in American society in which information is passed on inaccurately. Many literate Americans have difficulty comprehending that some people are astute observers and have sharpened and well-trained memory skills. I don't know any culture in which "hearsay" is thought of as acceptable oral history. Those who would do so would not be regarded as reliable

sources of information. Within Dakota culture this is referred to as *keyapi*, and everyone understands that information passed on in this vein is questionable and remains so until it is verified or validated using our internal mechanisms.

11. Charles Eastman, *Indian Boyhood* (1902; reprint, New York: Dover, 1971), 43.
12. Bernard Fontana, "American Indian Oral History: An Anthropologist's Note," *History and Theory* 8, no. 3 (1969), 370.
13. Joanne Rappaport, *The Politics of Memory: Native Historical Interpretation in the Colombian Andes* (1990; reprint, Durham NC: Duke University Press, 1998).
14. Eve Ball, *Indeh: An Apache Odyssey* (Norman: University of Oklahoma Press, 1980), xiv.
15. David William Cohen, "Undefining of Oral Tradition," *Ethnohistory* 36, no. 1 (Winter 1989), 16.
16. While Oyaṭe Yaŋke might be translated as "Sits with his People," "Sits among his People," or "Sits for his People," Dakota names are highly personal and if possible should be translated by the individual possessing the name or those who have heard what translation he or she prefers. Literal translations do not always capture the meaning of the name. For example, my father's Dakota name, Ed Hdi Nażiŋ, literally would translate as "Returns Home Standing At" (making little sense), but the appropriate translation is "One Who Stands in the Place of His Brother." In this case it is necessary to know the story behind the name. He had an older brother who died at the age of three by eating apples off a tree that had been sprayed with pesticide. When my father was born his great-grandfather, Iŋyaŋg Mani Hokśida, lifted him in his arms and pronounced in Dakota, "Deṭaŋhaŋ Ed Hdi Nażiŋ eciyapi kṭe," or "From this day forward he will be called One Who Stands in the Place of His Brother."
17. Deloria, *Red Earth White Lies*, 19.
18. Western culture seems only to accept mystery or miracles in a religious context, not in a historical or scientific one. From a Dakota perspective, miracles are accepted as possibilities and truths in all contexts.
19. Anton Treuer, ed., *Oshkaabewis Native Journal* 3, no. 1 (Spring 1996), 120.
20. Luci Tapahonso, *Blue Horses Rush In* (Tucson: University of Arizona Press, 1997), xiii–xiv.
21. Stevens, *Decolonizing Tribal Histories*, 271.
22. Stevens, *Decolonizing Tribal Histories*, 248.
23. Keith Basso, *Wisdom Sits in Places: Landscape and Language among the Western Apache* (Albuquerque: University of New Mexico Press, 1996), 31.
24. Basso, *Wisdom Sits in Places*, 31. Basso's work is a demonstration of the positive, quality work that can be produced when scholars work jointly with Native peoples in collaborative projects. In this case, the Western Apache have received a valuable record of their history and language, a portion of it just for their purposes and undisclosed to the public, and Basso has produced tribally endorsed and insightful publications.

25. Greg Sarris, *Mabel McKay: Weaving the Dream* (Berkeley: University of California Press, 1994), 135.
26. "Oren Lyons: The Faithkeeper," interviewed by Bill Moyers, Public Affairs Television, 1991, video recording.
27. Vine Deloria, *God Is Red* (New York: Dell, 1973), 76.
28. Deloria, *God Is Red*, 78.
29. Deloria, *God Is Red*, 116–17.
30. *New Standard Encyclopedia* (Chicago: Standard Educational Corporation, 1990), 8:182.
31. Deloria, *Red Earth White Lies*, 37–60.
32. James W. Loewen, *Lies My Teacher Told Me: Everything Your American History Textbook Got Wrong* (New York: Touchstone, 1995), 12.
33. Loewen, *Lies My Teacher Told Me*, 12.
34. Greg Sarris, "'What I'm Talking about When I'm Talking about My Baskets': Conversations with Mabel McKay," in Sidonie Smith and Julia Watson, eds., *De/colonizing the Subject: The Politics of Gender in Women's Autobiography* (Minneapolis: University of Minnesota Press, 1992), 30.

Chapter 2

1. Linda Tuhiwai Smith also discusses the questions asked by Indigenous activists such as, "Whose research it is? Who owns it? Whose interests does it serve? Who will benefit from it? Who has designed its questions and framed its scope? Who will carry it out? Who will write it up? How will its results be disseminated?" as well as questions more difficult to judge such as, "Is her spirit clear? Does he have a good heart? What other baggage are they carrying? Are they useful to us? Can they fix up our generator? Can they actually do anything?" see Linda Tuhiwai Smith, *Decolonizing Methodologies: Research and Indigenous Peoples* (London: Zed Books, 1999), 10. Also, Dr. Robert Venables, a historian I respect tremendously, commented to me that he has been placed in the position of accounting for his research in a formal forum with Onondaga people many times. He also commented that he never studies anything he's not asked to study. Because of his respect for the people who are often at the center of his research, he also is respected by them and they have a mutually beneficial relationship. He has been a great resource for Haudenosaunee people to call upon, especially in legal battles.
2. Stephen R. Riggs, *A Dakota-English Dictionary* (St. Paul: Minnesota Historical Society Press, 1992), 94.
3. The University of Minnesota, for example, has strong Dakota and Ojibwe language programs, which have been in existence since the 1970s. Indiana University regularly offers Lakota, and Arizona State University offers Navajo to interested students. The University of Colorado, University of Oklahoma, University of Nebraska, and University of South Dakota have also taught Native languages.

4. David E. Jones's *Sanapia: Comanche Medicine Woman* (1972; reprint, Prospect Heights IL: Waveland Press, 1984) is a dramatic example of a scholar's complete lack of sensitivity and understanding of his privileged position as an adopted son and of the culture he was attempting to present. He repeatedly describes the Comanches in extraordinarily offensive terms (i.e., their marriages are explained as "generally unstable," their social and political organization as "rudimentary," their "nature of subsistence is tenuous," providing for an "elaboration of hunting magic," that they have a "vaguely defined Great Spirit," a "lively ghost fear," a "poorly developed notion of the afterlife," "crude" dwellings, their women occupy an "inferior position in the society," and that they are "without war patterns" [8-9]). Clearly, Jones had little understanding of and respect for Comanche people or culture; instead, he gives credence to the notion that Comanches are an inferior and inept people in virtually all aspects of living.

5. Smith, *Decolonizing Methodologies*, 191. Smith also quotes Graham Smith's summary of Kaupapa Maori research, saying that it "1. is related to 'being Maori'; 2. is connected to Maori philosophy and principles; 3. takes for granted the validity and legitimacy of Maori, the importance of Maori language and culture; and 4. is concerned with the struggle for autonomy over our own cultural well-being" (185).

6. See Maude Kegg, *Portage Lake: Memories of an Ojibwe Childhood* (Edmonton: University of Alberta Press, 1991) and *Oshkaabewis Native Journal* 1, no. 2 (1990). Also see Earl Nyhom and John Nichols, *A Concise Dictionary of Minnesota Ojibwe* (Minneapolis: University of Minnesota Press, 1995). In addition, the *Oshkaabewis Native Journal*, edited by Anton Treuer, has an impressive collection of Ojibwe language texts in each issue.

7. William Moss, "Oral History: What Is It and Where Did It Come From?" in David Stricklin and Rebecca Sharpless, eds., *The Past Meets the Present: Essays on Oral History* (Lanham MD: University Press of America, 1988), 12.

8. Eastman, *Indian Boyhood*, 164.

9. James B. LaGrand, "Whose Voices Count? Oral Sources and Twentieth-Century American Indian History," *American Indian Culture and Research Journal* 21, no. 1 (1997), 75.

10. LaGrand, "Whose Voices Count?" 75–76.

11. Vansina, *Oral Tradition as History*, 196.

12. See http://www.shobannews.com/idaho_natives/nez_perce.html.

13. See Vansina, *Oral Tradition as History*, 55.

14. Peter Novick, *That Noble Dream: The "Objectivity Question" and the American Historical Profession* (New York: Cambridge University Press, 1988), 1.

15. For some written discussion of this see Devon Mihesuah, ed., *Natives and Academics: Researching and Writing about American Indians* (Lincoln: University of Nebraska Press, 1998), 17. Personally, I have had both faculty and graduate students suggest to me that I was too close to my subject and should, therefore, find a topic I could look at more objectively. In speaking with other Native historians, it is clear that my ex-

perience is not unique; other Native scholars receive the same kinds of "suggestions" in their research and writing about their own people.

16. Fanon, *Wretched of the Earth*, 77.
17. Paulo Freire, *Pedagogy of the Oppressed*, 30th anniversary ed. (New York: Continuum, 2001), 45.
18. This is making reference to a paper I first heard Roger Echo-Hawk present at the 1994 Western History Association Conference in Albuquerque, New Mexico, entitled "The Battlefield of Origins: Bringing the Bering Strait into Ancient Indian History." Also, see Roger Echo-Hawk, "Kara Katit Pakutu: Exploring the Origins of Native America in Anthropology and Oral Traditions" (M.A. thesis, University of Colorado, 1994), and Roger Echo-Hawk, "Forging a New Ancient History for Native America," in Nina Swidler et al., eds., *Native Americans and Archaeologists: Stepping Stones to Common Ground* (Walnut Creek CA: AltaMira Press, 1997), 88–102.
19. See the *Holy Bible: The New King James Version* (Nashville: Thomas Nelson, 1984): "Jesus said to him, 'I am the way, the truth, and the life. No one comes to the Father except through me'" (John 14:6).
20. Michael Dorris, "Indians on the Shelf," in Calvin Martin, ed., *The American Indian and the Problem of History* (New York: Oxford University Press, 1987), 102.
21. Anna Lee Walters, *Ghost Singer* (Albuquerque: University of New Mexico Press, 1988), 138.
22. For example, in the area of Dakota history, texts such as Roy Meyer's *History of the Santee Sioux: United States Indian Policy on Trial* (Lincoln: University of Nebraska Press, 1967) makes a valuable contribution to the understanding of Dakota-white relations, and Meyer makes no pretense of speaking for the Dakota or from their perspective.
23. Theodore S. Jojola, "On Revision and Revisionism: American Indian Representations in New Mexico," in Mihesuah, *Natives and Academics*, 177–78.
24. Stevenson, *Decolonizing Tribal Histories*, 240–41.
25. Smith, *Decolonizing Methodologies*, 9.
26. For example, it is my understanding that the Hocunk of Wisconsin made the decision that the Hocunk language is for Hocunk people and advocate that non-Hocunk scholars should not study their language.
27. Probably the most flagrant demonstration of this belief is the long-held academic perception that even Indigenous remains and sacred objects are open for collection, study, and display in spite of what should be the obvious "ownership" of these items by Indigenous Peoples.
28. For an excellent discussion on how to formalize regulations for scholars at the institutional level, see Devon Mihesuah, "Suggested Guidelines for Institutions with Scholars Who Conduct Research on American Indians," *American Indian Culture and Research Journal* 17, no. 3 (1993), 131–39.
29. See Ramón A. Gutiérrez, *When Jesus Came, the Corn Mothers Went Away: Marriage, Sexuality, and Power in New Mexico, 1500–1846* (Stanford: Stanford University

Press, 1991), and *American Indian Culture and Research Journal* 17, no. 3 (1993), 141–77 for Pueblo commentaries on his work.
30. Ted Jojola, "Commentaries on *When Jesus Came, the Corn Mothers Went Away: Marriage, Sexuality and Power in New Mexico, 1500–1846*, by Ramón Gutiérrez," *American Indian Culture and Research Journal* 17, no. 3 (1993), 143.
31. Deloria, *Red Earth White Lies*, 44.

Chapter 3

1. Pežihuṭazizi Wahoȟpi Wohdakapi Uŋspe may be translated as "Yellow Medicine Nest Where Speaking Is Learned." The name was based on the successful preschool "language nests" of the Maoris and Hawaiians.
2. Ngũgĩ wa Thiong'o, *Decolonising the Mind: The Politics of Language in African Literature* (Oxford: James Currey, 1986), 26.
3. Teresa McCarty, Lucille J. Watahomigie, and Akira Y. Tanamoto, "Introduction: Reversing Language Shift in Indigenous America—Collaborations from the Field," *Practicing Anthropology* 20, no. 2 (Spring 1999), 2.
4. Stephen Greymorning, "Running the Gauntlet of an Indigenous Language Program," in Jon Reyner, Gina Cantoni, Robert N. St. Clair, and Evangeline Parsons Yazzie, eds., *Revitalizing Indigenous Languages* (Flagstaff: Northern Arizona University, 1999), 6.
5. Stephen R. Riggs, *A Dakoṭa-English Dictionary* (St. Paul: Minnesota Historical Society Press, 1992), 533. This dictionary was originally published in 1890 by the Department of the Interior, U.S. Geographical and Geological Survey of the Rocky Mountain Region, as *Contributions to North American Ethnology*, vol. 7.
6. Riggs, *A Dakoṭa-English Dictionary*, 563.
7. Brenda Child, *Boarding School Seasons* (Lincoln: University of Nebraska Press, 1998), 28.
8. bell hooks, *Teaching to Transgress: Education as the Practice of Freedom* (New York: Routledge, 1994), 169.
9. In my own language work I have heard fluent speakers describe being taught not to speak the language in public, and I've witnessed other negative attitudes toward the language because of the shame remaining from boarding-school experiences. Indian people were taught to believe their languages were inferior to English and that they were no longer useful. Many others literally had the language "beaten out of them," so they could no longer remember their native language.
10. Ngũgĩ wa Thiong'o, *Moving the Centre: The Struggle for Cultural Freedoms* (Oxford: James Currey, 1993), 37.
11. Ngũgĩ wa Thiong'o, *Moving the Centre*, 32–33.
12. Darrell R. Kipp, *Encouragement, Guidance, Insights, and Lessons Learned for Native Language Activists Developing Their Own Tribal Language Programs* (Browning MT: Piegan Institute, 2000), 7–8.

13. James Brooke, "Indians Striving to Preserve Their Languages," *New York Times*, 1999.
14. Immersion education refers to being completely "immersed" in the language in the educational setting. There are no language lessons per se; rather, typical educational lessons are offered in the native language instead of English. Immersion schools attempt to reproduce the first language environment in a school environment.
15. Smith, *Decolonizing Methodologies*, 163.
16. See the Te Kohanga Reo Web site at http:\\www.kohanga.ac.nz/history.html.
17. At the "Focusing on Native Languages Conference" sponsored by the American Indian Institute, College of Continuing Education, University of Oklahoma, and held April 25–29, 1999, in Missoula, Montana, Dr. Stephen Greymorning showed participants a video from his personal collection obtained during his visits to New Zealand.
18. Rita Avila Elasser, "Nurture in the Language Nest: Punana Leo Preschools Ride the Renaissance in Hawaiian Speech," *Hawaii Magazine*, June 1995, 68.
19. "Looking Horse Proclamation on the Protection of Ceremonies," *Indian Country Today* 22, issue 46 (March 13, 2003).
20. Anna Wierzbicka, *Understanding Culture through Their Key Words: English, Russian, Polish, German, and Japanese* (New York: Oxford University Press, 1997), 15–16.
21. Wierzbicka, *Understanding Culture*, 5.
22. Daniel T. Rodgers, "Keywords: A Reply," *Journal of the History of Ideas* 49, no. 4 (Oct.–Dec. 1988), 670–71. See also Daniel T. Rodgers, *Contested Truths: Keywords in American Politics since Independence* (New York: Basic, 1987).
23. For example, at the Dakota Summit held in 1998 at Upper Sioux, a Dakota elder used the phrase Mitakuyapi Owas'iŋ, "All My Relations," as a way to justify the acceptance of the Chricoran Siouan Nation of South Carolina (who were claiming to be long-lost Dakota relatives) as members of the Dakota Oyate or Nation. Because there were those present who were in disagreement over the wisdom of quickly accepting this group as Dakota, the rhetoric around this heavily laden phrase was quite interesting.
24. In the town of Granite Falls, Minnesota, a marker is placed outside the Yellow Medicine County Museum with the description of the "World's Oldest Exposed Rock: Site of some of the oldest exposed rock in the world. Geologists estimate this Granitic Gneiss was formed 3,800,000,000 years ago." However, the *Geology of Minnesota: A Physical Geology Laboratory Manual* (Edina MN: Burgess International, 1990) states: "The oldest rocks in North America are the Montevideo and Morton Gneisses of the Minnesota River Valley which have radiometric dates of approximately 3.6 billion years" (62). While there is a slight discrepancy in the actual age of the rock (3.6 vs. 3.8), the claim that they are some of the oldest rocks in the world is accurate. The only other site where older rocks have been found, dated at 3.98 billion years, is in West Greenland.
25. Dale Childs, guest speaker at "An Evening of Dakota Stories," sponsored by the Dakota/Lakota Language Society at the University of Minnesota, March 1989.

26. Charles A. Eastman, *The Soul of the Indian* (Lincoln: University of Nebraska Press, 1985), 105–6.
27. Tim O'Halloran, with translators Doris Pratt and Eli Taylor, *Iapi unki tanin hdu kśan: Ite icupi owapi* (Burlington, Ontario: Hayes Publishing, 1987).
28. Doris Pratt and Eli Taylor, *Dakota Word Dictionary* (Manitoba: Banner Printing, 1986), 1.
29. Smith, *Decolonizing Methodologies*, 39.
30. Ngũgĩ wa Thiong'o, *Moving the Centre*, 39.

Chapter 5

1. Ella C. Deloria, *Speaking of Indians* (Vermillion: University of South Dakota, State Publishing, 1983), 17–18.
2. American Indian sign language uses the same idea to convey veracity or truth.
3. Dale Childs, from the Prairie Island Dakota Reservation near Red Wing, Minnesota, used to relate this story of the Bdewakantunwan Dakota emergence. Though he is no longer with us, I was fortunate enough to hear it from him on a number of occasions (at storytelling events, conferences, and Dakota gatherings).
4. Concentration camps were set up in Mankato to hold the men who had been tried for war crimes by Sibley's military tribunal while they were awaiting execution orders from President Lincoln, and also at Fort Snelling where approximately 1,600 Dakota people were held before their forced transportation and relocation to a reservation in Crow Creek, South Dakota. For accounts of the 1862 war, see Kenneth Carley, *The Sioux Uprising of 1862* (St. Paul: Minnesota Historical Society Press, 1976), and Roy W. Meyer, *History of the Santee Sioux: United States Indian Policy on Trial* (Lincoln: University of Nebraska Press, 1993).
5. Meyer, *History of the Santee Sioux*, 135.
6. Today, only about 1,200–1,500 Dakota people reside on the four Dakota reservations in Minnesota (Prairie Island, Prior Lake, Upper Sioux, and Lower Sioux). In an oral-history account relayed to the author by Elsie M. Cavender in 1990, Lazarus Skyman, son of Chief Mahpiya Wicasta, was the first to return from Canada to the Upper Sioux area twenty-five years after the 1862 war, making his arrival about 1887.
7. Makato Icu (Where They Get Blue Earth) refers to the area around Mankato, Minnesota. The city of Mankato has retained the ancient Dakota word for the land there, as has the town of Blue Earth, also in that region of Minnesota.
8. This place name, Cansayapi (Painting the Trees Red), is associated with the Lower Sioux Reservation, outside of Morton, Minnesota, and makes reference to the large number of redwoods in the area. The city of Redwood Falls also takes its name from the Dakota word for the area.
9. Pezihutazizi (Yellow Medicine) is the name for the Upper Sioux Community outside of Granite Falls, Minnesota. Historically, the yellow medicine grew in abundance in this area, and Dakota people would gather it to use for healing purposes. It has been

identified as moonseed or *Menispermum canadense* in Alma R. Hutchens, *Handbook of Native American Herbs* (Boston: Shambhala, 1992), 236.
10. *Wakan* is a word that can have many different connotations, but usually is translated as *mysterious, sacred,* or sometimes *holy.*
11. While Dakota people believe that all beings have a right to exist, this does not imply that we were never in conflict with other nations or that we never killed other spiritual beings such as plants or animals in order to sustain our lives. It does, however, mean that the notion of extermination of any other life form would be in violation of Dakota principles.
12. This belief in the divinity of language and oral tradition is common to other Indigenous Peoples as well. For another example, see Stevens, *Decolonizing Tribal Histories,* 248–49.
13. *Tak Wakan,* or *Taku Wakan,* may be translated as *Something Sacred* or *What Is Mysterious.* In this case it refers to the man encountered by the Dakota warriors in this first story. Although he had human qualities, he was referred to in this way because the Dakota men witnessed him performing miracles and having incredible knowledge, even about their reason for traveling such a great distance from their home.

Chapter 7

1. The one change made involved moving the story on the origin of the waehdepi to a later chapter in the text because of its length.
2. Walker, *Lakota Belief and Ritual,* 267.
3. Michael Yellow Bird, "Model of the Effects of Colonialism," Office for the Study of Indigenous Social and Cultural Justice, University of Kansas, Lawrence, 1998.
4. Wilson D. Wallis, *The Canadian Dakota* (New York: Anthropological Papers of the American Museum of Natural History, 1947), vol. 41, part 1, 42.
5. Riggs, *A Dakota-English Dictionary,* 218.
6. Eugene Buechel and Paul Manhart, eds., *Lakota Dictionary* (Lincoln: University of Nebraska Press, 2002), 132.
7. *Collections of the Minnesota Historical Society* (St. Paul: Ramaley, Chaney, 1872), 1:234–35.
8. Fred M. Hans, *The Great Sioux Nation* (Chicago: M. A. Donohue, 1907), 59.
9. Deloria, *Speaking of Indians,* 23.
10. Eastman, *Soul of the Indian,* 41.
11. William K. Powers, *Oglala Religion* (Lincoln: University of Nebraska Press, 1977), 196–97.
12. Samuel Pond, *The Dakota or Sioux in Minnesota as They Were in 1834* (St. Paul: Minnesota Historical Society Press, 1986), 137. This was originally published in the *Minnesota History Collections,* vol. 12.
13. Ella Cara Deloria, *Waterlily* (Lincoln: University of Nebraska Press, 1988), 220.
14. Eastman, *Soul of the Indian,* 38–39.

Chapter 9

1. Deloria, *Speaking of Indians*, 45.
2. Deloria, *Speaking of Indians*, 20.
3. Of course these are understandings of the world that will most likely never be validated by Western science, and there is no way to "prove" this Dakota reality to others. However, experiences such as these are completely taken for granted within Dakota culture in that they are accepted as perfectly normal occurences. In addition, nothing remains "impossible" with assistance from spiritual beings.
4. This story of Naomi Cavender's was recorded in March 1992 at her home in Minneapolis, Minnesota.
5. This account of the *iŋyaŋ śkaŋ śkaŋna* was recorded in an interview with Elsie Cavender in the fall of 1990 at her home on the Upper Sioux Reservation, Minnesota.
6. Deloria, *Waterlily*, 98–99.
7. See Angela Cavender Wilson, "Reclaiming our Humanity: Decolonization and the Recovery of Indigenous Knowledge," in Devon Mihesuah and Angela Wilson, eds., *Indigenizing the Academy: Transforming Scholarship and Empowering Communities* (Lincoln: University of Nebraska Press, 2004), 77–79.
8. For example, Richard White has acknowledged this difference in perception but has chosen to dismiss the inexplicable as historically unworthy, stating: "I do not believe that the Winnebagos walked above the earth, nor that the prophet [Tenskwatawa (Shawnee)] turned his belt into a snake," and admits that in "making this narrative decision, I failed to convey a full Winnebago understanding of significant events.... It is precisely this kind of narrative conundrum that writing Native American history forces historians to face." While this passage comes from Russell Thornton, ed., *Studying Native America* (Madison: University of Wisconsin Press, 1998), 227–28, Winona Lu-Ann Stevenson includes an interesting discussion of this issue in her dissertation, *Decolonizing Tribal Histories* (University of California, Berkeley, 2000), 9.

Chapter 11

1. Meyer, *History of the Santee Sioux*, 131.
2. See Annette Atkins, "How a War Was Hatched," *Minneapolis Star Tribune*, August 18, 2002.
3. Ngũgĩ, *Moving the Centre*, 84.
4. Ngũgĩ, *Moving the Centre*, 96–97.
5. While this may seem a bold generalization, the U.S.-Dakota War of 1862 has been of particular interest to me, and I have yet to see any written historical texts that depict the thirty-eight Dakota hanged at Mankato as patriots and heroes. I would be thrilled to be proven wrong.
6. Because Dakota oral tradition still has this effect on the younger generations, even today the thirty-eight hanged at Mankato are discussed reverently. Even young people view them as leaders who were fighting for their people, in spite of what these

same young people are exposed to in the school curriculum, history texts, historical markers, and many public education programs.
7. "Counting coup" is a reference to striking an enemy, alive or dead, usually with a "coup stick."
8. Charles Alexander Eastman, *Indian Scout Craft and Lore* (New York: Dover, 1974), 129–30. This book was originally published by Little, Brown in 1914 under the title *Indian Scout Talks: A Guide for Boy Scouts and Camp Fire Girls*.
9. M. Z. Rosaldo, "The Use and Abuse of Anthropology: Reflections on Feminism and Cross-cultural Understanding," *Signs: Journal of Women in Culture and Society* 5, no. 3 (1980), 393.
10. Deloria, *Speaking of Indians*, 26–27.
11. In reference to his desire to avenge the death of family members in war, Charles Eastman commented: "The thought of love did not hinder my ambitions. I had a vague dream of some day courting a pretty maiden, after I had made my reputation, and won the eagle feathers" (*Indian Boyhood*, 244).
12. Eastman, *Indian Boyhood*, 115.

Conclusion

1. *Mayanipi* may be translated as *you all walk, walked* or *you all carry, carried*. The *te* on the end is a contraction of *kte*, which indicates the future tense. When this phrase is used metaphorically, it indicates how you will live your life, whatever you carry or walk with in the future.
2. *Brandon Sun*, Wednesday, January 13, 1999, p. 13.
3. For further information, see the Mahkato Wacipi Web site at http://www.turtle track.org/MahkatoWacipi/index.htm.
4. Peter Passi, "Pow Wow Fixture 'Eli' Taylor Dies at Home in Canada," *Ikce Wicasta: The Common People Journal*, Spring 1999, 4–5.
5. Ngũgĩ, *Moving the Centre*, 54.

Works Cited

Primary Sources

Cavender, Elsie. Interviewed by Waziyaṭawiŋ Angela Wilson, tape recording, Fall 1990, Upper Sioux Community, Granite Falls, Minnesota.

Cavender, Naomi. Interviewed by Waziyaṭawiŋ Angela Wilson, tape recording, March 1992, Minneapolis, Minnesota.

Taylor, Eli. Interviewed by Waziyaṭawiŋ Angela Wilson, tape recording and videocassette recording, Sioux Valley Reserve, Manitoba, Canada, January 1992. The original videos (seven tapes) and audiocassettes (nine cassettes) are in Angela Wilson's private collection; videotape copies are housed in the American Indian Studies Department at the University of Minnesota.

Secondary Sources

Anderson, Gary Clayton. *Kinsmen of Another Kind: Dakota-White Relations in the Upper Mississippi Valley, 1650–1862*. Lincoln: University of Nebraska Press, 1984; reprint, St. Paul: Minnesota Historical Society Press, 1997.

Anderson, Gary Clayton, and Alan R. Woolworth. *Through Dakota Eyes: Narrative Accounts of the Minnesota Indian War of 1862*. St. Paul: Minnesota Historical Society Press, 1988.

Atkins, Annette. "How a War Was Hatched." *Minneapolis Star Tribune*, August 18, 2002.

Ball, Eve. *Indeh: An Apache Odyssey*. Norman: University of Oklahoma Press, 1980.

Basso, Keith. *Wisdom Sits in Places: Landscape and Language among the Western Apache*. Albuquerque: University of New Mexico Press, 1996.

Beuchel, Eugene, and Paul Manhart, eds. *Lakota Dictionary*. Lincoln: University of Nebraska Press, 2002.

Bixler, Margaret. *Winds of Freedom: The Story of the Navajo Code Talkers of World War II*. Darien CT: Two Bytes, 1992.

Brandon Sun, obituary for Eli Taylor, Wednesday, January 13, 1999.

Brooke, James. "Indians Striving to Preserve Their Languages." *New York Times*, 1999.

Carley, Kenneth. *The Sioux Uprising of 1862*. St. Paul: Minnesota Historical Society Press, 1976.

Child, Brenda. *Boarding School Seasons*. Lincoln: University of Nebraska Press, 1998.

Childs, Dale. Guest speaker at "An Evening of Dakota Stories," sponsored by the Dakota/Lakota Language Society at the University of Minnesota, March 1989.

Cohen, David William. "Undefining of Oral Tradition." *Ethnohistory* 36, no. 1 (Winter 1989), 16.

Collections of the Minnesota Historical Society (St. Paul: Ramaley, Chaney, 1872), vol. 1.

Deloria, Ella C. *Speaking of Indians*. Vermillion: University of South Dakota, State Publishing, 1983.

———. *Waterlily*. Lincoln: University of Nebraska Press, 1988.

Deloria, Vine, Jr. *God Is Red*. New York: Dell, 1973; reprint, Golden CO: Fulcrum, 1999.

———. *Red Earth White Lies: Native Americans and the Myth of Scientific Fact*. New York: Scribner, 1995.

DeMallie, Raymond J. "Male and Female in Traditional Lakota Culture." In Patricia Albers and Beatrice Medicine, eds., *The Hidden Half: Studies in Plains Indian Women*. Lanham MD: University Press of America, 1983.

Dickason, Olive Patricia. *Canada's First Nations: A History of Founding Peoples from Earliest Times*. Toronto: McClelland & Stewart, 1992.

Dorris, Michael. "Indians on the Shelf." In Calvin Martin, ed., *The American Indian and the Problem of History*. New York: Oxford University Press, 1987.

Eastman, Charles. *Indian Boyhood*. 1902. Reprint, New York: Dover, 1971.

———. *Indian Scout Craft and Lore*. 1914. Reprint, New York: Dover, 1974.

———. *The Soul of the Indian*. 1911. Reprint, Lincoln: University of Nebraska Press, 1985.

Echo-Hawk, Roger. "The Battlefield of Origins: Bringing the Bering Strait into Ancient Indian History." Paper presented at the annual meeting of the Western History Association. Albuquerque, New Mexico, October 1994.

———. "Forging a New Ancient History for Native America." In Nina Swidler et al., eds. *Native Americans and Archaeologists: Stepping Stones to Common Ground*. Walnut Creek CA: AltaMira Press, 1997.

———. "Kara Katit Pakutu: Exploring the Origins of Native America in Anthropology and Oral Traditions." M.A; thesis, University of Colorado, 1994.

Elasser, Rita Avila. "Nurture in the Language Nest: Punana Leo Preschools Ride the Renaissance in Hawaiian Speech." *Hawaii Magazine*, June 1995, 68.

Fanon, Frantz. *The Wretched of the Earth*. New York: Grove Press, 1963. Originally published under the title *Les damnés de la terre* (Paris: François Maspero, 1961).

Fixico, Donald, ed. *Rethinking American Indian History.* Albuquerque: University of New Mexico Press, 1997.

Fontana, Bernard. "American Indian Oral History: An Anthropologist's Note." *History and Theory* 8, no. 3 (1969), 370.

Freire, Paulo. *Pedagogy of the Oppressed.* 1970. New York: Continuum, 2001. Originally published in 1970 as *Pedagogía del oprimido.*

Geology of Minnesota: A Physical Geology Laboratory Manual. Edina MN: Burgess International, 1990.

Gonzales, David. Editorial. *Minneapolis Star Tribune,* December 25, 1997.

Greymorning, Stephen. "Focusing on Native Languages Conference." Sponsored by the American Indian Institute of Continuing Education, University of Oklahoma. Missoula, Montana, April 25–29, 1999.

———. "Running the Gauntlet of an Indigenous Language Program." In Jon Reyner et al., eds., *Revitalizing Indigenous Languages.* Flagstaff: Northern Arizona University, 1999.

Gutiérrez, Ramón. *When Jesus Came, the Corn Mothers Went Away: Marriage, Sexuality, and Power in New Mexico, 1500–1846.* Stanford: Stanford University Press, 1991.

Hans, Fred M. *The Great Sioux Nation.* Chicago: M. A. Donohue, 1907.

Henige, David. *Oral Historiography.* London: Longman, 1982.

Hinderaker, John H., and Scott W. Johnson. "Were Sioux Hanged in 1862 Patriots, or Murderers and Rapists?" *Minneapolis Star Tribune,* January 5, 1998.

Holy Bible: The New King James Version. Nashville: Thomas Nelson, 1984.

hooks, bell. *Teaching to Transgress: Education as the Practice of Freedom.* New York: Routledge, 1994.

Hoxie, Fred. *Parading through History: The Making of the Crow Nation in America.* New York: Cambridge University Press, 1995.

Hutchens, Alma R. *Handbook of Native American Herbs.* Boston: Shambhala, 1992.

Jacobs, Sue-Ellen, Wesley Thomas, and Sabine Lang, eds. *Two-Spirit People: Native American Gender, Identity, and Spirituality.* Urbana: University of Illinois Press, 1997.

Jojola, Ted. "Commentaries on *When Jesus Came, the Corn Mothers Went Away: Marriage, Sexuality, and Power in New Mexico, 1500–1846,* by Ramón Gutiérrez." *American Indian Culture and Research Journal* 17, no. 3 (1993), 143.

———. "On Revision and Revisionism: American Indian Representations in New Mexico." In Devon Mihesuah, ed., *Natives and Academics: Research and Writing about American Indians*. Lincoln: University of Nebraska Press, 1998.

Jones, David E. *Sanapia: Comanche Medicine Woman*. Prospect Heights IL: Waveland Press, 1984.

Kawano, Kanji. *Warriors: Navajo Code-Talkers*. Flagstaff: Northland, 1990.

Kegg, Maude. *Portage Lake: Memories of an Ojibwe Childhood*. Edmonton: University of Alberta Press, 1991.

Kipp, Darrell R. *Encouragement, Guidance, Insights, and Lessons Learned for Native Language Activists Developing Their Own Tribal Language Programs*. Browning MT: Piegan Institute, 2000.

LaGrand, James B. "Whose Voices Count? Oral Sources and Twentieth-Century American Indian History." *American Indian Culture and Research Journal* 21, no. 1 (1997), 75–76.

Lockhart, James. *The Nahuas after the Conquest: A Social and Cultural History of the Indians of Central Mexico*. Stanford: Stanford University Press, 1992.

Loewen, James W. *Lies My Teacher Told Me: Everything Your American History Textbook Got Wrong*. New York: Touchstone, 1995.

Looking Horse, Arvol. "Looking Horse Proclamation on the Protection of Ceremonies." *Indian Country Today* 22, issue 46, March 13, 2003.

Lyons, Oren. "Oren Lyons: The Faithkeeper." Interviewed by Bill Moyers. Videocassette. Public Affairs Television, 1991.

Mahkato Wacipi. http://www.turtletrack.org/MahkatoWacipi/index.htm.

McCarty, Teresa, Lucille J. Watahomigie, and Akira Y. Tanamoto. "Introduction: Reversing Language Shift in Indigenous America—Collaborations from the Field." *Practicing Anthropology* 20, no. 2 (Spring 1999), 2.

Memmi, Albert. *The Colonizer and the Colonized*. Expanded ed. 1965. Boston: Beacon Press, 1991.

Meyer, Roy. *The History of the Santee Sioux: United States Indian Policy on Trial*. Lincoln: University of Nebraska Press, 1967.

Mihesuah, Devon. *Natives and Academics: Researching and Writing about American Indians*. Lincoln: University of Nebraska Press, 1998.

———. "Suggested Guidelines for Institutions with Scholars Who Conduct Research on American Indians." *American Indian Culture and Research Journal* 17, no. 3 (1993), 131–139.

Moss, William. "Oral History: What Is It and Where Did It Come From?" In David Strickland and Rebecca Sharpless, eds., *The Past Meets the Present: Essays on Oral History*. Lanham MD: University Press of America, 1988.

New Standard Encyclopedia. Chicago: Standard Educational Corporation, 1990. s.v. "History."

Ngũgĩ wa Thiong'o. *Decolonising the Mind: The Politics of Language in African Literature.* Oxford: James Currey, 1986.

———. *Moving the Centre: The Struggle for Cultural Freedoms.* Oxford: James Currey, 1993.

Novick, Peter. *That Noble Dream: The "Objectivity Question" and the American Historical Profession.* New York: Cambridge University Press, 1988.

Nyhom, Earl, and John Nichols. *A Concise Dictionary of Minnesota Ojibwe.* Minneapolis: University of Minnesota Press, 1995.

O'Halloran, Tim, with translators Doris Pratt and Eli Taylor. *Iapi unki tanin hdu kṡan: Ite icupi owapi.* Burlington, Ontario: Hayes Publishing, 1987.

Oshkaabewis Native Journal 1, no. 2 (1990).

Passi, Peter. "Pow Wow Fixture 'Eli' Taylor Dies at Home in Canada." *Ikce Wicasta: The Common People Journal,* Spring 1999.

Paul, Doris A. *The Navajo Code Talkers.* Pittsburgh: Dorrance Publishing, 1998.

Pond, Samuel. *The Dakota or Sioux in Minnesota as They Were in 1834.* St. Paul: Minnesota Historical Society Press, 1986.

Powers, William K. *Oglala Religion.* Lincoln: University of Nebraska Press, 1977.

Pratt, Doris, and Eli Taylor. *Dakota Word Dictionary.* Manitoba, Canada: Banner Printing, 1986.

Rappaport, Joanne. *The Politics of Memory: Native Historical Interpretation in the Colombian Andes.* Durham NC: Duke University Press, 1998.

Riggs, Stephen R. *A Dakota-English Dictionary.* 1890. Reprint, St. Paul: Minnesota Historical Society Press, 1992.

Rogers, Daniel T. *Contested Truths: Keywords in American Politics since Independence.* New York: Basic, 1987.

———. "Keywords: A Reply." *Journal of the History of Ideas* 49, no. 4 (Oct.–Dec. 1988), 670–71.

Romano, Joseph J., and James E. Pizzuto. *Geology of Minnesota: A Physical Geology Laboratory Manual.* 6th ed. Department of Geology, University of Minnesota. Edina MN: Burgess International, 1990.

Rosaldo, M. Z. "The Use and Abuse of Anthropology: Reflections on Feminism and Cross-cultural Understanding." *Signs: Journal of Women in Culture and Society* 5, no. 3 (1980), 393.

Sarris, Greg. *Mabel McKay: Weaving the Dream.* Berkeley: University of California Press, 1994.

———. "'What I'm Talking About When I'm Talking About My Baskets': Conversations with Mabel McKay." In Sidonie Smith and Julia Watson, eds., *De/colonizing the Subject: The Politics of Gender in Women's Autobiography.* Minneapolis: University of Minnesota Press, 1992.

Shoemaker, Nancy, ed. *Negotiators of Change: Historical Perspectives on Native American Women.* New York: Routledge, 1995.
Silko, Leslie Marmon. *Storyteller.* New York: Arcade, 1981.
Smith, Linda Tuhiwai. *Decolonizing Methodologies: Research and Indigenous People.* London: Zed Books, 1999.
Stevenson, Winona Lu-Ann. *Decolonizing Tribal Histories.* Ph.D. diss., University of California, Berkeley, 2000.
Tapahonso, Luci. *Blue Horses Rush In.* Tucson: University of Arizona Press, 1997.
Te Kōhanga Reo National Trust. "Te Kōhanga Reo: History." New Zealand. http:\\www.kohanga.ac.nz/history.html.
Trask, Haunani-Kay. *From a Native Daughter: Colonialism and Sovereignty in Hawai'i.* Honolulu: University of Hawai'i Press, 1999.
Treuer, Anton, ed. *Oshkaabewis Native Journal* 3, no. 1 (Spring 1996), 120.
Vansina, Jan. *Oral Tradition as History.* Madison: University of Wisconsin Press, 1997.
Vogel, Virgil J. *American Indian Medicine.* Norman: University of Oklahoma Press, 1970.
Walker, James R., with Raymond J. DeMallie and Elaine A. Jahner, eds. *Lakota Belief and Ritual.* Lincoln: University of Nebraska Press, 1991.
Wallis, Wilson D. *The Canadian Dakota.* Vol. 41, part 1. New York: Anthropological Papers of the American Museum of Natural History, 1947.
Walters, Anna Lee. *Ghost Singer.* Albuquerque: University of New Mexico Press, 1988.
White, Richard. "Indian Peoples and the Natural World: Asking the Right Questions." In Donald Fixico, ed., *Rethinking American Indian History.* Albuquerque: University of New Mexico Press, 1997.
―――. "Using the Past: History and Native American Studies." In Russell Thornton, ed. *Studying Native America.* Madison: University of Wisconsin Press, 1998.
Wierzbicka, Anna. *Understanding Culture Through Their Key Words: English, Russian, Polish, German, and Japanese.* New York: Oxford University Press, 1997.
Wilson, Angela Cavender. "American Indian History or Non-Indian Perceptions of American Indian History?" *American Indian Quarterly* 20, no. 1 (Winter 1996).
―――. "Power of the Spoken Word: Native Oral Traditions in American Indian History." In Donald L. Fixico, ed., *Rethinking American Indian History.* Albuquerque: University of New Mexico Press, 1997.

———. "Walking into the Future: Dakota Oral Tradition and the Shaping of Historical Consciousness." *The Forum* (Canadian Oral History Association) 19–20 (1999–2000).

Yellow Bird, Michael. "Model of the Effects of Colonialism." Office for the Study of Indigenous Social and Cultural Justice, University of Kansas, Lawrence KS, 1998.

Source Acknowledgments

An earlier version of chapter 1 appeared as "American Indian History or Non-Indian Perceptions of American Indian History," in *Natives and Academics: Researching and Writing about American Indians*, Devon Mihesuah, ed. (Lincoln: University of Nebraska Press, 1998) and in *American Indian Quarterly* 20.1 (Winter 1996): 3–5.

An earlier version of chapter 2 originally appeared as "Power of the Spoken Word," in *Rethinking American Indian History*, Donald L. Fixico, ed. (Albuquerque: University of New Mexico Press, 1997), 101–16.

Parts of chapter 5 and the conclusion originally appeared as "Walking into the Future: Dakota Oral Tradition and the Shaping of Historical Consciousness," in *Oral History Forum* vol. 19–20 (1999–2000): 25–36.

Index

akicitapi, 20, 184
alcohol, 87, 130
Anawangmani, Simon, 197
autobiographies, as-told-to style of, 38
Atkins, Annette, 198

Ball, Eve, 29
Basso, Keith, 32, 250n24
Battle of Wood Lake, 7
Bdewakaŋtuŋwaŋ, 4, 8, 96
Bdoṭe, 32, 96
Bering Strait Theory, 45–46
Blackface, George, 184, 192–95, 202, 203
Blacksmith, Jacob, 225
Blacksmith, Jim, 121
Blackwood, Evelyn, 230
boarding schools, 53, 69, 96, 219, 220, 224, 225, 232–33; as genocide, 54
Boarding School Seasons (Child), 53
bounties, 8, 96–97, 179
Brandon (Manitoba) Sun, 237
Brandon University, 4
Briggs, Bruce, 58
Brooke, James, 55

Caŋsayapi, 73, 74, 97
caŋṭe, 37–38
Cardinal, Harold, 48
Caske Cistiŋna, 32
Caske Taŋka, 32
Cattaraugus Seneca Nation, 48
Cavender, Elsie (Two Bear), xi, 2, 31, 65, 95, 155n18, 179–80
Cavender, Gary, 2
Cavender, Naomi (Bear), xi, 10, 64, 66, 128, 178–79, 180
Ceglar, Shelly, 56
Child, Brenda, 53
Childs, Dale, 63
Christianity, 3, 6, 12, 46, 53, 61, 230, 231
Cloudman, Chief, 179
code-talkers, 20, 184, 202, 203; Navajo, 184, 196
Cohen, David William, 29

collective memory, 26, 28
College of St. Scholastica (Duluth MN), 56
colonialism, 13, 14, 52, 130, 239; academy as institution of, 45; and colonialist mindset, 133; and impact on Dakota people, 6
colonization, 127, 130, 135, 203; and colonizer/colonized relationship, 24, 16–17, 239; of history, 16–17, 170; Indigenous complicity in, 233; intellectual, 36, 56, 181; justification for, 198
Communion of Saints, 167
concentration camps, 7, 96, 248n13, 256n4
A Concise Dictionary of Minnesota Ojibwe (Nichols and Nyholm), 39
Contested Truths: Keywords in American Politics Since Independence (Rodgers), 60–61
counting coup, 200
creation/transformation, 45–46
critical consciousness, 14, 15, 21, 131
Crow Creek, 7, 256n4
cultural loss, 8, 236
cultural property rights, 49
cultural survival, 183, 235, 236, 240

Daklugie, Asa, 29
Dakota-English Dictionary (Riggs), 37, 53, 241
Dakota-English Dictionary Project (DEDP), 56, 61, 241
Dakota language: computer font, ix, 241; orthography, 241–43; translation of, 4
Dakota people: identity of, 8–9, 17; reservations and reserves, 8
Dakota Summit, 8, 55, 248n16
Dakota Word Dictionary (Taylor and Pratt), 65
Davenport IA, 7
decolonization, 12, 66, 127, 130, 136, 199–200, 239–40; Dakota terms for, 15; global movement for, 13, 21; literature on, 13; meaning of, 1, 13–14
Decolonizing Methodologies: Research and Indigenous People (Smith), 18
Deloria, Ella, 12, 17, 92–93, 132, 133–34, 174, 175, 180, 201

Deloria, Vine, Jr., 24, 30–31, 33–34, 35, 49
DeMallie, Ray, 230
diaspora, 97
Dickson, Olive, 218
Dorris, Michael, 46
Dowlin, Bruce, 237
Dunnigan, Tim, ix, 241
Duta, John, 137, 150–52, 153nn10–11, 176–77, 195

Eastern Dakota Bands Treaty Council, ix, 14
Eastman, Charles Alexander, 17, 28, 40, 64, 131, 132, 133, 134, 200, 202; on oral tradition, 27
Echo-Hawk, Roger, 45–46, 253n18
education, 224, 227–28, 233–34, 238
ehaŋna woyakapi, 20, 63, 65, 68, 102, 114, 118, 138, 142, 143, 149, 152, 158, 184, 203
ethnic cleansing, 8
ethnocide, 7, 54
extermination, 6, 8. *See also* bounties

Fanon, Frantz, 13, 45
flight to Canada following U.S.-Dakota War, 8, 30, 96–97
Fontana, Bernard, 29
Fort Snelling concentration camp, 7. *See also* concentration camps
Free Press (Mankato MN), 237
Freire, Paulo, 6, 45

gatekeeping scholars, 49
generosity, as Dakota virtue, 174
gender roles within Dakota culture, 201–2
genocide, 54; justification for, 198. *See also* bounties; extermination
Ghost Singer (Walters), 47
Gibbons, Tom, 56
gift-giving ceremonies, 174, 181
God Is Red (Deloria), 33–34
Gonzales, Dave, 198
granite gneiss, oldest known, 63, 255n24
Greymorning, Stephen, 52
Grotto Foundation, 59
Gutiérrez, Ramón, 49

haŋbdeceya ceremony, 46
Hapa, Herb, 184, 192–95, 202, 203
Harper, Elijah, 205n3, 218–19, 226
healing, 171–75; approaches to, 172
Henige, David, 26, 40
heyoka, 204, 212, 217, 221

Hinderaker, John H., 198
historians: academic vs. tribal, 41–42, 44, 249n10; mechanisms for evaluating, 44, 47; responsibilities of tribal, 42, 236–37; working with Indigenous languages, 25–26, 238
historical consciousness, 17, 19, 36, 101, 169, 197
history: academic discipline of, 17, 21, 22, 26, 169; as conduit of colonization, 170; broadening definitions of, 41–42, 238; colonialist interpretations of, 198, 238; conceptions of, 169; definitions of, 34–35; double standards in, 24, 48; future of, 50; and history/myth dichotomy, 28–29, 31, 100, 182, 238; and internal validation mechanisms, 43; irrelevance of, 35; oral vs. written, 36, 41, 48, 197; recentering of, 239; validation of, 36
History of the Santee Sioux (Meyer), 197
hituŋkaŋkaŋpi stories, 63–64, 65
Hocak Wazija Haci Language & Culture Program, 56
hooks, bell, 53
humanism, 3, 232, 235

Iašica (Germans), 193, 194
identity, 8–9, 17, 19, 21, 92, 101, 137, 169, 170, 182
Ihaŋktuŋwaŋ, 4, 184
Ihaŋktuŋwaŋna, 4
ikçe wicašta, 22, 222
Ikce Wicasta: The Common People Journal, 237
imperialism, 61
Indeh (Ball), 29
Indian Boyhood (Eastman), 202
Indigenous-centered framework, 22
Indigenous intellectual control, 48, 49
Indigenous knowledge recovery, 1, 130; of language, 66, 239
Indigenous language(s), 12, 18, 19, 25–26, 39, 49, 202; CD-ROMs for, 56, 58; crisis state of, 51, 52, 55; cultural shame associated with, 54; as decolonization tool, 66; every person has different, 77; keywords in, 60–61; and language immersion, 57, 59; and language trainees, 59; as link to culture and worldview, 51, 52, 59, 60; and master/apprentice programs, 59; preservation and revitalization of, 52, 55, 56, 66; punishment for speaking, 53, 54; in scholarship, 38; and using colonizer's language, 51–52
Indigenous perspective, 23, 29, 31, 46, 47–48, 92

inipi, 20, 59, 118–21, 122, 135–36, 216n22
intellectual property rights, 49
internalization of teachings, 232, 235
invasion, 5; justification for, 169, 198
iŋyaŋ śkaŋ śkaŋ, 20, 21, 137, 149–56, 157, 170, 171, 175–80, 182, 217. *See also* taḳ śkaŋ śkaŋ
ituh'aŋ, 174, 181
Iwakci Okodakiciye, 112–13, 129–31

Jacobs, Sue-Ellen, 229
Johnson, Scott W., 198
Jojola, Theodore S., 48, 49
Jones, David E., 252n4

Kaupapa Maori of New Zealand, 38–39
Kegg, Maude, 39
kinship, 175, 236; Dakoṭa terms of, 62–63, 93–94
Kipp, Darrell, 55
koda (friend) relationship, 180

LaFortune, Richard, 59
LaGrand, James, 41
Lake Andes Preschool Immersion Program (MN), 59
Lakoṭa, 4, 5
Lawrence, Lorenzo, 197
Lies My Teacher Told Me (Loewen), 35
Lincoln, Abraham, 7, 198
linear time, 33–34
Little Crow, Chief, 8, 149; death of, 8
Little Crow, Willie, 138–42, 149, 170, 172
Lockhart, James, 25
Loewen, James W., 35
Looking Horse, Arvol, 59, 61
Lower Sioux, 6
Lyons, Oren, 33

Maȟpiya Wicaṡṭa, 179
Makato Icu, 73
Mankato MN, 124, 215; powwow, 2, 216n21, 237, 238
Manifest Destiny, 198
Maori: language, 57–58; researchers, 38–39
mass execution, 7
Mato, John, 178
Mato Nuŋpa, Chris, xi, 2, 10, 56, 90n48, 100, 111n12, 139n3, 208n9, 215n20, 221; Dakoṭa name of, 250n16
Mazakutemani, Paul, 197
Mazomani, 32

McKay, Mabel, 33, 36
McKay, Neil, 15
Meech Lake Accord (1990), 205–6, 218, 226
Memmi, Albert, 16
memory as a gift, 3, 98, 232
menstruation, 135–36
methodology of narratives, 9–12, 40, 238
Meyer, Roy, 197, 253n22
Mihesuah, Devon, x, 252n15, 253n28
military tribunal formed by Sibley, 7
Minisoṭa Makoce, 5, 96
Minneapolis Star Tribune, 198
missionaries, 6, 12, 32, 52, 61, 115, 126, 133, 207n5
Mitaḳuyapi Owas'iŋ, 62
mnemonic devices, 32
moccasin game, 4, 238
Moss, William, 40
Moyers, Bill, 33

Nakoṭa, 4
neocolonialism, 13, 14, 52
Ngugi wa Thiong'o, 11, 13, 51, 54, 66, 198–99, 232, 239
Nichols, John, 39
Novick, Peter, 44
Nyholm, Earl, 39

Oak River Indian Day School, 107
objectivity, 44–45
Oċeti Saḳowiŋ, 5, 64
Ojibwe language, 39, 56
oḳicize stories, 64–65, 184, 191, 202, 203
Omaha Society, 102, 112–13, 114n20, 129–30
Ominsky, Alan, ix, 241
oppression, 6, 183; justification for, 169
Oral Historiography (Henige), 26
oral history, 26; analysis of, 47; connection to oral tradition, 41; definition of, 27, 40; differing versions of, 46–47; as raw data, 42; and relation to language, 60; veracity of, 29, 31
oral tradition, 16, 18, 126; and conceptions of time, 31–34; connection to academic discipline of history, 17, 23–25; connection to oral history, 41; comprehension of, 100; definition of, 27, 40, 181; as divinely ordained, 28, 98, 99, 232; function of, 35; inclusion of wakan, 170, 175, 180; interrupted transmission of, 232, 235–36; legitimacy of, 182; narrative strategy for, 126; privileging of, 1, 169; and subversion of colonialism,

oral tradition (*continued*)
199; in supplemental role, 16, 169; training for, 27–28, 44, 96, 181; validation of, 36, 169
Ota Kuteda, 211, 212
Other Day, John, 197
Owen, Amos, 216

Passi, Peter, 237
The Past Meets the Present (Moss), 40
patriotism, 117–18, 128
Peacemaker, 33
Peżihuṭazizi Ode, 74, 97
Peżihuṭazizi Wahoḣpi Wohdaḳapi Uŋspe, 51, 57
Piegan Institute, 55
Pine Ridge, 131
Pinkham, Josiah, 44
Pond, Gideon, 12
Pond, Samuel, 12, 133, 134
Poor Dog, 178
Prairie Island Reservation, 63, 216n21
Pratt, Donald, 117n25
Pratt, Doris, 15, 65–66
Protection of Ceremonies Ominiciyapi, 59

racism, 36, 53; within academia, 24
Ramsey, Governor Alexander, 7
Rappaport, Joanne, 29
Reading and Writing the Lakota Language (White Hat), 12
reciprocity, 38
Red Earth, Michael, 231
Red Earth, White Lies (Deloria), 35
religious imperialism, 6, 126
repatriation, 7
research ethics, 37–41
resistance, 127, 182, 200, 219, 239
reverse verification process, 36
Rice, Julian, 12
Riggs, Stephen, 12, 32, 37, 53, 130, 131, 241
Roberts, Isabel, 179
Roberts, John, 179
Rodgers, Daniel, 60
Rosaldo, M. Z., 201
Running Walker, Caske (Harry), xi, 11, 62

Sanapia: Comanche Medicine Woman (Jones), 252n4
Sarris, Greg, 33, 36
scholarly accountability, 18, 37, 48, 49

Schommer, Waḣpetuŋwiŋ Carrie, xi, 2, 10, 11, 59, 65, 100, 111n12, 214n16, 221, 229
self-determination, 18, 39, 234, 236
Seven Council Fires, 5
Shakopee Mdewakanton Dakoṭa, 58–59
shape-shifting, 30
Sibley, Henry Hastings, 7, 198
Silko, Leslie Marmon, 16
Sioux Valley, 2, 4, 55, 107, 112, 129, 136
Sisituŋwaŋ, 4
Skyman, Lazarus, 179–80
Smith, Graham, 252n5
Smith, Linda Tuhiwai, 13, 18, 38, 48, 57, 66
Speaking of Indians (Deloria), 201
spiritual run, 198
Stabilizing Indigenous Languages Conference (1999), 58
stories: internalization of, 94, 219; as living, 36; and marking the listener, 64; significance of, 43; as transmission of culture, 36; and truth/myth dichotomy, 63
swearing, 121–22

taḳ šḳaŋ šḳaŋ, 137, 138, 140, 153, 155, 171, 176, 182, 209n11, 210–11. *See also* iŋyaŋ šḳaŋ šḳaŋ
Tapahonso, Luci, 31
Taylor, Edna, 134, 138–41, 170, 238
Taylor, Eli: adoption of, 2; childhood, 68–71, 102–14, 126–28, 142–43, 172; death of, 4, 237; honorary doctorate received by, 4; marriages of, 102, 114–16; in Omaha Society, 129; purpose in project, 9; training in oral tradition, 96
Te Kohana Reo, 57
That Noble Dream (Novick), 44
thirty-eight Dakota men, 7, 20, 184, 197–200, 203, 219, 258n5. *See also* U.S.-Dakota War of 1862
Thomas, Peg, 59
Tituŋwaŋ, 4–5
traders' papers, 247n9
traditional copyright, 48
translation, 9–11, 12, 19
Trask, Haunani-Kay, 14
treaties, 5, 248n11
trickster, 30
truth, 46, 60, 95, 169, 175
two-spirit, 221, 229, 230
two-worlds, 45, 116, 134–36

Understanding Culture through Key Words (Wierzbicka), 60
United Nations Convention on the Prevention and Punishment of the Crime of Genocide, 54
Uŋkṭomi, 30, 64, 141, 142
Upper Sioux, 32, 51, 55–58, 129, 131, 244–45. *See also* Upper Sioux Resolution of Support
Upper Sioux Resolution of Support, 49, 244–45
U.S.-Dakoṭa War of 1862, 5, 96, 97, 131, 179, 197–200, 240; Battle of Wood Lake, 7, 32; beginning of, 6; causes of, 5–6; flight to Canada after, 8, 30, 96–97; thirty-eight Dakoṭas, 7, 20, 184, 197–200, 203, 219, 258n5

Vansina, Jan, 25, 26, 40, 42–43
Venables, Robert, ix, 251n1

waehdepi, 20, 137, 158–59, 164n28, 180, 182, 215
waekihdepi, 164–65
Waȟpekuṭe, 4
Wahpeton Reserve (Saskatchewan), 8, 158
Waȟpetuŋwaŋ, 4–5, 92
Wallis, Wilson, 130
Walters, Anna Lee, 47
Waŋ Duṭa, 142–43, 213–14
wapetokça (miracle), 184, 187–88, 191
wapiya (healing), 20, 138
warfare, 64, 131

Wašicu, translation of, 247n1
Wasicuna, Glen, 59
Waterlily (Deloria), 133, 180
Wayak Hiyaye Wiŋ, 127
Western Apache, 32
Wheeler, Winona, 13, 15, 31, 32, 48
When Jesus Came the Corn Mothers Went Away (Gutiérrez), 49
Whipple, Bishop Henry, 7
White, Richard, 25, 258n8
White Buffalo Calf Pipe, 59, 133
White Buffalo Calf Woman, 132–33
White Cloud, Peter, 137, 153–54, 177
White Elk, Charles, 15
White Hat, Albert, Sr., 12
white privilege, 220
Wierzbicka, Anna, 60
Willard, George, 186
Williamson, John, 12, 32
wiŋkṭa, 21, 221–22, 228–31
wiwaŋyak wacipi, 20, 122–24, 135–36
women, 201–2; and marriage, 131, 133–34; participation in inipi by, 135–36; and rites of passage, 131; societies for, 112–13, 129–31; status of, 131–36, 201
World War I, 20, 117, 120n29, 128, 137, 150, 152, 176, 184, 185, 191–92, 202
World War II, 120, 137, 153, 154, 176, 177, 196

Year of Reconciliation (1987), 198
Yellow Bird, Michael, x, 14, 130

Zuni History Project, 48

IN THE CONTEMPORARY INDIGENOUS ISSUES SERIES

Indigenous American Women:
Decolonization, Empowerment, Activism
By Devon Abbott Mihesuah

Indigenizing the Academy:
Native Scholars and Scholarship on Natives
Edited by Devon Abbott Mihesuah and Angela Cavender Wilson

Remember This!
Dakota Decolonization and the Eli Taylor Narratives
By Waziyatawin Angela Wilson
With translations from the Dakota text by
Wahpetunwin Carolynn Schommer

www.ingramcontent.com/pod-product-compliance
Lightning Source LLC
Chambersburg PA
CBHW062003220426
43662CB00010B/1212